THE DICTATOR'S DILEMMA

THE DICTATOR'S DILEMMA

*THE CHINESE COMMUNIST PARTY'S
STRATEGY FOR SURVIVAL*

BRUCE J. DICKSON

GEORGE WASHINGTON UNIVERSITY

OXFORD
UNIVERSITY PRESS

OXFORD

UNIVERSITY PRESS

Oxford University Press is a department of the University of Oxford. It furthers
the University's objective of excellence in research, scholarship, and education
by publishing worldwide. Oxford is a registered trade mark of Oxford University
Press in the UK and certain other countries.

Published in the United States of America by Oxford University Press
198 Madison Avenue, New York, NY 10016, United States of America.

© Oxford University Press 2016

First issued as an Oxford University Press paperback, 2018

CIP data is on file at the Library of Congress
ISBN 978-0-19-022855-2 (hardcover); 978-0-19-069219-3 (paperback)

3 5 7 9 8 6 4
Printed in Canada by Marquis

In memory of
Mike Oksenberg, Jim Millar, and Lee Sigelman
Mentors too soon gone

CONTENTS

Acknowledgments   ix

1. Introduction: The CCP's Strategy for Survival   1

2. The Heavy Hand of the State   31

3. Mass Line for Modern Times   96

4. Serving the People   164

5. Generating Support   214

6. Defining Democracy   262

7. Will the Party Survive?   301

Appendices   323
Bibliography   327
Index   341

ACKNOWLEDGMENTS

THE ORIGINAL IDEA FOR this book came from a conversation with Shen Mingming, professor in the School of Government and director of the Research Center for Contemporary China (RCCC) at Peking University. He told me about a man he met while visiting a town in China. The man was full of complaints about the town's leaders. He clearly felt they were only out for themselves, did not act in the best interests of the town, and did nothing meriting praise. Shen pointed out that he drove into the town on a newly paved, multi-lane main road that connected the town to other towns and markets. Surely the town's leaders deserved credit for this. But the man dismissed the construction of the new road, saying the construction company was in cahoots with the town's leaders. According to him, the only reason the government approved the project was that the head of the construction company was the brother of the town's top official. Even the building of this important infrastructure project, which brought easier transportation and greater economic opportunities, was not enough to change this man's assessment of the sorry state of the town's government.

This story inspired the central questions of this book. A key part of the Chinese Communist Party's strategy for survival is promoting economic development, improving personal prosperity, and enhancing quality of life in order to generate popular support, but does the public give the Party credit for its policies? Why have repeated public opinion surveys revealed support for a regime despite many examples of corrupt officials, governance failures, and public protest? Above all, how secure is the Party's hold on power? Will its strategy for survival prove to be indefinitely successful, or simply postpone its inevitable demise?

Answers to these questions require detailed information about Chinese public opinion. Fortunately for me, Shen's RCCC is China's premier public opinion survey center. Together with the RCCC's team of experts, we designed a nationwide probability sample of urban China and developed a survey questionnaire to examine the questions addressed in this book. In addition to Shen, I would like to thank Yang Ming, Yan Jie, Chai Jingjing, and the many dedicated grad students who worked in the center. In different ways, they helped in the drafting of the questionnaire, its implementation in 50 cities across China, and the interpretation of the results.

The survey was first conducted in 2010 and then repeated in 2014. Coming two years before and two years after the change of national leaders in 2012, these surveys provide before and after pictures of the public's assessment of economic, political, and social conditions in China. In particular, they let us see how the priorities and policies of China's current leader, Xi Jinping, have influenced public opinion toward the regime as a whole.

Because survey research involves a small army of researchers who work on the questionnaire, select the sample of cities and individuals to create a representative sample, travel around the country to interview people face-to-face, and then enter the responses into a database, it is an expensive style of research. For providing the funds necessary to complete this work, I wish to thank the National Science Foundation (award #SES-0921570), the Smith Richardson Foundation (award #2014-0041), and the Elliott School of International Affairs of George Washington University. And because managing grants requires greater attention to detail than I can muster, I want to thank Matt Greiger, Matt O'Mara, and Joyce Tso of the Sigur Center for Asian Studies. They paid the contracts, hired the research assistants, and prepared the financial reports required by the project's sponsors. Their expert handling of the project's logistics allowed me to concentrate on its substance.

Over the years, I have given talks related to the themes and findings of this book at a variety of universities and think tanks and have benefited enormously from the discussions. For this, I would like to thank the people at the University of Wisconsin, University of Pittsburgh, Villanova University, University of Pennsylvania, University of Iowa, Indiana University, University of Toronto, School of Oriental and African Studies, Fudan University, Shanghai Jiaotong University, Korea University, East Asia Institute (Seoul), Seoul Forum on International Affairs, University of Hong Kong, Peking University, Duke University, and of course my own school, George Washington University.

Many people have made helpful comments on various parts of the argument and evidence. Andrew Nathan and David Shambaugh read the entire manuscript and made innumerable suggestions for revisions. I have also benefited from conversations and feedback from many friends and colleagues, including Yuen Yuen Ang, Steve Balla, Brandon Bartels, Mayling Birney, Meina Cai, Yun-han Chu, Joe Fewsmith, Evgeny Finkel, Mark Frazier, Mary Gallagher, Pete Gries, Henry Hale, Enze Han, Tim Hildebrandt, Ron Inglehart, Jing Yijia, John Kennedy, Scott Kennedy, Lai Hairong, Pierre Landry, Eric Lawrence, Lianjiang Li, Zhou Liao, Liu Mingxing, Jie Lu, Xiaobo Lu, Melanie Manion, Meng Tianguang, Carl Minzner, Minxin Pei, Allison Quatrini, Tom Rawski, Ben Read, Bill Reissinger, Tony Saich, Victor Shih, John Sides, Yeling Tan, Wenfang Tang, Paul Wahlbeck, Jeremy Wallace, Yuhua Wang, Marty Whyte, and Dali Yang.

I have had the good fortune to work with several talented graduate students on this project. Jackson Woods was involved from the start and provided valuable input on the sampling design, the questionnaire, data collection, data analysis, and the interpretations I gave to the data. Chunhua Chen joined the project midway, collecting and analyzing data, doing additional background research, and providing a useful reality check on the main themes of the book. Both of them worked on revising the questionnaire for the second wave of the survey and read the entire manuscript in draft form. I quite literally could not have done it without them.

At Oxford University Press, I would like to thank Dave McBride for championing the book and providing judicious editing; Katie Weaver for keeping the process moving along; and Kate Nunn for overseeing the copyediting and production process.

Above all, I would like to thank my family, Benita, Andrew, and Caitlin, for enduring my trips to China without them and tolerating the long book-writing phase. Maybe one day I will write the novel they keep asking for.

This book is dedicated to the memory of three mentors, Mike Oksenberg, Jim Millar, and Lee Sigelman. Each of them had their lives cut short by cancer. Mike was my advisor at the University of Michigan. With his knowledge of the intricacies of policy making and elite politics in China, he was a reliable source of inspiration and ideas. His passion for Chinese politics was surpassed only by his love for Michigan football. His legacy is the dozens of China specialists he helped train during his years at Columbia, Michigan, and Stanford who went on to work in universities, think tanks, foundations, and government agencies. When I arrived at GW, Jim Millar was director of its Institute of European, Russian, and Eurasian Studies and I was housed in his center. Over the years, I benefited in countless ways from his advice and support. When I later became director of the Sigur Center for Asian Studies, he provided the model I tried to emulate. Lee Sigelman was chair of the political science department when I was hired at GW. He had a "Hundred Flowers" approach to scholarship: he did not care what you studied or what methodology you used as long as you did it well and got it published in respected outlets. He had a wicked sense of humor, an unerring editorial eye, and a generous spirit. His style of leadership continues to shape our department even now that he is gone. Although Jim and Lee did not always see eye to eye as administrators, they became close friends as they underwent treatments together. For their dedication to young scholars and the example of their scholarship, this book belongs to the three of them.

THE DICTATOR'S DILEMMA

I

Introduction

The CCP's Strategy for Survival

IN THE WAKE OF the Tiananmen demonstrations in 1989, the days of the Chinese Communist Party (CCP, or simply the Party) seemed numbered. While reformers within the Party favored accepting the protestors' initial demands— recognition that they were patriotic and a dialogue between student representatives and Party and government leaders—hard-liners ultimately prevailed. They imposed martial law, ousted top leaders who sought compromise over violence, and sent in the People's Liberation Army against unarmed demonstrators. Hundreds and perhaps thousands were killed in the sudden and unexpected crackdown. By using indiscriminate violence against those who had engaged in peaceful protests for weeks, the Party severely damaged its legitimacy at home and its reputation abroad. Many China watchers predicted the imminent downfall of the Party. Despite such dire forecasts, the Party has remained in power to the present day, more than three decades after the grim events of 1989. In a more general sense, China watchers have predicted the collapse of the Party and the onset of democratization throughout the post-Mao period. And yet the Party survives. Why has a party that seemed to face such long odds managed to survive for so long?

In the popular imagination, China's political system is a brutal authoritarian regime that represses its critics, is riddled with corrupt and venal officials, and is in danger of collapse if it does not sustain rapid economic growth. That image contains much that is true, but it overlooks the image that is most prominent for most people in China: a regime whose policies generate resentment and protest, but nevertheless enjoys a surprisingly high level of popular support; a regime that consults with a wide range of specialists, stakeholders, and the general public in a selective but yet extensive manner; a regime that tolerates and even encourages a growing civil society, even while restricting which interests can organize and which groups can operate; and a regime that is seen as increasingly democratic by the majority of its people, even though it does not allow political competition and its leaders are not accountable to the electorate. China's population may prefer change, but they prefer that it occur within the existing political framework. That is an image familiar to China specialists, but not to those whose knowledge of contemporary China is limited to the Western media. When we look at Chinese politics from these perspectives, we get a very different picture of the Party and the regime it governs, even while recognizing the repressive, corrupt, and dysfunctional aspects of the regime.

Those who have predicted collapse and democratization rightly noted the challenges facing the regime, but wrongly discounted its ability to adapt to changing conditions. Like all ruling parties, the Party's primary goal is to remain in power. Its strategy for survival is a combination of carrots and sticks. On one hand, it promotes economic growth—and more importantly raising standards of living for most but not all Chinese—in order to create support. On the other, it harshly represses real and perceived threats to the regime, including not just dissidents and democracy activists but also bloggers, businesspeople, and religious believers. It monitors the flow of information to limit the public's awareness of past and present events and raise the cost of collective action. These are familiar aspects of authoritarian regimes like China's.

But the Party also generates popular support in ways besides economic growth. It creates a sense of patriotic pride for the country's accomplishments and its growing international influence. It selectively embraces aspects of China's traditional heritage. It co-opts newly emerging economic and social elites into the Party and other political institutions. In contrast to those who say there has been no political reform in China, the Party has initiated a variety of reforms that have substantially changed state-society relations. They have not made the country more democratic, and they were not intended to do so. At best, they can be considered as consultation without accountability, but they do provide the public with input into the policy-making process that was generally lacking in the past. For those who steer clear of the red lines of Chinese politics, such as publicly criticizing Party leaders and their policies or organizing public protests, the state is less intrusive and less repressive than during the Maoist era. But for those who consciously (and sometimes inadvertently) step over the line, the state continues to be a powerful and oppressive force.

Recognizing the Party's strategy for survival—a combination of legitimation, co-optation, and repression—is the first step in understanding the prospects for regime change in China. Each element of the Party's survival strategy presents a dilemma. In seeking popular support, short-term gains may create long-term challenges. Rising living standards may produce a desire for more accountability from the Party and government. Relaxing controls over society to encourage economic growth and reduce the costs of repression may create demands for even greater openness. Implementing limited political reforms may lead to expectations for more ambitious reforms. In co-opting new elites into the Party, it may weaken its cohesiveness and bring potential threats into the Party where they may challenge the status quo. In handling real and perceived threats, it must calibrate its coercive tools: Too little and the threat may spread, too much and it may alienate its supporters, even turning them into opponents. Each of these steps presents a dilemma common to authoritarian regimes: rather than solidifying its hold on power, it may instead create greater challenges.

Recognizing how the public responds to the separate parts of the Party's survival strategy is the next step. This book is designed to lay out both the Party's survival strategy and the public's response to it. To this end, throughout the book, I rely on two nationwide surveys of public opinion in urban China that I designed and implemented in 2010 and 2014 (see appendix 1 for full details). Taking place two years before and two years after the change in the country's political leadership in 2012, these surveys provide before-and-after snapshots of the Chinese public's assessment of the regime's performance.

Public opinion surveys can reveal valuable information, but they have to be handled with care, especially when done in an authoritarian country like China. People living in authoritarian regimes may be reluctant to give their honest opinions, especially on politically sensitive questions. A key theme of this book—who does and who does not support the regime—is certainly a sensitive question. In this context, we must be careful in what we ask and how we ask it. That means avoiding questions that would elicit preprogrammed answers, questions that are too complex for a survey context, and questions that are known to be off-limits, such as Tibet, the Tiananmen Square protests of 1989, and approval ratings for specific Chinese leaders. With these restrictions in mind, public opinion surveys can offer unique insights. The greatest advantage of survey research is that it allows us to not simply state how many people agree and disagree with a particular question, but more importantly to see what influences people's responses. Do differences in age, education, income, and gender influence how people think and behave in China as they do in other countries? Are Party members different from the rest of society? Survey research is the best way of answering these kinds of questions.

Public opinion surveys are not the only means for gleaning public opinion. Interviews are also informative and allow more in-depth investigation of the questions at hand. The survey data are therefore supplemented by focus-group interviews conducted in four cities: Beijing and Wuhan in 2013, and Guangzhou and Chongqing in 2014. The cities were chosen to capture regional and economic differences. In each city, separate groups of local officials and residents were interviewed on a variety of current affairs topics. These focus group interviews complement the public opinion data and provide some local context on key issues.

Scanning the Internet and social media can also provide a window into public opinion in China, and this is a popular tool for journalists. But just as what is trending on Twitter is not a reliable indicator of American public opinion, focusing only on Internet discussions may not be the best way of deciphering public opinion in China. It is easy to find critical views on the Chinese Internet. Many are eloquent and colorful, even profane and threatening, but they may not represent public opinion as a whole. In order to understand the public's response to the

Party's survival strategy, and therefore the prospects for regime change, public opinion surveys offer new insights that are too often overlooked.

Regimes can collapse for reasons other than their survival strategy and public opinion. Above all, elite splits can result in a coup or civil war. After a long reign, authoritarian regimes can experience political decay, causing them to collapse from within. What looked to be a strong and durable regime can collapse in short order. But if leaders want to govern and modernize their countries and not simply cling to power, they have to build and maintain popular support. That is the situation the Party in China is in, and this book investigates both its survival strategy and how the public is responding to it.

I. Explaining the CCP's Survival Strategy

Much of the recent literature on the survival of authoritarian regimes has limited applicability to China. China lacks the abundant natural resources that have allowed some regimes to survive without needing to court popular support.[1] Patrimonial practices reward family members and political supporters with key jobs and the perks those jobs control,[2] but nepotism and favoritism have declined in post-Mao China; official appointments are increasingly based on merit and professional accomplishments, not simply ideological conformity or personal ties.[3] Rather than dividing the political opposition through wedge tactics,[4] the Party has attempted to eliminate it, aggressively defending its monopoly on

[1] Michael L. Ross, "Does Oil Hinder Democracy?" *World Politics*, Vol. 53 (April 2001), pp. 325–361.

[2] Eva Bellin, "The Robustness of Authoritarianism in the Middle East," *Comparative Politics*, Vol. 36, No. 2 (January 2004), pp. 139–157.

[3] Cheng Li, *China's Leaders: The New Generation* (Lanham, MD: Rowman & Littlefield, 2001); Andrew J. Nathan and Bruce Gilley, *China's New Rulers: The Secret Files* (New York: New York Review Books, 2001); Andrew J. Nathan, "Authoritarian Resilience," *Journal of Democracy*, Vol. 14, No. 1 (January 2003), pp. 6–17; Pierre Landry, *Decentralized Authoritarianism in China: The Communist Party's Control of Local Elites in the Post-Mao Era* (New York: Cambridge University Press, 2008).

[4] Ellen Lust-Okar, "Divided They Rule: The Management and Manipulation of Political Oppression," *Comparative Politics*, Vol. 36, No. 2 (January 2004), pp. 159–179.

political organization. China does not have competitive elections for the most important political posts, and therefore its leaders do not have to manipulate those elections or employ power-sharing arrangements to stay in power.[5] China remains a prominent example of what Larry Diamond calls a "closed political regime": It lacks meaningful elections, and all positions of political influence are controlled by the ruling party.[6]

In the Maoist era (1949–1976), the Party was a revolutionary party committed to remaking society in line with Mao's ideological and political preferences. The result was the political campaigns that defined his years as China's leader, above all the Great Leap Forward and the Cultural Revolution. In the post-Mao period, the Party changed directions. It abandoned the political campaigns and ideological debates of the past and adopted economic modernization as its key task. It no longer described itself as a revolutionary party but instead characterized itself as China's "ruling party" (*zhizheng dang* 执政党). The shift from being a revolutionary party to a ruling party was not just a rhetorical shift; it signified a change in the Party's survival strategy that had been underway for much of the post-Mao period.[7] No longer was the Party determined to transform society, reshaping it to conform to its ideological vision. Instead, the Party was determined to remain the party in power, repressing threats to its power—not class enemies, but threats to political stability—and generating popular support by promoting economic modernization, embracing nationalism and traditional values,

[5] Jason Brownlee, *Authoritarianism in an Age of Democratization* (New York: Cambridge University Press, 2007); Beatriz Magaloni, *Voting for Autocracy: Hegemonic Party Survival and its Demise in Mexico* (New York: Cambridge University Press, 2008); Jennifer Gandhi, *Political Institutions under Dictatorship* (New York: Cambridge University Press, 2008); Steven Levitsky and Lucan Way, *Competitive Authoritarianism: Hybrid Regimes after the Cold War* (New York: Cambridge University Press, 2010); Dan Slater, *Ordering Power: Contentious Politics and Authoritarian Leviathans in Southeast Asia* (New York: Cambridge University Press, 2010).

[6] Larry Diamond, "Thinking about Hybrid Regimes," *Journal of Democracy*, Vol. 13, No. 2 (April 2002), pp. 21–35.

[7] For discussion of how this change in labeling also signified a change in governing style, see Timothy R. Heath, *China's New Governing Party Paradigm: Political Renewal and the Pursuit of National Rejuvenation* (Burlington, VT: Ashgate, 2014).

and co-opting newly emerging economic and social elites into the Party. All this was designed to legitimize its continued status as China's ruling party.

Evaluating the prospects for regime change in China begins with understanding the Party's survival strategy and its relationship with society. That strategy includes a combination of repression, legitimation, and the co-optation of new elites into the Party. There is no consensus on the proper balance between repression, legitimation, and co-optation. Each is part of the Party's survival strategy, but the balance is constantly shifting and each presents its own dilemma.

Repression

Repression has been a key part of the communist regime in China, as it is in all authoritarian regimes. It represses real and perceived threats, including dissidents, bloggers, lawyers, journalists, people of faith, and ethnic minorities. It censors the flow of information by monitoring social media, banning mention of sensitive topics on the Internet, removing critical posts, and blocking access to foreign websites. It restricts the population's ability to move around the country through the household registration (hukou 户口) system; although this system has been weakened as a consequence of economic reform, it still limits life opportunities in real and profound ways. It also controls the population in a particularly invasive way: enforcing the one-child policy. This policy has been modified over the years in response to public protest, but it is often enforced in brutal ways. Repression is a hallmark of authoritarian regimes and a key part of the Party's strategy for survival.

However, repression is costly. It requires the state to devote substantial resources (time, talent, money) to monitoring and sanctioning unwanted activities. It also risks alienating people who otherwise might support the regime. Consequently, over time it has been used more selectively to sustain the Party. It no longer uses massive political campaigns to expose and punish alleged political enemies, as it did in the Maoist era (1949–1976). In order to repress and even preempt political challenges without relying entirely on coercive powers, the Party more commonly restricts access to "coordination goods," such as restricting the types of groups that can operate openly, screening the people who serve in public positions, and limiting the flow of information via the media and the Internet.[8] These tactics have been successful in stifling the emergence of organized political opposition and preventing the formation of sustained social movements.[9] In recent years, the Party has again expanded its use of coercive tools, resulting in a more repressive political atmosphere. However, focusing on coercive tools alone misses a crucial fact about politics in China: The Party remains in power not only because it has been able to eliminate or at least suppress all viable alternatives,[10] but also because it enjoys a remarkable degree of popular support.

Sources of Legitimacy I: Material Interests

The most common assumption about the Party's survival is that its popular support is a consequence of economic development. Throughout the post-Mao reform era, the Party has focused on the pragmatic goal of economic development, in contrast to the ideological goal of defeating class enemies that was the hallmark of the Maoist period. The implicit social contract of the post-Mao years has been that the party-state would reduce political controls over everyday life and allow people to pursue economic prosperity in exchange for political quiescence, and ultimately political support. Most observers contend that economic development is the main basis for political support and regime legitimacy.[11] However, GDP levels are too blunt a proxy for development and ignore the many negative consequences—corruption, pollution, inequality, unemployment—that not only accompany rapid growth but also trigger resentment and public protest.

[8] Bruce Bueno de Mesquita and George W. Downs, "Development and Democracy," *Foreign Affairs*, Vol. 84, No. 5 (September/October 2005), pp. 77–86.

[9] Kevin J. O'Brien, ed., *Popular Protest in China* (Cambridge, MA: Harvard University Press, 2008).

[10] Adam Przeworski, "Some Problems in the Transition to Democracy," in Guillermo O'Donnell, Philippe C. Schmitter, and Laurence Whitehead, eds., *Transitions from Authoritarian Rule, Vol. 3: Comparative Perspectives* (Baltimore, MD: Johns Hopkins University Press, 1986).

[11] For the most in-depth analysis of this perspective, see Teresa Wright, *Accepting Authoritarianism: State-Society Relations in China's Reform Era* (Palo Alto, CA: Stanford University Press, 2010).

In fact, in contrast to the conventional wisdom that economic growth is the key source of the Party's legitimacy, economic growth has led to unexpected results for the regime. As chapter 5 shows in more detail, the public opinion survey data show that neither levels of per capita GDP nor rates of growth increase trust and support in China's main political institutions—the Party, the government, and the people's congress (China's legislature)—at either the central or local level. However, individuals who have seen their incomes rise in recent years and believe they will continue to grow in the years ahead are more likely to support the regime. This highlights a paradox common to authoritarian regimes: What is necessary to legitimate the Party in the short run (such as higher incomes) may de-legitimate it in the long run as people's interests change as their standards of living improve and the grievances that accompany rapid growth accumulate. This is also an important finding for the Party: Slower economic growth is not a threat to its popular support so long as incomes continue to rise. The surveys were conducted while the economy was already slowing down and suggest that regime support is influenced by changes in individual incomes but not aggregate growth. These arguments are supported with the survey data throughout the book, and especially in chapter 5.

Sources of Legitimacy II: Local Political Reforms

Another way the Party has tried to generate popular support is by reforming the links between state and society, the subject of chapter 3. The desire to be legitimate affects not only what the Party does, but also how it governs. Although China has not embarked on political reforms on the same scale as its economic reforms, China's leaders have introduced greater consultation and deliberation into the policy process. During both the decision-making process and the local implementation of policy, party and government officials consult with other individuals and groups outside the state in a selective but yet extensive manner.[12] These interactions often lead to revision of policy initiatives

---

[12] Andrew Mertha, "'Fragmented Authoritarianism 2.0': Political Pluralization in the Chinese Policy Process," *China Quarterly*, No. 200 (December 2009), pp. 995–1012; Ann M. Florini, Lai Hairong, and Yeling Tan, *China Experiments: From Local Innovations to National Reform* (Washington, DC: Brookings Institution, 2012).

before they are publicly announced, and modifications as they are implemented. At the national level, the Party solicited public comment via the Internet before announcing its nationwide healthcare reform in 2009.[13] More ambitious reforms are occurring at the local level. With the guidance of academics James Fishkin and Baogang He, residents of the city of Wenling in Zhejiang province participate in an intense review of policy needs and priorities and then make recommendations for the city's budget, which are then ratified by the local people's congress.[14] Similar efforts to encourage more public involvement in the policy process have been encouraged as a means of restoring the Party's traditional use of the "mass line" and improving state-society relations. As Shaoguang Wang has pointed out, however, the public is not always a part of the policy process.[15] The Party is only willing to consult with society when the policies do not concern core political issues or the survivability of the Party.

One of the prominent features of contemporary China is the Party's intolerance of an autonomous civil society. At the same time, local party and government leaders encourage the activities of some nongovernmental organizations (NGOs) in order to improve the provision of public goods, while still suppressing other civil society groups with more overt political agendas.[16] The number of formally registered NGOs in China is now over half a million, with estimates of more than twice that many unregistered but active groups. These groups often operate with the encouragement of local officials. Local NGOs can be

[13] Steven J. Balla, "Information Technology, Political Participation, and the Evolution of Chinese Policymaking," *Journal of Contemporary China*, Vol. 21, No. 76 (April 2012), pp. 655–673.

[14] Joseph Fewsmith, *The Logic and Limits of Political Reform in China* (New York: Cambridge University Press, 2013).

[15] Shaoguang Wang, "Changing Models of China's Policy Agenda Setting," *Modern China*, Vol. 34, No. 1 (January 2008), pp. 56–87.

[16] Jonathan Schwartz and Shawn Shieh, eds., *State and Society Responses to Welfare Needs in China* (New York and London: Routledge, 2009); Patricia Thornton, "The Advance of the Party: Transformation or Takeover of Urban Grassroots Society?" *China Quarterly*, No. 213 (March 2013), pp. 1–18; Jessica Teets, "Let Many Civil Societies Bloom: The Rise of Consultative Authoritarianism in China," *China Quarterly*, No. 213 (March 2013), pp. 19–38.

partners with the state in providing public goods and services, especially in areas like job training, literacy programs, and disaster relief. Some of these groups are able to attract money and supplies from foreign governments and foundations, giving local officials another incentive to cooperate with them.

Despite several decades of far-reaching economic reforms, political reforms have been much more limited. They have changed state-society relations in important ways, but they have not made the regime more democratic—and were not intended to. They are often overlooked by outside observers who believe the only meaningful political reforms are democratizing ones. Political reforms in China are designed to make the current regime work better and, to some degree, more responsive to public opinion, but without becoming accountable to the public and without surrendering the Party's monopoly on political organization. Moreover, their full significance may not be felt until later. As people become accustomed to participating in these limited ways, they may come to expect broader participation and representation. If so, the short-term benefits may be outweighed by long-term costs. Even these limited political reforms still deserve attention and evaluation because they provide important insights into the Party's strategy for survival.

Sources of Legitimacy III: Public Goods

The positive link between governance and popular support is conventional wisdom in democratic polities, where elected officials seek to provide more public goods in order to be reelected. As a result, democracies tend to provide more public goods to their citizens than authoritarian regimes.[17] Leaders in authoritarian regimes also want to remain in power, but they face different incentives for achieving that goal. Rather than being disciplined by the threat of losing elections, the

[17] Adam Przeworksi et al., *Democracy and Development: Political Institutions in the World, 1950–1990* (New York: Cambridge University Press, 2000); Amartya Sen, *Resources, Values, and Development* (Oxford, UK: Blackwell, 2004); Stephan Haggard and Robert R. Kaufman, *Development, Democracy, and Welfare States: Latin America, East Asia, and Eastern Europe* (Princeton, NJ: Princeton University Press, 2008); Morton H. Halperin, Joseph T. Siegle, and Michael M. Weinstein, *The Democracy Advantage: How Democracies Promote Prosperity and Peace* (New York: Routledge, 2010).

threat to authoritarian leaders is more likely to come from potential challenges from other sets of elites. Therefore, in most authoritarian regimes, rational politicians distribute private goods—such as plum jobs and access to scarce goods and services—to their elite supporters rather than the public at large. In the words of Bueno de Mesquita and his coauthors, "bad policy is good politics" for authoritarian leaders.[18]

China's leaders are not following the "bad policy is good politics" strategy of political survival. Although it is true that the main beneficiaries of economic development have been those with close connections to the Party, especially the sons and daughters of high-ranking officials, the regime has also been providing greater amounts of public goods, such as education, healthcare, and poverty alleviation, in recent years. From the perspective of China's leaders, the main threat they face is not from insiders but from political discontent in the population at large.[19] As a result, efforts to govern better are designed to improve the quality of life and thereby promote political stability.

Providing more public goods is an alternative to economic growth for enhancing the popular support of the Party.[20] This is the focus of chapter 4. Although most discussions of legitimacy in contemporary China state that economic growth is the primary basis for the regime's legitimacy, the regime itself has a more varied strategy. Economic growth alone is too thin a reed to build legitimacy upon. Growth cannot last forever; it is susceptible to ups and downs beyond the state's control, as demonstrated by the 2007–2008 international financial

[18] Bruce Bueno de Mesquita, Alastair Smith, Randolph M. Siverson, and James Morrow, *The Logic of Political Survival* (Cambridge, MA: MIT Press, 2003).

[19] David M. Lampton, *Following the Leader: Ruling China, from Deng Xiaoping to Xi Jinping* (Berkeley, CA: University of California Press, 2014).

[20] Vivienne Shue, "Legitimacy Crisis in China?" in Peter Hays Gries and Stanley Rosen, eds., *Chinese Politics: State, Society, and the Market* (New York: Routledge, 2010), pp. 41–68; Bruce Gilley, "Legitimacy and Institutional Change: The Case of China," *Comparative Political Studies*, Vol. 41, No. 3 (March 2008), pp. 259–284; Bruce Gilley and Heike Holbig, "The Debate on Party Legitimacy in China: A Mixed Quantitative/Qualitative Analysis," *Journal of Contemporary China*, Vol. 18, No. 59 (March 2009), pp. 337–356; Teresa Wright, *Accepting Authoritarianism: State-Society Relations in China's Reform Era* (Palo Alto, CA: Stanford University Press, 2010).

crisis and the stock market volatility of 2015. Moreover, the beneficiaries of growth are too often corrupt and venal officials, who undermine the Party's claims to legitimacy. On the other hand, providing public goods addresses societal needs not met by growth alone, potentially benefits a wider range of the population, and may provide an alternative and more durable source of regime support. When the corrupt practices and heavy-handed tactics used by local officials to promote growth threaten to de-legitimate the regime, providing public goods may help restore legitimacy.

Sources of Legitimacy IV: Political Values

Regime support may also be based on nonmaterial sources. Jie Chen's study of Beijing residents showed that democratic beliefs and a desire for political reform diminished political support, but that nationalist sentiments and a preference for political order contributed to political support.[21] Other studies have similarly found growing nationalism in China, and examined the Party's efforts to promote and utilize it in different ways.[22] Promoting the Party as the defender of the nation's interests is a key element in its strategy for survival: To be patriotic is to support the Party.

Until the early 20th century, Confucianism had been the dominant philosophical tradition for over two millennia. It influenced patterns of governance in China and also shaped interpersonal relationships in families and throughout society. Although the Party tried to eradicate Confucian traditions during the Maoist era (1949–1976), in the post-Mao period, it has resurrected some of these traditions to legitimize its policies and practices. Party leaders have adopted slogans with Confucian origins to describe their goals and now celebrate Confucius' birthday as

[21] Jie Chen, *Popular Political Support in Urban China* (Stanford, CA: Stanford University Press, 2004).

[22] Suisheng Zhao, "A State-Led Nationalism: The Patriotic Education Campaign in Post-Tiananmen China," *Communist and Post-Communist Studies*, Vol. 31, No. 3 (September 1998), pp. 287–302; Peter Hays Gries, *China's New Nationalism: Pride, Politics, and Diplomacy* (Berkeley, CA: University of California Press, 2004); James Reilly, *Strong Society, Smart State* (New York: Columbia University Press, 2012); Jessica Chen Weiss, *Powerful Patriots: Nationalist Protest in China's Foreign Relations* (New York: Oxford University Press, 2014).

a national holiday. Along with its program of economic modernization, the Party has also embraced nationalism and Confucian traditions as part of its survival strategy. But public opinion may not be as amenable to this revival of Confucian values. The public opinion data presented in chapter 5 show that the changes underway in urban China, especially higher levels of education and increased mobility, are undermining the salience of Confucian values as a source of regime support.

Sources of Legitimacy V: Co-optation

Institutional ties to the state are also designed to generate regime support. As the Party shifted its political agenda from class struggle to economic modernization, it also shifted its recruitment strategy. It replaced the officials appointed in the Maoist era who had more ideological zeal than practical skills.[23] During the reform era, it appointed to official positions those who possessed the necessary professional skills to foster economic growth, which in turn was intended to produce popular support. In addition, it recruited new members from the social groups it relied on for support, in particular, college students, urban professionals, and private entrepreneurs.[24] This recruitment strategy has created institutional links between the Party and the beneficiaries of economic reform. My previous research showed that co-opted elites support the status quo.[25] But is this true for Party members as a whole? The survey

---

[23] Hong Yung Lee, *From Revolutionary Cadres to Party Technocrats in Socialist China* (Berkeley, CA: University of California Press, 1990); Melanie Manion, *Retirement of Revolutionary Cadres in China: Public Policies, Social Norms, Private Interests* (Princeton, NJ: Princeton University Press, 1993).

[24] Andrew G. Walder, "The Party Elite and China's Trajectory of Change," *China: An International Journal*, Vol. 2, No. 2 (September 2004), pp. 189–2009; Gang Guo, "Party Recruitment of College Students in China," *Journal of Contemporary China*, Vol. 14, No. 43 (2005), pp. 371–393; Bruce J. Dickson, "Who Wants to Be a Communist? Career Incentives and Mobilized Loyalty in Contemporary China," *China Quarterly*, No. 217 (March 2014), pp. 42–68.

[25] Bruce J. Dickson, *Red Capitalists in China: The Party, Private Entrepreneurs, and Political Change* (New York: Cambridge University Press, 2003); *Wealth into Power: The Communist Party's Embrace of China's Private Sector* (New York: Cambridge University Press, 2008); *Allies of the State: Democratic Support and Regime Support among China's Private Entrepreneurs* (Cambridge, MA: Harvard University Press, 2010), coauthored with Jie Chen.

data presented in chapter 5 show that it is: Party members as a whole have higher levels of regime support than nonmembers. They are also expected to show their loyalty to the Party in various ways, such as voting, volunteering, and making charitable donations, but this is the result of the Party's mobilization efforts more so than its members' genuine support.

II. Rethinking the Conventional Wisdom on China

The following chapters describe these elements of the Party's survival strategy and the public's response to it in more detail. The main findings challenge the conventional wisdom on contemporary China in several ways. First, they challenge the accepted idea that economic growth is the primary basis for the Party's legitimacy. That may have been the case early in the reform era, but after more than three decades of economic modernization, economic growth is no longer a reliable source of popular support. That is why the Party's survival strategy has become more diversified. In the study of American politics, scholars and pundits debate whether voting behavior is most influenced by aggregate economic conditions (known as "socio-tropic" factors) or individuals' pocketbook factors. Are election results determined by changes in overall GDP growth or personal incomes? Although China does not have elections, a similar distinction is important for understanding the link between economic factors and regime support. As chapter 5 shows, improvements in family income are highly correlated with regime support, but GDP growth is not. This has important implications for the Party's survival strategy: As the Party weans the economy off massive stimulus spending and infrastructure investments, slower growth need not produce a legitimacy crisis as long as individual incomes continue to rise. But if pocketbook factors also decline, levels of regime support are also likely to fall.

Second, they challenge the conventional wisdom that the Party rules primarily through repression. While survey data alone cannot determine precisely how much repression is responsible for the Party's survival, they do allow us to get some indication of how repression influences public opinion and regime support. Repression is definitely part of the Party's toolkit, but it is used more selectively than in the

Maoist period. Since 2008, however, coercive tools have impacted a wider range of the population, targeting people and activities that were previously tolerated. This presents a dilemma for the Party: It may eliminate some threats, but it also threatens to alienate people who would otherwise be regime supporters.

Third, they challenge the conventional wisdom that no political reforms have accompanied economic reform. In fact, various political reforms have been implemented that change the nature of state-society relations, even though they have not changed the regime itself. Instead, they have created new opportunities for the Party to consult in limited but important ways with stakeholders and the general public on specific types of issues, such as national healthcare reform and local budget priorities.

Fourth, they challenge the conventional wisdom that there is no civil society in China. The Party certainly does repress some civil society groups, but it tolerates and promotes others. The amount of repression and toleration varies in two ways: Some periods of time are more conducive to civil society development, and some cities have been more open to civil society organizations than others. The number of civil society groups has continued to grow even as the state cracks down on some groups. The key to understanding this seeming inconsistency is recognizing that neither the state nor civil society is monolithic in China. Some parts of the state promote the development of civil society, while others repress it. Some parts of civil society may pose a threat to the regime, but others want to partner with it. We need to abandon the idea that civil society is an inherently democratic agent. An active civil society can coexist with an authoritarian regime, even though the relationship is less predictable than in democratic regimes.

Finally, they challenge the conventional wisdom (especially as portrayed in the Western media) that the Chinese people are fed up with the Party, impatient for reform, and ready for democracy. Survey data and focus group interviews certainly reveal grievances on a host of policy issues, such as healthcare, education, the environment, and food safety, but they also see signs of improvement in at least some of these areas. More importantly, chapter 6 will show that most Chinese believe the regime has become increasingly democratic throughout the post-Mao period and expect it to become even more so in the near future. "Democracy" is defined differently by most people in China than it is in the West. This presents challenges to would-be democratizers: Not only do they face resistance from the state, they also face indifference and even resentment from those in society who believe the country is already moving in the right direction.

III. Debating Prospects for Change in China

The prospects for political change in China have been a constant source of scrutiny and debate in the academic and policy communities. The main point of contention has been whether the regime is fragile and in danger of collapse or if it is adaptable and resilient.

Most of the analyses of China's domestic politics portray a system in permanent crisis, where the Party relies on coercion and economic growth to maintain its fragile hold on power, is unable and unwilling to initiate political reform, and is paralyzed by fear of social unrest that could cause not only the collapse of the regime but the dissolution of the country. These problems are real, but China watchers have consistently underestimated the Party's ability to cope with these challenges. As a result, the image of China portrayed in much of the recent literature does not fit the reality that most Chinese confront on a daily basis.

Many studies focus on the fragility of the regime. Gordon Chang's *The Coming Collapse of China* gained great notoriety because of its bold prediction that the Party was incapable of change and would collapse within five or at most ten years (the Party survived both deadlines).[26] Chang correctly pointed out the challenges facing the Party, but was wrong on every prediction he made: China did not go to war with Taiwan; society did not revolt after China joined the World Trade Organization; the banks and stock market did not collapse; and above all the Party did not fall from power. Despite the litany of problems Chang identified, the Party survived because it was able to adapt. Similarly, Susan Shirk's *China: Fragile Superpower* captured a central paradox of contemporary China: It is simultaneously externally powerful and internally fragile.[27]

[26] Gordon Chang, *The Coming Collapse of China* (New York: Random House, 2001).

[27] Susan Shirk, *China: Fragile Superpower: How China's Internal Politics Could Derail Its Peaceful Rise* (New York: Oxford University Press, 2007).

She portrayed the Party and its leaders as fearful of public opinion and the potential for nationalism and popular protest to threaten the nation's stability and the Party's hold on power. She presented the Party as a passive bystander, threatened by a host of threats and challenges, but not doing anything to cope besides using coercion, control, and censorship. Minxin Pei's *China's Trapped Transition* offered an engaging account of why political reform did not accompany economic reform, as so many China watchers expected.[28] He gave a detailed depiction of the corrupt nature of Chinese politics: Its leaders are kleptocrats, out for their own interests and intent on accumulating as much wealth as possible before the regime collapses. He concluded that China's leaders are now trapped, unable to fully reform the economy and unwilling to democratize the political system. But for every case of kleptocracy, there is another example of a local leader who is committed to governing better or who has experimented with political reform (although not democratization). Although he pointed to examples of governance failures, this kind of perspective cannot explain the Party's commitment to improved governance that began about the time his book was published, or the far-reaching anticorruption campaign begun in 2013.

Other works focus on the secretive, internal aspects of the Party. David Shambaugh provided one of the most in-depth looks at the Party's organization and its internal debates about what it needed to do to survive.[29] He situated his account in the lessons drawn from the collapse of the Soviet Union and other East European communist states. He showed that the Party exhibited symptoms of both atrophy and adaptation, with adaptation being the more prominent trend. But Shambaugh subsequently noticed a reversion to atrophy after 2008, and in 2015 he predicted: "We are witnessing the endgame of communist rule in China."[30] While he offered a detailed examination of

---

[28] Minxin Pei, *China's Trapped Transition: The Limits of Developmental Autocracy* (Cambridge, MA: Harvard University Press, 2006).

[29] David Shambaugh, *China's Communist Party: Atrophy and Adaptation* (Berkeley, CA, and Washington, DC: University of California Press and Woodrow Wilson Center Press, 2009).

[30] Shambaugh, "The Coming Chinese Crackup," *Wall Street Journal*, March 6, 2015. See also his longer study, *China's Future* (Cambridge, UK: Polity, 2016).

the Party's internal debates and dynamics, he paid less attention to its efforts to govern better or improve relations with society. These are the key elements of the Party's survival strategy and are crucial for evaluating its future prospects. In a similar fashion, Richard McGregor looked almost exclusively at the internal operations of the Party, emphasizing its secretive nature, its control over the government and key sectors of the economy, and its preoccupation with avoiding negative publicity, including public protests.[31] These internal elements are important for understanding the Party, but they ignore its external relationships with the rest of society.

In contrast to these predictions of collapse and democratization, other scholars have concluded that the Party is adaptable, even resilient, and is likely to remain in power indefinitely. The most prominent is Andrew Nathan, who popularized the "authoritarian resilience" perspective.[32] While not denying the continued role of factions and personal relationships, he argued that the appointment of officials has become more meritocratic, rewarding good performance and not just good connections. Above all, he argued that China's political system has become more institutionalized in its policy process and the selection of top party and government leaders. The regime has also created new input institutions that allow new interests to be represented and shape state-society interactions. In a similar fashion, Dali L. Yang has argued that China has been enhancing its state capacity through institutional development and greater professionalism.[33] The result is a more responsive state, although one that is still without accountability. Elizabeth Perry identifies the Party's institutions for recruiting members, appointing officials, channeling public opinion, building coalitions, and creating divisions within society. Many of these originated in the pre-1949 era and remain a source of regime durability.[34]

[31] Richard McGregor, *The Party: The Secret World of China's Communist Rulers* (New York: HarperCollins, 2010).

[32] Andrew J. Nathan, "Authoritarian Resilience," *Journal of Democracy*, Vol. 14, No. 1 (January 2003), pp. 6–17.

[33] Dali L. Yang, *Remaking the Chinese Leviathan: Market Transition and the Politics of Governance in China* (Stanford, CA: Stanford University Press, 2004).

[34] Elizabeth J. Perry, "Studying Chinese Politics: Farewell to Revolution?" *China Journal*, No. 57 (January 2007), pp. 1–22.

Other scholars have combined a variety of adjectives to describe China's political system. Kenneth Lieberthal used "fragmented authoritarianism" to depict a policy-making process with extensive negotiating between central and local levels of government and between ministries and departments at each level.[35] Anne-Marie Brady coined the term "popular authoritarianism," which "combines one-party rule with close attention to public opinion."[36] In an interesting twist, she claimed that China has a post-communist society but still has a communist government.[37] Xi Chen described the interactions between state and society as creating a "contentious authoritarianism," in which some protests are successful in reaching their goals and others are suppressed.[38] Baogang He, Stig Thøgersen, and Jessica Teets revived "consultative authoritarianism," a phrase earlier used by Harry Harding to describe limited political reforms.[39] In these different ways, the adaptability of the Party and its regime has been identified by a variety of scholars, even if their findings are not well known outside the academic world.

The critique of the authoritarian resilience perspective has been intense in academic circles. Some question the degree to which the Chinese political system has become institutionalized, pointing instead to the continued influence of prominent individuals and factions. Cheng Li argues that "the CCP's 'authoritarian resilience' is a stagnant

[35] Kenneth Lieberthal, "The 'Fragmented Authoritarianism' Model and Its Limitations," in Kenneth Lieberthal and David M. Lampton, eds., *Bureaucracy, Politics, and Decision Making in Post-Mao China* (Berkeley, CA: University of California Press, 1992). See also Kenneth Lieberthal and Michel Oksenberg, *Policy Making in China: Leaders, Structures, and Processes* (Princeton, NJ: Princeton University Press, 1988); Mertha, " 'Fragmented Authoritarianism 2.0.' "

[36] Anne-Marie Brady, *Marketing Dictatorship: Propaganda and Thought Work in Contemporary China* (Lanham, MD: Rowman & Littlefield, 2009), p. 194.

[37] Brady, *Marketing Dictatorship*, p. 6.

[38] Xi Chen, *Social Protest and Contentious Authoritarianism in China* (New York: Cambridge University Press, 2012).

[39] Baogang He and Stig Thøgersen, "Giving the People a Voice? Experiments with Consultative Authoritarian Institutions in China," *Journal of Contemporary China*, Vol. 19, No. 66 (September 2010), pp. 675–692; Jessica C. Teets, *Civil Society under Authoritarianism: The China Model* (New York: Cambridge University Press, 2014); Harry Harding (*China's Second Reform: Reform after Mao* (Washington, DC: Brookings Institution, 1987).

system, both conceptually and empirically, because it resists much-needed democratic changes in the country."[40] Bruce Gilley argues that economic development has produced high levels of legitimacy in China at present, but is also leading to changes in political values that may require the Party to adopt institutional changes, specifically democratization, to accommodate popular demands.[41] Minxin Pei argues that many scholars are mistaking signs of fragility for resilience: "the principal reasons for the CCP's survival since Tiananmen have been robust economic performance and consistent political repression," but not its adaptability.[42] While recognizing that regime change may not be imminent, Li, Gilley, and Pei predict a democratic future for China.

In a general sense, skeptics of the Party's adaptability and resiliency see democracy as the solution to China's problems. Forecasts of China's democratization are problematic in several ways. Some turn legitimacy into a tautology: Only democracies are legitimate (because of the consent of the governed); China is not a democracy; therefore the current regime is not legitimate. But this ignores other sources of the Party's legitimacy, such as material interests, cultural values, and improved governance. Others conflate their preference for what they *want* to happen with a prediction of what is *likely* to happen. Few would disagree that democracy is a preferable form of government, but the prospects for a stable democracy in China are unknown and unknowable.

Forecasts of democratization also assume that democracy is the only alternative to Party rule. But the end of an authoritarian regime is not necessarily the onset of a democratic one. Following the collapse of communism in Eastern Europe and the Soviet Union, only ten of the 29 countries became stable democracies. Some were non-communist but still authoritarian regimes; some were unstable democracies; and others were hybrid regimes, with some of the trappings of democracy

[40] Cheng Li, "The End of the CCP's Resilient Authoritarianism? A Tripartite Assessment of Shifting Power in China," *China Quarterly*, No. 211 (September 2012), p. 595.

[41] Bruce Gilley, "Legitimacy and Institutional Change: The Case of China," *Comparative Political Studies*, Vol. 41, No. 3 (March 2008), pp. 259–284.

[42] Minxin Pei, "Is CCP Rule Fragile or Resilient?" *Journal of Democracy*, Vol. 23, No. 1 (January 2012), p. 39.

but still authoritarian in many of their practices.[43] Following the Arab Spring of 2011, only Tunisia became democratic, and the full consolidation of democracy there remains uncertain. Other countries that experienced mass uprisings—Egypt, Libya, Syria, Yemen—experienced either new forms of authoritarianism, prolonged instability, or a mix of both. We should not assume that democracy is the inevitable alternative to communist rule in China.

Finally, predictions of China's democratization assume that Chinese society prefers democracy to the status quo. But many Chinese fear the dramatic drop in living standards and economic prospects that transpired in post-communist Russia. Democracy as currently practiced in the United States, East Asia, Europe, and elsewhere does not inspire confidence that democracy is the answer to China's problems. Surprisingly, and as explained in chapter 6, most Chinese believe that their country already has a high level of democracy, are satisfied with the quality of current democracy, and are optimistic about further increases in democracy in the near future. Rather than an inherent desire for democracy now, most Chinese are willing to be patient and wait for it to unfold gradually. As Tianjian Shi concluded, "the way Chinese people understand democracy leaves their government great space to maneuver. This space, I would argue, constitutes the micro-foundation of authoritarian resilience in China."[44]

Cheng Li takes the critique of the resilient authoritarian perspective further by saying that it is unreliable because its advocates are "American China analysts," "foreign observers," and "academics in the West" with an overly simplistic understanding of Chinese politics.[45]

---

[43] Of the 29 formerly communist countries in Central Europe and Eurasia (including the countries that were once part of the Soviet Union), at most, ten can be considered to be democracies: Bulgaria, Czech Republic, Estonia, Hungary, Latvia, Lithuania, Poland, Romania, Slovenia, and Slovakia. Bulgaria, Hungary, and Romania belong to the EU, which requires members to be democracies, but Freedom House reports declining levels of democracy in these countries. In other words, the vast majority of former communist countries did not become democracies, but rather developed new forms of authoritarian rule after the end of communism.

[44] Tianjian Shi, *The Cultural Logic of Politics in Mainland China and Taiwan* (New York: Cambridge University Press, 2015), p. 220.

[45] Cheng Li, "The End of the CCP's Resilient Authoritarianism?" pp. 596–597.

This is problematic for at least two reasons. First, it assumes that a country can only be understood in terms of its own history, and that the experience of other countries provides no insight into a country's political trajectory. To a large degree, every country is unique, with distinctive political traditions that frame how current issues are understood and put limits on the range of options that leaders choose from. But no country is totally unique: The issues confronting one country's leaders are often similar to those in other countries, at present or in the past. Chinese scholars and political leaders from the 19th century to the present have looked abroad for examples to learn from, borrow from, and emulate. Even when the differences are more pronounced than the similarities, comparison can still provide insight into why one option was adopted in one country and a different one in another country. That is the fundamental logic of comparison, beginning with John Stuart Mill and continuing up to now in most of the social sciences. Whether cases are mostly similar or mostly different, comparison still aids our understanding. China is indeed distinctive and in some ways unique, as are other countries in their own ways. But as a large, rapidly growing, and modernizing country with an authoritarian political system, there are points of comparison and contrast that can be illuminating. For example, although corruption and inequality are seen as enormous problems in China, in comparative terms, China is more typical of countries at its level of development. Far from being exceptional, levels of corruption and inequality in China—while unquestionably high— are about par for the course.

The second problem with the assertion that Chinese scholars offer more credible insights on Chinese politics is that it assumes they share the same perspective on the nature of the CCP regime, and foreign scholars hold another. But in fact, there is a vibrant debate among China specialists, regardless of their nationality. Among the most influential scholars on the resiliency side of the debate are Chinese scholars such as Tianjian Shi, Dali L. Yang, Lai Hairong, and Shaoguang Wang. The main critics of that perspective include Western academics like Bruce Gilley, David Shambaugh, and Joseph Fewsmith. For each of them, as for others engaged in the debate, their conclusions are based on a careful analysis of available information, which is often incomplete and ambiguous. The debate that has developed is due to the ambiguous nature of the information at hand; as Shambaugh put it, there are elements of both atrophy and adaption in the Party and the Chinese political system as a whole. Which one is primary and which is secondary, which is on the ascendant or in decline, is the essence of the debate. If the data were incontrovertible, there would be no debate. The solution to the debate is continued research and analysis, the identification of new facts and trends, and not the assertion of credibility based on national origin alone.

IV. Why It Matters

No country presents a greater test of theories of regime change and continuity than China, and no country has greater potential to impact U.S. policy interests than China. One of the key goals of U.S. foreign policy has been the promotion of democratization around the world. Promoting regime change often backfires. In some cases, it produces chaos and instability instead of a consolidated democracy. In other cases, it replaces one authoritarian regime with another form of authoritarianism. Overt American support for regime change often produces anti-American sentiments. Especially in a country where nationalism is strong, as it is in China, people are more likely to be suspicious of U.S. actions than supportive. This is also a problem faced by NGOs: Accepting international funding makes them look unpatriotic and the tool of foreign governments.

Throughout the post-Mao period, China watchers in the academic and policy communities have predicted the collapse of the Party and the onset of democratization. And yet the Party survives. Those who predicted collapse and democratization rightly noted the challenges facing the regime, but they wrongly discounted its ability to adapt to changing conditions. Others have expected that China's extensive economic reforms, including privatization of the domestic economy and integration into the global economy, would trigger political reforms. Indeed, after the normalization of U.S.-China relations in the 1970s, U.S. policy-makers encouraged reform in China and trade with China as means of promoting eventual democratization. However, China has defied those predictions and remains a one-party authoritarian regime.

The findings from this project have several important implications for U.S. policy toward China. First and foremost, they offer a different perspective on the prospects for political change in China. The conventional wisdom is that Chinese society is unhappy with the status quo, angry about corruption, inequality, and other policy issues, and therefore impatient for political change. This perspective was particularly prominent in the run-up to the 18th Party Congress in 2012, when the once-a-decade leadership change occurred. It is most common among journalists and other China watchers who rely on isolated interviews, anecdotes, and Internet postings, none of which are reliable sources of information on public opinion more generally. In contrast, public opinion surveys portray a very different image, one in which there is frustration about a variety of policy issues, but nevertheless a surprisingly high level of regime support. The examples provided throughout this book indicate that public opinion has not changed in a fundamental way. This suggests that the conventional wisdom of an angry society and a fragile regime may well be wrong. The Party may have a level of popular legitimacy that will let it survive despite frequent complaints about the quality of governance. Grumbling about the cost of healthcare and access to quality schools is unlikely to lead to calls for regime change. Indeed, many Americans complain about the same things.

Second, many policy-makers assume that promoting the economic development of China will hasten its democratization. This has been the assumption behind the support for economic reform in China and trade with China.[46] Bill Clinton defended his human rights policy toward China by arguing that "the impulses of the society and the nature of the economic change will work together, along with the availability of information from the outside world, to increase the sphere of liberty over time. I don't think there is any way that anyone who disagrees with that in China can hold back that, just as eventually the Berlin Wall fell. I just think it's inevitable."[47] Similarly, George W. Bush also promoted trade as the basis for political change in China: "trade with China will promote freedom. Freedom is not easily contained.

[46] James Mann, *The China Fantasy: How Our Leaders Explain Away Chinese Repression* (New York: Viking, 2007).

[47] Made at a January 28, 1997, press conference; transcript available at the American Presidency Project, http://www.presidency.ucsb.edu/ws/index.php?pid=54449, accessed August 29, 2015.

Once a measure of economic freedom is permitted, a measure of political freedom will follow."[48] However, Chinese leaders have the opposite assumption: They expect that economic growth will bolster their popular support, not threaten their hold on power. The evidence presented in chapter 5 reveals a crucial distinction: Greater individual prosperity produces higher regime support, but aggregate indicators of prosperity and growth do not. More importantly, higher incomes are closely correlated with perceptions of the current level of democracy in China and satisfaction with it. So far at least, rising prosperity is not creating widespread demands for Western-style liberal democracy.

Finally, we should not assume that liberal democratic values are truly universal, or that they in particular are widely shared in China. While foreign governments and human rights organizations decry the increased use of coercion and censorship, these tactics do not face the same level of resistance within China. The fear of chaos remains a prominent part of Chinese political culture, making the Party's policies to maintain stability popular in society. Dissidents and activists are too often seen as troublemakers more than heroes, not just by the state but by society as well. Censorship is more likely to be met with resignation than anger.

These types of political values can change, but value change is often slow. It can occur in several ways. The first is generational replacement. The formative experiences of each political generation may be different, creating distinctive assumptions about how the world works that persist into later years. This is the slowest process of change, occurring as one cohort replaces another in the population. As is shown throughout the rest of this book, this type of change is clearly underway in China, with systematic consequences for political beliefs.

Second, individual experiences shape political values. Exposure to the international environment through education, travel, consumption of foreign goods, or simply surfing the web can cause values to change, at least for the people with direct experience. Throughout the post-Mao

[48] "In Bush's Words: 'Join Together in Making China a Normal Trading Partner,'" *New York Times*, May 18, 2000, http://www.nytimes.com/2000/05/18/world/in-bush-s-words-join-together-in-making-china-a-normal-trading-partner.html, accessed August 29, 2015.

era, the U.S. government has encouraged students from China to study in American schools, with the expectation that this would bring about pro-Western and pro-democracy values. In some cases, this has worked, but the effect has been muted because so many Chinese students have chosen to remain in the U.S. after graduation rather than return home to a less desirable economic, political, and environmental situation. In other cases, students from China have not had positive experiences in the U.S. They can feel isolated by language and culture in both their classes and communities. Even when they feel comfortable, Chinese students are often surprised to see how China is viewed in the U.S. and how other students in their classes discuss it. In response, they are more inclined to be defensive than critical. Simply studying, living, and working abroad does not ensure a change of values. Even Chinese-Americans born and raised in the U.S. tend to be patriotic and patient, and unknowingly repeat the core elements of modernization theory: China is too poor, too rural, and its cultural level is too low. Once those things change, China will be ready for democracy, but not yet. As a result, they support engagement with China instead of isolation and pressure to force political change, in sharp contrast to Cuban refugees who supported the blockade of Cuba in order to isolate and weaken the government there.

A third way in which values can change is through some traumatic event, such as war, economic crisis, or social upheaval. Unlike the other two types of value change that work at the cohort or individual level, traumatic events can affect the entire population suddenly and dramatically. The Cultural Revolution in China is one example of this kind of national trauma because just about everyone was affected in one way or another. People learned that they should not blindly trust their leaders and that they needed to think for themselves in order to survive. Even friends and family could not be counted on. Participants in the 1989 demonstrations in Tiananmen Square and elsewhere in China learned that patriotic and peaceful protests could end in tragedy. In the wake of June 4, Chinese and foreign observers suddenly became clear about what the Party was willing to do to hold on to power. But even the lessons of the Cultural Revolution and 1989 are not passed down from one generation to another. Parents are unwilling to share their experiences with their children, and the full accounts of these events are not taught in Chinese schools and universities. The first time that many young Chinese learn the details is in classes at foreign universities. The Party limits information on past events and blocks alternative perspectives in order to prevent these traumatic events from becoming common knowledge.

We do not have a good sense of how much support is necessary for a regime to remain in power. As Adam Przeworski pointed out, there are numerous regimes that survive without legitimacy, regardless of how it is defined.[49] But regimes that do not want to simply survive but also achieve developmental goals must also have the cooperation of the people they govern. The Party is seeking cooperation in a variety of ways, by providing new avenues for consultation in the policy process, providing greater amounts of public goods, appealing to nationalist and traditional beliefs, and co-opting new elites. This also creates a dilemma for the Party: As it adapts, it may create expectations for even more changes. Those who get used to participating in decision-making may not be content with consultation; they may also come to expect accountability from decision-makers. Recipients of public goods may be less willing to accept the intrinsic inequalities with which they are dispensed. As the Party cultivates nationalist sentiments to bolster its popular support, patriotism may give way to anti-foreign sentiments that make negotiation and compromise with other countries more difficult. Policy success carries the seeds of future challenges, as people take what they have for granted and want more. Co-opted elites may try to change the Party from within instead of simply being loyal supporters. The "revolution of rising expectations" may lead to rising costs for cooperation in the future. But there is little sign of that at present.

* * *

Although various recent studies have portrayed the Party as fragile, in danger of losing power, and facing a society that has grown impatient for genuine democratization, other studies have revealed a different

---

[49] Adam Przeworski, "Some Problems in the Transition to Democracy," in Guillermo O'Donnell, Phillippe C. Schmitter, and Laurence Whitehead, eds., *Transitions from Authoritarian Rule, Vol. 3: Comparative Perspectives* (Baltimore, MD: Johns Hopkins University, 1986), pp. 47–63.

picture, one in which the Party has changed its recruitment strategy, institutionalized its leadership succession process, generated popular support with a combination of material and cultural appeals, and is in the process of improving its quality of governance and rebuilding its relationship with society. The success of such initiatives is not yet known and they deserve more attention.

Just as China's leaders face a dilemma in deciding how to open up without losing their grip on power, the case of China presents a conundrum to specialists, pundits, and casual observers alike. It continues to defy expectations that economic growth leads to democracy. Many have been searching for signs of imminent democratization in China, but have done so largely in vain. When signs are seen, they are at the margins, in obscure locations, and consist of local innovations that rarely diffuse to other parts of the country, even though they get lots of attention from scholars and the media.[50] For example, at the bottom of the political system, village elections have been the focus of numerous studies, but these have not scaled up to counties and cities, much less to national institutions.[51] Although most Chinese see the country as increasingly democratic, there are few hints of democracy in the way that term is understood and practiced in the West. In considering the prospects for regime change in China, outside observers need to be aware of sources of support, as well as reasons for resentment.

Although we may debate whether China's authoritarian regime is truly resilient, there can be no doubt that it has been durable. In evaluating the durability of the Party and the regime it governs, we need to consider not only its fragile, secretive, and repressive nature, but also how it copes with economic and social change. In order to understand its fate, we have to first understand its strategy for survival and the public's response to it. That is what the rest of this book is designed to do.

---

[50] Bruce Gilley, "Democratic Enclaves in Authoritarian Regimes," *Democratization*, Vol. 17, No. 3 (June 2010), pp. 389–415; Joseph Fewsmith, *The Logic and Limits of Political Reform in China* (New York: Cambridge University Press, 2013); Ann M. Florini, Lai Hairong, and Yeling Tan, *China Experiments: From Local Innovations to National Reform* (Washington, DC: Brookings Institution, 2012).

[51] Kevin J. O'Brien and Suisheng Zhao, eds., *Grassroots Elections in China* (New York and London: Routledge, 2010).

In the chapters that follow, the different elements of the Party's survival strategy will be analyzed and public opinion data will be presented to show what does and does not resonate with members of Chinese society. Chapter 2 describes the different forms of repression, including crackdowns against dissidents and groups the Party sees as a threat, censorship over the flow of information, and controls over the population. Chapter 3 then looks at interactions between state and society, specifically local political reforms and China's evolving civil society. Changes in the provision of public goods, including education, healthcare, and poverty alleviation, are the subject of chapter 4. How the different elements of the Party's survival strategy—legitimation, co-optation, and repression—influence regime support is examined in chapter 5. Public perceptions about democracy and democratization in China are presented in chapter 6. Finally, the book concludes by considering the prospects for regime change in China and what the fate of the Party means for both academic debates and policy choices.

2

The Heavy Hand of the State

REPRESSION HAS BEEN A key part of the survival strategy of the CCP, as it is for all authoritarian regimes. For many outside observers, this is the most familiar feature of the Party's rule and the trigger for many of China's public protests. It is therefore the appropriate place to begin describing the Party's survival strategy and the public's response to it. Recognizing the Party's use of repressive tactics is necessary to understand what keeps it in power, but it is not sufficient for understanding its survival strategy as a whole. As subsequent chapters make clear, it also seeks the public's support in a variety of ways, even as it aggressively defends its monopoly on political power.

The Party harshly represses real and perceived threats to the regime, including not only democratic activists, but also lawyers, scholars, bloggers, and religious believers. It monitors and limits the availability of information to frame the public's awareness of past and present events and to make collective action more difficult.[1] However, coercion is costly. It requires large amounts of manpower and resources to carry out. It incurs international costs as foreign governments and other groups criticize human rights abuses. More importantly, it risks antagonizing people who are otherwise apolitical or potential supporters of the regime.

---

[1] Bruce Bueno de Mesquita and George W. Downs, "Development and Democracy," *Foreign Affairs*, Vol. 84, No. 5 (September/October 2005), pp. 77–86.

Consequently, over time, repression has been used more selectively to sustain the Party. For people who openly criticize and challenge the Party, repression can be swift and harsh. But most Chinese steer clear of the red lines of Chinese politics. For them, the Party's coercive controls are less oppressive because they are not used indiscriminately, as they were in the Maoist period and the immediate aftermath of the 1989 demonstrations. The heavy hand of the state is less visible and less threatening, and the range of freedoms, while far from complete, is broader than in the past. This change has not been smooth and linear, and recent years have seen the Party take a more forceful response to its critics. The tightening of political space began while Hu Jintao was head of the Party and accelerated after Xi Jinping succeeded him in 2012.[2] The line between what the Party will and will not tolerate (what Tang Tsou called the "zone of indifference"[3]) is always fuzzy, and people who operate near the line can find themselves targets of the repressive arm of the state.

In a related fashion, the Party also tries to restrict access to information through censorship of the media, the Internet, and even text messages. At the same time, the Chinese people have access to increasingly diverse sources of information. The Party has tight control over *People's Daily*, its official newspaper, and broadcast media, but most local newspapers and magazines are less encumbered by the Party's control. China's media environment is increasingly commercialized, and journalists and editors have to be mindful of both what the Party wants them to publish and what their readers want to read. The Internet is available to an ever-increasing number of people. In 2015, almost 670 million Chinese were online.

Like the story of the Dutch boy trying to stop a leaking dike by putting his fingers into the holes, only to find a new leak somewhere else, so too does the Party face the constant challenge of restricting the flow of information, only to find that new technology and greater access to different media increase the difficulty of controlling the message. It

[2] See Willy Wo-Lap Lam, *Chinese Politics in the Era of Xi Jinping: Renaissance, Reform, or Regression?* (New York and London: Routledge, 2015), esp. chapter 3.

[3] Tang Tsou, *The Cultural Revolution and Post-Mao Reforms: A Historical Perspective* (Chicago: University of Chicago Press, 1986).

is a never-ending challenge: The Party, determined to block access to information about local, national, and international events, faces off against citizens determined to gain access to information and share it with others. The gains on one side are quickly offset by innovations on the other, as they engage in a protracted game of cat and mouse, except that this is not a game. The stakes are quite high for some of the players. While some will have their blog posts taken down or their Internet accounts canceled, others will end up under house arrest or in prison.

The Party seeks to control not only information, but also other aspects of daily life. Although the post-Mao reforms have given people the opportunity to move in search of better housing, jobs, and in general improve the quality of their lives, the Party still restricts other options. Access to healthcare and education is not just tied to where people live, but also to where they were born. The government issues a person's household registration, or *hukou* (户口), which designates a person as either "agricultural" or "non-agricultural" (in other words, rural or urban) and indicates what province and city or county they were born in; for those with a rural *hukou*, it also designates the village. Once officially registered, their *hukou* is difficult to change, even if they no longer live in their place of birth. Although hundreds of millions of people have migrated from the countryside to urban areas in search of better-paying jobs, they are often unable to get healthcare and education because their *hukou*, their formal household registration, remains in the villages they left behind. There have been some significant reforms of the *hukou* system, but the state has been unwilling to do away with it altogether. It may not control where people live and work, but it still controls the amount of public goods that urban governments have to provide and perpetuates the unequal opportunities that are determined by where people are born and not by where they currently live. It has become a prominent issue of social justice in China.

Even more controversial has been the continuation of the one-child policy, which for most of the post-Mao era restricted married couples to having just one child (over the years, exceptions were made for people in various situations, as is outlined below, and in October 2015 was changed to a two-child policy). This policy has been the source of intense and often violent conflicts between local officials and people who try to evade the policy. The enforcement of this policy has led to international criticism regarding human rights violations. It has also created a skewed gender balance: Because most couples prefer sons, males far outnumber females among the younger cohorts. Although the state has relaxed some of the policy's provisions, it has not rescinded it altogether for fear of a population explosion.

Corruption is a different form of heavy-handedness by the state. Throughout the post-Mao era, corruption has grown apace with the economy as a whole. Examples abound of low-level, mid-level, and high-level officials using their formal posts to accumulate huge fortunes for themselves, their families, and their friends. The Party has repeatedly declared its intention to get serious about cracking down on corrupt practices, but to little effect. When Xi Jinping became China's leader in 2012, he launched a new anticorruption campaign that has been notable for its intensity and its targets of investigation. But like similar campaigns of the past, the campaign is aimed at Xi's potential rivals as much as it is aimed at eradicating corruption, and many of the targets of the campaign are subject to the same harsh treatment and extralegal punishment that are used against those in society who challenge the Party.

In the rest of this chapter, these key features of Party rule in China—repression, coercion, censorship, population control, and corruption—will be examined in more detail. In particular, this chapter focuses on both the Party's strategy and the popular reaction to the Party's often heavy-handed tactics.

I. Repression

Repression has been part of the Party's toolkit since before it became the ruling party in 1949. During the early 1940s, when the Party's headquarters were in the remote city of Yan'an in Shaanxi province, Mao forcefully weeded out critics and potential threats to his personal authority. Party members went through a three-year campaign known as the "Yan'an rectification," which involved lengthy political study and criticism/self-criticism methods, in which people criticized others while also admitting their own mistakes. In the course of this campaign, coercion was used to elicit confessions, approximately 40,000 were expelled from the party for not being in step with Mao, and an untold number were executed, including Wang Shiwei, a prominent journalist who wrote an essay criticizing Mao and the privileges granted to Party elites.[4]

After the CCP won the civil war and became the ruling party, it used a series of political campaigns to implement new policies and establish the Party's authority throughout the country and in every aspect of people's lives. Land-reform programs in the early 1950s reallocated land in the countryside and also included harsh sessions of struggle against former landlords. At these meetings, party officials encouraged peasants to recount their suffering at the hands of landlords. The purpose was to strip the old elites of both their land and social status. Estimates of the numbers of landlords who died during land reform vary widely, but somewhere between one and two million were probably executed.[5]

As the uncontested ruling party, the CCP used land reform and the nationalization of industry and commerce in the 1950s to consolidate its authority and promote its ideological goals, especially the elimination of private property, which Marx said was the essence of communism. Following this initial transition, Mao invited feedback from China's intellectuals in what became known as the "Hundred Flowers Movement," named after a Confucian saying: "let a hundred flowers bloom, let a hundred schools of thought contend." Instead of offering constructive suggestions on practical matters, intellectuals offered fundamental criticism of the political system itself: the intrusion of ideology into scientific research, the interference of party officials, many of them poorly educated and even illiterate, in the work of the government and universities, and the necessity of intellectual freedom unconstrained by political orthodoxy. These criticisms challenged core elements of the new communist system in China and were more than Mao and other Party leaders were willing to tolerate. The Anti-Rightist Campaign turned the table on the Party's critics; instead of addressing their complaints, Mao responded by attacking them as "rightists," counter-revolutionaries who wanted to do away with the Party (in contrast, correct thinking was

[4] Dai Qing, *Wang Shiwei and "Wild Lilies": Rectification and Purges in the Chinese Communist Party, 1942–1944* (Armonk, NY: M.E. Sharpe, 1994); Michael Lynch, *Mao* (London and New York: Routledge, 2004), p. 121.

[5] Frederick C. Teiwes, "Establishment and Consolidation of the New Regime," in Roderick MacFarquhar, ed., *The Politics of China*, second edition (NY: Cambridge University Press, 1997), p. 36.

labeled "leftist" because it supported the Party's ideology). Over half a million scientists, academics, writers, and government officials were labeled as rightists, with most of them fired from their jobs and sent to jail or labor camps.[6] In the post-Mao period, most of those accused of being rightists were rehabilitated, some posthumously.

Subsequent political campaigns targeted alleged class enemies. Even after private property in the countryside and the cities had been eliminated, the Party waged class struggle campaigns against real and imagined enemies. "Class" came to be defined in many ways other than wealth and property: Those who had relatives living abroad, those whose ancestors were landlords, capitalists, or officials in pre-1949 governments, and even those who listened to Western music or read Western literature could be accused of being class enemies—"capitalist roaders"—and consequently attacked, fired, and imprisoned. During the Cultural Revolution, indiscriminate witch hunts against supposed class enemies damaged careers and tore families apart, as children were pressured to denounce their parents. As more and more people realized that innocent people—including themselves, family, and friends—were being punished without cause, a sense of disillusionment set in. As Party-sponsored coercion and repression affected most people in one way or another, the Party's reputation was damaged. Repression may target and eliminate threats to the Party, but as it grows to target those who do not pose a threat to the Party and even those who support it, it creates disillusionment and resentment, in effect creating the very things that it tries to suppress.

In the post-Mao era, China's leaders announced the end of class struggle and mass campaigns and the beginning of economic modernization as the key task of the Party. For those who hoped that political reform and even democratization would accompany economic reform, the CCP had a quick reply: Economic reform would not come at the expense of the Party's monopoly on power. As the Party's leaders were debating the initial economic reform policies in 1978, the "Democracy Wall" movement gave voice to both hopeful and critical appeals to the Party. Whereas some called for the rehabilitation of Cultural Revolution victims, others argued for wide-ranging political reforms. In reply, Deng

[6] Teiwes, "Establishment and Consolidation of the New Regime," p. 82.

Xiaoping declared the "Four Cardinal Principles" that would guide the Party's policies: the socialist road, the people's democratic dictatorship, the leadership of the CCP, and Marxism-Leninism and Mao Zedong Thought. This put strict limits on the types of political debates and activities that the Party would allow. In the years afterward, the Party loosened its control over many aspects of everyday life, allowing more diversity in the economic, social, and cultural realms. However, it was also clear that the Party would repress all threats to its hold on power, but it did so in a more selective manner than during the Maoist era.

This insistence on the Party's unquestioned hold on power was nowhere more apparent than in the response to popular protests that began in April 1989, first in Beijing's Tiananmen Square and then spreading to over 300 other cities nationwide. The initial demands of the protestors—fighting corruption and inflation—seemed consistent with the Party's own goals, but CCP leaders like Deng Xiaoping who had suffered during the Cultural Revolution saw clear similarities to that earlier campaign and were determined not to let it happen again. Rather than offering negotiations, they denounced the peaceful protests as "turmoil." The demands of the protestors soon spread to more political issues and even demands for the resignation of top leaders. Participation in the protests expanded from the college students at the beginning to people from all walks of life, including workers and even government employees, who joined the marches with signs identifying what ministry or department they were from. The foreign media reported that millions of people were joining the almost-daily marches in Beijing. With the protests growing and the unity of the top leadership and the state apparatus as a whole coming apart, the government announced martial law in Beijing and, after several weeks of delay, sent tanks and armored personnel carriers through downtown Beijing and Tiananmen Square during the night of June 3–4, firing indiscriminately into unarmed crowds of people. As Melanie Manion described it, "This combination of severity and near randomness is the essence of political terror."[7] Several hundred and perhaps as many as several thousand

[7] Melanie Manion, "Introduction: Reluctant Duelists—The Logic of the 1989 Demonstrations and Massacre," in Michel Oksenberg, Marc Lambert, and Lawrence Sullivan, eds., *Beijing Spring 1989: Confrontation and Conflict* (Armonk, NY: M.E. Sharpe, 1990), p. xli.

people died, almost all of them on the streets leading to the square. Thousands of others were arrested for their participation, and top leaders were purged from office. Zhao Ziyang, general secretary of the CCP at the time of protests and an advocate of compromise with the demonstrators, remained under house arrest until his death in 2005. Other liberals in the Party and government had their careers derailed, and many intellectuals fled into exile abroad.

This tragic outcome to a peaceful protest sent a clear message to Chinese society and foreign observers: The Party was prepared to use any means necessary to defend its monopoly on political power. Since 1989, there have been no sustained, nationwide social movements in China. The number of protests grew in later years, from 32,000 in 1999 to 87,000 in 2005, at which point the Chinese government stopped reporting the annual figure. Although the government no longer publicized the number of protests, the number continued to grow. Sociologist Sun Liping estimated there were 180,000 protests in 2010. More notable than the number of protests has been the relatively narrow scope of demands. Protestors have generally been careful to limit their demands to local grievances, in particular local officials who were not implementing central policies properly, and not raise broader political issues that would trigger a 1989-like response.

In the years after 1989, the Party continued to use repression as part of its strategy for survival, but used it more selectively. Rather than going after entire classes of people as part of an ideological campaign, the Party targeted its coercive powers at individuals, normally in reaction to what they wrote, said, or did. The Party dealt harshly with challenges to its political monopoly. In 1998, veteran political activists (some of whom were involved in the 1989 protests) attempted to form the China Democracy Party. The Party's leaders were arrested and sentenced to prison terms of 11 to 13 years, and other CDP members received shorter sentences. Two of the best-known leaders, Wang Youcai and Xu Wenli, were later exiled to the U.S.; others went into exile in order to avoid imprisonment. As a means of dampening dissent in China, this was a successful tactic.[8] It removed potential threats to

---

[8] China also bans scholars from visiting China in retaliation for actions or publications that the government finds objectionable. Perry Link and Andrew

the regime and potential leaders of an opposition movement. Once in exile, these activists lost credibility among the activists who remained in China and thought the exiles were out of touch with recent trends within the country. As an additional boon to the Party, the exiled dissidents fought among themselves for status and influence. Even in exile, they could not form a unified opposition to the CCP.

Tighter Restrictions on Political Space

The level of repression in China fluctuates in two interrelated ways. The first is through cycles of liberalization and repression (*fang* 放 and *shou* 收), with each cycle lasting several years. This has been a prominent feature of Chinese politics since the beginning of the post-Mao era.[9] China is currently in a period of enhanced repression that began in 2008 after the international financial crisis and accelerated after Xi Jinping became CCP general secretary in 2012. One of the most tangible indicators of this is the number of political prisoners, which spiked in 2008 and remained high in subsequent years. During Xi Jinping's first year in office (2013), the number of arrests and indictments for "endangering state security" was three times higher than in Hu Jintao's first year (2003).[10]

The level of repression also fluctuates at predictable points in time, such as important Party and government meetings, diplomatic summits, anniversaries of past events, and international events. Chinese leaders carefully stage-manage political events, such as the National Party Congress (which meets every five years) and annual meetings of the National People's Congress and the Chinese People's Political

---

Nathan have been blacklisted for their criticisms of China's human rights record and for their involvement in the editing and publication of *The Tiananmen Papers* (New York: Public Affairs, 2001), reportedly internal documents concerning the 1989 demonstrations in Tiananmen Square. Nathan was also coeditor (with Bruce Gilley) of a later book, *China's New Rulers: The Secret Files* (New York: New York Review Books, 2002). The same individual smuggled out of China the documents that were published in *The Tiananmen Papers* and *China's New Rulers*.

[9] Richard Baum, "The Road to Tiananmen: Chinese Politics in the 1980s," in MacFarquhar, ed., *Politics of China*, pp. 340–471.

[10] Dui Hua Foundation, http://www.duihuahrjournal.org/2015/01/state-security-indictments-cult-trials.html, accessed March 17, 2015.

Consultative Congress (referred to as the "two meetings" because they are held simultaneously), and diplomatic events, such as visits by heads of state or major international organizations like the Olympics in 2008 and the Asia-Pacific Economic Cooperation summit in 2014. Security measures also increase around major anniversaries, such as the 1949 founding of the People's Republic (October 1, or National Day) and the 1989 crackdown in Tiananmen Square (June 4). Before and during these events, known dissidents and potential troublemakers are placed under house arrest or forced to leave town and warned not to communicate with journalists. When these tactics fail to deter efforts to gain attention, they may be arrested. The Party also worries that the deaths of former leaders, such as members of the Gang of Four or former CCP General Secretary Zhao Ziyang, could be used as a pretext for public protests and takes necessary precautions. Such concerns are not totally illusory: The deaths of Zhou Enlai in 1976 and Hu Yaobang in 1989 led to large-scale protests that challenged the status quo of the times. When the Party ignores an anniversary, it can provide an opening for protests. In 2008, it inexplicably made no preparations before the anniversary of the Tibetan uprising of 1959, and the result was large-scale violence in Tibet that led to international protests and the potential disruption of the Beijing Olympics.

Finally, foreign events can trigger increased repression in China. During the Arab Spring of 2011, the Party ramped up its repression to preempt any potential for the protests to spread to China. The Party prefers to prevent protests rather than suppress them once they occur, but uses heavy-handed tactics to do both.

Since 2008, the Party has ratcheted up its use of repression. It began harassing "rights defense" (*wei quan* 维权) lawyers who had sued the state for human rights violations, taking them in for questioning, revoking their law licenses, and even threatening to revoke the licenses of law firms they worked for if they were not fired. It cracked down on civil society groups that promoted legal rights and political freedoms, and even some that only had the potential to be involved in political issues. (At the same time, the number of civil society groups continued to grow, a paradox explored in the next chapter.) Numerous members of a loosely aligned "New Citizen's Movement" that called for greater transparency (in particular, demanding that party and government leaders reveal their wealth) were arrested and sentenced to up to seven years in jail.

The most prominent target was Xu Zhiyong, one of China's best-known rights defense lawyers and a frequent critic of the Party's failure to uphold the country's constitutional rights. In 2003, he was one of the few people ever elected as an independent delegate to a local people's congress. That same year, he fought against the secret detention system used for migrant workers and petitioners. He cofounded the Open Constitution Initiative (OCI) in 2005, registering it as a consulting firm because it could not register as a nongovernmental organization (see chapter 3 for more on the registration challenges of China's NGOs). The OCI took on public interest cases (e.g., representing families whose children died or became seriously ill after consuming milk and baby formula tainted with the chemical melamine). In 2009, the Beijing government charged the OCI with tax evasion and shut it down. Xu was briefly taken into custody in connection with the tax-evasion charges, but then released. Xu and several colleagues later formed the New Citizens' Movement, a loose-knit network of lawyers, scholars, and civil rights advocates promoting constitutionalism, political reform, and official transparency. He wrote an open letter to Xi Jinping calling for Party and government officials to disclose their wealth. Although Xi had launched an anticorruption campaign along the same lines, Xu was arrested and charged with "assembling crowds to disrupt public order." In January 2014, he was sentenced to four years in prison.

Gao Zhisheng is another prominent rights defense lawyer whose Christian beliefs influenced his work on behalf of China's disadvantaged. Although the Chinese government once championed him, he later became targeted by it. In 2001, the Ministry of Justice named him as one of China's ten best lawyers, in recognition of his pro bono work on behalf of victims of medical malpractice and people who had lost their homes without adequate compensation. But once he began defending members of the Falun Gong spiritual group and antigovernment protestors, the government closed his law firm, revoked his law license, and put him and his family under surveillance. He was detained and "disappeared" several times, and was given a three-year suspended sentence for subversion in December 2006. He was detained again in 2007 after writing to leaders of the European Union and the U.S. Congress to recommend a boycott of the 2008 Olympics in Beijing over China's human rights violations. Gao reported he was severely beaten during several long periods of detention. While Gao was in custody, the Chinese government did not reveal his whereabouts but issued cryptic statements saying that he had lost his way and was where he should be. He briefly reappeared in spring 2010 and told reporters that he would not continue his previous work. He then disappeared again, and in December 2011, the government revealed that he was serving a prison sentence after violating his probation. He was released from jail but placed under house arrest in August 2014 and reportedly was in bad health after years of mistreatment.

In 2008, Liu Xiaobo was arrested for his role in drafting "Charter 08," an online petition calling for greater democracy and the end of one-party rule in China. Although he was not the only person responsible for drafting the charter, he was the only one imprisoned afterward. Liu had previously been arrested and imprisoned three other times for political activities, including during the 1989 demonstrations. On December 25, 2009, he was convicted of "inciting subversion of state power" and sentenced to 11 years in prison. For his years of nonviolent protest, he was awarded the Nobel Peace Prize in 2010, but was unable to accept the prize because he was in prison. His wife Liu Xia was also prevented from attending the award ceremony and has been under constant surveillance during her husband's imprisonment.

What triggered this crackdown on individuals who had previously been tolerated and even publicized? Party leaders have always been vigilant in preserving their monopoly on political power, but two international events seemed to accentuate their willingness to use repressive tools. First of all, China's leaders have been fearful of the "color revolutions" that have challenged and in some cases overthrown authoritarian regimes, such as the Orange Revolution in Ukraine and the Jasmine Revolution in Tunisia that triggered the Arab Spring. Party leaders are determined to prevent color revolutions from spreading to China, and to limit the influence of foreign interests promoting political change. Second, the international financial crisis that began in 2007 seemed to make China's leaders more confident in their strategies for economic development and political survival. Its economy slowed down in the wake of the financial crisis, but avoided the recession and prolonged hardship that many Western countries experienced. China's leaders became less willing to accommodate Western advice on economic policy, more assertive in foreign policy, and more repressive in maintaining domestic order and stability. Beginning in 2010, official spending on internal public security surpassed the military budget. Even though most observers believe actual spending on both public security and the military is higher than the official budget, the dramatic boost in public security spending symbolized the Party's commitment to defending its political monopoly and suppressing threats to it. Patricia Thornton describes this crackdown as the "advance of the Party," a takeoff on the more familiar phrase "advance of the state, retreat of the private," which began with the 2007 international financial crisis. The advance of the state, retreat of the private generally refers to economic trends, specifically the boost given to state-owned enterprises at the expense of private firms, but the "advance of the Party" is also appropriate for its repression of private groups of various kinds.[11]

Spending on public security rose rapidly during Hu Jintao's tenure as the Party's general secretary, and in 2010, surpassed the officially reported military budget. Between 2008 and 2013 (the most recent year of available data), spending on public security rose 93 percent, indicating the Party's growing concern for maintaining order. But that is only one dimension of the Party's survival strategy. As chapter 4 shows in more detail, government spending on public goods rose even faster. Spending on education increased by 144 percent, healthcare by 122 percent, and social welfare by 113 percent.[12] The Party's investment in public security definitely increased sharply, but its investment in public goods increased even faster. To properly understand the Party's survival strategy, we need to consider all of its aspects.

[11] Patricia M. Thornton, "The Advance of the Party: Transformation or Takeover of Urban Grassroots Society?" *China Quarterly*, Vol. 213 (March 2013), pp. 1–18.

[12] Spending data on internal security, defense, education, and social welfare are taken from the Chinese Statistical Yearbook, various years, available on China Data Online. In the most recent edition of the Chinese Statistical Yearbook, healthcare spending is combined with family planning, which prevents it from being compared to previous years. Growth in the government's spending on healthcare is therefore calculated from the World Bank's World Development Indicators using Purchasing Power Parity (PPP) values, which attempt to correct for differences in the cost of living across countries.

The Party's reaction to the Arab Spring of 2011 illustrates its determination to prevent challenges to political stability and regime survival. It was worried that protests against authoritarian regimes in the Middle East might inspire similar protests in China. In response to anonymous calls on the Internet to hold protests in various Chinese cities (none of which amounted to anything),[13] it tightened its surveillance of political activists and increased the presence of uniformed and plainclothes police. For a time, it banned Internet searches including the word "jasmine" even though it is the name of a popular variety of tea and also a traditional folk song. At one point, it reportedly also blocked the word "tomorrow" in order to prevent people from getting information about a rumored event. Ai Weiwei, one of China's best-known avant-garde artists, used his Twitter account to make fun of people who were afraid of jasmine, an oblique statement implying support for protest. He was later detained when attempting to board an international flight at the Beijing airport. Rather than charge him with subversion or disrupting public order, he was instead charged with tax evasion. He remained in custody until he promised to pay back taxes worth millions of dollars. (In a show of support, people threw money over the wall surrounding his property to help pay the back taxes.) His passport was confiscated, preventing him from leaving the country, and was not returned to him until July 2015.[14] He promptly left China; whether for a short trip or an indefinite stay was not immediately known.

[13] One such call suggested the popular Wangfujing shopping district in Beijing as a site for protests. Among the people who showed up was Jon Huntsman, U.S. ambassador to China, who claimed he was just doing some shopping. A popular joke at the time said that 100 people responded to a call for protest: 90 policemen, nine foreign journalists, and the U.S. ambassador.

[14] This was not the first time the state punished Ai for his political activities. After using his blog to compile information on over 5,000 children killed when their schools collapsed in the 2008 Sichuan earthquake, his blog was shut down. In August 2009, while in Sichuan to testify on behalf of a colleague also investigating the collapse of school buildings, he was taken into custody and reportedly beaten. During a trip to Germany soon afterward, he was treated for a cerebral hemorrhage. He was placed under house arrest in November 2009 to prevent him from attending a party to protest the closing of his Shanghai art studio, which was demolished a few months later.

The Party may have overreacted to the potential ripple effects of the Arab Spring in China. In the end, there was little public support for similar demonstrations in China. The Arab countries were too far away—geographically and culturally—to inspire protests in China, and the economic stagnation that contributed to popular resentment toward Arab leaders was not present in China, which had experienced several decades of rapid growth. But the Party's strong response shows its determination to preempt any challenges to its authority, no matter how remote.

Once Xi Jinping became general secretary in 2012, the political tightening increased.[15] Civil society groups came under closer scrutiny, especially those that received foreign funding. More lawyers and activists, many of them involved in the New Citizen's Movement and other groups promoting citizens' rights, were arrested. Over 200 lawyers and support staff were taken into custody and questioned in July 2015, marking a significant uptick in the Party's use of coercive tools. In order to better control the flow of information, the state issued new regulations on social media to limit their ability to evade government monitoring. The state also put tighter controls on streaming videos, especially of foreign movies and television shows, to limit exposure to Western culture. In May 2013, the CCP's Document No. 9 announced seven topics that were forbidden from discussion online and in classrooms: universal values, civil rights, civil society, press freedoms, judicial independence, past mistakes of the communist party, and the newly wealthy and politically connected capitalist class. This ban was designed to prohibit the discussion of a wide range of political reforms.

The increased repressive atmosphere had a broad impact on public opinion. Even people who posed no threat to the Party were reluctant to criticize local or national leaders for fear of retaliation. The CCP's determination to repress critical voices has led to an increase in the public's fear of retaliation for criticizing the regime. This rising fear is reflected in the public opinion surveys used throughout this book (for details on the survey, see appendix). These surveys allow two types of comparisons: between levels of the state and between points in time. First of all, there

---

[15] Sarah Cook gives a thorough overview of increased repression under Xi in her *The Politburo's Predicament: Confronting the Limitations of Chinese Communist Party Repression* (New York: Freedom House, 2015).

is little variation in levels of fear for criticizing the CCP, central government, or local governments (see figure 2-1). There is slightly higher fear for criticizing local governments, but not dramatically so. Criticism of local government is more likely to be heard or reported, and people are also more likely to criticize their local governments. Fewer respondents say they never criticize their local governments, compared to those who never criticize the CCP or central government. Looking at each point in time separately, most respondents reported they have little or no apprehension when criticizing the regime.

However, when comparing the responses in 2010 and 2014, the data suggest that the expansion of repression under Xi Jinping led to some increase in levels of political fear. The percentage of those who had little or no fear dropped by almost 15 percent, and those who were very or pretty apprehensive increased by 50 percent (admittedly from a low starting point). Even so, less than 10 percent of all respondents reported high levels of political fear in either 2010 or 2014. Despite the increased repressive atmosphere of China's political system, the vast majority of respondents still report they have little or no fear when making political criticisms.

However, if never criticizing the regime is an indirect measure of political fear (i.e., people do not criticize the regime because they fear

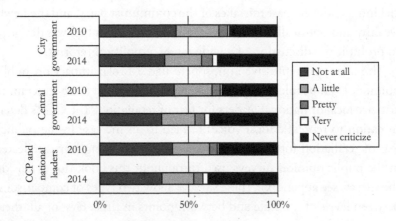

FIGURE 2-1 Levels of Political Fear, 2010 and 2014.
Q: Normally, are you apprehensive when you chat with others and criticize the _____?
Source: Public Goods and Political Support Surveys.

retaliation), then the data show a sharp increase between 2010 and 2014. Those who say they never criticize the regime increased about 20 percent. This suggests that the CCP's efforts to prohibit criticism of the party and its policies may be having some effect. Never criticizing the party and government could also be due in part to a lack of interest in politics. Most of the people who say they never criticize also report that they never talk about national affairs, even with friends or family. Most of them never go online, and if they do are less likely to browse for news or follow social media than other respondents. They are older, have lower levels of education, are more likely to be female, and are less likely to be CCP members or to know the name of the mayor of their city or even the prime minister, all of which indicate that they are less likely to participate in or even discuss politics. Indifference is undoubtedly part of the explanation, but the level of indifference is unlikely to have changed between 2010 and 2014. What has changed is the level of repression against critics of the regime. As Hirschman famously showed, when criticism (what he called the voice option) becomes more costly, loyalty—or more precisely, silence that may only seem like loyalty—becomes a more popular response.[16] With the CCP's increased repression of critical and dissenting views, many in society may be choosing to remain silent.

The Party often describes its repressive tactics in euphemistic ways, such as maintaining stability (wei wen 维稳) and achieving a "harmonious society," the latter phrase drawn from earlier Confucian traditions. Some in China use these benign-sounding phrases to mock them and the practices they disguise: Those who do not willingly maintain stability "get harmonized." But this is bitter humor: Getting harmonized can mean loss of employment, confiscation of computers, books, and notes, inability to communicate with family and friends, surveillance, house arrest, imprisonment, and sometimes simply disappearance into

---

[16] Albert Hirschman, *Exit, Voice and Loyalty: Responses to Decline in Firms, Organizations, and States* (Cambridge, MA: Harvard University Press, 1970). Another response to unsatisfactory situations is exit, often referred to as "voting with your feet." Many officials and businessmen have moved their families, financial savings, and in some cases themselves out of the country, mostly to escape China's risky political environment in recent years.

"black jails," secret facilities where people are detained without being formally charged and without their families being notified.

While this ratcheting up of repression has drawn criticism from within China and abroad, the general public seems to share their leaders' concerns about maintaining order and stability. The fear of chaos is one of the hallmarks of traditional Chinese political culture, and that fear is still prominent in Chinese society.[17] Fears of instability remain high and have even increased in recent years (see table 2-1). While those in favor of political liberalization decry the Party's recent attempts to stymie dissent and protest, there is also broad support for its stated goals throughout society.

Limits on Religious Freedoms

The Chinese government officially recognizes five religions: Buddhism, Taoism, Islam, Protestantism, and Catholicism (Protestants and Catholics are treated as separate religions and not two variants of Christianity). Each religion has a government-sponsored church managed by the government's Religious Affairs Bureau. These official churches are responsible for training new church leaders and overseeing worship services. Training involves some theological study, but more importantly political indoctrination to ensure that ultimate loyalty is to earthly authority in Beijing. Appointments to leadership posts are also more about political loyalty than theological knowledge or religious faith.

As the political suppression of religion eased in the post-Mao period, religious practices resumed. Churches and temples reopened, and the numbers of worshippers increased. Buddhism remains the largest religion, with between 200 and 250 million people who identify themselves as Buddhist or who practice folk religion (the two are largely synonymous in China). Outside of Tibet, Buddhists face little government pressure, and most Chinese Buddhists do not revere the Dalai Lama (the situation in Tibet is examined later). The number of Christians in China has grown dramatically in the post-Mao era, but the precise number is hard to pin

---

[17] Fear of political instability is by no means unique to Chinese culture. At the time of the Arab Spring, many media reports also identified fear of instability as a core element of political culture in Egypt and other countries.

TABLE 2-1 Fears of Instability in China (numbers in table are percentages)

	Strongly Agree		Agree		Disagree		Strongly Disagree	
	2010	2014	2010	2014	2010	2014	2010	2014
If a country has multiple political parties, that could lead to social chaos.	9.9	13.7	50.4	53.5	35.0	29.2	4.8	3.7
Locally, if there were many groups with different points of view, that could influence local stability.	6.6	10.5	56.4	54.4	34.1	31.3	3.0	3.8
Demonstrations can easily turn into social upheaval, threatening social stability.	11.6	15.1	60.2	61.9	26.0	20.8	2.2	2.1

Source: Public Goods and Political Support Surveys.

down. According to the state-sponsored churches, there were approximately 25 million Protestants and 6 million Catholics in 2012. Unofficial estimates put the numbers much higher, with most around 50 million and a few over 100 million. Many of the Christians not counted in the official number worship in underground or house churches.

The Party has viewed the revival of religion with concern, for several reasons. First, religion offers a separate set of values for people to live by, and these values are normally not compatible with the Party's ideology. Many dissidents and rights defense lawyers in China are Christian, and they see the promotion of human rights as both a moral and a spiritual cause. The CCP itself is officially atheistic, and even though some of its members are undoubtedly religious, no leader has been identified as a person of faith. Second, in China's past, religion has been the basis for popular uprisings that engulfed large areas of the country, such as the Taiping Rebellion in the 19th century. Third, religion is often tied to ethnicity, in particular Tibetan Buddhism and the Moslem Uyghurs in Xinjiang, two groups that have pushed for greater autonomy if not outright independence. Finally, Christianity is seen as a Western tradition, and the Party has long been wary of Western values leading to a "peaceful evolution" that would turn public opinion against the Party.

Catholicism is of particular concern, not only for spiritual reasons but also for matters of sovereignty. The Chinese government and the Vatican have been deadlocked on the issue of appointing bishops and cardinals: Beijing demands the right to appoint all officials within its boundaries, and Rome insists that the Pope alone has the authority to appoint Catholic leaders. Occasionally, bishops and cardinals are appointed under a tacit agreement in which the Vatican indicates which individuals it approves of and Beijing announces the actual appointment. But Beijing frequently appoints Catholic leaders without the Vatican's approval (some have been excommunicated as a result), and the Vatican appoints leaders to the underground church without Beijing's consent (many are later placed under house arrest or imprisoned). Relations between China and the Vatican have been strained over this issue, and the prospects for improving ties, much less establishing formal relations, remain uncertain. The Vatican is also one of the few states in the world that still has diplomatic relations with Taiwan, another issue that irritates China's leaders.

The tensions between China's leaders and the Vatican are occasionally on public display. For example, in July 2012, Thaddeus Ma Daqin was ordained as an auxiliary bishop in Shanghai. His appointment had the approval of both Beijing and the Vatican. At his ordination ceremony, he surprised those in attendance by announcing his resignation from the Chinese Patriotic Catholic Association, the organization sponsored by the Chinese government to manage the Catholic Church in China. He was immediately taken into custody and placed under house arrest at a seminary, where he underwent extensive questioning. He has not been seen in public since his ordination ceremony was cut short after his surprise announcement.

In addition to the officially recognized churches, many Chinese Christians worship in underground and house churches. China's house churches are more spiritual and in some cases more evangelical congregations than the staid and reserved official churches. Many pastors in house churches have limited theological training and therefore have unorthodox beliefs and practices. For example, members of the millennial Eastern Lightning believe that the wife of the founder is the second coming of Christ. The group has been known to kidnap members of rival Christian groups in order to force them to convert their allegiance to Eastern Lightning. Several members of Eastern Lightning, also known as the Church of Almighty God, were sentenced to death after beating a woman to death at a McDonald's restaurant when she refused their invitation to join their church. Leaders in the official churches often quietly work with house churches, providing theological and doctrinal education, as well as management skills. Worshippers frequently attend services in both official and underground churches.

The Chinese government makes it difficult for underground congregations to worship together. House churches only allow a small number of believers to gather in one place at a time. Some congregations have tried to rent larger spaces, with limited success. The Shouwang Church in Beijing is one of the largest and best-known underground churches with several thousand members. It has tried but failed to find an appropriately sized space for its worship services. In 2009, it signed a lease on a floor in an office tower, but the landlord later refused to hand over the keys after being pressured by the local government. However, he also refused to return the deposit the Shouwang Church paid him. To bring attention to their situation, the Shouwang Church organized outdoor services, beginning with an Easter service in April 2011. At many of these outdoor services, police have arrested worshippers and church leaders, and the founder of the church, Jin Tianming, was under house arrest for over a year.

While the Party frequently clamps down on underground Christian churches by arresting their leaders and closing and even bulldozing their buildings, under Xi Jinping, it began taking similar actions against the official Protestant and Catholic churches. In Zhejiang, a coastal province known for both its economic privatization and large Christian population, the government tore down crosses on tops of several churches, and issued demolition notices to over 100 churches, most of them part of the official church. Local officials claimed the crosses and buildings did not comply with zoning regulations, even though they had previously been approved.[18]

---

[18] The top Party official in Zhejiang, Xia Baolong, formerly served as Zhejiang's deputy party secretary and when Xi Jinping served as Zhejiang's party secretary (2002–2007).

The Suppression of Falun Gong's "Evil Cult"

The Falun Gong spiritual movement has been a particular target for the Party's repressive actions. In 1999, Falun Gong mobilized approximately 10,000 of its supporters in a day-long silent protest that surrounded Zhongnanhai, the walled compound in Beijing where many of the top party and government leaders live and work. This brazen but orderly and well-coordinated protest stunned Party leaders, especially Jiang Zemin, who was general secretary at that time. He pushed for a crackdown against Falun Gong that lasted several years. The Party denounced the group as an "evil cult," blocked access to its website, and banned its name in web searches. It imprisoned some of its members and sent others to labor camps and psychiatric hospitals, where many were reportedly tortured. At its peak, Falun Gong had tens of millions of members, according to most estimates, ranging from retirees to local party, government, and military leaders. Many of them joined because of the social and spiritual aspects of the group (it began during the qigong craze of the early 1990s, when many began practicing this traditional form of exercise and meditation), but the Party's harsh crackdown led to resistance from some of its most committed members. Falun Gong remains banned in China today, and sporadic resistance continues.[19]

As opposed to other groups who complain the Party is not democratic enough, Falun Gong's charge against the Party is that it is not Chinese enough. The group criticizes the Party for abiding by a foreign ideology—Marxism-Leninism—and not being sufficiently grounded in Chinese tradition. Its proposed solution is not to introduce democratic institutions into contemporary China, but to restore older traditions of governance.[20]

[19] Falun Gong is perhaps more prominent abroad than it is in China. The Shen Yun Performing Arts group, the *Epoch Times* newspaper, and New Tang Dynasty Television are all affiliated with Falun Gong in the U.S.

[20] Caylan Ford, "Tradition and Dissent in China: The Tuidang Movement and Its Challenge to the Communist Party," master's thesis, George Washington University, 2011.

Tibet and Xinjiang

The western provinces (formally, "autonomous regions") of Tibet and Xinjiang and the Party's policies toward them are roughly analogous:

- Both were promised a high degree of autonomy in the early 1950s, only to have that promise later taken away.
- Both are predominately non-Han, although the percentage of Han in their populations has been growing steadily, especially in the urban areas. Uyghurs are the largest ethnic group in Xinjiang, but today they make up less than 50 percent of the population.
- Both are distinguished by the combination of ethnic and religious identity: Tibetans are predominately Buddhist, and Uyghurs are predominately Moslem. In contrast, most Han do not identify with a religious faith.
- Both have had ongoing protests that often turned violent, for greater autonomy from Beijing's control (personified by the leadership of the Party secretary, a Han Chinese appointed by Beijing).
- Both experienced a brief period of relaxation in the 1980s, when then CCP General Secretary Hu Yaobang promised them more control over their regions.
- Both have seen economic development as a consequence of the "Open Up the West" policies that began in the 1990s, but many Tibetans and Uyghurs believe the benefits of those policies have disproportionately gone to recent Han immigrants, some of whom were sent by Beijing, others of whom chose to go west in pursuit of economic opportunities.
- Both occupy large sections of Chinese territory. Tibet makes up almost 13 percent of the PRC's landmass, and Xinjiang almost 17 percent. Xinjiang is rich in natural resources, especially oil, gas, and coal. Tibet is the origin of many of Asia's most important rivers, including the Yangtze, the Mekong, and the Irrawaddy.

For all these reasons, Beijing is determined to maintain control over both Tibet and Xinjiang, even though its strict policies have occasionally triggered violent reactions from local people.

Despite these similarities, events in Tibet and Xinjiang are unrelated, and there is no evidence of cooperation between Tibetans and Uyghurs, whether within China or in exile, to push for greater autonomy for their regions. They may have common aspirations, but they do not have common efforts.

TIBET

Tensions between Tibetans and the Chinese government go back to early in the People's Republic.[21] In 1951, the Tibetan government and the new communist government in Beijing signed an agreement, commonly known as the "Seventeen Point Agreement," which included the protection of the existing political system, religious practices, and customs in Tibet, while also declaring that Tibet was part of China. Despite this agreement, suspicions grew over Beijing's long-term objectives. In 1959, an armed uprising was quickly suppressed by Chinese troops. After this, the Dalai Lama, Tibet's religious and political leader, and roughly 80,000 of his followers fled across the border into India, where they set up their religious and political headquarters in Dharamsala. For its part, the CCP renounced the Seventeen Point Agreement, carried out forceful land-reform policies, and sent the military into Tibet to root out resisters to the new order, resulting in tens of thousands of deaths and injuries. Others were sent to labor camps, where many stayed for over 20 years before being released. The Party also closed most monasteries in Tibet and forced most monks and nuns out of their religious institutions. Tibetans held many government posts, but the more important Party posts were held by Han officials appointed by Beijing.

After a brief thaw in the early post-Mao era, when Deng Xiaoping met with the Dalai Lama's brother and allowed groups of Tibetan exiles to visit Tibet, a more hard-line policy resumed by the late 1980s. CCP leaders in Tibet denounced the Dalai Lama and his supporters. Frequent street protests calling for Tibetan independence and the return of the Dalai Lama were quickly suppressed, with most protestors

---

[21] Robert Barnett, "Tibet," in William A. Joseph, ed., *Politics in China: An Introduction*, second edition (New York: Oxford University Press, 2014), pp. 401–427.

arrested and reportedly tortured while in jail. In 1989, a large-scale protest led to the imposition of martial law in Tibet (this was unrelated to demonstrations in Tiananmen Square, which also ended in martial law). Photos of the Dalai Lama were banned. Tibetan monks and nuns were forced to undergo "patriotic education" campaigns in which they were required to denounce the Dalai Lama and swear loyalty to Beijing.

In addition to suppressing many aspects of Tibetan religious beliefs and practices, the Party embarked on an ambitious "Open Up the West" program of economic development in the western areas of China, including Tibet. This involved large construction projects for roads, railroads, mining, and commercial development. This led to a flood of Han Chinese into Tibet to take advantage of the new economic opportunities and jobs available there. By 2010, roughly one-third of the people living in Tibet's urban areas were non-Tibetans. On top of the resentment toward Beijing's religious and social policies, Tibetans also grew frustrated at being left out of the economic development in Tibet.

Tensions flared again in 2008, on the 49th anniversary of the 1959 uprising. Several hundred monks marched to protest Beijing's policies toward Tibet. When rumors circulated that some of the monks had been beaten after their arrest, their supporters went through the streets of Lhasa burning Chinese-owned businesses and beating up Chinese migrants, 18 of whom died. Chinese troops took over the city by force, and the Tibetan government in exile claimed that up to 80 Tibetans were killed in the process. In the subsequent days, over 100 additional protests occurred. The Chinese government shut down phone and Internet access to Tibet, banned foreign journalists and tourists, and renewed denunciations of the Dalai Lama. These heavy-handed policies led to international criticism of China on the eve of the Beijing Olympics that in turn triggered a nationalistic response from China's media and society at large, usually quick to reject Western criticism of China's domestic affairs.

Although there have been no reports of protests after 2008, over 100 Tibetans have used self-immolation as a symbolic form of protest and resistance.[22] Most of these occurred outside the boundaries of

---

[22] According to the International Campaign for Tibet, 132 Tibetans self-immolated, 108 of whom died. See http://www.savetibet.org/resources/fact-sheets/self-immolations-by-tibetans/, accessed October 5, 2014.

the Tibetan Autonomous Region, in the adjoining areas of Sichuan, Gansu, and Qinghai that are part of greater Tibet, the large region in southwest China that was traditionally under Tibetan influence (one self-immolation took place in Beijing).

When the current Dalai Lama passes away, an intense conflict is likely to emerge between the Chinese government and the Tibetans over selecting the next Dalai Lama. Tibetans believe the Dalai Lama is reincarnated in another person, and there are traditional practices for selecting the new Dalai Lama. The current Dalai Lama has said that the next might be living outside Tibet, may be female, or that he may choose not to reincarnate. The Chinese government rejected those statements and said that it alone would select the next Dalai Lama according to traditional Tibetan practices. This could create a situation where there are two rival Dalai Lamas, one recognized by the Tibetans and another appointed by the Chinese government. Just as the government tries to force Tibetans to renounce the Dalai Lama and swear their allegiance to Beijing, it would also likely demand that Tibetans accept the Dalai Lama selected by the government.

A similar battle already took place over the Panchen Lama, the second-highest Lama in Tibetan Buddhism. When the former Panchen Lama died, the Dalai Lama identified a boy in whom he said the Panchen Lama had been reincarnated. But Beijing rejected that announcement and selected another boy to be the Panchen Lama. He was sent to Beijing to undergo religious and political education under the close supervision of the government and away from the influence of the Dalai Lama and his supporters. The boy selected by the Dalai Lama was immediately taken into custody by Chinese authorities and has not been seen since. A similar scenario could easily unfold over the identification of the next Dalai Lama, but it would likely be more intense because it would focus on the most important spiritual leader of the Tibetans.

After Xi Jinping became China's top leader, the Dalai Lama made several conciliatory gestures, trying to reach an accommodation that might allow him to return to Tibet and perhaps prevent a clash over the next Dalai Lama. Beijing rejected those overtures and the suggestion that private discussions were underway to allow the Dalai Lama to visit Tibet. Instead, it called on him and others to abandon their efforts to seek Tibetan independence.

Efforts by the Chinese government to limit the Dalai Lama's influence extend to international affairs. It strongly criticizes meetings between the Dalai Lama and the White House or congressional leaders, and frequently registers its protest by suspending official exchanges and diplomatic meetings. The South African government has repeatedly denied a visa to the Dalai Lama, reportedly at the behest of China. In 2011, Archbishop Desmond Tutu celebrated his 80th birthday and invited numerous international figures, including the Dalai Lama. When the South African government did not grant the Dalai Lama a visa, Bishop Tutu denounced the South African government as no better than the former apartheid regime. A planned meeting of past winners of the Nobel Peace Prize in 2014 was canceled when the South African government again did not grant the Dalai Lama a visa. In both cases, the South African government did not formally reject the Dalai Lama's visa application; it simply took no action on his request, and he eventually withdrew his application. The meeting of Nobel laureates was later held in Rome in December 2014, but even Pope Francis declined a request from the Dalai Lama to meet, "for obvious reasons" according to a Vatican spokesman—not threatening the Vatican's efforts to improve relations with China.[23]

XINJIANG

The economic policies and political campaigns that swept China during the Maoist era also affected Xinjiang, although Uyghur-Han ethnic tensions and the possibility of Soviet intervention seem to have dampened their impact a bit.[24] In the post-Mao period, economic reforms were late in coming to Xinjiang, but it was a key part of the "Open Up the West" initiative beginning in the 1990s. Uyghurs held some positions in the government, but Hans controlled the more important Party positions. Ethnic tensions led to sporadic but mostly small-scale and peaceful protests during the 1990s and into the 2000s. But as the demands of the protestors for more autonomy went unmet, the protests grew more violent, though they were still

[23] "Pope Declines Dalai Lama Meeting in Rome," BBC News, http://www.bbc.com/news/world-europe-30455187?print=true.

[24] Enze Han, *Contestation and Adaptation: The Politics of National Identity in China* (New York: Oxford University Press, 2013), pp. 43–44.

generally small. In 1996, Beijing launched the first of several "Strike Hard" campaigns in Xinjiang, aimed at criminal activity (e.g., drug trafficking) but also political dissent and separatist activities. Uyghurs were also blamed for terrorist attacks outside Xinjiang, such as bus explosions in several cities. After the September 11, 2001, terrorist attacks in the U.S., China began its own antiterrorist program in Xinjiang. It persuaded the U.S. and the United Nations to designate the little-known East Turkestan Independence Movement as a terrorist group and used this designation as justification for increased repressive actions against Uyghurs in Xinjiang and elsewhere in China.

In July 2009, one of the bloodiest protests since the Cultural Revolution broke out in Xinjiang's capital city, Urumqi. The clash was triggered by a brawl between Han and Uyghur workers on the other side of the country, in Guangdong's Shaoguan city. The fight began after a group of Uyghurs allegedly raped two Han women, a story later revealed to be false. Two Uyghurs were killed and hundreds injured. Angered by the lack of a police response to the brawl and the labor policies that compelled many Uyghurs to leave Xinjiang, hundreds of Uyghurs began a peaceful march on July 5 that later escalated into violence. Clashes between the protestors and the People's Armed Police, as well as Han civilians, resulted in 197 deaths, most of them Han Chinese, and over 1,700 wounded, according to Beijing's official report (overseas Uyghur groups claimed that many more Uyghurs were killed). On July 7, Han Chinese staged a counter-protest to demand a stronger response to the Uyghur attacks, and beat Uyghurs they encountered on the streets. By July 9, the protests ended, but tensions remained high. Beijing initially cut off phone and Internet access to Xinjiang, but unlike the 2008 protests in Tibet, CCP leaders soon reopened communication links and even organized groups of foreign journalists to go to Urumqi to investigate the conflict.[25] Afterward, over 1,500 Uyghurs were taken into custody, and at least 26 were sentenced to death.

[25] Later that summer, I asked an official from the Central Propaganda Department what the CCP had learned from its response to the Tibetan protests, and how it changed its response in Xinjiang. He denied there was any difference.

A subsequent series of events led to the imposition of a prolonged crackdown in Xinjiang. In October 2013, a car crashed into a crowd of tourists in Tiananmen Square, killing two and injuring dozens. The three occupants of the car died when it burst into flames. This attack in the symbolic center of the country was a psychological blow for many Han Chinese, as well as the regime. In March, knife attacks at Kunming's railway station left 29 dead and 140 injured; Beijing blamed Uyghur separatists for the attacks. In April, a small group of people attacked passengers at Urumqi's railway station with knives and explosives. Xinhua reported that three people died, including two of the attackers, and 79 were injured. In May, a pair of suicide bombers in Urumqi killed 39 and injured over 90. In July, another group armed with axes and knives attacked civilians and clashed with police in Xinjiang. China's official media later reported that 96 people died, including 59 of the attackers killed by security forces. In response to this series of attacks, Beijing launched a new crackdown that it announced would last more than a year. It quickly arrested hundreds of people who were accused of planning or participating in the separate attacks, and over 30 were executed or sentenced to death. It banned fasting during Ramadan and the wearing of beards, headscarves, and other traditional Moslem clothing in public. It gave a life sentence to Ilhan Tohti, a prominent Uyghur scholar at Minzu University in Beijing, one of the few moderate voices among the leading Uyghurs. In so doing, it indicated it was prepared to stifle any dissent or opposition, regardless of how mild, in order to solidify control over Xinjiang.

Just as the Chinese government routinely blames the Dalai Lama and his exiled supporters for protests in Tibet, it also blames Uyghur exiles for planning violent protests in Xinjiang. If there is a leader of the Uyghurs in exile, it is probably Rebiya Kadeer, who once was appointed to a national advisory body in China but later was removed and imprisoned for her criticism of Beijing's policies in Xinjiang. In 2005, she was released from prison and deported. The next year, she became president of the World Uyghur Congress. However, she lacks the moral authority of the Dalai Lama, who remains the spiritual leader of Tibetans. She also lacks his international stature, the result of decades of touring the world and promoting peace. Both are dedicated to promoting the interests of their people in China, but both also face Beijing's reluctance to begin meaningful negotiations.

In order to repress alternative voices on Xinjiang, the Party also targets foreign scholars. The contributors to a 2004 book on Xinjiang[26] were repeatedly denied visas to travel to China after the book's publication. A few were later granted visas, but only after writing or stating to embassy officials that they opposed independence for Xinjiang. Many of the so-called Xinjiang 13 were also critical of their universities' leaders and the book's editor for not doing enough to push the Chinese government on this issue.[27] For people who rely on field research in China, the prohibition on entering the country was devastating.

II. Censorship

Limiting the flow of information is a common characteristic of authoritarian regimes. Autocrats censor information in several ways. First, they prevent their citizens from learning about events within their country or around the world that might trigger dissatisfaction or protests. Second, they use news media and social media to send out their own information about domestic and foreign affairs in order to shape public opinion. Third, they limit their citizens' ability to speak out—either in print or online—against their leaders, to spread information about sensitive issues, and above all to organize collective

[26] S. Frederick Starr, ed., *Xinjiang: China's Muslim Borderland* (New York: Routledge, 2004).

[27] Daniel Golden and Oliver Staley, "China Banning U.S. Professors Elicits Silence From Colleges Employing Them," *Bloomberg News*, August 10, 2011, http://www.bloomberg.com/news/2011-08-11/china-banning-u-s-professors-elicits-silence-from-colleges.html, accessed November 2, 2014. Daniel de Vise, "U.S. Scholars Say Their Book Led to Travel Ban," *Washington Post*, August 20, 2011, http://www.washingtonpost.com/local/education/us-scholars-say-their-book-on-china-led-to-travel-ban/2011/08/17/gIQAN3C9SJ_story.html, accessed November 2, 2014. In private conversations with a few of the Xinjiang 13, the main problem with the book was not so much its content, which was mainstream scholarship, but the background of the book's editor, S. Frederick Starr, who is an expert on Russia and Central Asia, and previously served as an advisor to the Reagan and Bush administrations and on a Pentagon review board. From their perspective, it was the suspicion of U.S. government support for the project that most riled China's leaders.

action against the government.[28] Advances in technology make these efforts at censorship increasingly difficult, but they also provide new ways for the state to reach out to the public in addition to suppressing critics. Many have expected the Internet to be the technology that will unleash public opinion and the flow of information that will bring down authoritarian regimes. But the Internet also gives the state new ways to control information and convey its viewpoint more widely and in some ways more effectively than ever before.[29] In Freedom House's 2015 ranking of Internet freedom around the world, China was dead last.

Controlling the Message through Media Control

In contemporary China, all broadcast and most print media are state-owned and under the jurisdiction of the CCP's Propaganda Department and the government's Ministry of Propaganda.[30] The Propaganda Department regularly gives out instructions about which stories can and cannot be covered, and what editorial lines to convey.[31] Editors and reporters who do not comply with these instructions can be suspended, fired, and even imprisoned. In order to make sure that budding journalists are loyal agents of the Party, it appoints former propaganda officials

[28] Gary King, Jennifer Pan, and Margaret E. Roberts, "How Censorship in China Allows Government Criticism but Silences Collective Expression," *American Political Science Review*, Vol. 107, No. 2 (2013), pp. 326–343.

[29] Marc Lynch, "After Egypt: The Limits and Promise of Online Challenges to the Authoritarian Arab State," *Perspectives on Politics*, Vol. 9, No. 2 (June 2011), pp. 301–310.

[30] In 1998, the CCP changed the English name of the Propaganda Department to the "Publicity Department" in order to give it a more neutral and less pejorative connotation. However, the Chinese name, *xuanchuan bu* 宣传部, remained the same. For an overview of the propaganda bureaucracy, see David Shambaugh, "China's Propaganda System: Institutions, Processes and Efficacy," *China Journal*, No. 57 (January 2007), pp. 25–58.

[31] These are typically given through verbal instructions, not in written form; see Anne-Marie Brady, *Marketing Dictatorship: Propaganda and Thought Work in Contemporary China* (Lanham, MD: Rowman & Littlefield, 2009), p. 19. These instructions are collected by the China Digital Times website under the heading "Directives from the Ministry of Truth" (http://chinadigitaltimes.net/china/directives-from-the-ministry-of-truth/).

as deans of journalism schools.[32] China has the largest number of journalists in prison in the world, most of whom are freelance journalists who do not work for the official media but are still subject to the Party's censorship policies and punished for violating them.

China's media are state-owned, but that does not mean they are necessarily loyal agents of the state. Beginning in the 1980s, the Party made most newspapers and magazines responsible for their own profits and losses. In the Maoist era, most newspapers and magazines were sold by subscription to local party and government offices. In the reform era, the Party dropped the requirement that these offices subscribe to numerous publications, thereby subsidizing their operations, and instead pushed them to sell to consumers and allowed them to accept advertising. In order to sell more copies and attract more advertising revenue, they printed tabloid-style articles on the rich and famous, as well as the misdeeds of the politically prominent. Corruption, extramarital affairs, abuses of authority, and the haughty behaviors of sons and daughters of Party, government, and military leaders became fodder for China's commercialized media. These stories often invited retaliation from their targets in the state who were not accustomed to having their official actions and private lifestyles exposed in public. While local leaders chafed at the stories, central leaders found that commercialized media provided valuable information on local misconduct.

The central leadership occasionally punishes local media when they are too critical or stray too far from the Party line. In 2006, the state shut down *Freezing Point*, a supplement to *China Youth Daily*, after it published an article that criticized the content of history textbooks for middle schools, suggesting they presented a skewed and overly nationalistic treatment of the late 19th and early 20th centuries. The Southern Media Group, which includes both *Southern Daily* and *Southern Weekend*, frequently angered local and central leaders with exposé articles and strong defense of press freedoms. Its fight for press freedom culminated in January 2013, when employees of *Southern Weekly*,

[32] Damon Yi and Any Qin, "Appointment at Chinese Journalism School Highlights Growing Party Role," *New York Times*, Sinosphere blog, August 25, 2014, accessed August 26, 2014. This is an outgrowth of the "Fudan model," where Fudan University's journalism school partnered with the local propaganda office.

another subsidiary, went on strike to protest government censorship; a new year's editorial calling for constitutional rights was replaced with one praising the Party. This followed a year in which over 1,000 of its articles were reportedly censored or deleted altogether. After the editor in chief was replaced, the paper's coverage and editorial lines became tamer.

While the commercialized media occasionally publish sensational stories, their editorial lines generally follow the Propaganda Department's directives. According to Daniela Stockmann, this leads to a surprising result: The reading public sees the commercialized media as more credible than the official media and is therefore more willing to believe the news it reads there. But because the content of most articles follows the official line, readers absorb the official line even if they do not realize it. In short, commercialized media do not provide an independent perspective on current events, but merely convey the official line through a more credible channel.[33]

Foreign media that carry critical or embarrassing stories are also censored. The *New York Times* revealed that then–Prime Minister Wen Jiabao's family had accumulated assets worth more than $2.7 billion.[34] Before Xi Jinping became head of the CCP in 2012, Bloomberg News reported that his extended family had business investments worth hundreds of millions of dollars, although none of those holdings were directly traced to Xi, his wife, or daughter.[35] The websites of both the *New York Times* and Bloomberg News were blocked after these stories, and their journalists were forced to leave China when they were unable to renew their visas. In order to protect its access to China, Bloomberg News reportedly told its reporters to focus on business-oriented stories and avoid political stories that would anger China's leaders.

---

[33] Daniela Stockmann, *Media Commercialization and Authoritarian Rule in China* (New York: Cambridge University Press, 2012).

[34] David Barboza, "Billions in Hidden Riches for Family of Chinese Leader," *New York Times*, October 12, 2012, http://www.nytimes.com/2012/10/26/business/global/family-of-wen-jiabao-holds-a-hidden-fortune-in-china.html?pagewanted=all&_r=0, accessed October 7, 2014.

[35] "Xi Jinping Millionaire Relations Reveal Fortunes of Elite," Bloomberg News, June 29, 2012, http://www.bloomberg.com/news/2012-06-29/xi-jinping-millionaire-relations-reveal-fortunes-of-elite.html, accessed October 7, 2014.

The Great Firewall of Internet Censorship

More common than press censorship has been censorship on the Internet. Dubbed the "Great Firewall," it blocks access to numerous websites, including foreign media, critical blogs, social media, pornography, and even the websites of foreign universities. Because of the large number of blocked websites, most Chinese users have access to a Chinese intranet, with many foreign websites blocked and Chinese websites like Baidu (百度), Renren (人人), and Sina Weibo (新浪微博) substituting for Google, Facebook, and Twitter. At the same time, the number of Internet users has grown exponentially, from less than 2 percent of the population in 2000 to 48 percent in 2014. The numbers of Internet users and the state's efforts to monitor and censor the web are growing in tandem.

In 2009, the Ministry of Industry and Information Technology announced a new requirement that Green Dam Youth Escort software be installed on new computers. This software was allegedly designed to block access to pornography on the Internet, but it also blocked access to many kinds of other websites involving political, legal, and human rights issues. It also created a log file of all the websites visited, potentially allowing the government to more easily monitor where users went on the Internet. After a public backlash and the refusal of some computer manufacturers to include the software, the government backed off a bit, making the software a requirement for computers in schools and Internet cafes but voluntary for other users. Many Chinese complained about this heavy-handed effort at censorship, and how it made the computers run slower and be more prone to crash. Eventually, the government tacitly ended the program by defunding it. This episode captures both the government's ambition to limit and monitor access to information on the Internet and the intense pushback from Chinese society.

At the same time, Internet users in China use various ploys to get around censors. A common tactic is the use of homonyms and euphemisms for sensitive words and the names of party and government leaders. One of the best-known examples of this was an Internet sensation in 2009 that described a facetious battle between a "grass mud horse" and "river crab," which were two homonyms for "screw your mother" and "harmony" (as in "harmonious society," Hu Jintao's slogan promoting stability and a euphemism for censorship online). The coverage of this battle involved not only Internet posts, a popular video, and cartoons, but also sales of t-shirts, posters, and other memorabilia with images of the mythical grass mud horse. In this way, those in the know were able to express their attitudes toward political repression through satire, instead of directly challenging the Party's heavy-handed policies and actions. Once the authorities caught on, the grass mud horse was added to the list of banned terms.

For the technologically savvy, using proxy servers and virtual private networks (VPNs) allows them to get around the Great Firewall. VPNs are particularly popular among ex-pats and foreign businesses in China because they allow them to access Facebook, Google, the *New York Times*, and other popular websites that are blocked within China. When the government temporarily blocked access to VPNs during the Arab Spring protests in 2011, one of the companies sent an email to its customers warning that "there has been a disturbance in the force." The Party once again blocked access to VPNs starting in January 2015, part of its ongoing restrictions on accessing the Internet.

But many Internet users in China are unfamiliar with these alternatives. My colleague Steve Balla spent the 2008–2009 academic year in China on a Fulbright fellowship and gave public talks at dozens of Chinese universities. At one talk, he mentioned that he was keeping a blog about his family's experiences in China, and even though the website Blogspot was blocked in China, the students in the audience could easily access it through a proxy server. "What is a proxy server?" they asked. Although college students are normally the most up-to-date users when it comes to new programs and apps, not all of them are motivated enough to evade the government's censorship tactics.

Another important reason that most Chinese do not access websites outside China is that most of those sites are in English and other foreign languages. Most Internet users in China understandably prefer to read in Chinese. Even those who do use foreign websites do not necessarily find them more credible than domestic sources of information (see figure 2-2). Even among the youngest cohort (those who came of age after 1989's crackdown on demonstrations in Tiananmen Square and elsewhere in China), less than 40 percent trust Western media. They prefer to get their news from Chinese Internet portals like Sina,

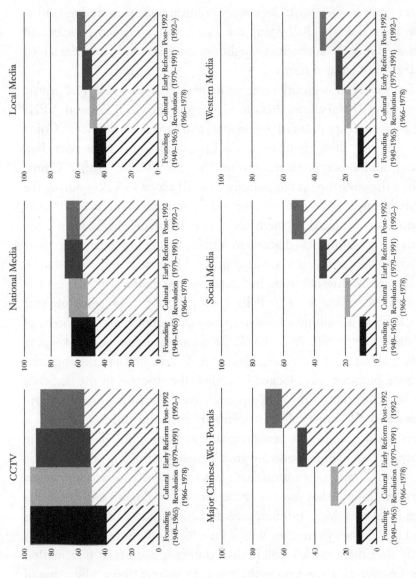

FIGURE 2-2 Trust in Media in Urban China, by Generation (bars represent percent who answered "trust a lot" (solid) or "some trust" (stripes) for each type of media).

Sohu, Tencent, and 163 (78.4 percent) or CCTV (73.5 percent). They even report more trust in national media like *People's Daily* and *Xinhua* and local media like *Southern Metropolitan Daily* (南方都市报) or the *21st Century Business Herald* (21 世纪经济报道) than Western media. Despite the Party's censorship over the Internet and the domestic media, these remain the preferred sources of information in China.

The Party's persistent censorship does not come cheap. It has to mobilize large numbers of people to support its efforts. The "Strong Country Forum" on the *People's Daily* website allows readers to voice their opinions on a variety of subjects, but within strict limits. The forum is managed at all times by at least six censors and one manager who monitor comments, censor or delete the ones they deem to be unacceptable, and actively guide the online discussions.[36] The Propaganda Department relies on retired CCP members from the propaganda, media, culture, or publishing worlds. Each person is assigned a TV station, newspaper, or magazine to follow. They report inappropriate content to provincial and central propaganda departments, which then decide on suitable punishments.[37] It supports an untold number of Internet users who participate in online discussions and are paid five *mao* for every comment they make that supports the Party and its domestic and foreign policies (hence they are often referred to as the *wu mao dang* [五毛党], or 50-cent party; five *mao* are half a yuan, or about eight cents in U.S. currency). It has also created phony web pages and Twitter accounts, supposedly by foreigners, that say nice things about China.[38]

The Party's dilemma in censoring the Internet is restricting political criticism and access to sensitive information without alienating people who rely on the Internet for other purposes. Most Internet users in China are not political activists, but instead use it to access email, shop, play online games, follow celebrities, and other nonpolitical pursuits (see table 2-2). In September 2014, the Chinese government shut down Instagram to prevent information about pro-democracy protests in Hong Kong from spreading throughout China. It may have achieved that goal, but at

[36] Brady, *Marketing Dictatorship*, p. 55.

[37] Brady, *Marketing Dictatorship*, pp. 22, 94.

[38] Andrew Jacobs, "It's Another Perfect Day in Tibet!" *New York Times*, July 21, 2014.

TABLE 2-2 What Do Chinese Do Online?

1.	browse news	74.2
2.	watch TV shows and movies	59.2
3.	chat (BBS)	49.2
4.	search for information	43.9
5.	read social media (WeChat, Weibo, Renren wang, etc.)	43.7
6.	shop	34.6
7.	play games	30.8
8.	email	26.3
9.	download movies, TV, music, and other entertainment programs	20.4
10.	read e-books	15.5
11.	maintain personal blogs	8.5

Source: 2014 Public Goods and Political Support Survey.

the cost of irritating people who were otherwise not politically inclined. "No one cared before what was happening over there in Hong Kong. We just wanted to quietly stalk our pop stars and get updates on ball games. But now that you've done this we have to care," wrote one blogger,[39] aptly summarizing the dilemma faced by the Party: As censorship and other forms of repression spread and affect a larger number of people, the Party runs the risk of turning people from neutrality to opposition.

---

[39] William Wan, "How One Night of Tear Gas in Hong Kong Just Shut Down Instagram in China," *Washington Post*, September 29, 2014, http://www.washingtonpost.com/blogs/worldviews/wp/2014/09/29/how-one-night-of-tear-gas-in-hong-kong-just-shut-down-all-instagram-in-china/, accessed September 29, 2014. As pro-democracy protests in Hong Kong were underway in fall 2014, over 40 political activists were taken into custody, and the state ordered publishers and bookstores to stop selling books by authors who may have been sympathetic toward the protests, even those who had not made any public statements about them. William Wan, "As Hong Kong Protests Challenge Beijing, Authorities Extend Backlash to Books," *Washington Post*, October 14, 2014, http://www.washingtonpost.com/world/asia_pacific/as-hong-kong-protests-challenge-beijing-authorities-extend-backlash-to-books/2014/10/13/813e8ccc-52d1-11e4-892e-602188e70e9c_story.html, accessed October 14, 2014.

Internet censorship even affects state-sponsored items. In February 2015, the Beijing Internet Association hosted a Chinese New Year celebration. The event included a performance of a new anthem sung by employees of the Cyberspace Administration of China, which is in charge of Internet regulation. Reminiscent of revolutionary songs of old, including orchestral music and uplifting lyrics, the song spread quickly on the Internet before being removed entirely a few days later. This new ode to the Chinese Internet itself fell victim to censorship. In February 2015, the documentary film *Under the Dome* was posted online and attracted over 100 million views on its first day. The film criticized China's environmental record, detailed the rising social and health costs associated with it, and blamed the politically powerful oil and steel industries for blocking the enforcement of environmental laws. Within a week, it was removed from the Internet, as were all articles mentioning it. Even though China's leaders have been extolling the dangers of pollution and the urgent need to deal with it, and even though the minister of the Environmental Protection Agency praised it when it was first released, and even though *People's Daily*, the Party's mouthpiece, published an interview with the film's maker Chai Jing and posted her video on its website, the video was too detailed in its description of pollution, too specific in criticizing the government for not enforcing its own regulations, and above all too popular for continued public viewing. Rather than risk a popular uprising over pollution, the censors chose simply to delete the video and all articles mentioning it, even the ones criticizing it.

Outsourcing Censorship

The leading Internet portals in China, such as Sina and Sohu, are privately owned but still subject to the government's censorship regulations. In a sense, the government has outsourced censorship to private companies that must monitor and police their own users in order to comply with the government's censorship policies. They block access to stories that the government prohibits and censor responses to search terms with sensitive words like Tiananmen, human rights, Falun Gong, and so on. In 2004, computer hackers discovered a list of banned words that was pre-installed in text messaging software. The list was not produced by the Propaganda Department, but by private

Internet companies based on instructions they had received from the Propaganda Department.[40]

In order to keep the government at bay, these companies have to engage in self-censorship of their own content, as well as their users' emails, blog posts, and search terms. Sina's Weibo (China's rough equivalent to Twitter) is one of the most popular micro-blogs in China. Rather than try to directly censor Weibo and similar social media, the Chinese government requires Sina and other micro-blog hosts to more carefully screen and censor their users' postings. In 2012, Weibo required all of its users to register with their real names in order to inhibit some of the extreme rhetoric that anonymity is known to allow. If comments could be traced to real names and not just fictitious user names, the fear of retaliation would presumably inhibit Weibo users from making political criticisms. But Internet users found it easy to get around this restriction.[41] The crackdown began in earnest in the fall of 2013, when a broad law against "spreading rumors or misinformation" went into effect. This had a particularly big impact on micro-bloggers with large followings (known as "Big V," the V referring to those whose real identities had been verified). The number of posts on Weibo declined sharply, due in part to the crackdown on content.[42] But more importantly, the appearance of a new app, WeChat (in Chinese, *weixin* 微信, meaning micro-message), that allowed people to send voicemail messages, as well as text messages, to other individuals or groups led many users to switch from Weibo. WeChat messages were less susceptible to government monitoring and censorship. But this was a short-lived free space. In summer 2014, the government announced new regulations on users of WeChat that limited the number of people in a group and allowed the government to unilaterally replace the head of a group. Although innovations allow Internet users to evade the Great Firewall,

---

[40] Brady, *Marketing Dictatorship*, p. 137.

[41] "China's Real Name Internet Part 5: 2013–2014," Fei Chang Dao, August 20, 2014, http://blog.feichangdao.com/2014/08/chinas-real-name-internet-part-5-2013. html, accessed July 27, 2015.

[42] "China Microblogging Site Weibo Sees Decline In Users," BBC News, January 17, 2014, http://www.bbc.com/news/world-asia-25775191, accessed July 27, 2015. See also King-wa Fu, Chung-hong Chan, and Michael Chau, "Assessing Censorship on Microblogs in China," *IEEE Internet Computing* 17, No. 3 (2013), pp. 42–50.

the state soon finds a way to reassert restrictions on the flow of information and ideas.

Even foreign Internet companies have been complicit in the Chinese government's censorship. Yahoo provided the email account information of several dissidents, leading to their arrest and conviction. Yahoo defended its actions by saying it must abide by the laws of the countries in which it operates. For years, Google agreed to censor search term results in order to do business in China, but in 2010, it moved its servers to Hong Kong after announcing that it and other U.S. companies had been targeted by a hacking attempt originating from China, including Gmail records of Chinese human rights activists. It had been willing to endure political pressure in China, but not the hacking of its computers. After its move to Hong Kong, Google provided uncensored search results; at the same time, the Chinese government blocked access to Google's search engine from within China, as well as access to Gmail and other email programs that use the Gmail platform.[43] Beginning in 2014, as the government's crackdown on intellectual freedom and foreign businesses in China increased, even access to Google documents became restricted, making it difficult for individuals and businesses to share files, spreadsheets, and calendars for meetings.[44]

While censorship has increased over the years, most Chinese Internet users report not being affected by it (see table 2-3; please note: 45.7 percent of the survey respondents reported they never went online; the percentages in the table refer only to Internet users). The vast majority report they have never experienced blocked websites and other forms of censorship, much less had their accounts canceled. Moreover, those who have experienced it are rather blasé about it. The most common response to censorship is "it doesn't matter" (*wusuowei* 无所谓) (48.6 percent), suggesting they are either resigned to government censorship, feel powerless to deal with it, or do not feel much affected by it. In a country where media censorship has been in place

---

[43] For example, my university's email uses the Gmail platform, making it inaccessible in China without a VPN.

[44] Keith Bradsher and Paul Mozer, "China Clamps Down on Web, Pinching Companies like Google," *New York Times*, September 2014, http://www.nytimes.com/2014/09/22/business/international/china-clamps-down-on-web-pinching-companies-like-google.html?_r=0, accessed October 14, 2014.

TABLE 2-3 Experience with Internet Censorship

Since the beginning of this year (i.e., 2014), have you had these experiences while on Weibo, QQ, Renren Wang, and other Internet social media?	Frequently	Sometimes	Rarely	Never
Web pages were blocked.	2.9	10.8	13.8	72.4
Items posted or forwarded were deleted.	1.4	9.1	12.7	76.9
Unable to post prohibited words or items that had not been screened.	0.5	4.1	7.1	88.3
Account was canceled.	0.3	3.0	5.8	91.0

Source: 2014 Public Goods and Political Support Survey.

for decades, it may not be too surprising that so many Internet users are willing to accept the limits imposed by the Great Firewall. But among those who had an emotional response, 33 percent were either angry, indignant, or both (respondents could select more than reaction). One former student told me that she always considered herself a patriot, except when she went online and grew angry at the censorship she encountered. But compared to the survey respondents, she was in the minority. Only 5 percent were worried by encountering censorship and only 1.5 percent reported feeling scared. While censorship often meets with public frustration, these responses indicate that it is also met with resignation.

Public opinion on the propriety of government regulation of the Internet in China shows seemingly contradictory opinions (see table 2-4). For example, 45.2 percent agree the government should totally control the Internet, but almost 90 percent believe this control should not come at the expense of infringing on individual freedoms or the right to free expression. Whether or not people use the Internet strongly influences their opinions on government control. Those who use the Internet are much less likely to agree that the government should totally control the Internet or that it should decide which opinions can be spread on the Internet. However, both users and non-users overwhelmingly agree that Internet supervision should not come at the expense of individual

TABLE 2-4 Public Opinion on Government Regulation of Internet

	Strongly Agree	Agree	Disagree	Strongly Disagree
The government should totally control the Internet.	13.1	32.1	43.3	11.5
The government should decide whether or not an opinion is able to be spread on the Internet.	7.0	24.5	53.4	15.1
Internet supervision should not come at the expense of infringing on individual freedoms.	27.3	60.4	10.4	1.9
Citizens have the right to free expression on the Internet.	26.6	58.8	13.1	1.5

Source: 2014 Public Goods and Political Support Survey.

freedoms or freedom of expression (although users are slightly more likely to strongly agree with those views).[45] In other words, there is a difference of opinion on the general propriety of government supervision over the Internet, but also general agreement that the government should not infringe on certain rights. The Party is less concerned about balancing these competing goals. Its desire to control the flow of information easily trumps the protection of individual rights.

III. Population Control

The Party tries to control not just political expression and the flow of information, but also private choices, such as where to live and work and when to have children. The two main mechanisms for these types of control are the *hukou* (household registration) system and the one-child policy.

The Hukou System: Institutionalized Discrimination

One of the tools used by the Party to control the population is the household registration system, known in Chinese as the *hukou*

---

[45] A difference of means test is statistically significant on the first two questions and negative on the other two questions.

system.[46] Depending on where people are born, their *hukou* designates them as either rural or urban and provides the location of their permanent residency, most often their place of birth. Originally, this system was designed to limit the mobility of the population and in particular prevent the flood of rural residents into cities. In the post-Mao era, restrictions on migration have eased, but the *hukou* system still largely determines many of the life opportunities available to people.

Under the central planning system of the Maoist era, the *hukou* system put strict limits on where people could live and work. There were no markets for housing, food, or permanent jobs; everything was allocated by the state. Housing was assigned to people and was often provided by a person's workplace. Food was often allocated with coupons, and people were unable to buy additional food with cash in stores or markets. People were normally assigned their work and could not easily transfer to different jobs. Even married couples who were assigned to jobs in different cities were not automatically entitled to transfer so they could live together. Rural workers could occasionally migrate to the cities for temporary jobs, but these were short-term stints allocated by the communes they belonged to. Their main residences remained in the countryside. During the Maoist period, a person's *hukou* was one of the most important determinants of life opportunities—receiving education, jobs, housing, food rations, and consumer goods. *Hukou* status also influenced marriage patterns: Those with an urban *hukou* were usually unwilling to marry someone with a rural *hukou* because they would not be able to live together in the city, and most urban *hukou* holders were unwilling to be permanently relegated to the countryside.

---

[46] On the establishment and evolution of the *hukou* system, see Tiejun Cheng and Mark Selden, "The Origins and Social Consequences of China's Hukou System," *China Quarterly*, No. 139 (September 1994), pp. 644–668; Fei-ling Wang, *Organizing through Division and Exclusion: China's Hukou System* (Palo Alto, CA: Stanford University Press, 2005); Jeremy L. Wallace, *Cities and Stability: Urbanization, Redistribution and Regime Survival in China* (New York: Oxford University Press, 2014), esp. chapter 4.

During the reform era, these constraints began to lessen, and the migrant population began to grow.[47] Millions of migrant workers moved from the countryside to the cities in search of manufacturing, construction, and service sector jobs. Food markets and small restaurants opened, giving people who were away from home easier access to daily food. Employers often built dormitories to house their employees and cafeterias to feed them. On construction sites, many workers lived in makeshift housing. As the stock of urban housing grew, people could rent apartments from landlords and were not limited to what was provided by their employers. The size of China's migrant population is estimated to be over 250 million, almost one-fifth of the country's population.

Although restrictions on mobility have eased, the *hukou* system remains in place. In the early reform period, migrant workers were technically in violation of the law and could be rounded up and sent back to their villages. This created one of the many paradoxes of the reform era in China: Urban employers desperately needed large numbers of unskilled and semiskilled workers to operate their factories and construction sites, and preferred hiring rural migrants who were willing to work long hours for little pay. At the same time, migrants were blamed for criminal activity and viewed with suspicion by urban governments and society alike.[48] This complaint is often made about illegal immigrants in the U.S., but there is an important difference: Migrants in China are PRC citizens. If migrants did not have their proper identification papers with them at all times, they could be taken into custody and forcibly returned to their villages, only to venture out again in search of urban jobs. Even though the work was hard and the pay was low, many with rural *hukou*, especially young people, still preferred the

---

[47] Migrants in China are often referred to as the "floating population," a more poetic-sounding name than simply "migrant population." However, the Chinese word *liudong* (流动) can be translated as either flow or move. It is in the translation of the word, not in the original Chinese, that the poetry is found.

[48] Dorothy J. Solinger, *Contesting Citizenship in Urban China: Peasant Migrants, the State, and the Logic of the Market* (Berkeley, CA: University of California Press, 1999).

higher standard of living, opportunities for upward mobility, and the excitement of city life.

A key turning point in the treatment of migrant workers by urban governments was the death of a young man named Sun Zhigang in 2003.[49] Sun was a recent college grad who found a job as a graphic designer in Guangzhou. Less than a month after arriving in Guangzhou, he was stopped on the street by police who took him into custody because he was not carrying his ID card. He called his friends from the police station, and they brought his ID card, proof of employment and housing, and bail money, but the police refused to release him. Sun was transferred to a detention center, one of hundreds around the country that were normally used for the unemployed, homeless, and people without papers. Sun died in the detention center. An autopsy showed that he had been beaten so badly that he went into shock and organ failure. Investigative reporting by the *Southern Metropolis Daily*, a hard-charging newspaper in Guangzhou, brought the case to light and created a national outcry. The secretive network of detention centers like the one Sun Zhigang died in was exposed to the public, and journalists in other cities turned up more stories of the brutal treatment of young people in these detention centers. In the end, the central government declared them to be illegal and ordered them closed.[50] But as is so often the case for whistleblowers, the top officials of the *Southern Metropolis Daily* were punished for putting the local leaders in such a bad light. The general manager was arrested and sentenced to 12 years in prison, later reduced to four. The editor in charge of the Sun Zhigang case, Cheng Yizhong, was arrested but released after about five months. He lost his job at the newspaper and later found work at the Chinese edition of *Sports Illustrated*.[51]

---

[49] Philip P. Pan, *Out of Mao's Shadow: The Struggle for the Soul of a New China* (New York: Simon and Schuster, 2008), pp. 247–267.

[50] One of the troubling aspects of this case is the attention it got because Sun had a college degree. If he had been a typical rural migrant with less than a high school education, his case may not have gained such notoriety.

[51] Cheng's penchant for exposés did not end there. While based in the western city of Chengdu, he broke the story of what became known as the "nail house," referring to a married couple that was "hard as nails" (*dingzihu* 钉子户). They

Although migrant workers are less subject to detention and repatriation than they were before the Sun Zhigang case, they still do not have equal rights as those with urban *hukou*. Above all, *hukou* status determines access to public goods. People with a rural *hukou* are entitled to the education and healthcare provided by their hometowns and villages, but if they move to a city, their access to public goods does not move with them. They are generally not able to send their children to local schools without paying tuition and fees, which they generally cannot afford. Groups of migrants have occasionally tried to set up their own schools to educate their children, but local authorities quickly shut them down. *Hukou* status also determines where people receive healthcare. If migrants or their family members become sick or get injured, they have to return to their original town or village where their *hukou* remains.

Given the size of China's migrant population and the need for labor mobility in a marketizing economy, many believe the *hukou* system has outlived its usefulness. While the central government is not ready to abandon the *hukou* system, it has encouraged local governments to experiment with *hukou* reforms. The State Council designated Chongqing as a "national experimental zone for integrating rural and urban development" in 2007. The Chongqing municipal government developed a system that allowed people to convert their *hukou* from rural to urban status, which would allow them to get a more generous share of public goods. Rural migrants were eligible to receive urban *hukou* if they met specific criteria—for example, if they worked or did business in Chongqing for more than five years or in suburban areas for more than three years; graduated from college or vocational school; were retired soldiers; or had their farmland expropriated for hydraulic power projects and were forced to move into the city. By 2013, 3.7 million migrant workers had received urban *hukou*, and by 2020, the

rejected what they considered to be inadequate financial compensation from a developer and refused to vacate their house. As a result, a construction pit was dug around their house, leaving it perched precariously on a thin tower of unexcavated dirt. Eventually, the city government and the couple negotiated a settlement (never revealed publicly), and the house was demolished. Although *Sports Illustrated* broke the story, what exactly it had to do with sports was never identified.

proportion of Chongqing's population with urban *hukou* was expected to rise from 29 percent to 60 percent. Guangdong's Zhongshan City adopted the country's first points-based *hukou* conversion system. People could earn points by having a good tax payment history, holding a professional degree, participating in charity work, etc.; conversely, they could lose points by misconduct and criminal behavior, and were ineligible if they were in violation of the one-child policy. This system was later extended to the entire province in 2010, and by March 2013, over 1.2 million rural migrants had received urban *hukou*. Shanghai also adopted a points-based conversion process, one that favored people with professional skills and entrepreneurial experience and consequently more supportive of economic development than social equity.

The main obstacle to *hukou* reform is the cost associated with providing public goods. In China, the majority of costs associated with education, healthcare, welfare, and other public goods is borne by local governments that cannot afford to begin offering them to millions of additional residents if the *hukou* system was fully reformed or even abandoned (public goods provision in China is the subject of chapter 4). In Chongqing, one of the leaders in *hukou* reform, the municipal government made local enterprises contribute 75 percent of the costs associated with providing social welfare to the millions of migrant workers who obtained urban *hukou* status, because the government could not afford to do it on its own. Local governments are already burdened with many unfunded mandates from Beijing. Without greater support from the central government, they may be reluctant to expand the numbers of people with urban *hukou* who are consequently entitled to receive the full range of public goods.

The One-Child Policy: The Extreme of State Control

China's family-planning policy is a major exception to the trend of declining state intrusion into the daily lives of most Chinese. Whereas most people in China have some degree of choice over where they live, where they work, where they get their information, what they do in their spare time, and so on, decisions on how many children to have—one of the most personal decisions individuals make—is still a matter of state policy.

The motivation behind the one-child policy was straightforward: China was experiencing rapid population growth that threatened to slow economic development. When the PRC was founded in 1949, China's population was just under 550 million. At the beginning of the reform era in 1981, its population had surpassed 1 billion and was projected to top 1.5 billion by 2000—triple the level of just 50 years before—unless new policies were put in place to reduce the birthrate. In order to achieve Deng Xiaoping's goal of quadrupling China's per capita GDP by the year 2000, China's leaders believed it was necessary to limit the number of children to just one per couple.[52] Beginning in 1979, this became official policy.

In order to ensure compliance with the policy, local officials monitor women's menstrual cycles. If they become pregnant after already having one or two children, they are pressured and in some cases coerced into having abortions. They are normally required to use some form of birth control, in most cases intrauterine devices, but in some cases they are sterilized. If couples have extra children, they are subject to heavily punitive fines, loss of jobs and even property, and may have to pay additional tuition in order for their children to attend school.

To make sure that local officials properly enforced the policy, it was made a "hard target" in their annual performance evaluations, equivalent to achieving economic growth targets (in later years, maintaining political stability was added as a third hard target). If they failed to limit the number of births in their jurisdiction, they faced a variety of penalties, including demotion. Enforcing the policy presented other risks: Officials were attacked and sometimes killed after forcing women to have abortions. Some had their houses set on fire, others had broken glass dropped on their rice fields so that when they planted rice seedlings, their bare feet would be shredded. Caught between the state's determination to implement the policy and the often violent reactions from people who were victims of it, some local officials colluded with families by not counting unauthorized births or by turning the collection of fines into a celebration of a new child. The result has been tremendous variation in the enforcement of the one-child policy. Where

---

[52] The goal of quadrupling per capita GDP by 2000 was surpassed. China's per capita GDP, measured in current $U.S., was $182 in 1979 and $949 in 2000. Using purchasing power parity, it was $182 in 1979 and $2,864 in 2000.

some local leaders use coercive means to achieve compliance with the policy, others use persuasive methods to encourage compliance, and others collude with local people to evade the policy.[53]

In one case that gained international attention, a blind self-taught lawyer named Chen Guangcheng tried to organize a class-action lawsuit against local officials in Shandong who used coercive measures in violation of the law, including late-term abortions, forced sterilizations, and the beating of relatives if women did not comply. He was arrested and convicted of damaging property and organizing people to disturb the peace (which referred to a street protest that happened while he was under house arrest, not his class-action lawsuit).[54] After more than four years in prison, he was released but kept under house arrest in his village. In order to monitor him and his visitors, his house was under surveillance day and night, with floodlights used to illuminate the house when it was dark. Despite these efforts, he was somehow able to escape one night and find his way to a rendezvous point outside the village, where a friend was waiting to whisk him away. He eventually made it to the U.S. Embassy in Beijing. Although he did not formally ask for asylum, he sought U.S. protection. After several days of tense negotiations between the State Department and the Chinese government, Chen was allowed to leave China, and he accepted a one-year fellowship at New York University.[55]

[53] Tyrene White, "Domination, Resistance, and Accommodation in China's One-Child Campaign," in Elizabeth J. Perry and Mark Selden, eds., *Chinese Society: Change, Conflict, and Resistance*, second edition (London and New York: Routledge, 2003).

[54] Pan, *Out of Mao's Shadow*, pp. 295–318.

[55] The story has a somewhat sad ending. As his one-year fellowship was nearing its end, Chen publicly criticized NYU for not extending it and implied that the university was responding to pressure from the Chinese government because NYU was opening a new campus in Shanghai. NYU denied the accusation and insisted the fellowship was intended to be only one year and was nonrenewable. In the end, Chen ended up at the Witherspoon Institute, a conservative think tank in Princeton, New Jersey.

Chen's family continued to suffer retaliation even after he left China. His brother was taken into custody for questioning and reportedly beaten. His nephew was arrested after attacking policemen with a knife when they broke into his house. He was convicted and sentenced to more than three years in prison.

In 2015, Chen released an autobiography, *The Barefoot Lawyer: A Blind Man's Fight for Justice and Freedom in China* (New York: Henry Holt and Co., 2015).

Chen's case raises an issue of central-local relations that concerns the one-child policy more generally. Either the central government was unable to prevent local officials from undertaking coercive actions that damage China's image at home and abroad, or it was unwilling to because local officials were simply doing the bidding of central leaders, who are willing to endure domestic and international criticism in order to suppress dissenting voices and enforce a deeply unpopular policy. Both scenarios are troubling.

Most of the violent reactions to the one-child policy have happened in the countryside, where the cultural preference for boys is strongest. There is a general belief that boys are necessary to maintain the lineage, provide labor in the fields, and support parents in their old age. With many young people leaving the villages and migrating to cities, and consequently leaving agriculture for industrial and service sector jobs, China's demographics are changing faster than the cultural norms.

In contrast, the one-child policy has been less contentious in cities. Birthrates in China's cities have fallen below replacement levels not as a result of the one-child policy but as a consequence of modernization. Urban women are choosing to have fewer children and sometimes no children in order to pursue their careers, maintain higher standards of living for the family, and save for the future.[56] This is causing some cities to rethink their family-planning policies. For example, instead of limiting the number of births, Shanghai now provides economic incentives for couples to have more children.

Societal reaction to this deeply unpopular policy eventually led to slight modifications. In recognition of the strong social norm on the importance of male offspring, especially in the countryside, families were entitled to have a second child if the first was a girl or had severe disabilities. If husband and wife were both only children, they could have a second child. Beginning in 2014, the policy was further amended, allowing couples to have a second child as long as one of the parents was an only child. Ethnic minorities are generally exempt from the one-child policy. In October 2015, the government announced that

---

[56] One consequence of this has been the rise of "little emperors": single children who are doted upon and spoiled by their parents, who pour all their hopes, dreams, and anxieties into their only children.

all couples would now be permitted to have two children. It is still try-ing to control the number of births, just relaxing the cap.

Unintended consequences also led to relaxation in the policy. One was the growing gender-ratio imbalance, which reached 119 boys for every 100 girls in 2000 (the normal ratio is about 105 boys for every 100 girls). The reasons for this imbalance are complex, and reliable data are scarce, so it is difficult to determine which reasons are primary and which are secondary. Part of the imbalance is due to abandonment, female infanticide, and gender-selective abortions; ultrasound tests made it possible to determine the sex of the fetus, and the preference for boys led to a dramatic skewing of the ratio of boys to girls.[57] Part of the gender-ratio imbalance is also due to parents choosing to not reg-ister the births of girls (and local officials who choose to look the other way).[58] Being unregistered means the girls are unable to go to school and have a very hard time finding jobs or a spouse. Another unintended consequence of the one-child policy was the changing age distribu-tion: With few children being born and later entering the workforce, there were fewer people to support those who retired. In 2009, there were 13 people of working age for every elderly person; by 2050, the ratio will decline to just 2:1, , at which time 40 percent of China's popu-lation will be over retirement age.[59] This will create a tremendous bur-den for the working-age population, which will be expected to produce the economic growth necessary to care for the elderly. Each working-age adult who is an only child will have to care for two parents and four grandparents (known in China as the 4-2-1 problem[60]). In addition, it will put additional pressure on the state to develop an adequate social security system of pensions, welfare, and healthcare, which will be an expensive proposition if fewer workers will be paying into it and greater numbers of elderly will be supported by it.

[57] A similar imbalance has occurred in India and South Korea due to the wide-spread use of ultrasound tests to detect the gender of the fetus.

[58] Shi Yaozhong and John J. Kennedy, "Delayed Registration and Identifying the 'Missing Girls' in China," *China Quarterly*, forthcoming.

[59] Tyrene White, "Population Policy," in William A. Joseph, ed., *Politics in China: An Introduction*, second edition (New York: Oxford University Press, 2014), p. 394.

[60] Another variant of the 4-2-1 problem describes each married couple (2) sup-porting two sets of parents (4) and their only child (1).

How effective has the one-child policy been? According to the World Bank's World Development Indicators, China's fertility rate declined from 2.8 live births per woman in 1979, when the policy first went into effect, to 1.7 in 2012. However, the fertility rate had been declining from the mid-1960s on, and it is difficult to sort out the impact of the policy from other socioeconomic changes underway in China, especially economic modernization, urbanization, and rising levels of education, all of which are also associated with declining fertility. Critics of the policy, both within China and abroad, argue that the same results could have been achieved through better education and incentives, instead of the heavy-handed and coercive way it was implemented in many areas of China.

Although the Chinese government has tinkered with the one-child policy to moderate some of its unpopular and unwanted effects, it has not changed its commitment to birth control. As Tyrene White put it, "Through all these changes and fluctuations in political atmosphere, the insistence on strict birth control never faltered. It was a constant in an otherwise volatile situation."[61] The government changed how it pursued the goal of limiting population growth, but not the goal itself.

IV. Corruption

Corruption is not as intensive or repressive as other examples of "the heavy hand of the state," but in a different sense reflects the abuse of power by party and government leaders. The need to give bribes in order to gain access to scarce goods and services, such as judicial rulings, business contracts and licenses, medical appointments, school admissions, etc., reflects the weak constraints on those in positions of influence. It is therefore one of the most corrosive factors undermining public trust in the Party. While the Party is more focused on officials who squander state resources on travel, banquets, houses, and cars for personal use (including apartments and condos for mistresses), and other illicit behaviors, the public is more concerned with cases of corruption that affect their own pocketbooks.[62] Although Party leaders

[61] White, "Population Policy," p. 383. See also Yijia Jing, "The One-Child Policy Needs an Overhaul," *Journal of Policy Analysis and Management*, Vol. 32, No. 2 (Spring 2013), pp. 392–399.

[62] Melanie Manion, *Corruption by Design: Building Clean Government in Mainland China and Hong Kong* (Cambridge, MA: Harvard University Press, 2004).

often refer to corruption as "a matter of life or death" for the Party, it is more like a chronic but (by itself) nonfatal disease. Throughout the post-Mao era, corruption has grown in scale and scope: More officials are involved, and the monetary amounts grow and grow.[63] For many, corruption is the grease that makes the economy grow and gives local officials a tangible incentive to engage in economic reform. At the same time, the Party's recurring efforts to clamp down on corruption are a form of repression aimed at its own members. Party and government officials charged with corruption are subject to the same repressive and extralegal practices as the rest of the population.

Corruption has plagued the Party from the founding of the People's Republic in 1949, but the nature of corruption has changed over the years. During most of the Maoist era, it was less about money because money was scarce. There were no markets in which to spend the money, and recurring campaigns against "capitalist roaders" made people wary of overt corruption. Instead, corruption was more about favors and preferential treatment—better fields, the first cut at ration coupons, a few creature comforts, and support during political meetings. At a time when virtually any thought or action could have political consequences, corruption was held in check by political campaigns and the likelihood of retaliation.

The commitment to economic reform in the post-Mao period provided new opportunities for corrupt practices.[64] Growing prosperity made more money available for bribes and gift-giving. The need to obtain approvals to open a business, receive loans, engage in trade, and limit taxes and fees allowed party and government officials to engage in extensive rent-seeking. Even official posts in the Party, government, and military bureaucracies were available for sale. The weak rule of law and the Party's reluctance to air its dirty laundry allowed corruption of various kinds to grow extensively.

At the beginning of the reform era, the Party resurrected its Central Discipline Inspection Committee (CDIC), which had been created in 1949 but discontinued during the Cultural Revolution. Although

---

[63] Andrew Wedeman, *Double Paradox: Rapid Growth and Rising Corruption in China* (Ithaca, NY: Cornell University Press, 2012).

[64] See in particular Minxin Pei's *China's Trapped Transition: The Limits of Developmental Autocracy* (Cambridge, MA: Harvard University Press, 2006).

an important institution, it did not have the status or clout of other Party organs, and its leaders were often not among the most politically powerful. It is not an autonomous body with full powers of investigation. At the central level, there has been an informal norm that the top Party leadership, essentially the incumbent and retired members of the Politburo Standing Committee and their children, are off-limits. At the local level, the discipline inspection commissions work under the authority of the local Party leadership. As a result, most investigations target lower-level officials.

When high-level Party leaders are charged with corruption, it is often the result of a political struggle. Corruption is so prevalent that being charged with accepting bribes or embezzlement is not seen as a sign of guilt as much as an indication that the individuals have lost the political support necessary to protect themselves. During the post-Tiananmen era, charging someone with corruption became the preferred means for removing them from office. In this way, the ouster of a leader is not seen as the result of divisions within the leadership—Party leaders have been careful to maintain a united front since the 1989 protests—but as individual wrongdoing.

During the early 1990s, Beijing Party Secretary Chen Xitong was seen as a potential rival to the new General Secretary Jiang Zemin. He was removed from office and charged with corruption in 1995 and later sentenced to 16 years in prison. After Hu Jintao replaced Jiang Zemin as general secretary in 2002, he adopted more populist policies to narrow the gap between the prosperous coastal areas and the less-developed inland provinces. Shanghai Party Secretary Chen Liangyu (no relation to Chen Xitong) challenged this shift in resources, and in 2006, he was removed from his post in Shanghai and on the Politburo. He was charged with misusing money in Shanghai's pension fund and sentenced to 18 years in prison.

In 2012, Bo Xilai was removed as party secretary in Chongqing and charged with accepting over 20 million yuan (approximately $3.6 million) in bribes, embezzling 5 million yuan, and covering up his wife's murder of a British businessman. All of which may be true, but most people interpreted his ouster as the result of his policies in Chongqing, which included an aggressive crackdown on organized crime, promoting "red culture" with the singing of revolutionary songs, and the "Chongqing model" of state-led development, egalitarian values, and increased spending on social welfare policies. These actions were remarkably popular in Chongqing and created support for Bo elsewhere, including among "new left" intellectuals and other Party leaders. He was even seen as a likely candidate for the Politburo's Standing Committee. But his economic and social policies were out of step with the rest of the leadership, and his popularity presented a potential challenge for the orderly transfer of power to a new generation of leaders, above all incoming General Secretary and President Xi Jinping. In 2013, he was convicted and sentenced to life in prison.

After Xi Jinping became general secretary, he launched an extensive anticorruption campaign. It targeted wasteful spending on official banquets and travel, and cracked down on bribes and gifts. The CDIC reported it confiscated 38.7 billion yuan (approximately $6.2 billion) between November 2012 and June 2015.[65] These were very popular measures and had an immediate effect. Restaurants and hotels that depended on official banquets and parties were forced to close when business suddenly and dramatically dropped off. Even traditional gifts took a hit. For example, mooncakes are a popular gift during the Mid-Autumn Festival. In recent years, boxes and baskets of mooncakes also concealed gifts of cell phones, jewelry, money, and even gold bars. With the anticorruption campaign in full swing, sales of mooncakes declined, and most stores stopped selling the more expensive boxes.[66]

Xi promised at the start of the campaign that it would not only target low-level officials but also capture several "tigers," high-level officials who are normally immune from investigations. In March 2015, the government released a list of 99 tigers, including four at the national level who were popularly referred to as "mega-tigers" (超级老虎).[67] The two biggest mega-tigers were Xu Caihou and Zhou Yongkang. Before retiring in 2013,

[65] Zhang Yi, "38.7b yuan in State assets recovered in campaign," *China Daily*, July 30, 2015, http://usa.chinadaily.com.cn/epaper/2015-07/30/content_21452545.htm, accessed July 30, 2015.

[66] An Baijie, "Mooncake Sales Wane as Anti-Graft Scrutiny Rises," *China Daily*, September 8, 2014, p. 6.

[67] "*Di jiushijiu 'hu' luoma jingshi le sha*? [Fall of the 99th 'Tiger' Sends What Message?]," *Zhongguo Wang* [China Net], March 21, 2015, http://media.china.com.cn/cmjujiao/2015-03-21/396575.html, accessed August 20, 2015. China Net is a "national key news site" under the authority of the State Council Information Office and National Internet Information Office.

Xu had been a Politburo member, vice chairman of the Central Military Commission, and a general in the People's Liberation Army. As a protégé of Jiang Zemin, he was able to maintain Jiang's influence in the military even after Hu Jintao had succeeded Jiang as CCP general secretary and CMC chair. Even though he was retired and being treated for cancer, Xu was taken from his sickbed in the hospital and placed under arrest. He admitted to accepting an unspecified but "extremely large" amount of bribes in exchange for promotions and other favors. He accumulated so much cash that 12 trucks were reportedly needed to remove the money from his house. In March 2015, Xu died while awaiting sentencing.

The biggest tiger in this anticorruption campaign was Zhou Yongkang. His arrest in 2014 broke one of the unwritten rules of Chinese politics: Members of the Politburo Standing Committee, the Party's top echelon of leaders, had previously been immune from prosecution. Before his retirement in 2012, Zhou had been the head of the extensive and powerful security apparatus, which includes police, courts, and intelligence agencies. Under Zhou's leadership, the security apparatus had grown to such an extent that by 2010, its annual budget exceeded even that of the military. Zhou was also a strong supporter of Bo Xilai and his Chongqing model. But other Party leaders were apparently worried that the security apparatus had become too independent, and they took several steps to limit its influence. When the new Politburo Standing Committee was announced in 2012, the number of members dropped from nine to seven, and Zhou's replacement as security czar was not included.

A new Central National Security Commission was created in 2013 with Xi Jinping as its chair, putting the security apparatus directly under his control. Several of Zhou's protégés, including Li Chuncheng, a former deputy party secretary of Sichuan, Jiang Jiemin, former chief executive of China Petroleum, and Li Dongsheng, former deputy minister of public security, were arrested as part of the investigation. In December 2013, Zhou's wife, his son Zhou Bin, daughter-in-law Huang Wan, and Huang's father Huang Yusheng were taken into custody.[68] Other relatives, including his brother, cousin, and nephew, were also placed under

---

[68] Jonathan Ansfield and Chris Buckley, "China Focusing Graft Inquiry on Ex-Official," *New York Times*, December 15, 2013, http://www.nytimes.com/2013/12/16/world/asia/china-presses-corruption-inquiry-of-powerful-former-security-official.html, accessed December 8, 2014.

investigation.[69] By March 2013, investigators had seized assets worth at least 90 billion yuan (almost $15 billion) from Zhou's family members and former associates. Much of this money came from investments in China's oil industry, where Zhou wielded great influence from his time as head of China's largest oil and gas company, China National Petroleum Corporation.[70] After months of rumors and speculation, the Party formally announced in July 2014 that Zhou himself was "under investigation for suspected 'serious disciplinary violation,'"[71] and was sentenced to life imprisonment in June 2015. In bringing down Zhou, his associates, and his family members, the Party signaled that even the highest-level leaders would be susceptible to corruption investigations, especially if they were seen as a threat to the incumbent top leader.

Additional arrests of mega-tigers came four months after the March 2015 list of 99 tigers and mega-tigers. Guo Boxiong was the highest-ranking officer in the People's Liberation Army (PLA) at the time of his retirement in 2012, and like Xu Caihou, he was vice chairman of the Central Military Commission and a Politburo member. In July 2015, the Politburo approved his expulsion from the Party and a criminal investigation of his receiving bribes in exchange for promotions within the PLA. Ling Jihua, former chief of staff of previous CCP leader Hu Jintao, was expelled from the CCP and charged with corruption in July 2015. Ling came under public scrutiny in 2012 when his son died after a high-speed crash in a Ferrari; he was found naked, and the two women in the car with him were either naked or scantily clad. Despite an official cover-up, the story was circulated widely, and Ling suffered political disgrace. He was not of the same stature as Zhou, Xu, or Guo, but his arrest indicated Xi's willingness to go after the personal network of Hu Jintao.

[69] Michael Forsythe, Chris Buckley and Jonathan Ansfield, "Investigating Family's Wealth, China's Leader Signals a Change," *New York Times*, April 19, 2014, http://www.nytimes.com/2014/04/20/world/asia/severing-a-familys-ties-chinas-president-signals-a-change.html, accessed December 8, 2014.

[70] Benjamin Kang Lim and Ben Blanchard, "Exclusive: China Seizes $14.5 Billion Assets from Family, Associates of Ex-Security Chief: Sources," Reuters, March 30, 2014, http://www.reuters.com/article/2014/03/30/us-china-corruption-zhou-idUSBREA2T02S20140330, accessed December 8, 2014.

[71] "Zhou Yongkang Investigated for Serious Disciplinary Violation," *Xinhua*, July 29, 2014, http://news.xinhuanet.com/english/china/2014-07/29/c_133518450.htm, accessed December 8, 2014.

During the summer of 2015, rumors continued to swirl that Zeng Qinghong and Li Yuanchao were either under investigation, under house arrest, or likely to be arrested. Zeng was Jiang Zemin's right-hand man for many years and was formerly on the Politburo's Standing Committee. Li is both an incumbent Politburo member and vice president, and comes from the same network as Hu Jintao and Ling Jihua. Targeting him would signify the open-ended nature of Xi's anticorruption campaign and also fuel suspicions that the goal of the campaign is to eliminate Xi's rivals more than address the problem of corruption within the Party. In January 2016, as this book was going into production, the CDIC announced that it was investigating Wang Bao'an, director of the National Bureau of Statistics, for "serious violations of party discipline," which is normally a euphemism for corruption. The National Bureau of Statistics is a government agency that among other things monitors the economy and determines the officially reported growth rates, which many believe to be inflated and unreliable. Whether this investigation concerned Wang's performance as director or his previous work at the Ministry of Finance was not immediately known.

When party and government leaders are accused of corruption, the consequences can be dire. Unlike government officials and businessmen in the U.S., those charged with corruption in China are subject to harsh treatment and even torture. When investigations start, the targets are often placed in the Party's own investigative system, known as *shuanggui* (双规, double designation, meaning they are detained at a designated time and place). They do not have the right to legal counsel and are separated from family. The purpose of *shuanggui* is to elicit confessions from those in detention. It is separate from the regular law enforcement system. Those charged with corruption or other violations of party discipline are not handed over to the courts until the Party completes its investigation , which usually ends with the accused being stripped of Party membership. During the most recent anticorruption campaign, the media reported that some officials had been driven to suicide, preferring death to *shuanggui*. The CDIC began leasing more office space and hired more people to handle the increased volume of investigations. It also bought padding for tables and walls, in order to prevent serious injuries during interrogations. A "clean government education center" in Jiangsu opened an exhibit of techniques and devices used throughout

Chinese history to torture corrupt officials. Being a Party member may have numerous advantages, but those benefits vanish once they are charged with corruption and expelled from the Party.

Despite all the media coverage of corruption in China, in comparative terms, China is not that exceptional. According to the World Bank's Global Governance Indicators, between 1996 and 2014 (the most recent year available), it fluctuated between the 32nd and 50th percentiles, and in the most recently reported year, it was in the 47th percentile, ahead of Sri Lanka, Belarus, New Zealand (Denmark was at the top of the list). In Transparency International's annual index of corruption around the world, China is also in the middle of the list: It was ranked 80th out of 175 countries in 2012, the year the anticorruption campaign began. Ironically, China *dropped* to 100 in the 2014 rankings as a consequence of the campaign, because it was deemed to be politically motivated and not in accordance with the rule of law. Not an exemplary record, to be sure, but comparing China with other countries in terms of corruption offers an important and often-overlooked perspective: While corruption is an important and corrosive issue within China, it is about par for the course.

The Party faces a dilemma in coping with corruption: Left unchecked, it would have damaging political, social, and economic consequences; but if it is dealt with too rigorously, it can damage the Party's legitimacy by exposing the extent of corruption at all levels of the state and give incentives to Party and government officials to flee the country with their embezzled assets to avoid prosecution. As Party elder Chen Yun once put it, "if we fight corruption too little, it will destroy the country, but if we fight it too much, it will destroy the Party." Publicly, China's leaders focus only on the first half of Chen's statement: Corruption left unchecked threatens the Party's survival. Corruption is often referred to as a matter of life or death for the Party. In his speech to the 18th Party Congress in November 2012, Xi Jinping said, "Facts prove that if corruption is allowed to spread, it will eventually lead to the destruction of a party and the fall of a government."[72] The Party's official paper, the *People's Daily*, cited a more ominous warning from Xi, saying that

[72] "Study, Disseminate and Implement the Guiding Principles of the 18th CPC National Congress," in Xi Jinping, *The Governance of China* (Beijing: Foreign Languages Press, 2014), p. 17.

"examples of the ruling group losing the people's support due to severe corruption are pervasive in China's history and that modern cases of ruling parties losing power due to corruption and decay that distances them from the people are too numerous to count."[73]

In comparing survey data about the prevalence of corruption before and during the anticorruption campaign, a contrary finding emerges: Respondents are more optimistic that the level of corruption is improving, but they are also more pessimistic about how widespread corruption is. In the 2010 survey, respondents were roughly equally split on whether corruption in their cities was getting better, worse, or staying the same (see table 2-5). In 2014, a sizable majority of respondents thought the situation had improved, and the percentages of those who thought there was no change or had gotten worse dropped accordingly. In both years, there was also a relatively high percentage of respondents who answered "don't know" or did not answer at all: 22.8 percent in 2010 and 24.3 percent in 2014.

Although most respondents thought the level of corruption was improving, they also thought more officials were corrupt (see table 2-6). This is especially apparent for the perceived scope of corruption among central government leaders, the "tigers" that were removed from office and formally charged with corruption. In 2010, respondents were evenly divided between those who thought corruption was common among central officials and those who thought it was rare, but in 2014, almost 70 percent thought it was at least somewhat common, and the percentage of those who thought almost all central officials were corrupt more than doubled. The change was less dramatic for local officials, in large part because respondents thought most local officials were corrupt even in the 2010 survey. By 2014, 84.1 percent thought corruption was at least somewhat common and almost one-fourth thought almost all local officials were corrupt.

This is the dilemma faced by Xi Jinping: The anticorruption campaign may be good for him but bad for the Party. It has proven to be popular with society, boosted public support for Xi himself, and

---

[73] "*Fanfu changlian guanxi dang he guojia shengsi cunwang*" (Anti-Corruption Is a Life and Death Matter for Party and Country), *People's Daily*, January 30, 2013, http://paper.people.com.cn/rmrb/html/2013-01/30/nw.D110000renmrb_20130130_2-02.htm, accessed August 20, 2015.

TABLE 2-5 Attitudes toward Corruption

Comparing recent years to five years ago, do you think the level of corruption in your city has:	2010	2014
Improved	35.5	60.4
No change	32.3	22.5
Gotten worse	32.2	17.1

Source: Public Goods and Political Support Surveys.

allowed him to consolidate his authority as China's new leader.[74] But exposing corruption on such a broad scale may prove to be bad for the Party in the long run. That many officials are corrupt surely comes as no surprise to most Chinese. Even before the start of Xi's campaign, most Chinese thought corruption was at least somewhat common among Party and government officials. But exposés of high-level officials provide juicy details on the amount of money changing hands and the numbers of underlings and mistresses involved. Such revelations tarnish the Party's reputation and diminish support for it. The impact of corruption on regime support will be examined in chapter 5.

A separate dilemma of fighting corruption is collateral damage to the economy. According to a local official in Guangzhou, because corruption was caused in part by the lack of institutional incentives, the campaign might lead to an economic downturn if local officials stopped launching new programs. On one hand, officials who are worried about being implicated in the corruption investigation think "if I do nothing, I won't make mistakes"; on the other hand, the lack of other incentives creates a "no corruption, no achievement" mindset.[75] By early 2015, Prime Minister Li Keqiang accused local officials of dereliction of duty for not implementing central initiatives to boost economic growth.[76] Whether

[74] There are no approval ratings for Chinese leaders. While public surveys can ask about political institutions and central and local officials as a whole, they cannot ask about specific leaders by name. Popular support for Xi is therefore based on anecdotal evidence.

[75] Focus group interview with local officials in Guangzhou, October 18, 2014.

[76] Zhao Yinan, "Local Officials Neglect Duties, Premier Says," China Daily, February 10, 2015.

TABLE 2-6 Popular Beliefs in the Prevalence of Corruption

	2010	2014
What do you believe is the scope of corruption among *central* government officials?		
Hardly any are corrupt.	8.2	3.7
Not too many are corrupt.	42.1	26.5
It is somewhat common.	41.7	53.1
Almost all are corrupt.	8.0	16.7
What do you believe is the scope of corruption among *local* government officials?		
Hardly any are corrupt.	1.4	1.4
Not too many are corrupt.	21.4	14.5
It is somewhat common.	61.7	60.5
Almost all are corrupt.	15.5	23.6

Source: Public Goods and Political Support Surveys.

local officials were afraid of making mistakes or were waiting for the corruption campaign to wind down so they could again solicit bribes, the ongoing anticorruption campaign made them reluctant to approve new projects, which in turn exacerbated the ongoing economic slowdown.

* * *

While China still lacks the rights and freedoms that people living in democracies take for granted, it is more open than it was in the past. That is one of the paradoxes of contemporary China. The Party continues to restrict its citizens' ability to speak freely, find information, obtain basic welfare, and determine the size of their families, but the restrictions have loosened considerably in response to popular resentment and an ever-changing social, economic, and technological environment. Compared to other countries, China lacks many basic freedoms; but compared to its own past, the degree of political and personal freedom has been expanding in fits and starts. Repression remains an essential element of the Party's strategy for survival, but it is used more selectively than in the past.

Since the beginning of the international financial crisis in 2007 and especially after new Party and government leaders took office in 2012/2013, the Party has reverted to a more typical authoritarian organization. In the past, many noted the incongruity between economic and social dynamism on one hand and political stasis on the other, and predicted that sooner or later political reform would have to catch up with economic reform and social change. Instead, the Xi era has seen an upsurge in repression and censorship. The Party has become more vigilant at monitoring and censoring speech in print, online, and even in the classroom. Professors have been warned against talking about certain topics with their students, and the presidents of leading universities—Peking University, Tsinghua, and Fudan—have pledged their loyalty to the Party. Bloggers, human rights activists, lawyers, and scholars have been harassed and arrested for criticizing the Party's policies. The Chinese government has cracked down on Christian churches, not just the unregistered house churches but also the official Protestant and Catholic churches. Most forcefully, it has increased pressure on Xinjiang's Uyghurs after a series of bombings and attacks that were blamed on the Uyghurs. It banned the wearing of Muslim headscarves in public and fasting during Ramadan and arrested numerous people for promoting terrorism and separatism, some of whom were executed. Whether these trends are part of a temporary effort to reassert Party supremacy and consolidate the authority of new leaders, or represent a basic change of strategy—more stick, less carrot—remains to be seen.

The tightening even extended to parts of the state. Xi launched an anticorruption campaign that captured numerous high-ranking and local officials and even a former member of the Politburo Standing Committee, the highest-level official ever charged with corruption in China. The Chinese Academy of Social Sciences, the government's main think tank, was accused of being "infiltrated by foreign forces" by the CDIC, the CCP's body for investigating corruption.[77] The *People's Daily*, the Party's official mouthpiece, also underwent investigation by the

---

[77] Adrian Wan, "Chinese Academy of Social Sciences Is 'Infiltrated by Foreign Forces': Anti-Graft Official," *South China Morning Post*, June 15, 2014, http://www.scmp.com/print/news/china/article/1533020/chinese-academy-social-sciences-infiltrated-foreign-forces-anti-graft, accessed October 1, 2014.

CDIC. Even People's Liberation Army officers were required to swear an oath of allegiance to Xi Jinping as commander in chief, signaling not only Xi's authority over the military but also the military's subordinate role to the Party. Just as the Party was actively tightening its control over society, Xi was consolidating his control over the political system.

These are the aspects of Chinese politics that are most familiar. However, focusing on coercive tools alone misses a crucial fact about politics in China: The Party remains in power not only because it has been able to eliminate or at least suppress all viable alternatives; it also enjoys a remarkable degree of popular support. Repression is definitely a part of the Party's strategy for remaining in power, but it also relies on different forms of legitimation and co-optation to generate support for the regime. That will be explored in the following chapters.

3

Mass Line for Modern Times

THE CCP RULES NOT through repression alone but also seeks some semblance of legitimacy. The desire to be legitimate affects not only what the government does, but also how it governs. Although China has not embarked on political reforms on the same scale as its economic reforms, China's leaders have introduced greater consultation and deliberation into the policy process and created more space for civil society. At the same time, the Party remains determined to integrate itself into society according to its own traditions, particularly the "mass line" and "party building." These Party traditions, which originated in the pre-1949 period, are intended to improve the quality of governance through greater but selective consultation with society and improve the Party's ability to monitor China's increasingly diversified society. This presents a dilemma for the Party: Invitations for more consultation may improve the implementation of policies, but they may also lead to expectations for greater participation, demands for new and protected rights, and calls for greater accountability, all of which would constrain the Party's authority and monopoly on political power. In many ways, the mass line and party building are outdated approaches for linking the Party with society and are of dubious effectiveness. But recognizing the continued importance of these Party traditions is essential to understanding the Party's strategy for survival.

This chapter looks at two key elements of the Party's survival strategy. First, it has initiated limited political reforms. During both the decision-making process and the local implementation of policy, Party and government officials consult with other elites, specialists, stake-holders, and the general public in a selective but still extensive manner. These interactions often lead to revision of policy initiatives before they are publicly announced and modifications as they are implemented. While politically significant, they fall far short of democratization; at best, they entail consultation without accountability. These reforms are limited not only in their goals but also in their reach. They often occur in isolated areas, and they do not diffuse as widely as economic reforms typically do. However, their full significance may not be felt until later. As people become accustomed to participating in these limited ways, they may come to expect broader participation and representation.

Second, the Party has managed the emergence of China's civil society. The number of non-governmental organizations (NGOs) in China has grown steadily, despite the Party's inconsistent approach to civil society. The Party is ambivalent about the growing prominence of civil society. It welcomes the help of some civil society groups, and local governments increasingly contract with NGOs to be service providers. But the Party is also wary of the NGOs' true intent and political impact. This chapter examines the ambiguous role of civil society in contemporary China, emphasizing a key point overlooked by most advocates of civil society development: To the extent that China's civil society groups improve the lives of those they help and increase their overall life satisfaction, their efforts can help to stabilize the regime and do not present an inherent threat to it.

More to the point, the mass line shows the tension between the different elements of the Party's survival strategy. It seeks both legitimacy (e.g., in the form of greater consultation) and the preservation of its political monopoly. The limited nature of political reforms to date and the Party's ambivalence toward civil society—helpful in social development and provision of public goods, though potential agents of regime change—reflect these competing elements.

I. The Mass Line Concept

The mass line concept was one of the quintessential elements of Mao Zedong Thought, the so-called Sinification of Marxism-Leninism. It tried to strike a balance between the autocratic tendencies of a Leninist party and the spontaneity of mass action. It was based on the idea that ideological rigidity would doom the Party to failure; instead, it had to be continually in touch with the masses, attuned to their interests and concerns, and willing to adjust the Party's goals and policies to the local context. In a nutshell, it was an interactive process of "from the masses, to the masses." As Mao described it, the mass line meant:

> take the ideas of the masses (scattered and unsystematic ideas) and concentrate them (through study turn them into concentrated and systematic ideas), then go to the masses and propagate and explain these ideas until the masses embrace them as their own, hold fast to them and translate them into action, and test the correctness of these ideas in such action. Then once again concentrate ideas from the masses and once again go to the masses so that the ideas are persevered in and carried through. And so on, over and over again in an endless spiral, with the ideas becoming more correct, more vital and richer each time.[1]

The mass line is a pragmatic approach to governing that involves consultation with society without requiring the Party to be accountable to it. As with many of Mao's ideas, the reality deviated from the ideal. The CCP was and is a vanguard party, not a mass party, and therefore prone to being out of touch with the wants and needs of most of society. In addition, complex bureaucracies are better at following routines than being flexible, and they often neglect to consider if their policies and procedures are conducive to diverse environments. During the post-1949 period, the Party launched repeated efforts to fight against bureaucratism, without much lasting success. In fact, Mao was so convinced that he was in touch with the masses that he assumed anyone who did not follow his line was in violation of the mass line. The resulting campaigns—the 100 Flowers Movement, the Great Leap Forward, and the Cultural Revolution—indicated that Mao had lost touch with the wants and needs of Chinese society. This was ironic vindication of the wisdom inherent in the mass line.

[1] "Some Questions Concerning Methods of Leadership," *Selected Works of Mao Tse-Tung*, Vol. 3 (Beijing: Foreign Languages Press, 1967), p. 119.

Even though many of Mao's policy goals were abandoned in the post-Mao era, many of the Party's reforms have been couched in terms of the mass line, and many of China's post-Mao leaders have emphasized it. China's leaders continue to use the mass line concept to legitimate—at least in the eyes of the Party—political reforms and experimentation. The mass line is so identified with Chairman Mao that one might think post-Mao reformers would want to jettison it, along with class struggle, mass campaigns, and other policies and practices from the Maoist era. But the Party has been ambivalent about Mao. Party leaders have abandoned the ideological goals that proved to be so devastating and divisive, and criticized to a limited degree his policies in the Great Leap Forward and the Cultural Revolution. At the same time, Mao is so essential to the Party's history and founding of the PRC that post-Mao leaders could not reject him entirely. (In contrast, Khrushchev could thoroughly vilify Stalin without undermining the legitimacy of party rule in the Soviet Union because Lenin, the founder of the party and regime, remained untouched.) In particular, the Party has maintained the more pragmatic approach to governing and interacting with society that Mao also periodically advocated. The purpose of the post-Mao reforms has been to improve relations between state and society, in part by adopting policies that will prove to be popular. The mass line is designed to do just that, and reforms to create more consultation, deliberation, and co-optation are easily legitimized by the mass line concept.[2] For example, describing reforms as improving transparency may seem risky or problematic to many Party and government officials, but framing them as a continuation of the mass line tradition makes it harder to oppose such reforms. The continued use of the mass line rhetoric may seem incongruous in an increasingly modern China—as do many aspects of the Party's ideology—but it helps legitimize many institutional innovations.

New slogans have been prominent throughout the post-Mao era: Deng Xiaoping's "Four Modernizations," Jiang Zemin's "Three Represents," Hu Jintao's "Scientific Development" and "Harmonious

---

[2] Xi Chen notes that another mass line institution, the petitioning (*xinfang* 信访) system, began under Mao and was revived in the post-Mao era; see *Social Protest and Contentious Authoritarianism in China* (New York: Cambridge University Press, 2012), pp. 89–131.

Society," and most recently, Xi Jinping's "China Dream" and "Four Comprehensives." But calls to uphold the Party's mass line tradition persist. At the closing session of the work conference that launched the reform era in December 1978, Deng said:

> During the drive to realize the four modernizations, we are bound to encounter many new and unexpected situations and problems with which we are unfamiliar. In particular, the reforms in the relations of production and in the superstructure will not be easy to introduce. They touch on a wide range of issues and concern the immediate interests of large numbers of people, so they are bound to give rise to complications and problems and to meet with numerous obstacles.... We will be able to solve any problem and surmount any obstacle so long as we have faith in the masses, *follow the mass line* and explain the situation and problems to them.[3]

Deng's successors all paid homage to the mass line. Jiang Zemin said the Party "should work hard to educate our leaders and cadres on mass opinion and the mass line" in order to rid the Party of "unhealthy trends of formalism, bureaucratism, extravagance and waste, and abuse of power."[4] Hu Jintao told the CCP's Central Committee that "Party committees, governments and cadres at all levels must stick to the party's 'mass line.' . . . It should be deeply recognized that the party's biggest political advantage is our close bond with the masses and that the biggest danger for us as the ruling party is disconnecting from the masses."[5] The CCP's

[3] Deng Xiaoping, "Emancipate the Mind, Seek Truth from Facts and Unite as One in Looking to the Future," speech delivered at the closing session of the central work conference that preceded the Third Plenum of the 11th Central Committee of the Communist Party on December 13, 1978, in *Selected Works of Deng Xiaoping, 1975–1982* (Beijing: Foreign Languages Press, 1984), p. 164, emphasis added.

[4] Jiang Zemin, "*Shenru jinxing qunzhong guandian he qunzhong luxian de jiaoyu*," (Deepen the Education on Mass Opinion and the Mass Line), speech delivered on December 5, 1995, at the CCP Central Committee work conference, in *On Party Building* (Beijing: CCPCC Party Literature Publishing House, 2001), p. 194.

[5] Hu Jintao, "*Zai dangde shiqijie wuzhongquanhui shang de jianghua*" (Speech Delivered at the Fifth Plenary Session of the 17th Central Committee), October 18, 2010, http://cpc.people.com.cn/n/2013/0530/c364600-21672949.html, accessed September 16, 2014.

current General Secretary Xi Jinping not only spoke in favor of the mass line but also initiated a new campaign in 2013 to study and implement it. According to Xi, "The goal of the party's campaign of 'Mass Line Education and Practice' is for all party members to remember and comply with the fundamental principle of serving the people whole-heartedly, to unify the people with exemplary working style, and to work hard to accomplish the goals set at the 18th CPC National Congress."[6] This campaign even has its own website: "massline.com" (qzlx.people.com.cn).

While there is undoubtedly a bit of lip service in these references to the mass line, it is a common refrain in Party pronouncements. In 2001, new experiments in tax reform were linked to the mass line: "During the reform, we must stick to the 'mass line,' respect the practices of the people and the grassroots level cadres, and constantly adjust and improve the reform plan and supportive measures."[7] The announcements of five-year economic plans are also opportunities to recall the Party's mass line traditions. In 2000, the Party's proposal on the 10th Five-Year Plan stated: "The key to achieving the goals of the tenth five-year plan and the new victory in building Communism with Chinese characteristics is to constantly improve the Party's ability to rule, especially the ability in mastering the big picture of economic and social development. . . . We must stick to the 'mass line,' expand the channels through which the Party bonds with the people, and find solutions from people's practices."[8] The announcement of the 12th Five-Year Plan in 2010 had a similar statement: "Leaders and cadres at all levels

---

[6] Xu Jingyao and Zhou Yingfeng, "*Dangde qunzhong luxian jiaoyu shijian gongzuo huiyi zhaokai Xi Jinping fabiao zhongyao jianghua*" (Xi Jinping's Important Speech at the CCP Work Conference on the Mass Line Education and Practice), June 18, 2013, http://news.xinhuanet.com/2013-06/18/c_116194026.htm, accessed September 16, 2014.

[7] State Council of the People's Republic of China, "*Guowuyuan guanyu jinyibu zuohao nongcun shuifei gaige shidian gongzuo de tongzhi*" (Notice of the State Council on Further Work in the Experimental Reforms of Taxes and Fees), March 24, 2001, http://news.eastday.com/eastday/zfgb/gwy/userobject1ai14906.html, accessed September 24, 2014.

[8] "*Zhonggong zhongyang guanyu zhiding guomin jingji he shehui fazhan dishige wunian jihua de jianyi*" (The Proposal of the CPC Central Committee for the Formulation of the Tenth Five-Year Plan for National Economic and Social Development), October 11, 2000, http://cpc.people.com.cn/GB/64162/71380/71382/71386/4837946.html, accessed September 24, 2014.

must follow the fundamental principle of serving the people whole-heartedly, stick to the party's 'mass line,' maintain the bond of flesh and blood with the masses, have a correct view of government perfor-mance, and work hard to achieve substantive outcomes that can with-stand the test of practice, people, and history."[9] In 2013, *People's Daily* highlighted the results of the Third Plenary Session of the Eighteenth Central Committee, which announced new economic reform initia-tives as "a new historical starting point. . . . We must put the party's 'mass line' into practice while comprehensively deepening the reform, so that the two facilitate each other."[10] Readers of such statements may choose to skim over them as empty verbiage, but the Party misses few opportunities to link its actions to the mass line tradition.

The mass line approach is not only legitimized by Party traditions, it is also a way of legitimizing new efforts to improve the quality of gov-ernance. Township officials are now required to spend several days each week living in the villages they govern in order to have a better under-standing of what is happening there.[11] Several multi-year programs are now in place to train local officials in the mass line concept, combined with academic studies of the efficacy of those programs. The underlying goal of the program is to improve governance and relations between local officials and the people they govern, but it is framed as emphasizing the mass line in order to get more support from party and government lead-ers.[12] Framed this way, it is hard for people to oppose or resist the goals of the program.

---

[9] *"Zhonggong zhongyang guanyu zhiding guomin jingji he shehui fazhan dishige wunian jihua de jianyi"* (The Proposal of the CCP Central Committee for the Formulation of the Twelfth Five-Year Plan for National Economic and Social Development), October 18, 2010, http://politics.people.com.cn/GB/1026/13066300.html, accessed September 24, 2014.

[10] Bao Xinjian, *"Jianxing qunzhong luxian yu quanmian shenhua gaige"* (Practicing the "Mass Line" and Carrying Out Reform in an All-around Manner), *People's Daily*, February 20, 2014, Sec. 16. Available at http://qzlx.people.com.cn/n/2014/0220/c364565-24412093.html, accessed September 24, 2014.

[11] Graeme Smith, "The Hollow State: Rural Governance in China," *China Quarterly*, No. 203 (September 2010), pp. 601–618.

[12] John James Kennedy and Yaojiang Shi, "Rule by Virtue, the Mass Line Model and Cadre-Mass Relations" in Shiping Hua, ed., *East Asian Development Model: The 21st Century Perspectives* (New York: Routledge, 2015).

The adherence to the mass line rhetoric also maintains the Party's primary role in policy-making and implementation. It may seek input from the masses, but in the end, it reserves the right to make most decisions and remain unaccountable to society. In China, there is no equivalent to the election of top leaders, let alone the traditions of initiative, referendum, and recall that are designed to provide accountability of elected officials to the people they govern. The mass line is therefore intended to enhance the Party's authority, not to constrain it. The result is best described as "consultative authoritarianism," a system that includes consultation in a selective manner, but remains distinctly authoritarian without direct accountability of the state to society.[13]

The debate over the mass line and proper forms of governance occasionally spills over from the ideological realm into broader circles. One example is a 2013 debate that ensued after Hu Angang, an influential scholar and government advisor based at Tsinghua University in Beijing, published an article in the overseas edition of *People's Daily* arguing that "people society" is more important than civil society. He linked people society with two of Xi Jinping's new initiatives: reviving the mass line and promoting the "China Dream." He argued that the mass line was superior to Western forms of government, in part because it was invented by the Chinese themselves and not borrowed from other countries, and because China's national conditions were different from those of the West.[14] The societal response online was sharply critical.[15] Many noted that Marxism, the basis for the Party's ideology, was itself imported from the West. This is a popular response when

[13] The term "consultative authoritarianism" was first applied to China by Harry Harding in *China's Second Reform: Reform after Mao* (Washington, DC: Brookings Institution, 1987), p. 200, who noted that the term comes from G. Gordon Skilling. More recently, it has been used by Jessica C. Teets in *Civil Society under Authoritarianism: The China Model* (New York: Cambridge University Press, 2014).

[14] Hu Angang, "*Renmin shehui weihe youyu gongmin shehui* (Why People Society Is Superior to Civil Society)," *People's Daily Overseas Edition*, July 19, 2014, http://paper.people.com.cn/rmrbhwb/html/2013-07/19/content_1270853.htm, accessed July 16, 2015.

[15] Cary Huang, "Leading Leftist Academic Mocked over 'Maoist' Op-Ed," *South China Morning Post*, July 20, 2013, http://www.scmp.com/news/china/article/1286519/leading-leftist-academic-mocked-over-maoist-op-ed, accessed July 16, 2015.

Party leaders decry Western influences in China. While the mass line concept may have been created in China, its logical underpinning—the need to seek feedback from society—is the essence of good governance anywhere.

II. Consulting the Masses

A key example of the updated mass line logic is seen in the Party's strategy for soliciting and incorporating public opinion into policy-making. New initiatives to allow members of society to decide on budget and policy priorities, use the Internet to solicit public comments on pending laws and regulations, and promote "open government" are legitimized not only by the mass line concept, but also by Mao's endorsement of flexibly adapting general policies to local conditions (a practice more common in the pre-1949 period when the Party was seeking popular support than after it had won the civil war).[16] These different modes of consultation are often used for trade-offs between policy goals (more money for roads or schools?) and technical issues (how should prescription drugs be priced and distributed?), but not structural reforms or core issues that affect the legitimacy of the Party (such as freedoms of speech, assembly, or organization).[17]

This consultative approach has several advantages. First of all, it promotes better governance. Budget transparency in particular has been a focal point for advocates of good governance reforms.[18] It provides societal input, especially from those with particular expertise in the question at hand. And it improves the likelihood of public support for final decisions, and thereby the legitimacy of the decisions and trust in the decision-makers. Earlier research on village elections found that greater transparency made it easier to implement even the most

[16] Sebastian Heilmann and Elizabeth J. Perry, eds., *Mao's Invisible Hand: The Political Foundations of Adaptive Governance in China* (Cambridge, MA: Harvard University Asia Center, 2011).

[17] Shaoguang Wang, "Changing Models of China's Policy Setting Agenda," *Modern China*, Vol. 34, No. 1 (January 2008), pp. 56–87.

[18] Ann Florini, Hairong Lai, and Yeling Tan, *China Experiments: From Local Innovations to National Reform* (Washington, DC: Brookings Institution Press, 2012), p. 139.

unpopular policies, including tax collection and enforcement of the one-child policy.[19]

Perhaps the most studied and well-documented case of local political reform is the experience of Wenling, a city in the coastal province of Zhejiang.[20] The city of Wenzhou in Zhejiang is well known as a successful case of economic reform and privatization, but Wenling has not had the same economic fame, even though it also prospered during the reform era. Instead, it became known for experimenting with various types of political reforms. Different towns adopted different varieties of consultative authoritarianism in the budget process, and these reforms were covered widely by China's media, as well as Chinese and foreign scholars.

Deliberating Policy Priorities

One of the approaches used in Wenling was deliberative polling, a technique developed by Stanford professor James Fishkin. The deliberative poll in Wenling's Zeguo township was equal parts political reform initiated by local leaders who wanted to innovate with political reforms and academic experiment carried out by foreign scholars who wanted to try out an established process in a new setting.

Beginning in 2005, party and government leaders in Wenling's Zeguo township convened a randomly selected group of 275 people to review, discuss, and rank the importance of various development projects, such as roads, parks, sewage treatment, and architectural renovation. In order to provide informed opinions, participants received briefing

[19] Kevin J. O'Brien, "Implementing Political Reform in China's Villages," *Australian Journal of Chinese Affairs*, No. 32 (July 1994), pp. 33–59; Thomas P. Bernstein and Xiaobo Lü, *Taxation without Representation in Contemporary Rural China* (New York: Cambridge University Press, 2003).

[20] The description of Zeguo's reforms is based on James S. Fishkin et al., "Deliberative Democracy in an Unlikely Place: Deliberative Polling in China," *British Journal of Political Science*, Vol. 40, No. 2 (April 2010), pp. 435–448; Baogang He and Stig Thogerson, "Giving the People a Voice? Experiments with Consultative Authoritarian Institutions in China," *Journal of Contemporary China*, Vol. 19, No. 66 (2010), pp. 675–692; Baogang He and Mark Warren, "Authoritarian Deliberation: The Deliberative Turn in Chinese Political Development," *Perspectives on Politics*, Vol. 9, No. 2 (Summer 2011), pp. 269–289.

materials on the pros and cons of each project. The deliberators met for an entire day. For part of the day, participants met in small groups of roughly 16 people; at other times, all participants met in a general meeting. The small group sessions were led by local teachers who were trained to lead discussion but not reveal their own preferences. At the end of the process, participants ranked roughly 30 different projects; because of budgetary limitations, only the top 12 received funding. The recommendations of the deliberators were then conveyed to the local people's congress, which voted in favor of the 12 projects. The local people's congress both approved the government's budget for the coming year and also identified the projects to be undertaken.

According to the organizers of this experiment, it provided several rewards.[21] It created a stronger community spirit as participants grappled with the difficult trade-offs between various projects. Participants in these deliberations came to value projects that benefited the town as a whole, and not just individual villages. It was more egalitarian, incorporating the views of the community, and not just the privileged elites. It gave Party and government officials a better sense of the priorities of local society, and how those priorities differed from their own. Zeguo's Party Secretary Jiang Zhaohua reported that "he was surprised at the difference between the local leadership's perception of what the people would want and what they actually wanted after deliberation." For example, participants in the deliberations placed less emphasis on image projects, such as building a park in the town square and planting flowers and trees to enhance the town's appearance, and put greater priority on environmental projects such as sewage treatment. In this sense, participants preferred "green" projects that directly cleaned up pollution but not greenery per se. Because the projects that were ultimately approved had the support of the community—or at least those randomly selected to deliberate—they were easier to implement and did not face the protests that occur with increasing frequency elsewhere in China.

At the same time, deliberative polling places great demands on the participants and organizers. Without detailed information, participants cannot make informed decisions about budget priorities. Organizers therefore

[21] Fishkin et al., "Deliberative Democracy in an Unlikely Place."

developed briefing materials on the pros and cons of the many projects under deliberation and led presentations and discussions with the participants. In some cases, they also arranged site visits so that the participants could see what was being proposed and why it was needed. Participants spent several days studying, debating, and deciding on budget priorities, which took them away from their regular jobs and daily activities. Local officials and people's congress deputies also spent several days with the participants, listening to their debates to gain a better understanding of their thoughts and priorities. The end result had notable benefits, but it required a high investment of time and resources. It is no wonder then that deliberative polling has not caught on more widely in China. (For that matter, it has not caught on very widely in democracies either.)

To be effective, it also requires the full commitment of local party and government officials. The first several deliberative polls were endorsed and promoted by the local party secretary, but when he was transferred to a new position, his replacement was less enthusiastic. The new leader at first dropped the practice, but after some outcry, he reinstated it. This speaks to the fragility of local political reforms: They are initiated by the Party and government, but without the ongoing support of local leaders, they may also be withdrawn. But it also speaks to the inherent dilemma of Party leaders about whether to initiate or endorse reforms in the first place. Once societal actors become familiar with the experience of consulting and deliberating on policy decisions, they may come to value it and resist having it taken away. Reforms to promote certain goals in the short run may have unanticipated and—from the perspective of party leaders—undesirable consequences in the long term.

Deliberative polling in Zeguo rank-ordered the various projects, but initially did not make decisions on how much should be spent on any of them. The goal was to decide where to spend the money, not how much should be spent. The neighboring town of Xinhe took a different approach.[22] At the annual meeting of the people's congress in 2006,

[22] Joseph Fewsmith, *The Logic and Limits of Political Reform in China* (New York: Cambridge University Press, 2013), pp. 142–169. Fewsmith notes that the new Party secretary was not native to Xinhe and faced opposition from the town's government leader. The Party secretary was concurrently head of the people's congress, so greater transparency and leverage over the government's budget also worked to his advantage.

deputies heard reports from "democratic consultation" meetings, which occurred every few months and were open to the public. These meetings allowed members of the community to discuss local issues and offer opinions on alternative solutions. In Xinhe, some of the democratic consultation meetings allowed participants to ask questions about specific line items in the government's budget, which is normally a carefully kept secret. People's congress deputies then questioned government officials about their proposed budget. Following a meeting between the financial affairs committee of the people's congress and various government officials, the government submitted a revised budget that more closely reflected the priorities of those in the democratic consultation meetings and the people's congress deputies. Whereas the result in Zeguo influenced the priority of projects, the result in Xinhe influenced how much was actually spent on a range of issues, including infrastructure and the town's vehicle fleet.

The reforms in Xinhe gained media attention and the support of higher-level officials, in large part because they concerned the transparency of the budget process and the people's congress oversight of government spending. Leaders in Wenling endorsed and publicized Xinhe's reform, and within a few years, six of Wenling's 11 towns were including public participation in the budgetary process (including Zeguo, which eventually incorporated budgetary transparency into its deliberative polling). Despite its apparent success and popularity, the Wenling model did not spread much beyond Wenling. Only a few other townships have adopted similar practices. Moreover, these reforms have not deepened even in Wenling.

In many ways, the experience in Wenling is typical of experiments with political reform elsewhere in China. First, they are initiated by state, not society, and moreover are often pushed by municipal and county leaders, not the towns and townships where they are actually carried out. They are also not always maintained by new leaders in the same locale. In other words, it is a top-down process, not built from the bottom up. Second, they typically do not get adopted by other locales (unlike local economic reforms, which do spread when they are effective). Local political reforms do not provide the same rewards that economic reforms do; economic reforms can boost economic growth, a key goal for local officials. Political reforms do not offer the same immediate and tangible results. Unless other communities share the same circumstances, the innovations are less likely to spread. If they do not solve local problems and do not provide rewards to local leaders, they are unlikely to be adopted elsewhere. Third, central leaders in Beijing rarely endorse local political reforms or encourage other localities to adopt them. In particular, under Xi Jinping, the Party has been less supportive of polling or elections to bring the public into the decision-making process, despite his promotion of the mass line after he became general secretary in 2012. As one Chinese scholar described it to me, Xi is trying to develop a mass line concept without the masses.

Local political reformers are rarely rewarded for their innovations. With fewer incentives to engage in political reform, they are less frequent and less significant than economic reforms. Because of these constraints, some organizations give awards or other types of recognition to encourage local reforms. One of the most prominent is the Innovations and Excellence in Chinese Local Governance Program, which is cosponsored by the CCP's China Center for Comparative Politics and Economics, the Center of Comparative Studies on Political Parties of the Central Party School, and the China Center for Government Innovations at Peking University. The sponsors of this award acknowledge its semi-official status and the political prominence that comes with it. Its director is Yu Keping, a prominent intellectual who formerly worked within the Party and an advocate for political reform within the existing political system. It gives out awards every other year to eight to ten organizations or local governments that have successfully introduced political reforms (including Wenling). Whereas the local innovations awards recognize successful cases of reform, other organizations evaluate the full range of local governments, including both pioneers and laggards. The Economic, Financial, and Governance Research Center at Tsinghua University released a report in June 2014 that ranked almost 300 cities in terms of their fiscal transparency. Unirule is a private think tank in Beijing that has also periodically ranked the transparency and quality of governance in cities.[23] Chinese officials are very sensitive to rankings, and these reports are designed to improve their performance. Officials whose cities rank low on the lists may take

[23] *2008 Report on Public Governance in China's Provincial Capital Cities* (Beijing: Unirule, 2009); *2010 Report on Public Governance in China's Provincial Capital Cities* (Beijing: Unirule, 2012).

steps to improve their rankings. Similarly, the lists provide information to central and provincial governments, which may then pressure low-ranking cities to improve their performance.[24]

National Reforms to Allow Public Comment via the Internet

Whereas Wenling provided examples of consultation and deliberation at the grassroots level, a more common mechanism for gathering public opinion on policy issues is the use of the Internet. Before the Chinese government adopts new laws and regulations, it provides opportunities for individuals and groups to submit opinions and recommendations. For example, the draft labor contract law received over 190,000 comments from the Internet, most from ordinary workers. These comments reportedly led to major revisions in the law that was finally adopted in 2006.[25] In late 2008, the National People's Congress posted the draft of the social insurance law on its website and invited public comment. During a 50-day period of public comment, the NPC received over 70,000 comments. Although the actual comments were not publicly revealed, the NPC and the media published summaries of the broad themes that the public was most concerned about.[26] Beginning in 2008, the NPC Standing

[24] The environment has similarly spawned efforts to reward individual firms and organizations for their green practices, as well as rank cities on the transparency of their information on environmental quality. Yanhong Jin, Hua Wang, David Wheeler, "Environmental Performance Rating and Disclosure: An Empirical Investigation of China's Green Watch Program," Policy Research Working Paper 5420 (Washington, DC: World Bank, Development Research Group, Environment and Energy Team, 2010); Peter Lorentzen, Pierre F. Landry, and John Yasuda, "Undermining Authoritarian Innovation: The Power of China's Industrial Giants," *Journal of Politics*, Vol. 76, No. 1 (January 2014), pp. 182–194.

[25] Jamie P. Horsley, "Public Participation in the People's Republic: Developing a More Participatory Governance Model in China" (2009), p. 9, available at http://www.law.yale.edu/intellectuallife/publicparticipation.htm, accessed July 28, 2014. The American Chamber of Commerce (AmCham) also submitted its recommendations. Whereas the Chinese government normally does not release the comments it receives (although it occasionally does summarize the broad themes), AmCham chose to release its recommendations publicly and faced backlash from many in China who felt its recommendations were biased in favor of enterprises (naturally, since the members of AmCham are U.S.-owned enterprises) and did not adequately defend workers' rights.

[26] Mark W. Frazier, "Popular Responses to China's Emerging Welfare State," in Peter Hays Gries and Stanley Rosen, eds., *Chinese Politics: State, Society, and*

Committee announced that it would post all draft legislation online for public comment. In some cases, it also describes the reasons for the draft law, its potential implications, and even the specific questions it wants recommendations about.[27] Similarly, the State Council posts draft regulations and solicits public comment before final revision and adoption.

The 2009 national healthcare reform illustrates well this consultative approach to decision-making.[28] After years of decline and underinvestment, the Chinese healthcare system reached its nadir in the early 21st century. In a 2000 study, the WHO ranked China third from last for the fairness of the amount of government spending relative to private spending (often referred to as out-of-pocket expenses by individuals) and 144th out of 171 countries overall.[29] After the SARS crisis of 2003, a report by the Chinese government in collaboration with the WHO described China's healthcare system as "basically unsuccessful," and the phrase was repeated widely in the state-run media.[30]

In 2006, the Chinese government created the Health Care System Reform Coordination Small Group (hereafter Health Care Coordination Group), an ad hoc body tasked with coming up with a proposal for a

the Market (London: Routledge, 2010), pp. 258–274. At the top of the list was the non-portability of pensions and other social welfare benefits. Because most benefits are paid by local governments, there are residential and employment restrictions on recipients. The result is that when people change jobs or move to new cities, their accumulated benefits do not travel with them. There was a strong preference for a national social security system that was not tied to work or residence, a burden the central government was reluctant to undertake.

27 Horsley, "Public Participation in the People's Republic," p. 9.

28 This case study of the healthcare reform process is based on Yoel Kornreich, Ilan Vertinsky, and Pitman B. Potter, "Consultation and Deliberation in China: The Making of China's Health-Care Reform," China Journal, No. 68 (July 2012), pp. 176–203; Drew Thompson, "China's Health Care Reform Redux," in Charles W. Freeman III and Xiaoqing Lu, eds., China's Capacity to Manage Infectious Diseases: Global Implications (Washington, DC: Center for Strategic and International Studies, 2009), pp. 59–80; Steven J. Balla, "Information Technology, Political Participation, and the Evolution of Chinese Policymaking," Journal of Contemporary China, Vol. 21, No. 76 (April 2012), pp. 655–673.

29 The World Health Report 2000: Health Systems: Improving Performance (Geneva: World Health Organization, 2000).

30 An Evaluation of and Recommendations on the Reforms of the Health System in China: Executive Summary (Beijing: State Council Development Research Council, 2005).

new national healthcare system. It initially consisted of ten government agencies with responsibility for healthcare, including the Ministry of Health, the Ministry of Labor and Social Security, and the National Development and Reform Commission (NDRC); its membership later expanded to 14 agencies.

After members of this body were unable to reach agreement on the general principles of healthcare reform, in March 2007, they sought proposals from Peking University, Fudan University, the NDRC, and three international organizations (the World Bank, the WHO, and McKinsey & Company, a major international consulting firm). Two months later, the Health Care Coordination Group requested additional proposals from Beijing Normal University and Renmin University, and a month after that, Tsinghua University submitted its own proposal. It solicited a tenth and final proposal from Guangzhou's Sun Yat-sen University in early 2008. None of these ten proposals were ever made public.[31]

From available information, it is not clear if this incremental process of soliciting multiple proposals was planned from the start or if the members of the Health Care Coordination Group sought additional and presumably different proposals when they were unsatisfied with what they had already received. Either way, this incremental approach to reform has been a hallmark of the general reform process in China throughout the post-Mao period. Policy-makers "cross the river by feeling for stones" rather than following a clear blueprint from start to finish.

To further promote and publicize their preferred policies, the various universities, government agencies, and think tanks held a series of conferences and other public events. Key players also wrote articles for and gave interviews in the state-owned media. Although reform proposals were submitted privately and their contents not made public, these later tactics were designed to influence decision-makers in a more public way. This is a specific form of public opinion—not the general public seeking to have its voice heard, but the more specialized views of experts and stakeholders trying to influence policy outcomes by both submitting private proposals and offering public commentary. Duckett

---

[31] Thompson, "China's Health Care Reform Redux," offers summaries of what the proposals most likely consisted of, based on media reports, previous statements and publications by the proposers, and interviews with likely authors.

and Langer's study of this process described the elite and media debates as "populist and paternalistic": "elites and the media spoke *for* 'the people' and debated their needs and benefits, but gave them little opportunity to voice their own views and preferences."[32]

In October 2008, the government announced the broad outline of the new healthcare plan. It was not a detailed document with operational details, but a description of the priorities of the plan, including universal coverage, a balance between traditional Chinese medicine and Western medicine, and more affordable prescription drugs. It posted this document on the NDRC website and invited public comment during a one-month window. In the end, it received almost 28,000 comments via the Internet. Over half of the people offering comments were medical professionals.

The new healthcare plan was formally announced in April 2009. How important were these three types of consultation—expert proposals, conferences and media reports, and public comment via the Internet—in shaping the final outcome? In an authoritarian regime like China's, there is no question that the final outcome was largely shaped by bureaucratic infighting. The different members of the Health Care Coordination Group favored different approaches to healthcare reform, and the final plan reflects a compromise among those different preferences. For example, the Ministry of Health favored a more supply-side approach with the government subsidizing and directly supplying healthcare services (similar to the U.K.'s National Health Service), whereas the Ministry of Labor and Social Security favored the demand-side strategy of insurance programs that would lower government expenditures. Although multiple conferences, workshops, and symposia were held on healthcare reform, the participants primarily reflected the preferences of the hosts and sponsors, rather than an open debate between opposing views. This reflects another aspect of the policy process in China: Much of the public debate is indirect, with each proponent only vaguely and implicitly referring to opposing views. Direct competition between opposing views, the pro-and-con

[32] Jane Duckett and Ana Inés Langer, "Populism versus Neoliberalism: Diversity and Ideology in the Chinese Media's Narratives of Health Care Reform," *Modern China*, Vol. 39, No. 6 (November 2013), p. 660

approach so familiar to talk shows, public hearings, and editorial pages in the U.S., is all too rare in China.

However, the process for soliciting information and feedback continued for almost two years, indicating that members of the small group sought more information in order to resolve their differences, as well as consider alternative proposals and perspectives. For example, the tenth and final proposal from Sun Yat-sen University is believed to be the only one incorporating the viewpoints of doctors, an essential group in the healthcare system but whose perspectives had not been explicitly represented previously. Before the final plan was announced, various stakeholders were given the opportunity to weigh in. People who offered their opinions during the one-month period of open comment on the Internet thought that decision-makers would be responsive to the views coming from government officials and medical professionals, but not to the general population.[33] In other words, this was a technocratic process of finding an appropriate solution to a grave problem, but a process that was open primarily to those in the government and key stakeholders.

The final plan also indicated the influence of key stakeholders. It called for government procurement of essential medicines to be done through open bidding, the position favored by the powerful pharmaceutical industry. In response to public complaints about the high costs of prescription drugs, the final plan called for accelerating reforms to bring prices down. The plan also called for institutional changes to improve the working conditions of medical professionals, who face the dual problem of overwork from hospital administrators and tensions with angry patients.

We do not have full information on the different steps of the process, and in particular, the contents of the ten proposals solicited by the Health Care Coordination Group, and we cannot definitively analyze the degree to which the final plan responded to the priorities and preferences of non-state actors. Nevertheless, the case of the 2009 healthcare reform does reveal a more open and consultative process that puts a modern spin on the Party's mass line tradition.

[33] Balla, "Information Technology, Political Participation, and the Evolution of Chinese Policymaking."

Open Government Information

Another initiative to expand state-society interactions in line with the mass line principle is the nationwide effort to introduce greater transparency into the work of the government. As early as 2003 and 2004, local governments such as Guangzhou and Shanghai adopted Open Government Information (OGI) regulations. Most local governments have joined the "e-government" movement and created websites to post information about their work. This has produced a flood of new information, although it is released at the state's discretion.

In 2007, the State Council issued national OGI regulations, requiring the government's administrative agencies to proactively provide information to the public and create mechanisms to allow citizens to request information. Unlike the Freedom of Information Act in the U.S., which is based on citizens' right to information, China's OGI regulations are designed to produce more efficient (technocratic) government, not necessarily a new right. Guangzhou and Shanghai adopted regulations that referred to citizens' "right to know" as the basis for their OGI provisions, but the regulations adopted by the State Council were tilted more in favor of protecting certain kinds of information and improving the quality of governance.[34] Because OGI is a regulation and not a law, state secrets take precedence, giving government agencies wide discretion in what they choose to keep hidden. Although most local governments now have their own websites for providing information and allowing citizens to post questions and comments, e-government in China is more about conveying information in a highly selective manner than responding to public opinion. The public's interest in receiving information is generally outweighed by the state's interest in keeping information secret in order to govern more effectively.

Nevertheless, OGI may be changing how people think about their rights relative to the state's authority. One indication of an emerging rights consciousness is the growing number of lawsuits stemming from the Administrative Litigation Law (ALL). According to Article 2 of the ALL, people have the right to sue the government when the actions of its agencies or officials infringe on citizens' "lawful rights and interests." This can include illegal land grabs, illegal detention, violating

---

[34] Florini, Lai, and Tan, *China Experiments*, pp. 128–129.

the property rights of enterprises, and other actions where government agencies do not comply with official laws and regulations. Since its adoption in 1990, the number of ALL cases per year has grown from 13,006 to 123,194 in 2013. People who believe they have a right to know take action to find out. Over half of Shanghai's ALL cases are OGI-related. But equally important, almost all have been unsuccessful.[35] Growing rights consciousness among society is running up against the state's desire to keep information secret.

OGI itself has not been a tremendous success, but it has allowed activists to successfully pursue their causes, at least in limited ways. Research by Greg Distelhorst found that—despite OGI regulations—most local governments do not respond to public requests for information.[36] Together with a Chinese research organization, they sent requests about traffic safety, teacher credentials, and consumer product safety to 60 local governments. Only 14 percent of the requests received replies within 30 days, twice the time specified in the OGI regulations. But Distelhorst also shows that activists can use the failure of local government to comply with OGI as a vehicle for advancing their causes. When OGI requests failed, activists sought remedy through the courts (via the ALL). When both the OGI and ALL failed, activists were able to publicize their causes through the media. They were able to get greater financial compensation for homeowners whose properties were demolished for urban redevelopment, more transparency on local education spending, and information about local anti-counterfeiting efforts. Similar to "rightful resistance," in which citizens are able to challenge local officials by pointing to central laws and regulations,[37] activists have used the OGI to make new claims against local governments that are unwilling to comply.

In a political system dominated by the Party, it is important to note that OGI applies only to administrative agencies of the government. The Party itself is not subject to OGI. Its decisions and processes are not open to public examination. In Beijing, even the location of the central Organization Department, a powerful but secretive department that

---

[35] Florini, Lai, and Tan, *China Experiments*, pp. 144, 155.

[36] Greg Distelhorst, "The Power of Empty Promises: Quasidemocratic Institutions and Activism in China," *Comparative Political Studies*, forthcoming.

[37] Kevin J. O'Brien and Lianjiang Li, *Rightful Resistance in Rural China* (New York: Cambridge University Press, 2006).

controls the Party's personnel assignments, is not widely known.[38] From its appearance, it is obviously of great importance: It has a long driveway, it is a physically imposing structure, and it was clearly expensive to build. I was part of a delegation that visited there in 2012. The head of the Organization Department at that time, Li Yuanchao, tried to convince my delegation that it was not as secretive as its reputation suggested. He alluded to its description in Richard McGregor's book *The Party*:

> The national headquarters of the Central Organization Department occupy an unmarked building in Beijing, about a kilometre west of Tiananmen Square along the broad sweep of Chang'an Avenue. No sign hangs outside indicating the business of the building's tenant. The department's general switchboard number is unlisted. Calls from landlines in the building to mobile phones do not display an incoming number, as is customary for ordinary phones, just a string of zeros.[39]

Li laughingly told us the description was inaccurate. As proof, he told us a long story about the more open process he had instigated for selecting and promoting officials within the Central Organization Department, allowing people to vote on candidates for top leadership positions.[40] But there is still no name on the building or the entrance gate to indicate what the building is. Even if Li was reforming how the Organization Department operated internally, it was still off-limits to public scrutiny, just as its building was not publicly identifiable.

NIMBY Disputes

When Party and government officials make decisions that affect public well-being without first consulting society in line with mass line traditions, the result can be "not in my backyard" (NIMBY) protests. This

[38] The same is true for the CCP's Propaganda Department; see Anne-Marie Brady, *Marketing Dictatorship: Propaganda and Thought Work in Contemporary China* (Lanham, MD: Rowman & Littlefield, 2009), p. 13.

[39] Richard McGregor, *The Party: The Secret World of China's Communist Rulers* (New York: Harper Perennial, 2010), pp. 71–72.

[40] This initiative was discontinued after Xi Jinping gave a series of speeches indicating that he preferred appointing officials rather than electing them. This was consistent with his general top-down leadership style, with little room for bottom-up participation.

is also a way of conveying public opinion to leaders, but because it results in public demonstrations, NIMBY disputes indicate that the mass line has broken down. This is not only a loss of face for the officials involved, because they have to reverse course in the wake of public protest, but it is also potentially damaging to their careers. Maintaining social stability is one of the hard targets that local officials have to meet, and NIMBY protests by definition produce instability. Here again, local officials confront a paradox: They need to promote economic growth (another hard target), but their heavy-handed efforts often create a NIMBY backlash that poses a threat to stability.

In recent years, numerous NIMBY protests have erupted around China, all prompted by the failure to involve the public in the decision-making process. In 2008, Shanghai officials announced their plan to build a maglev train that would connect Pudong International Airport in the eastern part of the city with Hongqiao Airport in the west and the city of Hangzhou farther west. The government made this announcement on its website, an example of selectively releasing information to the public but not involving them in the actual decision-making. The announcement provoked protests by residents over the costs of the train, its environmental impact on the communities through which it would be built, and the unilateral nature of the decision, made without consulting people in the affected areas. The protests were also notable for their novel approach. Because organizing public protests can be very risky for the organizers and the participants, supporters sent text messages inviting others to join them in a "stroll" through the downtown area. This got the point across by disrupting traffic and interfering with business, but it also lowered the risk of the protestors being arrested. Plans to build the train were later abandoned.

A plan to build a waste incinerator in Panyu (a district in Guangzhou) created fears about negative health effects in November 2009. Hundreds of people marched to the management commission office in the capital city of Guangzhou and then took a "stroll" to the Guangzhou municipal government building. When government officials asked to talk with representatives of the protestors, they replied they did not want to be represented (officials often arrest such representatives after the fact). After the protests ended, the Panyu district government immediately announced three hotlines and an email address for residents to express their concerns. The deputy mayor of Guangzhou went to Panyu to announce that the project would not go forward unless the majority of the residents agreed to it.[41] A CCTV report on the protests said that the cause was not the environmental and health risks posed by the incinerator, but inadequate transparency and consultation with the public.[42] In December 2009, the Panyu party secretary met with residents to announce that the project had been canceled and promised that "in the future, the location of such projects will need to be agreed by over 75 percent of the residents who live nearby."[43]

Several years later, another plan to build a waste incinerator in Hangzhou led to large protests. On May 10, 2014, several thousand people blocked the road to the site of the planned incinerator, and some later tried to block traffic on a nearby highway. When police arrived to break up the protests, dozens of police and protestors were injured and over 30 police vehicles were set on fire.[44] That same day, the government announced that the project would not go forward without the "understanding and consent" of the public. It promised to uphold the public's "right to know" and participation in the decision-making process in the future.[45] At the same time, over 50 protestors were later detained for their roles in the violent clashes with police.

[41] Xingyu You, "*Su Zequn: Ruo daduoshu shimin fandui, laji fenshaochang jue-buhui donggong*" (Su Zequn Said the Incinerator Would Not Be Built if Most Residents Oppose), Oeeee.com, November 24, 2009, http://gz.oeeee.com/a/20091124/807430.html, accessed January 27, 2015.

[42] "*Yangshi guanzhu lajichang shijian: Laji mianqian minyi shi huangjin*" (CCTV Reports on Incinerator Incident: Public Opinion Is the Most Important), Oeee.com, November 26, 2009, http://gz.oeeee.com/a/20091126/808894.html, accessed January 27, 2015.

[43] "*Guangzhou fanyu laji fenshao xiangmu yin jumin qianglie kangyi tingjian*" (Waste Incinerator Project Halted in Fanyu, Guangzhou over Residents' Strong Opposition), news.163.com, December 21, 2009, http://news.163.com/09/1221/07/5R1PFKMN000120GU.html, accessed January 27, 2015.

[44] "Incinerator Won't Be Built without Public Support: Official," News.xinhua.net, May 11, 2014, http://news.xinhuanet.com/english/china/2014-05/11/c_13332 5173.htm, accessed January 27, 2015.

[45] "*Hangzhou Yuhang tonggao jiufeng huanjing nengyuan xiangmu: Weihuo lijie yiding bukaigong*" (Authorities of Hangzhou and Yuhang Promised Not to Build the Jiufeng Incinerator without Public Understanding), People.cn, May 10, 2014, http://society.people.com.cn/n/2014/0510/c1008-25000964.html, accessed January 27, 2015.

Plans to build chemical plants have sparked protests in numerous cities, including Xiamen in 2007, Dalian in 2011, Ningbo in 2012, Kunming in 2013, and Maoming in 2014. In each case, local residents protested the environmental and health consequences of the plants, some wearing surgical masks to make their point. Protests began peacefully, but some ended in violence. In Maoming, police used clubs and tear gas to disperse crowds after they began to throw water bottles at the main government building. In response, the protestors set fire to police and government vehicles.[46] A few days after these protests, the government announced that the project would not commence without the consent of the public. It also revealed that some of the protestors had been detained and punished, and acknowledged that over a dozen others were "accidentally" injured by the police.[47] The Maoming protests fit a more general pattern: A unilateral decision by the government sparks protests that turn violent; the government then announces the cancellation of the project (although some are simply moved to a new locale) and promises to be more transparent and consultative in the future; and as a warning to others, it arrests several people to punish them for their participation in the protests.

In each of these cases and many others throughout the country, local officials had to either abandon or significantly modify their plans in light of the public outcry. Also in each case, the protests were the direct result of a decision made by local government officials without consulting the people whose lives and property would be affected by the project. Although the mass line concept may seem antiquated, local officials repeatedly learn what happens when they ignore its underlying premise: If you want people to go along with a policy or project, you have to bring them into the process. Otherwise, they are likely to resist the new initiative, either passively or, in the case of NIMBY protests, demonstrably.

[46] China Blog Staff, "Piecing Together China's Maoming Plant Protest," BBC News, April 2, 2014, http://www.bbc.com/news/blogs-china-blog-26847987, accessed January 27, 2015.

[47] Jutao Xu, "*Shizhengfu zuori zhaokai xinwen fabuhui*" (Municipal Government Held Press Conference Yesterday), People's Government of Maoming City, April 4, 2014, http://www.maoming.gov.cn/Item/31680.aspx, accessed January 27, 2015.

Significance

These various reforms should not be confused with democratization. At best, they can be considered as consultative authoritarianism, involving consultation without accountability. Participation is generally at the invitation of the state, and as the case of healthcare reform shows, the exact nature of outside proposals and recommendations is shrouded in secrecy. That eliminates the ability to trace the responsiveness of the state to popular demands. As a result, these local reforms have yet to change the Chinese political system into a truly responsive and accountable state. They may be moving China in that direction, but it still has far to go.

But we should not lose sight of several key points. First, the Party is increasingly reaching out to various organizations and individuals for input into the policy process. The reform policies are not just generated from ideological precepts or the dictates of individual leaders. Second, initial reforms are being modified in light of public opinion, especially those of specialists and stakeholders. When reforms do not involve the legitimacy of the regime, the Party is more willing to solicit and listen to outside voices and modify policies accordingly. Above all, as greater consultation leads to more transparency and in turn better governance, it may ultimately produce greater satisfaction with the policy process and support for the regime as a whole. This would also help address the growing incidence of NIMBY and other local protests against the arbitrary decisions of party and government leaders and thereby improve political and social stability. These are quality-of-life issues over and above the purely economic indicators of performance legitimacy, which are more easily measured (and are examined in chapter 5).

These reforms are not creating new rights, but they may be creating new expectations for more frequent and institutionalized consultation. So far, these reforms are more like gifts from the state rather than demands from society, but once they have been given, they are difficult to rescind. As opportunities for consultation become more common and routine, they may become an expected norm. And as people come to expect to be consulted in the policy process, they may well become inclined to hold decision-makers accountable when their preferences are not adopted and reforms do not achieve their intended goals. For now, this is a key part of the Party's dilemma: Will more consultation and greater transparency satisfy public opinion, or create demands for more responsiveness and accountability? Rather than allow the Party to speak for the people, the Chinese people may want to speak for themselves.

Public Opinion on Government Responsiveness

How do urban Chinese view their leaders? This is a potentially sensitive question in the Chinese context. Rather than ask people directly about the merits and shortcomings of leaders, the 2014 survey asked people "what qualities do you think the ideal government official should have?" As seen in table 3-1, the most valued attributes concern honesty and public welfare. Implicitly, these may be the attributes they find most lacking in their officials. In contrast, the ability to implement higher-level policies—the attribute most important in the evaluation of officials by their superiors—is ranked next to last.[48] These priorities hold true regardless of age: For all cohorts, honesty is always ranked first, "capable," "able to implement higher-level policies," and "good people skills" are ranked at the bottom, and the others are in the middle.

These priorities in the qualities of government officials are further reflected in questions about the kind of treatment people expect from the government (see table 3-2). Almost two-thirds of the respondents stated that government officials normally do not speak the truth. This fits the previous finding that honesty is the most desired attribute in an ideal official—it seems to be a rare occurrence among actual officials. Almost as many respondents agree that government officials do not care about their opinions, indicating that the Party's mass line concept is more rhetoric than reality. Less than half expect to receive equal treatment from the government. This is what we would expect from an authoritarian regime: Government officials are not accountable to the people and do not have much incentive to be responsive to them.[49] But

[48] The 2010 survey asked this question differently: From the same list of attributes, which three were most important. The rank ordering was largely similar: Honesty ranked first and "able to implement higher-level policies" and "good people skills" ranked last.

[49] On these questions, the respondents' characteristics matter: CCP members have a slightly more optimistic view of government officials; the youngest cohorts have a more cynical view. Education only matters on the question of whether

TABLE 3-1 Desired Attributes of Government Officials (percent who answered "very important")

1. Honest 廉洁	79.4
2. Able to treat people fairly 能够公正待人	75.5
3. Truthful, keeps promises 诚实守信	75.1
4. Serve the public interest 服务公共利益	73.4
5. Able to listen to the ideas of the people 能听取群众意见	72.6
6. Capable 有能力	68.5
7. Able to implement higher-level policies 能贯彻上级的政策	59.1
8. Good people skills 人缘好	40.8

Source: 2014 Public Goods and Public Support Survey.

TABLE 3-2 How Government Officials Treat the Public (percent who answered "agree" or "strongly agree")

Generally speaking, government officials normally speak the truth.	36.3
Government officials don't care much about the opinions of people like me.	38.7
Everyone can obtain equal treatment from the government.	45.7

Source: 2014 Public Goods and Public Support Survey.

it also suggests that most Chinese have not experienced government officials whose behavior is in keeping with the mass line principle.

III. Managing Civil Society

The traditional concept of the mass line treats "the masses" as individuals, not as members of groups and organizations. In contemporary China, the Party is increasingly engaged with a growing number of

officials care about people like them; those with college degrees are slightly more likely to say that officials do care (34.4 percent compared to 29.8 percent of the rest of the respondents). Those with college degrees have the communication skills and connections to interact with officials, but even so, the vast majority of college-educated respondents believe that government officials do not care about people like them.

NGOs (more often referred to as social organizations in China; here, the terms are used interchangeably). It is often said that China does not have a civil society. The absence of an organized opposition or social movements on behalf of political change leads many to conclude that civil society remains weak or even nonexistent. Efforts to form groups capable of challenging the state—ranging from the China Democracy Party to dissident movements such as Charter 08 or even the Falun Gong spiritual movement—have been quickly repressed, their leaders imprisoned, and their motives harshly criticized in the official media. Because the rise of civil society is seen as a precursor to political change, its absence in China seems to suggest that this part of the Party's survival strategy—maintaining its political monopoly by quickly and ruthlessly eliminating potential threats—has been successful.

If civil society refers to autonomous groups that are critical of political leaders and their policies, and even opposed to the regime, then this is largely true. The Party is hostile to such groups, which pose an existential threat to it. But this is not the only definition of civil society. If the notion of civil society is expanded to include the kinds of groups that make up civil society in democratic regimes—neighborhood groups, social organizations, philanthropic and faith-based organizations, etc.—then civil society in China is blooming. By 2013, China had over 500,000 registered social organizations (see figure 3-1), and by most estimates, at least twice that many unregistered but still active organizations.

Civil society is seen not only as a key factor in promoting the democratization of authoritarian regimes, it is also seen as an essential ingredient in creating a stable and well-governed democracy. How can the same factor lead to both political change and political stability? A key to resolving this paradox is recognizing that there are different dimensions of civil society, and each has different goals and consequences for the regimes in which they operate. In assessing the strength of civil society and its likely consequences in China, we need to distinguish between these different dimensions.

Scholars have highlighted these differences with different labels: sociological vs. political; the noncritical vs. critical sphere; the economic vs.

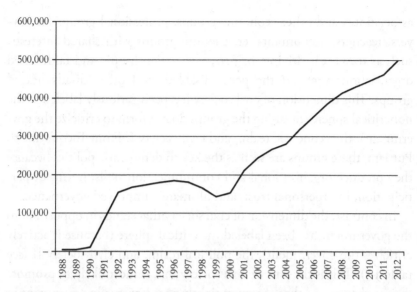

FIGURE 3-1 Number of NGOs in China, 1988–2012.

Sources: 1988–2003: China Civil Affairs Statistical Yearbook 2009, http://chinadataon-line.org/member/yearbooknew/yearbook/ybcdata.aspx?yc=F88F0ED0C6279E70F07E 4AB418BBF839&cc=P010Q&ft=619E3FE41E16A774; 2004–2012: Chinese Academy of Social Sciences, *Blue Book of Civil Organizations* (Beijing: Social Science Academic Press 2008, 2009/2010, 2011/2012). The total number of NGOs includes social organizations (社会团体), non-state (literally, "people-run") non-enterprise units (民办非企业), and foundations (基金会).

political realm; civil society I vs. civil society II.[50] Although the labels are different, the underlying logic is the same: Different groups form to pursue different kinds of interests, and their relationships with the state are consequently different. Civil society groups that organize on behalf of the economic and cultural interests of their members normally do not have political agendas. They may try to cooperate with the government in achieving their goals, or they may not interact with the government at all. In China, they include sports leagues, fan clubs, book clubs, and other social organizations; chambers of commerce, business

[50] Jonathan Schwarz and Shawn Shieh, eds., *State and Society Responses to Social Welfare Needs in China: Serving the People* (New York and London: Routledge, 2009); Yanqi Tong, "State, Society, and Political Change in China and Hungary," *Comparative Politics*, Vol. 26, No. 3 (April 1994), pp. 333–353; Gordon White, Jude Howell, and Shang Xiaoyuan, *In Search of Civil Society: Market Reform and Social*

associations, and other economic groups; professional groups for law-yers, teachers, accountants, etc.; leisure groups with shared interests, such as travel, car driving, or pets; and philanthropic and faith-based organizations that aid the poor, disabled, and other disadvantaged groups. This dimension of civil society has been variously labeled as the noncritical sphere (meaning the groups do not form to criticize the gov-ernment), the economic realm, and civil society I. From Tocqueville to Putnam, these groups are seen as the key to democratic politics because they produce organizational and communication skills, norms of par-ticipation, interpersonal trust, and ultimately improved governance.

In contrast, the dimension of civil society that stands in opposition to the government has been labeled the critical sphere (because it actively criticizes the government), the political realm, and civil society II (see table 3-3). This is the part of civil society that is most likely to promote regime change and that observers rightly note is virtually nonexistent in China. The Party zealously defends its monopoly on political organiza-tions, suppressing any that pose a challenge to the Party.

As described in chapter 2, since 2008, the Party ramped up its repres-sion of dissidents, rights lawyers, and others who were critical of the Party's policies and practices and sought to change them. Even though the Party has cracked down hard on some civil society groups, it toler-ated and even promoted others, and the number of NGOs grew steadily (see figure 3-1). One study described the Party's crackdown on civil soci-ety groups prior to the 18th Party Congress in 2012 as "a nearly schizo-phrenic effort to simultaneously restrict and foster development of civil society."[51] What explains the contradictions in the Party's approach to civil society? It largely depends on two separate factors: divisions within the state and the nature of the groups it faces. It actively represses

Change in Contemporary China (Oxford, UK: Oxford University Press, 1996); Michael W. Foley and Bob Edwards, "The Paradox of Civil Society," *Journal of Democracy*, Vol.7, No.3 (July 1996), pp. 38–52. John Tai also identifies the sociological use of civil society as an intermediate realm between the state and individual citizens, but without presupposing whether its purpose is to oppose, ignore, or cooperate with the state; see *Building Civil Society in Authoritarian China: Importance of Leadership Connections for Establishing Effective Nongovern-mental Organizations in a Non-Democracy* (New York: Springer, 2015).

[51] Florini, Lai, and Tan, *China Experiments*, p. 100.

TABLE 3-3 Different Realms of Civil Society Organizations in China

	Civil Society I	Civil Society II
Scope of activities	Economic, cultural, social	Political
Relationship to state	Interactive, cooperative, occasionally apolitical	Autonomous, critical
Impact on stability of authoritarian regime	Positive—can improve quality of governance, social well-being, and interpersonal trust. Supports status quo.	Negative—seeks change in nature of regime, which can lead to crackdowns and further resistance. Often supports democratization or other forms of regime change.
Examples	Business associations, professional associations, leisure groups, philanthropic and faith-based groups	Social movements, dissidents, critical intellectuals, rights defense lawyers
State response	Tolerate or promote	Repress

individuals and groups belonging to civil society II, but is more willing to tolerate and even cooperate with those in civil society I.

Divisions within the State

Despite the portrayal of China as a one-party state, the state is not a unitary actor. Some government agencies favor civil society development as part of their organization missions (for instance, the Ministry of Civil Affairs and the Ministry of Environmental Protection). In contrast, the public security apparatus, which is responsible for maintaining stability, sees NGOs as a potential threat and therefore prefers to limit the space available for them to operate in. Crackdowns on civil society groups are primarily done by the public security agencies, the coercive arm of the state.

Not only are there notable differences among government agencies, there is also an important distinction between the goals of the central leadership and those of local leadership. A key purpose of political reform has been to help the central leadership monitor the behavior of local officials so that their actions do not de-legitimate the regime as a whole.[52] For example, Beijing has been pushing for better environmental protection, which has created the opportunity for numerous environmental NGOs to operate. The Ministry of Environmental Protection is more supportive of local environmental NGOs because it is understaffed and cannot monitor local compliance with national regulations, and local NGOs are in a better position to monitor local officials.[53] But local leaders often see these groups as bothersome and an obstacle to achieving their primary goal of spurring economic growth. In China, as in most countries, officials and businesspeople see a trade-off between the immediate goal of economic growth and the long-term need to limit the environmental damage that rapid growth creates. Businesses complain that abiding by environmental regulations raises their operating costs and lowers their profits. Local officials complain that their limited resources and staff expertise prevent them from monitoring compliance with environmental regulations. More importantly, because economic growth is one of the hard targets that local officials must meet as part of their annual reviews, they have little incentive to enforce environmental regulations that reduce economic growth. The result is that the central government may welcome the activities of environmental NGOs, but local officials may see them as detrimental to their primary goals and therefore restrict their ability to operate.

Differences within Civil Society

The second factor in explaining the state's response to civil society concerns the different types of civil society. How NGOs are treated by the state depends in large part on whether the NGOs' missions are in line with the state's own goals. When they are seen as complementary, the state can be encouraging and cooperative, but when they are in conflict, the state shows little tolerance. Many Chinese NGOs are engaged in providing education, healthcare, job training, and legal aid. NGOs often have the enthusiasm, determination, commitment, and technical

----

[52] "It is not unusual for central state agencies to encourage NGOs to be more confrontational with local governments" to help monitor them. Florini, Lai, and Tan, *China Experiments*, p. 152.

[53] Florini, Lai, and Tan, *China Experiments*, pp. 142–144.

expertise that local governments lack. These groups do not pose an imminent threat to the Party, and at least some local officials have seen the benefits of partnering with them as service providers. Over time, NGOs have proven to be useful in achieving the state's goal of improving public goods and social services, giving local officials an incentive to work with them.[54] Local governments particularly tolerate NGOs that serve communities (such as migrants and the elderly) for which they do not have resources.

To improve their relationships with the state, NGOs may also choose to prioritize the goals that are consistent with the regime's priorities in order to be more effective. For instance, gay men's groups have framed their activities in terms of public health—limiting the spread of HIV/AIDS—instead of equal rights, which would likely be seen as confrontational and invite repression.[55] Faith-based organizations have emphasized the beneficial services they provide rather than the spiritual calling that inspires them. At the same time, they see charity work as not only a social service but also a spiritual practice. In a largely covert and non-confrontational manner, their work is a principled protest against the regime's priorities and restrictions on religion.[56]

Equally important, NGOs are a separate source of revenue for providing public goods. Budget constraints are a major motivation for local leaders to partner with NGOs in service delivery. Local governments in China face a host of unfunded mandates. The central government has repeatedly issued new policies requiring increased spending on public education, healthcare, environmental regulation, and other important policy areas without providing the funds to implement them. The central government pays only 30 percent of budgetary expenditures in China, whereas the different levels of local governments (provinces, municipalities, counties/cities, and townships/towns) make up the

[54] Anthony J. Spires, "Contingent Symbiosis and Civil Society in an Authoritarian State: Understanding the Survival of China's Grassroots NGOs," *American Journal of Sociology*, Vol. 117, No. 1 (July 2011), pp. 1–45; Teets, *Civil Society under Authoritarianism*.

[55] Timothy Hildebrandt, *Social Organizations and the Authoritarian State in China* (New York: Cambridge University Press, 2013), p. 14.

[56] Susan McCarthy, "Serving Society, Repurposing the State: Religious Charity and Resistance in China," *China Journal*, No. 73 (July 2013), pp. 48–72.

other 70 percent. This is way out of proportion compared to the practices of other countries. In developing countries, the local governments provide 32 percent of expenditures, and in developed countries, only 14 percent.[57] In the U.S., the federal government accounts for almost 60 percent of all government spending.[58] To make matters worse, even though local governments in China are responsible for providing most public goods and services, they have limited fiscal authority to raise taxes and fees to pay for them. One solution that some local leaders have hit upon is working with NGOs, especially those that receive foreign funding from the World Bank, the Ford Foundation, the Gates Foundation, and other groups dedicated to human and social development. In an environment in which local governments are often starved for cash, these foreign sources of funding can supplement the government's coffers. However, it is also true that many local governments also see these foreign sources as slush funds that they can dip into for all sorts of reasons, not just their intended purpose. Local governments even encourage groups to form in order to attract foreign funding, and then take a portion of the money and materials (such as computers and other equipment).[59]

These two dimensions of civil society are not mutually exclusive. Groups organized for one purpose can be quickly converted to another, a process that scholars refer to as "institutional conversion."[60] The noncritical realm can become critical when the opportunity arises. Groups that organize for cultural or recreational purposes can adopt political agendas. For example, in the U.S. civil rights movement, churches originally formed for worship became the bases for publicizing information

---

[57] Pierre F. Landry, *Decentralized Authoritarianism in China: The Communist Party's Control of Local Elites in the Post-Mao Era* (New York: Cambridge University Press, 2008), pp. 3–9; Teets, *Civil Society under Authoritarianism*, p. 45.

[58] In the 2014 fiscal year, the U.S. federal government accounted for 58.2 percent of total government spending; see http://www.usgovernmentspending.com/year2014_r, accessed August 25, 2014.

[59] Hildebrandt, *Social Organizations and the Authoritarian State in China*.

[60] Kathleen Thelen, "How Institutions Evolve: Insights from Comparative Historical Analysis," in James Mahoney and Dietrich Rueschemeyer, eds., *Comparative Historical Analysis in the Social Sciences* (New York: Cambridge University Press, 2003), pp. 208–240.

and mobilizing protest marches. Labor unions that were originally formed to negotiate higher wages and better work conditions later tried to influence the political system itself, whether by endorsing candidates for elected office or lobbying for new legislation.

This is the dynamic that is most worrisome to the Party. It recognizes the need for certain civil society groups because they provide essential goods and services. At the same time, it is wary that these groups can develop political goals. For example, the Party has allowed certain environmental groups to operate as long as they limit their actions to publicizing "reduce, reuse, recycle" programs, but it does not want them to publicize the sorry state of China's air and water or criticize the government for encouraging an economic growth strategy that has ravaged China's environment. It is also aware that environmental movements in the former Soviet Union and Taiwan played leading roles in promoting regime change.

In addition, the Party is also ambivalent about groups that serve the needy or disadvantaged in various ways. Throughout China, national and local groups have organized to serve the needs of migrant workers who become ill, are injured on the job, or are not paid what they are owed. Those who migrated from the countryside to cities are generally not entitled to receive health insurance, education, unemployment insurance, or other public goods. These goods and services are determined by *hukou* status and generally provided to people only in the place where they are formally registered, and not necessarily where they reside, as described in chapter 2. One reason NGOs have been so important for helping migrants is that the state generally ignores them and even harasses them. Legal aid centers help people understand their legal rights and navigate the legal system, especially when party or government officials are the culprits.[61] Philanthropic groups and faith-based organizations run homes for orphans and the elderly, offer aid to the poor and disabled, and provide relief to victims of natural disasters. On one hand, the Party welcomes the efforts of these groups to address pressing needs. On the other hand, if these groups are more effective and more popular than government offices tasked with the same responsibilities, they can represent an implicit rebuke to the state.

---

[61] Jeffrey Becker, *Social Ties, Resources, and Migrant Labor Contention in Contemporary China: From Peasants to Protestors* (Lanham, MD: Lexington Books, 2014).

By promoting public welfare and social justice, these groups also indirectly challenge the policies that produce these needs. It is then a small step from aiding the victims of these policies to criticizing the policies and the politicians who make them.

In a one-party political system, the party prefers to control many activities, including charity work. Most charitable donations are supposed to be channeled through official charities, many of which have reputations for being wasteful and even corrupt. The reputation of the Red Cross Society of China was seriously damaged by a 2011 scandal involving Guo Meimei, a woman who claimed to work for the Red Cross Society and shared details of her life of luxury on the Internet. Many assumed her Maserati, Hermès handbags, and Beijing villa were paid for by the Red Cross Society. Even though she later admitted she did not work for the Red Cross, it was later revealed that she was the girlfriend of one of its board members, who subsequently resigned.[62] But the damage to the Red Cross was done. In the aftermath of the scandal, the Red Cross Society received few individual donations. In the days immediately after the 2013 earthquake in Sichuan, the Red Cross Society received only 142,800 yuan in donations, while Jet Li's One Foundation, a private foundation profiled below, raised over 15 million yuan.[63] The Red Cross Society was not the only government-sponsored charity that experienced scandals over its operations. China's other major official charity, the China Charity Federation, was accused of money laundering for businessmen in 2011, and was mocked by netizens as the "China Money Laundering Federation."[64] The China

[62] She was arrested in July 2014 for gambling on World Cup games. After her arrest, CCTV broadcast Guo Meimei's confession, in which she blamed her fabricated Red Cross story on her own vanity.

[63] Julie Zhu, "China Earthquake: Donors Prefer Private Charities over Public," *Financial Times*, April 22, 2013, http://blogs.ft.com/beyond-brics/2013/04/22/china-earthquake-donors-prefer-private-charities-over-public/?#axzz2mW1quciR, accessed January 27, 2014.

[64] "*Na shenme lai zhengjiu ni, 'Guanfang cishan*?"(What Can Save You, 'Official Charities'?), Southcn.com, August 19, 2011, http://www.southcn.com/nfdaily/finance/content/2011-08/19/content_28601311.htm; Bei Fang, "*Cishan zonghui chengle xiqian zonghui?*" (Has the China Charity Federation Become the Money Laundering Federation?), Iqilu.com, August 19, 2011, http://pinglun.iqilu.com/yuanchuang/2011/0819/534914.shtml, accessed October 4, 2014.

Women's Development Foundation was also involved in a corruption scandal in 2011.[65] The charities' efforts to defend their activities against these rumors only served to fuel the public's distrust of them.[66] Many government-sponsored charities suffered sharp drops in donations following this series of scandals.[67]

Finally, there are a large number of organizations that fall between the state and civil society. In China, they are often referred to as "mass organizations" and more generally are called "government-organized nongovernmental organizations," or GONGOs. These include the All-China Women's Federation, the All-China Federation of Trade Unions, and the All-China Federation of Industry and Commerce (ACFIC). The budgets and key personnel for these groups are provided by the state. There is a much wider array of groups that may be organized by their members but have close ties with these Party-sponsored mass organizations. For example, there are many business associations that represent private entrepreneurs as a whole, different industrial or commercial sectors, and even different localities. These groups may work closely with the ACFIC, raising product quality, adopting industry standards, and lobbying the government for policy or regulatory changes.[68]

In a similar fashion, the Party has created national religious organizations to monitor and constrain worship and other religious activities, including theological training for new pastors. In recent decades, Christian house churches and other places of worship have grown rapidly, but the leaders of some of these churches are poorly trained and often self-taught. Members of the official churches (the Three-Self Patriotic Church for Protestants and the Patriotic Catholic Association

[65] Li Ying, "*Hongshi zihui xinren weiji boji qita guanfang cishan jigou*" (Red Cross' Public Trust Crisis Affects Other Public Charities), Qingdaonews, August 12, 2011, http://www.qingdaonews.com/gb/content/2011-08/12/content_8899562.htm, accessed October 4, 2014.

[66] "*Hongshi zihui gongxinli queshi: Guanfang cishan jigou cun tizhi kunju*" (Red Cross Lost Credibility: Public Charities' Institutional Predicament), CCTV.com, July 5, 2011, http://news.cntv.cn/china/20110705/103266.shtml, accessed October 4, 2014.

[67] Karla W. Simon, *Civil Society in China: The Legal Framework from Ancient Times to the "New Reform Era"* (New York: Oxford University Press, 2013), pp. 323–324.

[68] Scott Kennedy, *The Business of Lobbying in China* (Cambridge, MA: Harvard University Press, 2005).

for Catholics) often work quietly with leaders of house churches to improve their biblical knowledge and organizational skills and avoid the heterodox and even heretical teachings that some of China's underground church leaders have become known for.

The larger point is this: Interactions between civil society groups, GONGOs, mass organizations, and the state are not necessarily adversarial in China. Civil society groups by and large recognize that their survival and success depend on maintaining good relations with Party and government officials. The Party is ambivalent about civil society, but over time, the number of NGOs and the scope of their activities have grown. But this growth is largely limited to the types of groups that fall into the civil society I category: those with economic, social, or cultural interests that do not directly challenge the political status quo. These groups do not challenge the state and in many cases try to cooperate with it. Instead of presenting an organized opposition, these groups are better seen as partners—at least for the time being.

Natural disasters often provoke an upsurge of volunteers and donors wanting to help in the relief efforts. When a devastating earthquake struck Sichuan's Wenchuan county in 2008, people around the country instantly mobilized to send money, supplies, and volunteers to the area. The sudden appearance of often ad hoc social organizations then triggers renewed speculation on whether they portend the long-anticipated rise of civil society in China, followed sometime later by reports on why these spontaneous movements did not coalesce into more permanent civil society groups or social movements. The assumption behind much of this speculation is that a "true" civil society is incompatible with authoritarian regimes, so that the sudden increase in organized voluntary activity may be an indicator of political foment leading to regime change. Such speculation misses the mark for two reasons: One, the Party quickly reacts to limit the potential challenge from such groups; and two, these groups rarely exhibit political ambitions beyond the tragedy that inspired them.

The implications of this trend are also clear: Because these groups are willing to partner with the state instead of opposing it, their actions do not pose a threat to the political status quo. According to Hildebrandt, "Leaders of Chinese NGOs do not work to change the rules of the game, but instead play by them."[69] They are more dedicated to addressing social problems than achieving political change. Moreover, they may even stabilize it. Just as Putnam found that a robust civil society improved the quality of governance in democratic regimes, the same kinds of groups may have a similar effect on China's authoritarian regime. But not all groups in civil society are the same, and the consequences of their actions are also not the same. Civil society II seeks regime change by harnessing shared resentments and organizing opposition, whereas civil society I accepts the status quo as given and tries to work within those rules to achieve its goals. By providing valuable social welfare goods and services, China's NGOs may reduce resentment toward the Party and its policies and therefore promote political stability. To the extent it is successful, an active and expanding civil society I may facilitate regime survival in China and in other countries instead of the change that people expect from civil society. That is why distinguishing types of civil society groups and the state's response to them is so essential.

Coping with Civil Society

The Party's main tool for restraining and monitoring China's civil society has been the registration process. In 1998, the state established strict regulations for registering NGOs.[70] In order for groups to legally operate, they had to find a state-affiliated unit willing to serve as their sponsor (often despairingly referred to as the mother-in-law) and then register with the Ministry of Civil Affairs. At the beginning, few NGOs were able to find sponsors. The potential sponsors were worried that they would be held responsible, politically as well as financially, if the NGOs they sponsored ran into trouble. The result was a mismatch between the growing numbers of social organizations seeking sponsors and the limited number of government organizations willing to be

---

[69] Hildebrandt, *Social Organizations and the Authoritarian State in China*, p. 60.

[70] The best discussion of these original regulations is in Tony Saich, "Negotiating the State: The Development of Social Organizations in China," *China Quarterly*, No. 161 (March 2000), pp. 124–141. Later revisions are documented in Simon, *Civil Society in China*.

sponsors. But most NGOs tried to register in order to obtain a variety of benefits, including opening bank accounts and the ability to seek funding from the government, private foundations, and foreign organizations. This gives NGOs a certain freedom of action, not only in the programs they administer but also in the sources of funding they pursue. Registration means state oversight, but in other ways, it also creates independence.

When Chinese NGOs were unable to find a sponsor, many found ways around the regulations. A common tactic was to register as a for-profit private enterprise or a non-enterprise unit (a category that includes healthcare, education, and other professional services), or even as a consulting firm. This had the advantage of letting them operate in the open, but it also had several disadvantages. First, they had to demonstrate an initial capital investment, something start-up NGOs had little of. Second, as enterprises, they could seek new investors, but they could not solicit donations from government agencies, foreign foundations, or even Chinese citizens. Third, they were expected to be profitable, selling goods or merchandise like other enterprises, but not to run training or aid programs for the groups they targeted. When these organizations operated more like the NGOs they truly were, they risked being shut down by the local government they were registered with as an enterprise.

An alternative tactic was to operate as an unregistered NGO. This had a different set of advantages and disadvantages. On one hand, unregistered NGOs enjoy a degree of independence in terms of their staffing and operations. In some cases, local governments may even encourage NGOs to form but not register. For example, registered groups can receive foreign funding that is often funneled through central government agencies, but unregistered groups get money funneled through local governments. Local leaders therefore encourage the formation of groups that seek foreign funding, which the leaders then utilize for public goods and private gain. They are more motivated by getting foreign funding than battling the problems the funding is intended for. This is a common occurrence and by no means limited to China. In informal conversations with people who work with international foundations, most are not too concerned about corruption in China. They recognize that some of their funding goes into the pockets of local Party and government officials, but not on the same scale as in some other countries. Money may get diverted from healthcare programs to repair a school or pave a road, but those are also important developmental needs. In the end, enough of their funding gets to the designated NGOs that they can still make a difference.

On the other hand, unregistered NGOs exist in a precarious gray area and can be shut down as soon as they are discovered by the authorities or lose the support of officials who previously chose to look the other way. Ironically, unregistered NGOs may attract more oversight from local leaders suspicious of their activities and goals. These NGOs may be unregistered, but they are not invisible. Unregistered NGOs also face the risk of having their money and equipment confiscated at any time. These uncertainties limit the scale of their operations and their ability to raise money. But for many NGOs, this is preferable to not operating at all.

A second restriction on the number of NGOs was the requirement that only one organization could represent a particular interest in a given locality. If two groups formed to support the local soccer team, they would be forced to merge, or one would be forced to disband. This corporatist-style policy was designed to limit the number of NGOs in any one locality and eliminate competition between NGOs. Over time, this tool of control was reduced and eventually removed, but the underlying logic—limit the number of groups active in an area to reduce competition and conflict and increase the state's ability to regulate, control, monitor, and cooperate—remained. Moreover, this provision is often the basis for repression of potential threats to the Party. Above all, the All-China Federation of Trade Unions' status as the official representative of workers has been the basis for the Party's quick and often harsh repression of efforts to organize new and autonomous labor unions.

Over time, these restraints on the growth of civil society proved unworkable. The number and diversity of NGOs grew rapidly. Equally important, the results of their work indicated that they were committed to economic and social improvement. Although the Party continued to be wary of an unregulated civil society, it also came to recognize its potential to play a complementary role to the work of the government. In 2003, the Third Plenum of the 16th Central Committee approved the Party's intention of "standardizing and developing, according to marketization principles, all types of industry

associations, commercial associations, and other autonomous organizations."[71] The following year, the Fourth Plenum approved a resolution to strengthen the Party's governing capacity. As part of this effort,
it declared that it would "give play to the role of social bodies, sector
organizations, and social intermediary organizations in providing services, reflecting demands, and regulating behavior; and form a joint
force for social management and services."[72]

This new supportive attitude toward civil society allowed local governments to introduce innovations in the registration and management
of NGOs. In particular, local reforms made it easier for NGOs to register without having a sponsoring agency. The province of Guangdong,
in southeast China adjacent to Hong Kong, was a leader in liberalizing
regulations concerning civil society, just as it had previously been at
the forefront of economic reforms. In December 2005, the Guangdong
government announced a new policy concerning the regulation of
industry associations that included a provision that "work supervising
units" should only guide, but not intervene in, the work of industry
associations, and that new industry associations could apply directly
for registration without the previously required sponsor.[73] In 2010, the
provincial government extended the scope of civil organizations that
were allowed to register without a sponsor from industry associations
to chambers of commerce, charities, and economic, science, and technology organizations.[74] By 2012, the provincial government allowed
all social organizations to register with the Civil Affairs Department

[71] Central Committee of the Communist Party of China, "*Zhonggong zhongyang guanyu wanshan shehuizhuyi shichang jingji tizhi ruogan wenti de jueding*" (Decision of the Central Committee of the Communist Party of China on Several Issues in Improving the Socialist Market Economic System), October 14, 2003, http://www. people.com.cn/GB/shizheng/1024/2145119.html, accessed May 12, 2014.

[72] "Text of CPC Central Committee Decision on Enhancing Ability to Govern," Xinhua, September 26, 2004, in World News Connection, http://wnc. eastview.com/wnc/article?id=35815079, accessed April 7, 2015.

[73] http://www.gd.gov.cn/wsbs/jmbs/mjzz/bszn/200606/t20060617_2149.htm, item 11.

[74] Zhong Liang, "*Gaige zai nanfang: Guangdong dui shehui zuzhi de guanli gaige*" (Reform in the South: Guangdong's Reform in NGO Management), last modified December 30, 2011, http://finance.ifeng.com/news/region/20111230/5376808.shtml, accessed May 15, 2014.

without needing to find a sponsor first.[75] This more liberal and inviting political environment encouraged NGOs from elsewhere in the country that had been unable to find a sponsor to move to Guangdong, as will be shown later in the case studies.

Besides Guangdong, the central government encouraged other localities to experiment with civil society reforms, in particular to make it easier to register without a sponsoring agency. In 2008, the Ministry of Civil Affairs designated Shanghai, Shenzhen, Guangdong, Yunnan, Xinjiang, and Qingdao as "innovation pilot points" and authorized them to reform their policies for registering and managing social organizations. This follows the pattern used for many economic reforms: Begin on an experimental basis in specific localities and, when it is clear which experiments are successful, have the central government approve them and turn local experiments into national policy.[76] For example, in 2002, Shanghai established a new Municipal Office for the Development of Industry Associations to supervise all industry associations of the city (this office was later incorporated into the Shanghai Municipal Social Service Bureau in 2005). The Jing'an district government within Shanghai authorized the Federation of Social Organizations to be the sponsoring agency of all NGOs. Shanghai announced in 2008 that it would contract with NGOs to provide a wide variety of government services. The same year, the Innovations and Excellence in Chinese Local Governance Program gave a sub-district in Shanghai one of its awards for setting up an NGO Service Center that provides services to both society and the government.[77] The Beijing municipal government authorized the Federation of Trade Unions, the Communist Youth League, the Women's Federation, and 17 other official and semi-official

[75] "Regulations for Boosting Support for Developing Civil Society Organizations and Standardizing Their Management," released at the end of 2011 and took effect from July 2012; released by Dongguan city government, http://www.dg.gov.cn/dgsgw/s32146/201305/635117.htm, accessed January 26, 2015. See also Simon, *Civil Society in China*, pp. 330ff.

[76] Sebastian Heilmann, "From Local Experiments to National Policy: The Origins of China's Distinctive Policy Process," *China Journal*, No. 59 (January 2008), pp. 1–30; Heilmann, "Policy Experimentation In China's Economic Rise," *Studies in Comparative International Development*, Vol. 43, No. 1 (March 2008), pp. 1–26.

[77] Florini, Lai, and Tan, *China Experiments*, p. 106.

organizations to sponsor NGOs. In 2012, the Beijing municipal government designated four types of NGOs—industry and commerce, charity, social welfare, and social security—to register with the Civil Affairs Department without a sponsoring agency. The reforms in Guangdong, Shanghai, and Beijing were later adopted by other provinces and cities.

Generally speaking, business associations have been less restricted than other categories of social organizations. Party and government officials have long recognized the need to promote and cooperate with enterprises of all types: state-owned, private, joint ventures, and various hybrids. Where the private sector is most developed, such as the coastal provinces of Jiangsu and Zhejiang, local governments have relaxed registration requirements for business associations by allowing the local Federation of Industry and Commerce to be their sponsoring agency. In other areas where state-owned and collective enterprises are more prominent, such as in Hebei, the Federation of Industrial Economics also serves as the sponsor and supervising unit of business associations.[78]

Finally, in March 2013, the State Council of the central government issued a new policy on the "Institutional Reform and Functional Transformation Plan," which designated separate categories of social organizations (industry associations and organizations promoting science and technology, charitable contributions, social welfare, and community services) to register directly with Civil Affairs Departments without first obtaining approval from a supervising unit.[79] After more than two decades of local innovation, the central government followed the lead of local governments and finally removed a crucial barrier to the registration and operation of at least certain types of NGOs. Even though the Party had been actively repressing political activists, it was at the same time expanding the space afforded to NGOs. At both the national and local levels, through regulations and laws, there was greater allowance for the social welfare and charitable work of NGOs.

---

[78] "*Hebeisheng hangye xiehui jixu tingjin jingji zhuzhanchang*" (Hebei's Industrial Associations Continue to Play a Role in Economy), Chinanews.com, May 20, 2006, http://www.heb.chinanews.com/news/cjlt/2006-05-20/6934.html, accessed May 12, 2014.

[79] "State Council Circular Regarding Division of Labor in Implementing the State Council Institutional Reform and Functional Transformation Plan," http://www.gov.cn/zwgk/2013-03/28/content_2364821.htm, accessed January 26, 2015.

In China, there is often a notable gap between laws and their implementation, but the general direction of these reforms was to simplify the registration process, thereby letting NGOs organize, register, and operate more easily.

But the draft of a new NGO law threatened to reverse the liberalization of restrictions governing civil society. The Chinese government released an "Overseas NGO Management Law" in spring 2015 that would require international NGOs operating in China to find a government sponsor and register not with the Ministry of Civil Affairs but with the Ministry of Public Security.[80] Both of these provisions—finding a government sponsor and supervision by the public security apparatus—would undermine the progress of recent years and turn routine activities into potentially criminal behavior. This would have a chilling effect on the operations of international NGOs in China. The draft law was written so broadly that it would include any nongovernmental and not-for-profit organizations—such as private universities with operations in China—and their activities, including renting hotel space for academic conferences or conducting executive and professional training programs. As is now the norm, this draft law was posted for public comment; ironically, the period of public comment ended on June 4, the anniversary of the Tiananmen Square crackdown in 1989. At the time of this writing (August 2015), its final form was still not known. But it will be an important signal for how far the Party under Xi Jinping is willing to go in its repression of civil society.

Societal Responses to China's NGOs

In addition to restraints from the state, social organizations in China face resistance from the members of society they hope to serve. In a political environment where the state provides most public goods and services, people are often suspicious of groups that are not connected to the state. Moreover, the Chinese name for NGOs has the connotation of not just *non*governmental (*fei zhengfu* 非政府) but

---

[80] An English translation of the draft law was made available by the China Development Brief: http://chinadevelopmentbrief.cn/articles/cdb-english-translation-of-the-overseas-ngo-management-law-second-draft/, accessed August 3, 2015.

also *anti*-government (*fan zhengfu* 反政府). As noted in chapter 2, almost 65 percent of the respondents in both the 2010 and 2014 surveys believed that large numbers of social organizations with different points of view are a threat to social stability, which adds to their suspicions about the work of NGOs. Most Chinese simply do not trust NGOs: In the 2014 survey, only 38 percent trusted NGOs, ranking below local leaders and staff people and above only outsiders and strangers (see figure 3-2). Trust in officials declines through the political hierarchy: Central officials are trusted more than provincial officials, who in turn are trusted more than local officials, and finally staff people are trusted the least. But NGOs are trusted even less. This puts extra pressure on NGOs: Not only do they face pressure from party and government officials, they do not get much support from society either.

Focus group interviews conducted in 2013 (in Beijing and Wuhan) and 2014 (in Guangzhou and Chongqing) echoed these survey results. Focus group participants showed little confidence that NGOs could have any impact on the government's provision of public goods. Even though many local governments now contract out delivery of some public goods and services, the focus group participants believed that NGOs should not do the work of the government and would need to be supervised by the government in order to be credible (a view not surprisingly shared by many officials in separate focus groups). In the Chongqing focus group, some said that "public goods should be provided by the government because they are 'public,'" and others said

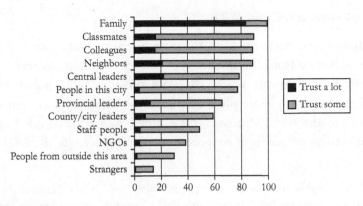

FIGURE 3-2 Levels of Trust.

Source: 2014 Public Goods and Political Support Survey.

that "you cannot expect ordinary people to take responsibility for the government." Only in Guangzhou, which has a relatively open environment for NGOs, did focus group participants believe that NGOs could play a positive role, but only if they were financially independent and not just an extension of the government. This would make NGOs more in line with the liberal expectations of civil society groups, but it would be very difficult in China's current environment. Facing skepticism and even opposition from both state and society, NGOs have been challenged to survive and succeed. Those suspicions may have declined somewhat over time, but NGOs continue to face an uphill battle.

Case Studies

Several brief case studies will illustrate these general patterns. These NGOs have been involved in different types of activities—disaster relief, needs of migrant workers, healthcare, and poverty alleviation, among others—but their experiences have been similar. They have been among the most visible and politically well-connected NGOs in China, but have had to operate in the same constrained environment that less fortunate NGOs confronted. All were hampered by difficulties getting registered as an NGO, and once they were registered, they had difficulties carrying out their programs.

RURAL WOMEN KNOWING ALL

One of the best-known, longest-lasting, and most successful NGOs in China has been Rural Women Knowing All. Despite its record of success and the strong political connections of its leaders, Rural Women Knowing All has faced many of the same problems encountered by less well-known and less well-connected NGOs.

Rural Women Knowing All began as a project connected to the *Rural Women Knowing All* magazine, the first monthly magazine dedicated to providing practical information on farming, animal husbandry, and small business operations to rural women. The magazine began publication in 1993 and was affiliated with the All-China Women's Federation (ACWF), a Party-sponsored mass organization. In 1996, it set up the Migrant Women's Club, the first NGO to target the needs of migrant women. It also held numerous literacy-promotion classes, teaching rural women how to read and write the names of their villages, types of medicine, crops, fertilizers, and even teaching them to speak Mandarin, the official spoken language, which allows them to communicate more effectively when they migrate to other areas of China.[81] It not only holds its own classes, but also trains teachers to continue and expand the programs. It has held community-building activities for rural women, teaching them how to care for children left behind by other migrant women, how to make and market folk art, how to utilize the legal system, and other practical skills.[82] The Migrant Women's Club also provides legal and financial assistance to migrant women who become sick or injured on the job or have their legal rights violated. More recently, it has been involved in the highly visible relief efforts after earthquakes in Sichuan in 2008 and 2013. This included counseling for women who lost children, organizing rebuilding efforts in the villages damaged by the earthquakes, and free training in Beijing for women who chose to migrate.[83]

The leaders of Rural Women Knowing All have substantial political experience. Its founder and current chair of the board of directors, Xie Lihua, was a People's Liberation Army veteran and worked for the ACWF when she founded the magazine that later launched Rural Women Knowing All. The former vice chair of the board and later secretary general of its Rural Women Development Foundation, Wu Zhiping, had previously served as deputy director of propaganda in Hubei's Suizhou city. A co-founder of the Practical Skill Training Center, Wu Qing, is the daughter of influential writer Bingxin (the pen name of Xie Wanying) and had previously served as a delegate in the Beijing Municipal People's Congress.

These political connections and past work experiences proved to be invaluable to its work. It maintained its reputation through personal ties and extensive public relations efforts. Rather than take on controversial or confrontational issues, it cooperated with state agencies in

[81] "*Nongcun funu saomang ji fazhan xiangmu guangkuang*" (Rural Women Literacy and Development Campaign), Rural Women, July 19, 2013, http://www.nongjianv.org/plus/view.php?aid=52, accessed January 27, 2015.

[82] Ibid.

[83] Guo Hong, "*Nongcun funu huzhu fazhan: Jiulongzhen nongjianu xiangmu*" (Rural Women Mutual Help: Rural Women Project at the Town of Jiulong), Ngocn.net, http://zt.ngocn.net/512-2013/7.htm, accessed January 27, 2015.

many of its programs. For example, when the Practical Skills Training Center started a scholarship program to provide vocational training and job placement in cities, it partnered with local branches of the ACWF and local governments in order to reach out to potential students and gain their trust.[84] Xie Lihua has frequently stated that one of the missions of Rural Women Knowing All is to help the government reduce illiteracy, specifically by focusing on a niche that is not well served by the national education system.[85]

Rural Women Knowing All's work has received numerous awards, as well as financial support from Chinese and foreign organizations. It was selected as the "Most Responsible NGO" by News China in 2006, as "Non-Profit of the Year" by the China Charity Festival in 2012, and its work in disaster relief was honored by the China Charity Foundation in 2010. Over the years, it has received grants from UNESCO, the World Bank, the Asia Foundation, Ford Foundation, the European Union, Microsoft, Exxon Mobil, and the embassies of the U.S., Germany, Japan, and Ireland.

Despite this background, it was unable to register with any government agency because there were no laws or regulations pertaining to this type of social organization. In 1998, the magazine created the Practical Skill Training Center for Rural Women, which was able to register as an educational institution with a local branch of the Beijing Bureau of Civil Affairs. Rural Women Knowing All was finally established in 2001 to coordinate the work of the Migrant Women's Club and the Practical Training Center. However, it did not fit any of the categories recognized by the Bureau of Civil Affairs and was unable to register as a social organization. Instead, it had to register as an enterprise with the All-China Federation of Industry and Commerce. Even though it saw itself as an NGO and operated as an NGO, its registration status as an enterprise hampered its operations. For example, NGOs registered as enterprises cannot accept foreign funding, but Rural Women Knowing

[84] Chen Chen, "*Lixing xuanze xiade xietong celue*" (Coordination under Rational Choice), Rural Women, http://old.nongjianv.org/web/project/seed/01(200308)/0106.htm, accessed January 27, 2015.

[85] Yang Tianxiao, "*Xie Lihua—Bianzhuan nongjianu de fuyinshu*" (Xie Lihua—Bringing Hope to Rural Women), Sohu.com, October 16, 2009, http://women.sohu.com/20091016/n267422115.shtml, accessed January 27, 2015.

All had been doing so for years. When it tried again to register with the Beijing Bureau of Civil Affairs, it was informally told the application was denied because of the previous "overseas assistance" it had already received. After many years of failed efforts getting officially registered in Beijing, the organization moved to Guangdong (one of the local governments that was authorized to reform its management of NGOs) and re-registered as the Rural Women Development Foundation Guangdong in 2013.

THE FUPING DEVELOPMENT INSTITUTE

The Fuping Development Institute (hereafter Fuping) describes itself as a "not-for-profit organization that pays attention to low-income groups, cultivates and supports successful social enterprises and social entrepreneurs, with the goals of improving poor people's welfare, increasing their access to equal opportunities, and promoting equitable social development."[86] It was founded in 2002 by two prominent economists: Mao Yushi, a liberal economist who cofounded the Unirule Institute of Economics after he retired from the Chinese Academy of Social Sciences, and Tang Min, a former student of Mao's and chief economist at the Asian Development Bank. It is formally registered as a "private non-enterprise unit" with the Civil Affairs Bureau in Beijing's Dongcheng district.

Some of Fuping's most successful programs have been in the area of micro-finance, which provides small loans to people to start or expand a business. Although Chinese law prohibits unauthorized micro-finance programs, Fuping found local governments willing to cooperate with its small-scale development projects. Nevertheless, because Fuping's micro-finance projects were not formally and legally recognized, they existed in a gray area and were vulnerable to government crackdowns. To avoid this possibility, Mao and Fuping created "small-sum loan companies" with capital he raised through his personal connections. These are small-scale yet ambitious programs. According to Shen Dongshu, president of Fuping and chairman of the Yongji Fuping Small-Sum Loan Company (the first of several such companies set up by Fuping),

---

[86] "*Fuping shi shei*" (Who Is Fuping), Fuping Development Institute, http://www.fdi.ngo.cn/fupingshishei, accessed January 27, 2015.

"we are more than a loan company—we are a development organization" promoting rural development through micro-finance.[87]

In addition to these programs in rural areas, it also runs training programs for migrant workers in urban areas and directly negotiates salaries with employers. Fuping takes credit for making one day off per week a contractual obligation.[88] It also set up an emergency relief fund for domestic workers who needed but could not afford medical care. In 2011, Fuping opened a kindergarten for the children of migrant workers in Beijing.[89] Each of these projects is related to Fuping's focus on poverty alleviation and social justice.

Like most other Chinese NGOs, Fuping does not see its role as confronting the state, but rather complementing it. Fuping's goals converge with the task of many local governments to alleviate poverty, which means that Fuping's work dovetails with local governments' need for better performance in poverty relief. Many of its programs benefit people from remote and mountainous areas not served by government programs. Because NGOs like Fuping aid the government in various ways, its leaders have also indicated they would welcome financial support for their work. Mao Yushi said in a 2012 interview that "the government should subsidize some private educational institutions. After all, they have eased some of the government's burden."[90]

Fuping also learned that it needed government support to be successful and overcome societal distrust. When it created its training school, it discovered that it could not recruit students because people did not trust an organization that was not affiliated with the state. Some villagers even suspected that Fuping's recruitment director was

[87] "*Yongji fuping xiao'e daikuan moshi diaocha*" (Yongji Fuping Small Grant Model Survey), Sina.com, January 19, 2010, http://news.sina.com.cn/c/sd/2010-01-19/101719498647.shtml, accessed January 27, 2015.

[88] Jiang Xueqing, "Helping the Poor to Help Themselves," *China Daily*, last modified June 27, 2012, http://europe.chinadaily.com.cn/china/2012-06/27/content_15524731.htm, accessed November 2, 2013.

[89] Thousand Trees Equal Education Partners, "Who We Are? What Do We Do?" Qianqianshu.org, http://www.qianqianshu.org/en/, accessed November 2, 2013.

[90] Xi Muge, "Mao Yushi Talks about Fuping School Phenomenon and Private Education in China," Sina.com, November 1, 2012, http://finance.sina.com.cn/roll/20121101/154913551830.shtml, accessed November 2, 2013.

involved in human trafficking.[91] To solve this problem, Fuping developed a "government-assisted nongovernmental operation" (*minban gongzhu* 民办公助) model of partnership with the poverty-alleviation office and the provincial branch of the ACWF of Anhui province in August 2002. For every migrant worker that Fuping trains, the provincial poverty-alleviation office would subsidize Fuping a tuition fee of 300 yuan, and the women's federation would reimburse the trainee 500 yuan for travel and physical examination.[92] In the following years, Fuping gradually established a recruiting network led by the poverty-alleviation offices of local governments in Anhui, Gansu, Hunan, and Henan provinces.[93]

THE SMILE ANGEL FOUNDATION

The Smile Angel Foundation (hereafter Smile Angel) focuses on corrective surgery for children born with cleft lips or palates and whose families cannot afford the surgery. It was established in 2006 with a one-million-yuan donation from Li Yapeng, a famous actor, and Faye Wong, a popular singer and actress, after their daughter was born with a cleft lip. They took their daughter to California for surgery because they felt China lacked the necessary surgical expertise. Afterward, they established Smile Angel in order to make the surgery available to more children in China. It began by partnering with eight hospitals around the country to minimize the amount of travel required by the children selected for surgery. Recognizing that many of the children needing surgery live in remote and often poverty-stricken areas, Smile Angel sent medical teams to Xinjiang, Tibet, Sichuan, and Hainan in order to perform surgery there. In 2012, it opened the Smile Angel Children's Hospital, China's first privately owned nonprofit hospital. During the

[91] Han Yong, "*Fuping xuexiao: Jingjixuejia yaobang qiongren zhuanqian*" (Fuping Institute: Economists Should Help the Poor Get Rich), Sohu.com, January 4, 2013, http://roll.sohu.com/20130104/n362381736.shtml, accessed November 2, 2013.

[92] Zhao Xiaojian, "*Fuping xuexiao: Yige feiyingli zhuzhi de zhongguoshi shengcun*" (Fuping Institute: a Not-for-Profit Organization's Survival in China), Infzm.com, last modified December 5, 2007, http://www.infzm.com/content/8078, accessed November 2, 2013.

[93] "*Fuping zuo shenme*" (What Does Fuping Do), Fuping Development Institute, http://www.fdi.ngo.cn/zuoshenme/community-anddomestic-services, accessed November 2, 2013.

hospital's first year of operation, it provided corrective surgeries to over 9,000 children.

Smile Angel's sponsoring agency is the Red Cross Society of China. Even after the Red Cross Society's reputation was damaged by the previously described scandal, Smile Angel chose to keep it as the foundation's sponsor. Li Yapeng described this decision in an online forum in 2012: "as a foundation providing assistance in medical treatment, we get more public support remaining in the Red Cross Society. Although we feel our hands are tied sometimes with a sponsoring work unit, the government-connected Red Cross Society lends us its credibility, which is lacking in the general environment for non-profit organizations in Chinese society today."[94] At the same time, Smile Angel took several steps to improve its professionalism and the quality of its operations. It hired professional full-time staff, shifted its fundraising strategy from relying primarily on individual donations to seeking contributions from enterprises and foundations, opened a Hong Kong branch that can operate more independently, hired the United Bank of Switzerland to manage its offshore accounts, and expanded its contacts with the United Nations and international charities.

The decision to open the Smile Angel Children's Hospital was based on making it easier to provide surgery to the children who needed it, but it first had to overcome bureaucratic hurdles. Smile Angel was so successful in bringing attention to the need for corrective surgeries, its original eight partner hospitals did not have the capacity to meet the need. In addition, Li wanted to combine surgery with post-surgical treatments like speech therapy, dental care, and psychological counseling, which the eight hospitals were not able to provide. Li hoped that a single hospital dedicated to the multiple needs of children with cleft lips and palates would prove to be more efficient and ultimately more successful.

In order to sustain its operations, the hospital provides four different types of care: (1) free treatment to at least 600 children each year; (2) expensive medical treatment to other patients who are covered by

[94] "Yanran tianshi jijin Li Yapeng fangtan" (Transcript of Interview with Li Yapeng about Smile Angel Foundation), People.com, June 26, 2012, http://live.people.com.cn/note.php?id=821120625145134_ctdzb_001, accessed January 27, 2015.

medical insurance; (3) low-cost medical care to "members" who donate at least 10,000 yuan to Smile Angel Foundation each year; and (4) routine medical care to the general public at rates comparable to other public hospitals.[95] The hospital also attracts doctors from the U.S. and Hong Kong who donate their time during short visits.[96]

Smile Angel addressed a serious need not identified or met by the government. Children born with cleft lips or palates are often abandoned because their parents cannot afford surgery or they believe that the conditions are not correctable. The government had not made it a priority either. Before 2012, it was not included in the Ministry of Health's Critical Illness Insurance Program. Li's work with Smile Angel has not only increased awareness that these are correctable conditions, but has also encouraged the government to include them on its list of covered health issues.[97]

In order to register the hospital as a nonprofit, it needed the approval of both the Ministry of Civil Affairs and the Beijing Bureau of Health. But a privately run nonprofit hospital was unprecedented in China, and the Chinese bureaucracy has a hard time coping with situations that are unprecedented. Many of the officials Li talked to were unwilling to take a risk on an experiment. They advised him to register as a for-profit hospital, which would be quickly and easily approved. But Li did not want the hospital's reputation damaged by claims that it was making a profit off the needs of the children. Eventually, through the use of his own social network and the support of high-level officials, including a former vice mayor of Beijing, the Smile Angel Children's Hospital was successfully registered as a nonprofit hospital.[98]

[95] Liu Muyan and Li Jia, "*Li Yapeng banyi: Mingxing pobing yigai zhidao*" (Li Yapeng Opened a Hospital: How a Celebrity Facilitates Health Reform), Bundpic.com, September 16, 2013, http://www.bundpic.com/2013/04/21683. shtml, accessed January 27, 2015.

[96] Hou Xuezhu and Huang Yingnan, "*Minban feiyingli yiyuan de yici tansuo*" (An Experiment by a Private Not-for-Profit Hospital), Jinghua.cn, July 2, 2012, http://news.xinhuanet.com/ent/2012-07/02/c_123355493.htm, accessed January 27, 2015.

[97] Yuan Ningchen and An Bixian, "*Li Yapeng: Yige gongyi xianfeng tanluzhe*" (Li Yapeng: a Pioneer in Charities), QQ.com, June 5, 2013, http://gongyi.qq.com/a/20130605/008354.htm, accessed January 27, 2015.

[98] Liu and Li, "Li Yapeng Opened a Hospital."

THE ONE FOUNDATION

The One Foundation was created in April 2007 by the movie star Jet Li, son of the late Bruce Lee. From its beginning, the One Foundation has been committed to disaster relief, children's welfare, and supporting other philanthropic organizations. Given Jet Li's fame and visibility, as well as his continued commitment to the foundation's work, it is one of the most recognized and trusted NGOs in China.

Li's goal was to make it a vehicle for fundraising and public participation in charitable activities. One of its key slogans—"1 person + 1 dollar + 1 month = 1 big family"—provided the name of the One Foundation and also alluded to its purposes: getting people committed to donating on a regular basis, even if only on a small scale. Another of its slogans—"Doing What I Can, Charity by All" (*jin wo suoneng, renren gongyi* 尽我所能，人人公益)—stated its goal of making philanthropy the work of individual members of society, not just the government, firms, and foundations.[99] The One Foundation also provides psychological counseling for victims of earthquakes and other natural disasters, builds playgrounds for children, and creates service networks for families with children with disabilities and special education needs.

At the time of its founding, the foundation's sponsoring agency was the Red Cross Society of China, giving Li's foundation the long and awkward formal title of the Red Cross Society of China Jet Li One Foundation Project. The One Foundation was not financially independent of the Red Cross Society and had to do its public fundraising in the name of the Red Cross Society. In order to raise money on its own, Li created the Jet Li One Foundation Charity Fund in Shanghai, one of the cities authorized by the central government to experiment in civil society management. Because the Shanghai branch was registered as an equity fund and not a fundraising charity, it continued to have difficulties receiving donations. Li tried but failed to reregister the One Foundation as an independent fundraising foundation.

Frustrated by his inability to carry out the foundation's goals, Li complained in a CCTV interview that "the Foundation is like a baby that

---

[99] "*Yijijin zhuanxing, shouzhong quxin yu gongzhong*" (The One Foundation Prioritizes Public Trust in Transformation), Ngocn.net, August 31, 2011, http://www.ngocn.net/home/news/article/id/80562, accessed January 27, 2015.

has been born but could not get an identification card" and as a result might have to shut down. The head of the Shenzhen Civil Affairs Bureau then contacted Li and invited him to register the One Foundation with his bureau and without the need for a sponsoring agency. As noted above, Shenzhen was one of the cities authorized by the Ministry of Civil Affairs to reform its management of civil society. The Shenzhen One Foundation was formally registered as a public fundraising foundation with an independent legal status in December 2010.

Five Chinese foundations contributed 10 million yuan apiece in startup capital: Shanghai Jet Li One Foundation Charity Fund, Lao Niu Foundation, Tencent Charitable Foundation, Vantone Foundation for Public Welfare, and Vanke Foundation for Public Welfare. These are the charitable arms of some of China's largest Internet, real estate, and commercial giants. In order to provide a steady stream of donations and to realize the goal of making it easy for individuals to donate regularly, the Shenzhen One Foundation developed an innovative program in cooperation with the China Merchants Bank (also registered in Shenzhen). Whenever someone signs up for a One Foundation Charity Credit Card, the foundation receives a donation and a smaller donation every time they charge at least 20 yuan. Cardholders are also registered as volunteers for the community service projects sponsored by the bank, and are notified when events are planned.[100] The One Foundation also partnered with Alipay, a subsidiary of Alibaba and the main provider of electronic payments in China (similar to Paypal in the U.S.). They produced an application that allows people to make online donations via their Alipay accounts, including automatic monthly donations.

Registering in Shenzhen also allowed the One Foundation to distance itself from the Red Cross Society after its reputation was tarnished by the 2011 scandal. As noted earlier, in the immediate aftermath of the 2013 earthquake in Sichuan, the One Foundation received donations worth more than 100 times what the Red Cross received.[101]

---

[100] "*Yijijinka aixin gongneng*" (Functions of the One Foundation Charity Card), China Merchant Bank, http://market.cmbchina.com/ccard/one/html/function. html; "*Juankuan xinxi*" (donation information), One Foundation, http://one-foundation.cn/juanzengshuju/index.html, accessed January 27, 2015.

[101] Zhu, "China Earthquake," *Financial Times*, April 22, 2013.

The One Foundation is the exception that proves the rule: Because its founder Jet Li is so famous, he has been able to get prominent individuals, companies, and foundations to support it. Recognizing that other NGOs lacked the One Foundation's access to funding, beginning in 2008, it selected up to ten "model" Chinese NGOs every year in the fields of environmental protection, education, poverty relief, public health, and disaster relief and gave each of them a development fund of one million yuan. Recipients have included Rural Women Knowing All and the Fuping Development Institute. According to Yang Peng, secretary general and board member of the foundation, "the One Foundation is an open platform for public good and the 'ministry of finance' of many NGOs, because it funds many organizations' projects." These partnerships with NGOs across the country have enabled it to quickly respond to groups in need.[102]

In order to remain active, Jet Li and his staff have been careful not to overstep or compete with the government. Li has stated that the government should always take the leading role in disaster relief efforts, while the work of NGOs like the One Foundation should be complementary.[103] "If NGOs and individuals 'compete' with the government to do charity, the outcome might be 'too much care, too little result.' What is needed is the synergy between all parties."[104] Following the 2013 earthquake in Sichuan, while the government was focused on search-and-rescue operations, the One Foundation delivered supplies where needed. According to Li, "when the government is saving lives, shouldn't NGOs go and collect trash to prevent pollution? Shouldn't NGOs try to build makeshift toilets for the affected people?"[105] After

---

[102] Lin Yi and Wu Jing, "*Yijijin zhuanyehua zhilu*" (Professionalization of the One Foundation), May 2013, http://www.gemag.com.cn/14/32267_1.html, accessed January 27, 2015.

[103] Tang Xunfang, "*Li Lianjie: Yijijin zai zhuangda ye wufa tidai hongshizihui*" (Jet Li Said the One Foundation Would Never Be Able to Replace the Red Cross), Ifeng.com, May 9, 2013, http://news.ifeng.com/mainland/detail_2013_05/09/25089454_0.shtml, accessed January 27, 2015.

[104] Lin and Wu, "Professionalization of the One Foundation" (full cite in fn. 102).

[105] Dong Yang and Zhang Yao, "*Zuo gongyi qishi shizai bangzhu ziji*," (Doing Public Welfare Is in Fact Helping Ourselves) People.com.cn, May 12, 2013, http://society.people.com.cn/n/2013/0512/c41260-21449550.html, accessed January 27, 2015.

the initial 72-hour emergency period, it shifted its efforts toward mid- and long-term projects, the "blind spots" that the government was not addressing, such as building children's playgrounds and providing psychological counseling.[106]

Summary

As seen in the brief overview and case studies above, the relationship between the state and China's growing civil society is characterized by bureaucratic rigidity, local flexibility, and popular ingenuity. Only groups that fit into predefined categories have been able to register easily, and even then bureaucrats have found reasons to deny registration applications. At the same time, some local leaders have promoted the formation and operation of NGOs, provided that their work is in line with the Party's priorities. NGO leaders have shown great creativity in how they organize and operate: Some are registered, some are not; some are registered as private enterprises because they could not register as social organizations; some have sought close cooperation with government agencies, others have sought greater autonomy. These experiences and strategies reflect the diversity of China's civil society organizations and the changing political and social environments in which they operate.

Party Building in China's Private Sector and Civil Society

The Party's approach to civil society has been very similar to the way it dealt with the private economy.[107] Both the rise of civil society and the emergence of a private sector are thought to pose a challenge to authoritarian regimes, and the Party has been determined not to be an example of social and economic change leading to political change. While it first tried to limit the scope of both civil society and the private sector, NGOs and private firms found creative ways around those restrictions.

---

[106] Xiang Jiaming and Zhou Xifeng, "*Lushan zhenzai zhongde minjian cishan yu guanban cishan*" (Private and Public Charities in the Lushan Disaster Relief), last modified April 25, 2013, http://focus.news.163.com/13/0425/09/8TA1J1EVo0011SM9.html, accessed October 11, 2014.

[107] The following discussion on party building in the private sector is based on my previous studies: *Red Capitalists in China* and *Wealth into Power*.

Over time, the Party shifted its strategy from controlling to managing and monitoring and even promoting them. It relied on its traditional practices of party building to integrate itself with NGOs and private firms, but adapted those practices to accommodate the changing social and economic environment. Whether those practices will be sufficient to accommodate social and economic change will be a crucial element in whether the Party's strategy for survival will succeed.

In many ways, the experiences of China's NGOs are similar to those of private enterprises. As private firms and civil society organizations began to form, they faced the immediate challenge of how to avoid being shut down by the state. In both cases, they developed creative ways to remain in operation. Private firms were illegal at the beginning of the reform era, having been eliminated in the 1950s. The state did allow individually owned enterprises known as *getihu* (个体户) to open and operate, but it set limits on their size: They could hire no more than seven workers outside their families. These were small-scale firms doing simple assembly work, manufacturing, repairs, and food service. But these firms quickly grew beyond their legal limits. Some therefore registered as collective enterprises, which are owned and managed by local governments. They were known as "red hat enterprises"; They were for all intents and purposes private firms, but because they were formally registered as collectives, they wore a politically correct red hat. By the late 1980s, private enterprises were allowed to register, making the wearing of red hats less necessary. Similarly, civil society organizations often had to register as firms, non-enterprise units (a category that includes hospitals and schools), or consulting firms, and were willing to do so in order to remain in operation. In both cases, this was a necessary but still risky tactic. Because their registrations did not match their realities, they were subject to being shut down and having their equipment and financial resources confiscated by the state. One key difference: Private firms did not need a sponsor in order to register, and by the mid-2000s, neither did some NGOs.

The Party was ambivalent about both the private economy and civil society. Both were seen as potential threats to the Party's hold on power and sparked heated debate within the Party about how to handle them. Eventually, Party leaders came to recognize that both the private economy and civil society—or at least some parts of it—were beneficial to the Party's desire to remain in power. The private sector provided jobs, growth, and increased tax revenue, and some civil society groups were helping by providing social welfare and monitoring local officials. Rather than see them as inherent enemies, the Party came to view them as potential allies, though it remained watchful for actions and trends that would indicate a challenge to its supremacy.

In order to keep a watchful eye on the private sector and civil society, the CCP relied on different aspects of Party-building. First, it created Party organizations in as many private firms and NGOs as possible. Any unit that had three or more Party members was expected to have its own Party organization, and if it had fewer than three, it should create a joint branch with other firms or NGOs. As the numbers of firms and NGOs began to proliferate, the Party recognized that it had a very weak presence in the most dynamic sectors. It therefore began campaigns to build Party organizations, giving it a greater capacity to monitor and manage private firms and NGOs. By its own accounts, it was successful in doing so: At the end of 2013, it had established Party organizations in 58.4 percent of all private firms and 42 percent of all social organizations.[108] Many of the others were too small to have their own Party organizations.

Traditionally, these kinds of Party organizations were meant to be the eyes and ears of the CCP, monitoring the activities of Party members and providing political and ideological training. In the reform era, Party organizations in the private economy and civil society were less political and more paternalistic. Part of the party building mission was helping these new economic and social organizations become successful. Instead of organizing political study, Party cells in firms and NGOs emphasized management skills, human resource development, and marketing strategies. The CCP has a nationwide network of Party schools that primarily train Party and government officials, but now also offer practical skills-based classes for private entrepreneurs, such as marketing, accounting, and human resources. Similarly, the Party has tried to improve the work of NGOs. In Shanghai, the local Party

---

[108] "CPC Membership Records Slower Growth," *Xinhua*, June 30, 2014, http://www.china.org.cn/china/2014-06/30/content_32814079.htm, accessed February 25, 2015.

has encouraged NGOs to hire professional staff, manage their finances more efficiently, and communicate with the public more effectively.[109] This paternalistic approach is not without merit: Because China lacked a private sector and civil society for most of the Maoist era and into the beginning of the reform era, no one had the opportunity to work in the family business or intern with an existing NGO. They did not develop the skills and experiences that would launch their careers. As a consequence, many of the early private firms and NGOs were small in scale, limited in their resources, and short-lived. The Party's paternalistic practice of party building was meant, at least in part, to stem this waste of scarce resources. This is certainly ironic, since the Party's efforts to constrain and control the private economy and civil society were also partially to blame for their inability to thrive, but as the Party came to recognize their importance, it also became more willing to cooperate with them.

The response of economic and social entrepreneurs to the Party is also similar. Some prefer to avoid the Party altogether because they do not want the Party to scrutinize their operations or squeeze them for bribes.[110] But most recognize that, in order to be successful in China, they need to be tied to the state in some way. At a personal level, this means regular formal and informal interactions with local Party and government officials in order to build rapport and mutual trust. This often spills over from building connections to outright corruption.[111] At the institutional level, this means hiring people who previously worked for the Party or government, or are friends and family of local officials. It is common for private firms and NGOs to hire former officials or appoint them to their boards of directors. This can help them navigate the often-murky world of Chinese politics and gives them easier access to influential decision-makers. Some resist having a Party presence in their firms and organizations, but others are willing to allow it because

[109] Patricia M. Thornton, "The New Life of the Party: Party-Building and Social Engineering in Greater Shanghai," *China Journal*, No. 68 (July 2012), pp. 58–78.

[110] Kellee S. Tsai, *Capitalism without Democracy: The Private Sector in Contemporary China* (Ithaca, NY: Cornell University Press, 2007); Hildebrandt, *Social Organizations and the Authoritarian State in China*.

[111] John Osburg, *Anxious Wealth: Money and Morality among China's New Rich* (Palo Alto, CA: Stanford University Press, 2013).

they recognize the benefits. Resisting party building can bring increased scrutiny and pressure, whereas allowing it can create goodwill with local party leaders. Moreover, because party building now emphasizes practical training and professional development, it offers tangible benefits. When the owners of a firm or leaders of an NGO are themselves CCP members, they may even be their own Party secretaries, further ensuring that the Party's presence is to their advantage.

A key difference in the party building strategies with the private sector and civil society concerns recruitment of new members. After initially banning the presence of private entrepreneurs in the Party (after all, communism was meant to overthrow capitalism), the Party changed its policy to actively recruit successful entrepreneurs and even adapted its ideology to legitimize the change. The "Three Represents" slogan, promoted by former CCP General Secretary Jiang Zemin and added to the Party's constitution in 2002, states that the CCP does not just represent the revolutionary classes in Chinese society—the workers, peasants, and soldiers—but also the advanced productive forces (a euphemism for the private sector), advanced culture, and the interests of the vast majority of the Chinese people. This is a very encompassing scope, representing a clear break in the Party's formal policy, but not necessarily in its actual behavior. Local Party officials had been recruiting private entrepreneurs into the Party even when the formal ban was in place. The "Three Represents" slogan brought formal policy in line with informal practice.

In contrast, the Party has not pursued social entrepreneurs as vigorously. It has been willing to work with them and partner with them, but it has not been as interested in co-opting them. It has not recruited them as aggressively or appointed them to official or honorary posts as frequently as private entrepreneurs. There are several reasons for this. First, private entrepreneurs provide material benefits—jobs, growth, taxes—to local officials, but the benefits provided by social entrepreneurs are less immediate, harder to measure, and therefore not as advantageous to local officials. Private entrepreneurs help local officials meet their hard targets, but social entrepreneurs only help to meet soft targets, such as raising literacy, lowering poverty and inequality, and improving the environment. Second, private firms are often much bigger than NGOs, whether in terms of workers, revenue, or scope of operations, and so co-opting them is not only more beneficial but also easier. The larger a firm is, the more likely that the owner is a Party member and the more likely they are to be members of the local people's congress or political consultative conference. NGOs are generally smaller in scale, and identifying which social entrepreneurs should be recruited into the Party or appointed to posts is a more difficult task. The CCP has been eager to build organizational ties with both the private sector and civil society, but it has not been as interested in bringing social entrepreneurs into the Party. Third, social entrepreneurs are less interested in joining the Party. Many of them became socially active because they saw needs being unmet by the state, and this disappointment affects their willingness to join the Party.

The CCP has relied on its tradition of party building to build ties with the private sector and civil society. This is the Party's tried-and-true method for monitoring key sectors of the economy and society. Rather than develop a new approach, it continues to draw upon Party traditions to address new situations. While this traditional approach may seem antiquated, the CCP has also adapted some of its party building practices to China's modernizing and diversifying environment. Party-building today is less about ideological indoctrination and more about practical issues of management and branding. In that sense, party building is more paternalistic than political, but it is still an effective tool for integrating the Party with economic and social organizations.

Not all of its party building activities are so high-minded. In recent years, the Party has also sponsored dances, sport and game competitions, and even speed dating to meet the needs of its members.[112] While the individual needs may be quite real, for the Party to engage in these activities seems to trivialize its organizational mission and in turn diminish its image. But they also reflect its paternalistic approach to party building in recent years. Whether hiring new employees or finding a mate, the CCP is serving as a matchmaker.

At the local level, variation in the Party's approach to civil society is related to local variation in private sector development. Whereas Guangdong pursued more liberal policies toward NGOs in keeping with its similarly liberal policies toward economic development, Shanghai took a more statist

---

[112] Patricia M. Thornton, "The Advance of the Party: Transformation or Takeover of Urban Grassroots Society?" *China Quarterly*, No. 213 (March 2013), pp. 1–18.

approach, also consistent with its state-led economic model.[113] More specifically, Shanghai pioneered a *Party*-led approach to managing civil society. The relationship between the Party and some NGOs in Shanghai is so close that Thornton describes them as "PONGOs"—Party-organized nongovernmental organizations. The local Party's management of NGOs involved not just reforms of the registration process, but also innovations in the practice of party building in the many "two new" organizations—new firms and new social organizations, in other words, the growing non-state sectors. It began a campaign to create Party organizations in the NGO sector, including Party cells to organize and monitor the Party members who worked there. By the end of 2008, when just over half of social organizations nationwide had Party cells within them, over 98 percent of Shanghai's eligible social organizations had reportedly accomplished party building goals.[114] This was not just to control their activities; it was also designed to improve their operations. The Shanghai CCP organization offered training to NGO leaders to improve their brand, hire more professional staff, manage their books more effectively, and in general become more effective and efficient in what they do.

Shanghai's approach to Party management of civil society may be a substitute for government oversight.[115] Chinese scholars have debated the Party's capability for managing social organizations.[116] Rather than

---

[113] Yasheng Huang, *Capitalism with Chinese Characteristics: Entrepreneurship and the State* (New York: Cambridge University Press, 2008).

[114] Thornton, "The Advance of the Party," pp. 7–8. The word "eligible" is often used as a fudge factor to increase the reported extent of party building. Factors influencing eligibility include the number of employees and especially the number of Party members among employees. It is usually not reported how many of the enterprises or social organizations meet these standards, making it hard to fully evaluate the extent of party building in these non-state units.

[115] In China's political system, the Party is not part of the government, even though most government officials are Party members. The Party and government often have parallel offices with similar responsibilities (e.g., the Party's Organization Department and the government's Ministry of Personnel both handle the appointment of officials). Most important, the Party always outranks the government; the Party secretary of a city or province outranks the mayor or governor, respectively. The actual division of labor between the Party and government can often be ambiguous.

[116] Thornton, "The Advance of the Party."

the "small government, big society" approach that was influential in the late 1990s when government agencies were downsized, Thornton dubs this approach the "big Party, small government, big society" model, in which the Party moved into activities that are normally handled by government agencies, and therefore required more ambitious party building efforts. Outside of Shanghai, the CCP's party building activities are less prominent. In Beijing, for example, a different relationship exists between the Party and civil society. NGOs have more autonomy, more vitality, and less CCP penetration.[117] This regional variation in the nature of civil society is another factor complicating a simple analysis of civil society in China. Discovering variation within China—not just over time but also across different areas of the country—is important for getting a holistic understanding of political and social trends.

* * *

The Party's relationship with society is still defined by its long-standing traditions of the mass line and party building. Chinese society in the post-Mao period has been changing rapidly, and these Party traditions have had to adapt accordingly. Soliciting ideas "from the masses" is now practiced through new forms of consultation on policy priorities. Providing information "to the masses" is part of the open government initiatives, which provide a modicum of transparency in an often-opaque political system. While these reforms may put restrictions on the discretion of policy-makers, they are legitimized by the Party's mass line, a practice that goes back to the pre-1949 years when the Party was trying to elicit popular support. The failure to abide by the logic of the mass line often results in local protests against government decisions.

Whereas the traditional mass line concept focuses on individual members of society, the Party has adapted the idea to now include civil society groups as well. Both the Chinese state and society have been skeptical of civil society, suspicious of its true intent and wary of its potential threat to stability. The Party still suppresses civil society II groups, such as opposition political parties and autonomous labor

---

[117] Jessica C. Teets: "Let Many Civil Societies Bloom: The Rise of Consultative Authoritarianism in China," *China Quarterly*, No. 213 (March 2013), pp. 19–38.

unions. These are the kinds of groups that are most likely to push for political change in China, and the Party does not tolerate them. But over time, it has become more willing to accommodate more civil society I groups that focus on economic, social, and cultural issues. These kinds of NGOs normally do not seek political change and are therefore overlooked by people looking for signs of civil society in China. But they deserve more attention because they play a growing role in contemporary China. NGOs better understand the needs of society and can be flexible in how they respond to those needs. To the extent that civil society I groups are successful at improving the quality of life of their members and the people they serve and reducing grievances against the state, they can help to stabilize the regime, and not pose an inherent threat to it. Local officials increasingly recognize this, and have been willing to partner with these groups to deliver public goods and services to the people who need them most. At the same time, the CCP has been actively recruiting members of these groups and building Party organizations in them in order to monitor their activities. This too is a long-standing Party tradition.

The emergence of a vigorous and effective civil society is not only beneficial in the present; it can be a valuable resource at a time of regime change. It provides organizations the regime can negotiate with, instead of just confronting an unruly mob. Similarly, it offers organizations within which society can mobilize, rather than rely on unorganized and extremist individuals. But to measure the strength of civil society solely in terms of its ability to create political change misses an essential element of China's civil society: While it faces restraints from both state and society, it is growing, and while it does not seek political change, it nevertheless plays an important if still marginal role in China's economic, social, and cultural development—marginal not because they are insignificant, but because they serve the needs of people on the margins of society that are not being adequately addressed by the state. To the degree that China's civil society is successful in meeting its goals, it may ironically help the Party survive.

At the same time, we have to recognize that these innovations by themselves are unlikely to change the existing political system. Neither the OGI reforms nor the revival of mass line traditions are fundamentally changing state-society relations in China. The crackdown against lawyers, begun under Hu Jintao and accelerated under Xi Jinping, shows the limits of the Party's co-optation strategy and its tolerance of critical voices. Even civil society I groups face obstacles, borne of the CCP's ambivalence toward civil society and the bureaucracy's slow response to social change. Recent efforts by Xi Jinping further constrain NGOs' abilities to meet pressing social needs. The Party may be updating its mass line concept, but it continues to resist being changed by the masses.

4

Serving the People

IN 2011, I PARTICIPATED IN a conference in Beijing on the fate of the CCP. Among the other participants were several scholars who lived and worked outside of China, and a much larger number of Chinese scholars, most of whom worked in the Party and government bureaucracies.[1] During my presentation, I began with the observation that the primary goal of the CCP, like all ruling parties, is to remain in power. This is a standard assumption in political science, one that would be noncontroversial if made at most any gathering of American scholars. But one of the Chinese participants at this conference strenuously objected to this statement. From his perspective, it showed how little foreign so-called experts on the CCP actually knew about the Party. The CCP's primary goal was *not* to remain in power, he assured me, but to serve the people. I should have known better.

"Serve the people" is the Party's official slogan, coined by Chairman Mao during the Chinese civil war, and it is still emblazoned on the entrance to Zhongnanhai, the Party and government compound in downtown Beijing. More importantly, serving the people has become part of the Party's survival strategy: By providing more public goods and governing better, the Party hopes to increase its popular support. You could argue that the Party can only serve the people if it remains

---

[1] Papers presented at this conference by David Shambaugh, Cheng Li, Yongnian Zheng, Kjeld-Erik Brodsgaard, Kerry Brown, and myself were published in a special issue of *China: An International Journal*, Vol. 10, No. 2 (August 2012).

in power. In that sense, staying in power is the precondition for serving the people. But in another sense, the opposite is also true: Serving the people is a prerequisite for the Party to remain in power. Providing more and better public goods—such as healthcare, education, and other social welfare policies—benefits the public well-being and in a very literal way serves the people. For the past decade or so, the Party has been committed to governing better, and one dimension of this is providing public goods. The expectation is that improved governance will create public satisfaction with the work of the government, which in turn will help legitimize the regime. In other words, improved public goods provision is part of the Party's strategy for survival.

In the absence of democratic institutions to monitor, reward, and punish their performance, authoritarian politicians are normally expected to seek their self-interest through corruption and rewards to cronies, rather than providing for the public welfare.[2] However, the Chinese state has actively promoted improved governance in recent years, with greater attention to quality-of-life issues to balance the primary focus on sustaining rapid economic growth. In doing so, the Party has opened itself to the "Tocquevillian paradox": The most dangerous time for autocrats is not when things are at their worst, but when they are starting to get better. When things are at their worst, people are focused on basic material interests and survival. But when things begin to improve, their expectations begin to rise even faster. Rather than give their leaders credit for improving their lot, they grow disgruntled because the regime cannot meet their new expectations. China's leaders are well aware of this paradox. Wang Qishan, a

[2] Bruce Bueno de Mesquita, Alastair Smith, Randolph M. Siverson, and James Morrow, *The Logic of Political Survival* (Cambridge, MA: MIT Press, 2003). Numerous other studies have also found that democracies spend more on public goods and social welfare than autocracies; see, e.g., Adam Przeworski, Michael E. Alvarez, Jose Antonio Cheibub, Fernando Limongi, *Democracy and Development: Political Institutions and Well-Being in the World, 1950-1990* (New York: Cambridge University Press, 2000), Amartya Sen, *Resources, Values, and Development* (Oxford, UK: Blackwell, 2004); Stephan Haggard and Robert R. Kaufman, *Development, Democracy, and Welfare States: Latin America, East Asia, and Eastern Europe* (Princeton, NJ: Princeton University Press, 2008), and John Gerring, Strom C. Thacker, and Rodrigo Alfaro, "Democracy and Human Development," *Journal of Politics*, Vol. 74, No. 1 (January 2012), pp. 1–17.

member of the Politburo's Standing Committee and head of the Central Discipline Inspection Commission (the Party's agency for investigating corruption), has studied Alexis de Tocqueville's analysis of the French Revolution and has urged other top officials to heed Tocqueville's warning.[3] The provision of public goods has been improving in China, but the Party may also fall victim to the "revolution of rising expectations."

This chapter analyzes the Party's use of public goods provision as part of its survival strategy and evaluates the results to date. Two themes will be prominent: First, there is tremendous variation in the provision of public goods in urban China, with dramatic changes over time and substantial differences across China's cities at present; second, the public gives a mixed evaluation to their local governments' provision of public goods, recognizing that the government is doing more but remaining disgruntled with what they receive. Special emphasis is given to healthcare and education, two of the most important types of public goods often used in international comparisons of human development. But first, it helps to put China's experience in perspective: How does its spending on public goods compare with other countries?

I. Putting China into Perspective

In many ways, the Party's record on providing public goods to its people is quite mixed. As will be shown later, there are huge discrepancies in spending on education, healthcare, and other types of public goods. There are disparities between cities and the countryside, between cities of different levels of economic development, and between permanent residents and migrants in cities. In addition, the Party's commitment to providing public goods has varied over time. But these patterns are not unique to China; they play out in many countries around the world. If we compare public goods in China to most Western countries, China's record looks poor. But if we compare it to countries at its own level of development, China looks better.

---

[3] William Wan, "Secretive Agency Leads Most Intense Anti-Corruption Effort in Modern Chinese History," *Washington Post*, July 2, 2014, https://www. washingtonpost.com/world/asia_pacific/secretive-agency-leads-most-intense-anti-corruption-effort-in-modern-chinese-history/2014/07/02/48aff932-cf68-11e3-937f-d3026234b51c_story.html, accessed August 30, 2015.

One key measure of a country's commitment to governance is the amount the government spends on healthcare, education, and other public goods relative to its GDP. This shows how much governments spend based on the size of the economy: The larger the economy, the more resources there are for the government to tap into to spend on public goods. When China is compared to other large economies, its commitment to public goods provision seems lacking. For example, governments in OECD countries spent on average 7.6 percent of their GDP on healthcare in 2013, whereas China's government spent only 3.1 percent. Government spending on education shows a similar gap: In 2011, OECD countries spent 5.2 percent of GDP compared to just 4.3 percent for China.[4] Critics of China's public goods provision allege that China should be spending much more on public goods, given that it is now the second-largest economy in the world.

Such comparisons can be misleading, however. OECD countries are all democracies, and democracies tend to provide more public goods to their citizens than authoritarian regimes do. The OECD countries are also the most urban, industrialized, and modern countries in the world, whereas China is in many ways still a developing country. China may have the second-largest economy in aggregate terms, but that is mostly a result of having the world's largest population. In per capita terms, China's economy ranked only 89th in 2014, just below the Dominican Republic and just above Grenada. This puts a different perspective on China's relative level of development: Although the total size of its economy puts it near the top of the list, its per capita GDP ($13,217 in 2014) puts China in the middle of the pack, in the company of countries with whom China is not often compared.[5] If we compare the Chinese government's public goods provision with other upper-middle-income countries, its performance is closer to the average (see table 4-1).[6] According to World Bank figures,

[4] Spending data come from the World Bank's World Development Indicators, except China's spending on education, which comes from China Data Online.

[5] The ranking is from the International Monetary Fund, using Purchasing Power Parity values, which correct for differences in cost of living. Using nominal values of per capita GDP, China ranks 79th, below Bulgaria and above Botswana, which are again not countries with which China is typically compared.

[6] The World Bank has four categories of countries based on per capita gross national income: low (less than $1,035 per capita GDP), lower middle ($1,036–$4,085), upper middle ($4,086–$12,615), and high (over $12,615).

TABLE 4-1 Comparing Spending on Education and Healthcare in China and other Countries

	Spending on education			Spending on healthcare		
	% of GDP, 2012 or most recent year	% of GDP, 2002–2012 growth	% of total government spending, 2012 or most recent year	% of GDP, 2013	% of GDP, 2003–2013 growth	% of total government spending, 2012 or most recent year
China	4.3	47.6	17.7	3.1	76.9	12.5
Low-income countries	4.1	27.1	15.9	2.6	29.0	12.1 (2010)
Lower-middle-income countries	4.4 (2010)	37.4	17.5 (2010)	1.6	14.7	6.6
Upper-middle-income countries	4.5 (2011)	8.3	13.9 (2011)	3.5	35.3	9.7 (2004)
High-income (OECD) countries	5.2 (2011)	2.1	12.1 (2011)	7.6	16.3	17.5

Sources: World Bank, World Development Indicators; data on education for China comes from China Data Online.

governments in upper-middle-income countries spent 4.5 percent of GDP on education, compared to China's 4.3 percent, but the ten-year rate of increase was almost six times faster in China (47.6 percent in China and 8.3 percent in upper-middle-income countries). Similarly, governments in upper-middle-income countries spent 3.5 percent of GDP on healthcare, above China's 3.1 percent. However, between 2003 and 2013, this figure grew more than twice as fast in China (76.9 percent compared to 35.3 percent in upper-middle-income countries). Considering that China's GDP was growing by more than 10 percent during most of these years, that is a dramatic increase. Even local officials in China are aware that public goods spending lags behind global norms. In a focus group interview, officials in Chongqing noted—without prompting—that China spent less on education and healthcare as a percentage of GDP than other countries, and therefore needed to invest more.

Another indicator of a government's commitment to public goods is how much it spends on them relative to total government spending.

This measures the government's commitment to specific public goods relative to other priorities in spending. The Chinese government spent more of its total expenditures on education than upper-middle- and even high-income countries. Comparisons of healthcare spending are a bit imprecise because the most recent year of data varies from 2004 to 2012. The most recent year available for upper-middle-income countries is 2004, when they spent 9.7 percent of their total budgets on healthcare; in that same year, China spent 10.1 percent. In 2012, the Chinese government spent 12.5 percent of its total budget on healthcare; in that year, lower-middle-income countries spent 6.6 percent, about half as much. Although these comparisons are not ideal because they cover different groups of countries in different years, China's performance looks good in comparison to other countries at similar levels of development.

A third indicator of a government's commitment to healthcare is how much the government spends compared to total spending on healthcare (the rest is spent by individuals and firms). In China, government spending accounted for 55.8 percent of total healthcare expenditures in 2013, comparable to upper-middle-income countries (56 percent). China's rate of increase between 2001 and 2011 (54 percent) was almost three times faster than other upper-middle-income countries (18.7 percent). Again, the Chinese government's spending on healthcare was typical of countries at its level of development, and its rate of improvement was much faster.

Government spending is one way of measuring public goods provision. Another way is to look at results of that spending. Governments can spend a lot on education and healthcare, but are their people better educated and healthier as a result? If we look at literacy and life expectancy (measures of education and healthcare, respectively), we find China is slightly above upper-middle-income countries (see table 4-2). Although China still has far to go in both its education and healthcare systems, as is described in more detail later in this chapter, it compares quite favorably to other countries at a similar level of development.

In short, while China's provision of public goods is not on par with OECD countries, it is quite comparable to countries at a similar level of development, and its rate of improvement on a variety of indicators is considerably better.

TABLE 4-2 Human Development Indicators,
China and the World

	GDP per cap (2014, PPP, current US$)	Life expectancy (2013)	Adult literacy (2010)
Low income	1,624	59.3	60.8
Lower middle income	6,101	66.6	70.5
Upper middle income	14,331	74.3	93.9
China	**13,217**	**75.4**	**95.1**
High income (OECD)	38,817	80.0	n.a.

Sources: World Bank, World Development Indicators.

II. Regional Disparities in Public Goods Spending within China

These cross-national comparisons pale in comparison to variations within China. In the 50 cities included in the Public Goods and Political Support Survey, government spending on education ranged from a low of 721 RMB per capita to a high of 4,960 RMB. Education spending as a share of local GDP also varied enormously, from a low of 0.7 percent to a high of 7.2 percent. As a share of government spending, education ranged from 10.2 percent to 35.7 percent. Overall local government expenditures are highly correlated with spending on education (.96), and range from 2,936 to 29,973 RMB per capita. These figures point to a basic fact about public goods provision in China: What a person receives largely depends on where they live. The difference between people who live in cities and those who live in the countryside has long been noted. But even among urbanites, the amount of public goods they receive depends on the specific city in which they live.

Although China's cities vary tremendously in their levels of government spending on overall expenditures and education in particular, there is consistency on a different dimension: Cities that spend a lot on education tend to spend a lot on other types of public goods, such as healthcare. The same holds true for the broad category of public security, which includes not only law and order, but also such things as public transportation, disease control, and building security. Spending on these three types of public goods is very highly correlated: Cities that spend relatively high amounts on one tend to spend high amounts on all of them. Or at least they did as of 2007. After that year, city-level spending on a wide range of categories stopped being reported. Spending on education is now the only type of public good available at the city level. Nonmonetary measures of public goods provision also show large differences, although not as extreme as reported spending. Student-teacher ratios range from 11.8 to 21.4. In the area of healthcare, the number of doctors per 1,000 people ranges from 1 to 10.1, and the number of hospital beds per 1,000 ranges from 2.1 to 13.4.

This presents a puzzle: Why do China's cities vary so much in the public goods they provide to their people? One main reason for this huge variation is similar to the cross-national comparisons: More prosperous cities tend to provide more public goods. The logic here is straightforward: The more prosperous a city (or a country) is, the more resources there are to pay for public goods.

However, just having a prosperous local economy is not sufficient to guarantee greater spending on public goods; local governments must also be able to tap into the economic resources in their communities. A second and more important explanation for the variation in public goods provision is therefore what political scientists call "state capacity," in this case, the ability to extract resources, primarily in the form of taxes. The higher the local government's state capacity (measured by the ratio of government revenue to local GDP), the more able it is to provide public goods. State capacity varies widely in China: Among the 50 cities in the Public Goods and Political Support Surveys, it ranged from a low of 2.5 percent to a high of 18.6 percent, with an average of 9.4 percent. It is important to note that state capacity is not simply a result of prosperity. The two have a relatively low level of correlation (.36), the result being that some of the cities with the highest state capacity did not have high per capita GDP, and some prosperous cities did not have high state capacity.

These two factors alone—prosperity and state capacity—explain most of the variation in public goods provision in urban China. In other words, if you know a city's per capita GDP and its ability to extract resources from the local economy, you can make a fairly accurate estimate of how much the government spends on public goods.

And if you know how much it spends on one type of public good, you have a good sense of how much it spends on some others. State capacity not only provides resources for public goods spending, it also supports the repressive aspect of the Party's survival strategy: Cities that spend more on education and healthcare also spend more on public security.

III. Variation Over Time

China's commitment to public goods provision not only varies in different parts of the country, it has also varied considerably over time. One thing has remained constant, however: What people receive in terms of public goods depends on where they live and where they work.

During the Maoist era, men and women who worked for state-owned enterprises (SOEs) became the aristocracy of Chinese labor, enjoying good-paying jobs, lifetime job security, and generous benefits, including housing, healthcare, education, various other subsidies and welfare benefits for themselves and their families, pensions when they retired, and the right to pass on their jobs to their children. These benefits were commonly referred to as the "iron rice bowl" because they met people's daily needs and could not be broken. Not all of China's workers were so fortunate. Those who had temporary or part-time contracts were not entitled to the same pay and benefits as permanent, full-time workers. Even those with full-time jobs in collective enterprises had lower wages and fewer benefits than SOE workers.[7]

Those who lived in the countryside were further disadvantaged. Agricultural jobs paid less than industrial jobs, and opportunities for earning extra income on the side were intermittent due to frequent policy changes. Rural workers occasionally got temporary jobs in urban factories, but these were short term and paid substantially less than full-time positions, although more than they earned from farming. Education was provided in schools that were often distant, poorly funded, and

[7] Andrew G. Walder, *Communist Neo-Traditionalism: Work and Authority in Chinese Industry* (Berkeley, CA: University of California Press, 1986), pp. 39–54; Elizabeth J. Perry, "Labor Divided: Sources of State Formation in Modern China," in Joel Migdal, Atul Kohli, and Vivienne Shue, eds., *State Power and Social Forces: Domination and Transformation in the Third World* (New York: Cambridge University Press, 1994).

staffed with unqualified teachers. Healthcare was largely in the hands of "barefoot doctors," paramedics who received minimal training in health and sanitation. And because the household registration system (*hukou*) determined where people could live, where they could work, and what public goods they had access to, mobility was sharply circumscribed.[8] Although many in the countryside desired to transfer their *hukou* from rural to urban status, that possibility was exceedingly rare.[9] Despite these discrepancies, China experienced marked progress in human development. Between 1950 (the year after the CCP took power) and 1982 (early in the post-Mao era), life expectancy rose from 35 to 67.5 years, and adult literacy rose from around 20 percent to 65.5 percent.[10]

With the beginning of the economic reforms in the late 1970s, the Chinese state searched for ways to boost economic growth and reduce its welfare commitments. China thus was part of a global trend in the 1980s and 1990s, when many governments sharply reduced their commitment to welfare spending for the sake of economic growth.[11] The state's commitment to healthcare, pensions, and a host of other public goods (but not education) decreased in order to devote more resources to promoting economic growth.

China's SOEs were a perpetual drain on the state's finances, requiring the state to heavily subsidize their operations. Most of them operated at a loss. Not only did they have obsolete technology, excess capacity, and the inefficiencies that often accompany monopolies, they were also responsible for paying high wages (at least compared to agriculture,

[8] William L. Parish and Martin King Whyte, *Village and Family in Contemporary China* (Chicago: University of Chicago Press, 1977); Anita Chan, Richard Madsen, and Jonathan Unger, *Chen Village: Revolution to Globalization*, third edition (Berkeley, CA: University of California Press, 2009).

[9] The alternative—switching from urban to rural *hukou*—was much easier, but few were willing to trade the economic and social opportunities that came with urban registration.

[10] Numbers for 1950 come from Hu Angang, *China in 2020: A New Type of Superpower* (Washington, DC: Brookings Institution, 2011); for 1982, from the World Bank's *World Development Indicators*, http://databank.worldbank.org/data/home.aspx, accessed July 16, 2013.

[11] Paul Pierson, "The New Politics of the Welfare State," *World Politics*, Vol. 48, No. 2 (January 1996), pp. 143–179.

collective enterprises, and the emerging private sector) and benefits to their workers. The Chinese government tried a number of reforms to improve the performance of SOEs, including new incentives for managers, shifting the burden of benefits and pensions from the enterprises to the local governments, making SOEs responsible for their own profits and losses, and eventually allowing them to lay off workers, but none of these initiatives made SOEs profitable. Beginning in the mid-1990s, the Party adopted the slogan of "grasp the large, release the small"— the state would maintain ownership and management control over the largest SOEs, especially those in strategic industries like energy, telecommunications, and aviation, but allow smaller firms to be sold off, merged with other firms, or even closed.[12] More than 30 million SOE workers lost their jobs and the benefits that came with them.[13] Many were unable to find new jobs in the private sector because of age and lack of skills, and many found that the pensions they were promised were cut or eliminated altogether.[14]

It helps to put this change into perspective. In the U.S., there are frequent complaints that China is stealing American jobs. Between 1995 and 2002, the number of American manufacturing jobs declined by almost two million (a different study found 2.1 million U.S. manufacturing jobs were lost due to trade with China between 2001 and 2010).[15] But the decline was even more severe in China: The number

[12] Edward S. Steinfeld, *Forging Reform in China: The Fate of State-Owned Industry* (New York: Cambridge University Press, 1998); Shahid Yusuf, Kaoru Nabeshima, and Dwight Perkins, *Under New Ownership: Privatizing China's State-owned Enterprises* (Palo Alto, CA, and Washington, DC: Stanford University Press and World Bank, 2006).

[13] Barry Naughton, *The Chinese Economy: Transitions and Growth* (Cambridge, MA: MIT Press, 2007), p. 184.

[14] Dorothy J. Solinger, "Labour Market Reform and the Plight of the Laid-Off Proletariat," *China Quarterly*, No. 170 (June 2002), pp. 304–326; Ching Kwan Lee, *Against the Law: Labor Protests in China's Rustbelt and Sunbelt* (Berkeley, CA: University of California Press, 2007); William Hurst, *The Chinese Worker after Socialism* (New York: Cambridge University Press, 2009); Mark Frazier, *Socialist Inequality: Pensions and the Politics of Uneven Development in China* (Ithaca, NY: Cornell University Press, 2010).

[15] Susan Baum, "So Who Is Stealing China's Manufacturing Jobs?" Bloomberg News, October 14, 2003, http://www.bloomberg.com/apps/news?pid=newsarchiv

of manufacturing jobs shrank by an estimated 16 million between 1995 and 2002, the years when SOE reform was underway, eight times more than in the U.S. during those same years. In some cases, those jobs went to other countries with even lower wages than China. More often, factories employed more workers than they needed, so workers who were laid off or forced into retirement were not replaced. While a large number of American firms outsourced their manufacturing jobs to China and other countries with low wages, China experienced an even larger net loss in industrial workers.

During this time, China's private sector was the source of most new jobs, new economic output, and new tax revenues. Many workers in the rapidly expanding private sector did simple assembly jobs, requiring few skills and earning low pay without benefits. Working conditions were often harsh, and turnover was high. But with upward of 150 million workers migrating from the countryside to the cities in search of jobs, China's private owners were quickly able to replace workers who quit their jobs. This is also what made China attractive to foreign investors and exporters: Workers were abundant, wages were low, and benefits were few.

Most migrants from the countryside sought work in private firms. Even though these were low-paying jobs compared to urban SOEs and collective enterprises, they were still better than what was available in the countryside. Many migrants worked long hours in unsafe conditions; worse, they were often not paid the money they were due or had deductions taken from their paychecks for rent, food, tardiness to work, and bad behavior. They typically lived in cramped quarters with other migrants, cut off from family and friends and even from the local population. They were willing to accept these miserable conditions because they were still better than what they had left behind. Migrants did not expect to work long-term in any one job; instead, they would save up enough money to move to another city or another job, or build up a nest egg that they would take back with them to their villages, where they would

e&sid=aRI4bAft7Xw4, accessed January 15, 2014. Robert Scott, "The China Toll," Economic Policy Institute, Briefing Paper #345, August 23, 2012, http://www. epi.org/publication/bp345-china-growing-trade-deficit-cost/, accessed January 15, 2014.

then have financial security, a new home, or even a new business.[16] They were less concerned about the absence of fringe benefits because they did not have them to begin with. They did not miss what they never had. Moreover, migrant workers were mostly young and therefore less worried about health insurance and pensions than older workers.

As a result of both SOE reform and the expansion of the private sector, many workers lost their good-paying jobs and the benefits that went with them. Newly created jobs did not pay as well, were less secure, and did not provide the same range of benefits as the SOE positions that had been eliminated. This set of conditions created a seemingly endless supply of cheap labor in the 1990s and early 2000s. It was a prominent part of the "China model" of export-led growth: Foreign companies set up manufacturing and assembly operations in China to take advantage of its surplus labor.

The situation changed around the time of the international financial crisis. Some workers lost jobs when factories suddenly closed; others chose to return to villages, unwilling to continue accepting low wages for monotonous and even dangerous jobs. At the same time, standards of living were improving in the countryside due to new income subsidies, the elimination of agricultural taxes, incentives to buy major consumer goods, and new infrastructure investments. What had been a labor surplus turned quickly into a labor shortage. Firms were forced to begin paying higher wages and even benefits in order to attract and retain the workers they needed.

Changing Priorities, Enduring Problems

During the 1990s, the Party and government were primarily focused on increasing economic growth, with heavy reliance on foreign trade, the expansion of the private sector, and major spending on infrastructure projects designed to stimulate subsequent development. These pro-growth economic strategies were successful in achieving high rates of growth, but they also created huge disparities in income. Whether

[16] For migrant women, financial independence also brings more autonomy from their husbands, and even in the choice of whom they marry. See Leslie T. Chang, *Factory Girls: From Village to City in a Changing China* (New York: Spiegel and Grau, 2009).

comparing urban and rural areas, coastal and inland areas, or individuals living in the same communities, the levels of inequality in China grew dramatically. At the beginning of the reform era, China had one of the lowest levels of economic inequality in the world. But that was because most people were equally poor. As China's economy began to grow, so did inequality. China's Gini coefficient[17] rose from 29.1 at the beginning of the reform era in 1981 to a peak of 49.1 in 2008, and an officially reported 47.4 in 2012 (unofficial estimates put the rate as high as 61 in 2010).[18] In comparison, the Gini coefficient in the U.S., where income inequality has grown markedly in recent years and become a political issue, was 45 in 2007. Compared to the other BRICS countries (Brazil, Russia, India, and South Africa), China is smack in the middle, above Brazil and South Africa (the most unequal country in the world) and below Russia and India.[19] Rising inequality in China also led to growing numbers of public protests against the consequences of these pro-growth strategies: the loss of jobs, pensions, farmland, and living spaces, and in general, a loss of security.

A new generation of leaders took over the top Party and government posts beginning in 2002, led by Hu Jintao as the CCP general secretary and Wen Jiabao as prime minister. These new leaders shifted policy priorities. Although still committed to rapid growth, they were also concerned about narrowing income gaps and opportunity gaps. They devoted new investments to inland areas that had not yet benefited from the rest of the country's rapid growth. They paid income subsidies directly into the savings accounts of rural

[17] The Gini coefficient is the most commonly used measure of inequality, with 0 indicating everyone has the same amount of wealth and 100 indicating one person has all the wealth and the rest have none. Some sources use a 0 to 1 range. The numbers are the same, only the decimal point changes.

[18] "China Gini Coefficient at .474 in 2012," accessed July 17, 2013; *Xinhuanet*, January 18, 2013, http://news.xinhuanet.com/english/china/2013-01/18/c_132111 927.htm, accessed July 16, 2013; the higher estimate is reported in "China's Gini Index at .61, University Report Says," *Caixin* Online, October 12, 2010, http://english.caixin.com/2012-12-10/100470648.html, accessed July 16, 2013. The World Bank estimated China's Gini coefficient at 37.0 in 2011, well below even the Chinese government's own estimate.

[19] This comparison uses CIA estimates.

residents in order to boost their standards of living and prevent local officials from skimming some of the money before it reached their hands. And they revived the government's commitment to providing public goods.

Under Xi Jinping, the Party's focus turned again toward rapid urbanization. By 2020, up to 60 percent of China's population is expected to be living in cities.[20] China already has regions that have become megacities, including one around Shanghai in the Yangtze delta and another in the Pearl River delta near Hong Kong that includes Guangzhou and Shenzhen. In 2015, the Politburo approved a plan that will combine the capital city of Beijing, the port city of Tianjin, and the surrounding area of Hebei province into a single megacity to be known as Jing-Jin-Ji, which will include approximately 130 million people. This strategy of rapid urbanization and the formation of megacities in particular will complicate the already difficult challenge of providing high-quality public goods to urban residents. And because large urban areas tend to be focal points for political opposition,[21] it will undoubtedly also require further adjustments in the Party's survival strategy overall.

Renewed Commitment to Healthcare

During the 1980s and '90s, the state's commitment to providing healthcare decreased. Absolute levels of government spending on healthcare increased, but healthcare costs increased even faster. This required individuals to pay an ever-increasing share of healthcare costs. Out-of-pocket expenses as a share of total health expenditures steadily climbed to a peak of 60 percent in 2001. Afterward, it declined to 33.9 percent in 2013 (the last year statistics are available from the World Bank; see figure 4-1). This brought China more in line with upper-middle-income countries, where out-of-pocket spending on healthcare averaged 31.9 percent.

[20] "China Unveils Landmark Urbanization Plan," *Xinhuanet*, March 6, 2014, http://news.xinhuanet.com/english/china/2014-03/16/c_133190495.htm, accessed August 12, 2015.

[21] Jeremy L. Wallace, *Cities and Stability: Urbanization, Redistribution and Regime Survival in China* (New York: Oxford University Press, 2014).

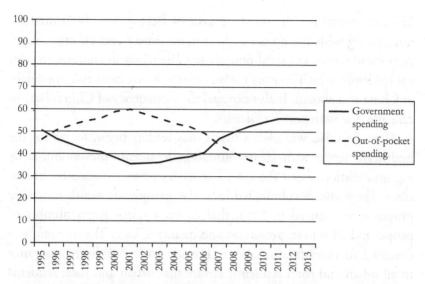

FIGURE 4-1 Government and Out-of-Pocket Spending on Healthcare, 1995–2013 (as percentage of total health expenditures).
Sources: World Bank, World Development Indicators.

The severe acute respiratory syndrome (SARS) crisis of 2003 revealed the dangers of the deteriorating public health system.[22] As the disease began to spread from south China where it originated to other areas of the country and even abroad, doctors and hospitals were slow to recognize the disease, and healthcare departments were slow to report on the growing number of cases. Local officials were reluctant to quickly disclose information, fearful that the news would cause public panic and also make them look bad for not being able to stop the spread of the disease. After an army doctor disclosed that SARS had reached military hospitals in Beijing, the government was forced to respond.

[22] Karen Eggleston, "*Kan Bing Nan, Kan Bing Gui*: Challenges for China's Health-care System Thirty Years into Reform," in Jean C. Oi, Scott Rozelle, and Xueguang Zhou, eds., *Growing Pains: Tensions and Opportunity in China's Transformation* (Palo Alto, CA: Walter H. Shorenstein Asia-Pacific Research Center, Stanford University, 2010). On SARS, see Karl Taro Greenfeld, *China Syndrome: The True Story of the 21st Century's First Great Epidemic* (New York: HarperCollins, 2006).

The minister of health and the mayor of Beijing were both fired for not dealing with the epidemic in a more timely and effective way.[23] Nationwide, over 120 local officials lost their jobs in connection with the epidemic, which eventually claimed over 8,000 cases and 774 deaths in China and abroad. It also exposed the inadequacy of China's healthcare and disease-reporting systems.

After the crisis was over, China's new leaders began to reform the healthcare sector with greater attention to disease prevention, sharing information about the spread of disease, and reducing healthcare costs. These efforts culminated in a new nationwide health insurance program, announced in 2009, that covers a much larger number of people and aims to improve cost and quality of care. The program was designed to meet five objectives: Provide basic healthcare insurance to all urban and rural residents; ensure that urban and rural residents receive equal coverage in this new system; improve the delivery and regulation of pharmaceutical drugs; enhance the primary care system; and use pilot projects to reform public hospitals. The government claimed that 95 percent of all urban and rural residents were covered by one type or another of health insurance by 2011,[24] although as will be shown, survey respondents reported a lower level of coverage. Moreover, the coexistence of three separate insurance schemes proved confusing and unwieldy. Many people faced difficulties getting treated or reimbursed for care when they were outside the city or village where their insurance was based. Although it remains a work in progress, the new healthcare system was gradually bringing more affordable and extensive care to a larger number of people. To further these efforts, the 12th Five Year

---

[23] For Zhang Wenkang, the ousted minister of health, this was the end of his career. He was not given another position and was not reelected to the CCP's Central Committee in 2007. Because he was identified with former General Secretary Jiang Zemin's "Shanghai Gang," a member of new General Secretary Hu Jintao's faction also got fired to keep the balance. However, for Meng Xuenong, this was a temporary step. After being fired as mayor of Beijing, he soon (but quietly) reemerged in a variety of Party and government positions, including governor of Shanxi, and was reelected to the Central Committee in both 2007 and 2012.

[24] Information Office of the State Council of the People's Republic of China, "*Zhongguo de yiliao weisheng shiye*" (Medical and Health Services in China), http://news.xinhuanet.com/politics/2012-12/26/c_114167248.htm, last modified December 26, 2012, accessed October 20, 2013.

Plan (covering the years 2011–2015) singled out healthcare (specifically biotech) as a "strategic emerging industry" that would get significant new investments.[25]

Expansion of Education Opportunities

Unlike healthcare, the Party has had a strong commitment to providing public education from the inception of the PRC. Education was highly politicized in much of the Maoist era, but basic literacy increased. In the post-Mao years, China's public education system became less politicized than during the Cultural Revolution, but political constraints still exist on what can be taught. The Party's view of history not only skews what is taught, but forbids certain subjects. In Document No. 9, a secret document issued in 2013, the Party identified a list of seven topics that are forbidden in the classroom, including democracy, freedom of speech, and the Party's past mistakes, which presumably include the Great Leap Forward, the Cultural Revolution, and the 1989 demonstrations.[26] In 2015, the state went a step further, warning against the use of imported textbooks with "Western values," which include discussions of democracy, civil rights, and a description of modern history different from the one extolled by the CCP (but not

[25] According to a Washington think tank, the 12th Five Year Plan "will support the development of innovative biotech products, high-end medical devices and patented medicines. The government will reportedly put forth a spending package of more than 12 billion RMB for R&D of new drugs from 2011–2015." See "China's 12th Five Year Plan: How It Actually Works and What Is in Store for the Next Five Years" (Washington, DC: APCO Worldwide, 2010), p. 7.

[26] Li Qi and William Wan, "China's Constitution Debate Hits a Sensitive Nerve," *Washington Post*, June 3, 2013, http://www.washingtonpost.com/blogs/worldviews/wp/2013/06/03/chinas-constitution-debate-hits-a-sensitive-nerve/, accessed January 17, 2014. The professor who originally revealed the seven banned topics was later fired from his job at East China University of Political Science and Law; see Andrew Jacobs, "Professor Who Advocated Free Speech Is Fired," *New York Times*, December 11, 2013, http://www.nytimes.com/2013/12/11/world/asia/chinese-professor-who-advocated-free-speech-is-fired.html?emc=edit_tnt_20131211&tntemailo=y, accessed December 12, 2013. Independent journalist Gao Yu was also convicted of leaking Document No. 9 to foreign reporters and sentenced to seven years in prison. In November 2015, her sentence was reduced to five years and she was allowed to serve the remainder of her sentence outside of prison.

Marxism, which is itself a Western import into China), and prohibiting professors from making comments in class that "defame the rule of the Communist Party, smear socialism or violate the constitution and laws."[27]

Throughout the post-Mao period, the Party invested additional resources in schools and teachers and expanded opportunities for high school and college education. China has a nine-year compulsory education system, and most urbanites now graduate from high school. Access to post-secondary education has also grown sharply. The number of students enrolled in vocational and technical schools increased from 9.9 million in 2000 to 15.4 million in 2011 (the most recent year available). In 2000, there were 5.6 million students enrolled in China's colleges and universities; by 2014, that had increased to 25.5 million, a more than fourfold increase in just 14 years. Between 2000 and 2013, the number of Chinese students studying abroad multiplied from 39,000 to 459,800.[28] Of the foreign students studying in the U.S. in 2013, 28.7 percent were from China.[29] These rising levels of education are reflected among the Public Goods and Political Support Survey respondents (see figure 4-2). For the youngest generation, over 82 percent have either a high school or college education. These numbers are expected to grow in coming years. As part of the 2010–2020 national guidelines for education reform and development, the government plans to increase the

---

[27] Andrea Chen and Zhuang Pinghui, "Chinese Universities Ordered to Ban Textbooks That Promote Western Values," *South China Morning Post*, January 30, 2015, http://www.scmp.com/news/china/article/1695524/chinese-universities-instructed-ban-textbooks-promote-western-values?page=all, accessed February 19, 2015. Several professors interviewed in summer 2015 said they never received a directive to stop using foreign textbooks. They also said that the days when a top official could simply make a speech and have everyone fall into line were over, at least in the education sphere.

[28] These numbers are taken from China Data Online, www.chinadataonline.org, accessed August 3, 2015.

[29] "Open Doors 2013: International Students in the United States and Study Abroad by American Students Are at an All-Time High," Institute of International Education, November 11, 2013, http://www.iie.org/Who-We-Are/News-and-Events/Press-Center/Press-releases/2013/2013-11-11-Open-Doors-Data, accessed February 5, 2015.

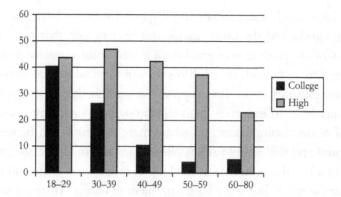

FIGURE 4-2 Rising Education Levels among Urban Residents, by Age Cohorts (bars in graph represent percentages).
Source: 2014 Public Goods and Political Support Survey.

high school enrollment rate to 90 percent and college enrollment to 40 percent.[30]

To achieve these ambitious goals, as of 2012, Beijing required local governments to spend 4 percent of GDP on education. This is an aspirational goal: In the 2014 survey, only seven of the 50 cities spent at least 4 percent of GDP on education. This will bring China closer to international standards (see table 4-1) and set a common standard for all localities. However, it will also perpetuate existing inequalities because poorer communities will spend less on education. A more equitable standard would be based on per capita spending, but this would put a greater burden on governments in less prosperous areas with fewer resources available to them. The central government is not providing additional spending to meet these education goals, so establishing a benchmark relative to GDP will make it easier for local governments to meet the target, even if it will not address regional inequalities in the quality of education.

The rapid increase of college enrollments came with attendant problems, such as finding qualified teachers and ensuring the quality of education.

---

[30] "*Guojia zhongchangqi jiaoyu gaige he fazhan guihua gangyao (2010–2020 nian)*" (Guidelines for the National Plan for Medium and Long-Term Reform and Development of Education 2010-2020), *Xinhua*, July 29, 2010, http://news.xinhuanet.com/edu/2010-07/29/c_12389320.htm, accessed February 13, 2014.

More importantly, there is currently a gap between the large numbers of new graduates and the much smaller number of jobs that require their skills. College grads expect good-paying jobs commensurate with their talents, not entry-level, low-skill manufacturing and service sector jobs. But desirable jobs are in short supply. The result is that college graduates in China have an extremely high unemployment rate. This problem is typical of developing countries, where there is a mismatch between the ambitions and skill sets of young college grads and the labor markets they face. That has also been true in the U.S. in recent years as the job market has been sluggish. But it is a bigger problem in China. There are so many unemployed college grads in China that they have been dubbed the "ant army" because, according to the person who coined the term, "They share every similarity with ants. They live in colonies in cramped areas. They're intelligent and hardworking, yet anonymous and underpaid."[31]

This expansion of educational opportunities, especially college education, is atypical of authoritarian regimes. According to Bueno de Mesquita and Downs, authoritarian regimes are more likely to limit access to higher education in order to limit the development of "coordination goods," which they define as "public goods that critically affect the ability of political opponents to coordinate but that have relatively little impact on economic growth." Coordination goods include political rights, human rights, press freedom, and access to higher education.[32] However, the Party is not following this model.[33] It is promoting the rapid expansion of higher education, not limiting it. Although the Party is not following Bueno de Mesquita and Downs' advice to limit access to higher education as part of its survival strategy, the logic of their argument still applies to the Party: Young people now possess larger amounts of coordination goods—the ability to communicate with others with the

---

[31] Chen Jia, "Despite Better Educations, 'Ants' Still Struggling," *China Daily*, December 14, 2010, http://www.chinadaily.com.cn/china/2010-12/14/content_11696624.htm, accessed December 12, 2013.

[32] Bruce Bueno de Mesquita and George W. Downs, "Development and Democracy," *Foreign Affairs*, Vol. 84, No. 5 (September/October 2005), pp. 77–86.

[33] In the years leading up to the Arab Spring, many authoritarian governments in the Middle East and North Africa were also improving the provision of public goods. See Steven Heydemann, "Upgrading Authoritarianism in the Arab World," Brookings Institution, Analysis Paper No. 13 (October 2007).

same interests and more importantly the ability to organize themselves to pursue their shared goals. The Party raised expectations that college degrees would lead to good jobs and better lives. With those jobs slow to materialize, the Party is vulnerable to the simmering dissatisfaction of young grads. In other countries, unemployed college grads have been at the forefront of public protests against their governments. If the Party cannot create suitable jobs for the growing number of college grads in China, it may face a similar challenge in the near future.

New Public Goods Challenges

As spending on traditional public goods grew, so did concern about other issues. Food safety became a prominent issue after several scandals involving tainted food. In 2008, approximately 300,000 babies became ill after drinking baby formula and powdered milk that contained melamine, a chemical added to foods to make it seem as though they have more protein than they actually do. Thousands developed kidney stones and kidney disease.[34] The previous year, pet food sold in the U.S. was found to contain melamine, causing hundreds of deaths and cases of kidney failure in cats and dogs. Many countries around the world banned the import of baby formula and dairy products from China due to safety concerns. Despite the government's claims that all stocks of melamine had been destroyed, reports of food products containing melamine continued in subsequent years. Consumers lost confidence in China's domestic dairy and infant formula industries, preferring instead to buy imported products. These developments led to new government regulations on dairy products and infant formula, as well as closer inspection of imported products, some of which were also found to be unsafe.[35] In other food scandals, used cooking oil was illegally recycled, sometimes from restaurants' drains, and resold. Walmart pulled donkey meat from its stores when it was discovered

[34] Andrew Jacobs, "China Pledges New Measures to Safeguard Dairy Industry," *New York Times*, November 21, 2008, http://www.nytimes.com/2008/11/21/world/asia/21milk.html?ref=melamine, accessed January 17, 2014.

[35] Laurie Burkitt, "China to Strengthen Infant-Formula Regulations," *Wall Street Journal*, December 25, 2013, http://online.wsj.com/news/articles/SB1000142405270230475350457927979792334738168, accessed January 17, 2014.

to contain fox meat. (Neither type of meat would appeal to American shoppers, but the intentional mislabeling caused an uproar in China.) Pork sold in Shanghai had an iridescent blue glow in the dark. Meat sold as lamb was actually rat meat. Much as Upton Sinclair's *The Jungle* led to new government inspection of the U.S. meat-packing industry, these food scandals in China threatened consumer confidence in China's food supply and pushed the Chinese government to investigate and punish the firms and people involved.

In recent years, the environment has moved to the top of the policy agenda as China's economic model began to take its toll. China heavily relies on coal for its energy needs and also relies on industries that are energy- and resource-intensive, such as steel and petrochemicals. For much of the reform era, the Chinese government saw pollution as an unfortunate but necessary byproduct of its rapid growth strategy. It preferred growth in the short run at the expense of the environment and resisted international pressure to change its energy policies to slow global warming. However, China's environmental degradation has reached a tipping point. In 2012 and following years, large areas of the country were blanketed with thick layers of smog. Flights were grounded, and the government advised people to stay indoors. Tourism in Beijing dropped because of concerns about its air quality. A study by scientists from China, the U.S., and Israel found that life expectancies in northern China were reduced by 5.5 years due to pollution caused by burning coal.[36] Air pollution originating from China even contributes to smog in the western parts of the U.S.[37]

China's leaders could no longer ignore the environmental consequences of its rapid growth policies, especially as the Internet allowed people to express their concerns about pollution and its health consequences. In

[36] Brad Plumer, "Coal Pollution in China Is Cutting Life Expectancy by 5.5 Years," *Washington Post*, July 8, 2013, http://www.washingtonpost.com/blogs/wonkblog/wp/2013/07/08/chinas-coal-pollution-is-much-deadlier-than-anyone-realized/, accessed January 22, 2014. Political scientist Andrew Gelman raised doubts about the statistical inference leading to the prediction of lower life expectancy; see http://andrewgelman.com/2013/08/05/evidence-on-the-impact-of-sustained-use-of-polynomial-regression-on-causal-inference-a-claim-that-coal-heating-is-reducing-lifespan-by-5-years-for-half-a-billion-people/, accessed August 5, 2013.

[37] William Wan, "Chinese Factories Affect U.S. Air: Pollutants Cross Pacific and Contribute to Smog in West, Study Finds," *Washington Post*, January 22, 2014, http://www.washingtonpost.com/world/study-pollution-from-chinese-factories-is-harming-air-quality-on-us-west-coast/2014/01/21/225e9b1e-8281-11e3-bbe5-6a2a3141e3a9_story.html, accessed January 24, 2014.

2012, the government directed major cities to begin monitoring air quality according to the global standard of counting particulates 2.5 microns or less in diameter, instead of 10 microns, which had been the norm in China. At the time of this directive, two-thirds of China's cities could not meet the new air-quality standard.[38] (The U.S. Embassy had been tweeting air quality reports based on the lower standard for years, a source of embarrassment to the Chinese government because the readings were much higher than the government's reports.) However, it is well known that central policies are often circumvented by local leaders, especially when the policies negatively affect economic growth.[39] Whether the recent environmental scares will be enough to bring about a true change of priorities remains to be seen.[40]

IV. Public Assessments of Public Goods

Improved delivery of public goods is part of the Party's new survival strategy, but how does the Chinese public evaluate its results? The public's assessment of public goods in China generally matches the aggregate trends described above: They recognize the existing problems with most public goods, believe that things are getting better, and give middling grades to the government's performance in each of these areas.[41] In fact, these assessments are interrelated. The respondents in the Public

[38] "Two-Thirds of Chinese Cities Cannot Meet Stricter Air Quality Standards: Vice Minister," *Xinhua*, March 1, 2012, http://news.xinhuanet.com/english/china/2012-03/02/c_131442222.htm, accessed March 28, 2012.

[39] Elizabeth Economy, *The River Runs Black: The Environmental Challenge to China's Future*, second edition (Ithaca, NY: Cornell University Press, 2010).

[40] Although China's environmental problems are severe and getting worse, the rest of the world is catching up to its pollution levels. In 2006, the World Bank reported that China had 16 of the 20 most polluted cities in the world. A similar list from the World Health Organization in 2013 included only four Chinese cities. Ritchie King and Lily Kuo, "Here Are the World's Worst Cities for Air Pollution, and They're Not the Ones You'd Expect," *Quartz*, October 18, 2013, http://qz.com/136606/here-are-the-worlds-worst-cities-for-air-pollution-and-theyre-not-the-ones-youd-expect, accessed January 17, 2014.

[41] These results are consistent with previous studies of public goods in urban China. See, for instance, Jie Chen, *Popular Political Support in Urban China* (Stanford, CA: Stanford University Press, 2004); and Tony Saich, *Providing Public Goods in Transitional China* (New York: Palgrave Macmillan, 2008).

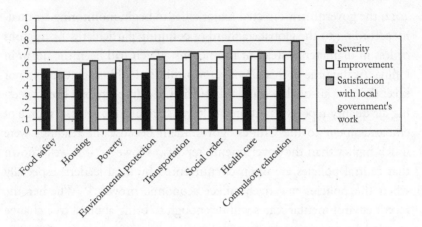

FIGURE 4-3　Public Assessments of Public Goods in Urban China, 2014 (0–1 scale).

Source: 2014 Public Goods and Political Support Survey.

Goods and Political Support Surveys were asked a series of questions about an array of public goods: How severe was the problem, had the situation improved in recent years, and how satisfied were they with the government's work in each policy area?[42] As seen in figure 4-3, the severity of the issues varied but within a small range. For each type of public good except food safety, respondents saw recent improvements, a bare majority for poverty alleviation, but more substantial majorities for other types of public goods, such as healthcare and education. The more severe the problem was perceived to be, the less satisfied respondents were with the government's work; conversely, the greater the improvement, the more satisfied they were with the government's work. These assessments are essential for understanding the provision

[42] The three questions had different responses, so they were standardized on a 0–100 scale by dividing the average values by the maximum possible values. For example, the severity of food safety was measured from 0 (not a problem at all) to 10 (extreme problem). The average of all responses was 5.46. That becomes a .546 on a 0–1 scale. Improvement was measured on a five-point scale (0 = a lot worse, 1 = a little worse, 2 = no change, 3 = a little better, 4 = much better). The average response was 2.08, or .52 on a 0–1 scale (2.08/4 = .52). Satisfaction was measured on a four-point scale (0 = very unsatisfied, 1 = not too satisfied, 2 = somewhat satisfied, 3 = very satisfied). The bar in figure 4-3 is the percent of respondents who were either somewhat or very satisfied, 51.5 percent.

of public goods in China: If serving the people has become part of the Party's strategy for survival, and not just a slogan, then the people should be able to evaluate the quality of public goods and the role of the government in providing them. As figure 4-3 indicates, they do.

Not only does the public's evaluation of public goods provision fit the general pattern outlined above (so-so, but getting better), they see the government bearing the primary responsibility for delivering these goods. Respondents were asked whether the government or individuals bore the main responsibility for these goods. With the exception of housing, the majority of respondents saw the government as bearing the main responsibility (see figure 4-4). Less than 10 percent saw individuals having sole or primary responsibility for any public good; the highest was poverty, with just 6.4 percent. For older respondents, this could be the "socialist legacy": In the past—and in their lifetimes—the state was committed to providing these kinds of public goods. For much of the Maoist era, markets and private firms did not exist, the state was the main source of all goods and services, and there were few alternatives for obtaining them if the state did not provide them. But the difference between older and younger respondents is minuscule: People of all ages see the main responsibility in the hands of the government. This sentiment is not simply nostalgia for the past, although it may be for some. Younger respondents, who did not experience the Maoist period,

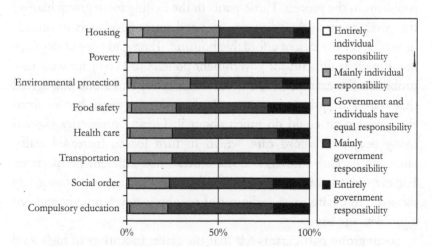

FIGURE 4-4 Responsibility for Providing Public Goods and Services.
Source: 2014 Public Goods and Political Support Survey.

have the same perspective: The government is primarily responsible for delivering public goods and services. That widespread sentiment makes public evaluations of public goods all the more salient. From the point of view of most Chinese, whatever problems exist, they are the government's responsibility to resolve.

Moreover, most Chinese saw the government's responsibility as larger in 2014 than in 2010. A larger percentage of the respondents saw the government as mainly or entirely responsible for each type of public good (except for food safety, which was not included in the 2010 survey). For example, environmental protection increased by 10.9 percentage points (from 54.4 percent to 65.3 percent), social order 6.6 points (from 70 to 76.6 percent), education 6.5 points (71.1 to 77.6 percent), and healthcare 5 points (70.1 to 75.1 percent). In sharp contrast to the "small government, big society" slogan of the past, most Chinese see a larger role for the government in providing all types of public goods.

Focus group interviews done in conjunction with the 2014 survey added greater precision to the survey findings. Across an array of issues, focus group participants said that it was the government's responsibility to solve the growing public goods problems, but they were not optimistic that a solution was likely. In all four cities, citizens complained that construction and redevelopment were poorly planned by the government. While it might be good in the long run, it created unnecessary problems in the process. Participants in the Beijing focus group blamed the government and no one else, not real estate developers or outside investors, for the lack of affordable housing. The rapid pace of development made it difficult for government policies to keep pace with new problems. For example, the citizens' focus group in Chongqing agreed that transportation was an increasingly severe problem, but doubted the government could do much about it. Greater prosperity allowed many people to afford cars, which in turn led to increased traffic jams and parking shortages. Local officials had different perspectives. For example, a transportation official in the Guangzhou focus group viewed traffic jams as an indicator of economic development, and not a problematic issue.

Focus group participants felt that the career incentives of high-level officials interfered with local efforts to improve the provision of public goods. The Chongqing focus group of citizens complained that officials only cared about growth and "image" projects like roads, but not other public goods like healthcare and education, because they "were not something to be seen, but to be lived with." But focus groups of officials deflected this criticism to higher levels. They blamed high-ranking officials who cared more about GDP growth, which their evaluations were based on, and the images of their cities than the actual welfare of the people. These views reflect the distinction between hard and soft targets in the evaluation process faced by Party and government officials.

Local officials in the focus groups also complained about the difficulties arising from competing interests and poor coordination between departments and different levels of the government. The result was poor enforcement of the central government's "good policies" and the dissatisfaction of ordinary people with their local governments. An official who worked in a community service center in Wuhan complained that local officials had to spend most of their time catering to the demands of higher-level officials instead of the people they were supposed to serve, making it hard to convey public opinions about public goods provision to higher-level officials.

Focus groups in all four cities (Beijing, Chongqing, Guangzhou, and Wuhan) highlighted the issue of food safety: They agreed that nothing on the market could be trusted as safe. Most said that they simply tried to do their best to distinguish between safe and unsafe products. In Guangzhou and Chongqing, the younger people in the citizens' focus groups were not too concerned about food safety, reflecting perhaps the feeling of invulnerability common among youths. They were more concerned about their tight work schedules and the good taste of restaurant food than they were worried about tainted cooking oil and other safety issues. But older people were more concerned about the safety of food and said they did not trust the quality of even well-known brands. A Guangzhou official who worked in the agriculture bureau said he did not trust any food bought in the city and only ate food from his rural hometown. Other Guangzhou officials said food safety concerns led them to eat at home instead of going to restaurants. Chongqing officials said the local preference for hot and spicy food presented an additional problem because the spices made it difficult to taste if the food had gone bad.

Most focus groups said the government needed to do more to address the problem "at the root." They saw the need for tougher laws and more stringent regulations in order to address this growing problem (only the citizens' focus group in Wuhan did not blame the government for the problem). But the nature of the food industry presented particular problems in dealing with safety and quality issues. Guangzhou and Chongqing officials said it was hard to monitor food safety because the number of street vendors, small restaurants, and small farms was so large and the supply chain so long. Available resources were also inadequate to undertake such a large new task. A Chongqing official said that when she worked in a department in charge of education and culture, her office was also put in charge of food and drug safety even though it lacked the resources and expertise to do the job properly. They had to accept the task, but were "extremely nervous" that they would make mistakes. According to one Guangzhou official, the government put too much importance on economic development and not enough on the people's interests. This led to the government blocking media coverage of food safety scandals, such as the tainted milk powder that caused kidney damage and, in a few cases, the deaths of infants.

In all four focus group cities, the environment was a major concern. Although the focus groups agreed that local governments were trying to address the problem, they also believed this work had started too late. In Wuhan, groups of both citizens and officials blamed the many construction projects in the city as the main cause of pollution. In Guangzhou and Chongqing, citizens and officials said pollution was somewhat better in recent years because many industrial firms had moved to second-tier cities. But this did not really solve the problem, it just moved it elsewhere. Citizens in the Chongqing focus group were satisfied with what the local government had done about pollution, but thought the central government needed to do more because pollution was a national problem needing national policies and should not be left to local governments to address.

Most participants in the focus groups thought public security was in decline. There were more traffic accidents, more frequent robberies and thefts, and slow response by the police. Some in the Guangzhou citizens' focus group even thought the police were colluding with thieves because they were unwilling to investigate thefts of smartphones and other small but expensive items, and because they refused to examine security camera footage even when it was available. Although the incidence of violent crime in China is relatively low, the public's perception is that it is on the rise. Train stations were identified in each city as being particularly unsafe. Even officials felt increasingly unsafe. In Chongqing, the focus groups of citizens and officials both said public safety was generally good, although the citizens' group also said it had been even better in the Bo Xilai era. Only the Guangzhou focus groups said that public safety had improved, the result of increased police patrols and more extensive public participation, such as volunteer neighborhood watch programs. Even so, one Guangzhou official blamed the media for the city's unsafe image: "The media are too liberal now. Some incidents would never have made it to the news in some other cities, but they do in Guangzhou." As noted in chapter 2, many local officials do not appreciate the media's coverage of local problems.

In assessing the overall quality of governance, officials and the general public had different perspectives. Those in the citizens' focus groups were frustrated but somewhat resigned to the situation. For example, focus group participants thought that access to education was unfair, but there was no point in trying to change the system because society was divided into different hierarchies depending on where people lived and what their social status was. On an array of policy issues, citizens felt that officials were trying to address problems, but there was not much that could be done; the pace of growth was too fast and the size of the population too large to truly solve many problems. In contrast, officials described more tension, even animosity, between state and society, with ordinary people feeling hatred toward officials, rich people, and the police (仇官，仇富，仇警). They were on the receiving end of vitriol from the most frustrated and the most vocal, and those experiences shaped their assessments of the situation. According to a Beijing official, "The government has not fulfilled its function of maintaining a minimally acceptable living standard for ordinary people. That is where the sense of injustice and inequality comes from."

Public Satisfaction with Healthcare

There are two main complaints about healthcare in China: It is difficult to obtain, and it is expensive.[43] In many cases, patients are required to

---

[43] Eggleston, "*Kan Bing Nan, Kan Bing Gui.*"

pay in cash before being treated because medical insurance is limited, in both the number of people who are insured and the types of medical care covered by the insurance. Hospitals and doctors have greater incentives to order expensive diagnostic tests and prescription drugs than lower costs for effective preventive care, such as immunizations.

Among respondents in the Public Goods and Political Support Survey, insurance coverage varied widely (see table 4-3). Those whose *hukou* registrations were in the same city they resided in were most likely to be insured. Others with an urban *hukou* but in a different city from where they resided were much less likely to be insured. There are dramatic differences across different types of *hukou* for the extent of medical and old-age insurance, and smaller but still notable differences for the percentages of people covered by housing subsidies and unemployment insurance. Between the 2010 and 2014 surveys, most groups of people reported drops in these levels, but urban migrants from other cities actually reported an increase. Although most of those with a rural *hukou* had some type of medical insurance, few were covered in the cities where they currently lived at the time of the survey. If they were severely ill or injured, they had to return to their villages for treatment. Having insurance was no guarantee of being able to use it. According to participants in the Wuhan focus group, the best hospitals did not accept insurance cards, so patients were required to pay for treatment out of pocket. In Guangzhou, the citizens' focus group said it was relatively easy to see a doctor, but it was still expensive. Although simple ailments could be treated at clinics and community hospitals, smaller hospitals could not be trusted to handle more serious cases.

The extent of insurance coverage tells only part of the story, however. More important is what that coverage includes: high deductibles and co-pays, limited coverage of major medical issues, and time-consuming and complicated procedures for getting reimbursed. Given a hypothetical situation in which a person was hospitalized, required surgery, and the care of a specialist, the vast majority of respondents in the Public Goods and Political Support Survey said they would have difficulty finding care and paying for it. Specifically, 78 percent of the respondents said they would have some or major difficulty paying for these medical expenses; 70.2 percent would have difficulty finding a specialist at a city hospital;

TABLE 4-3 *Hukou* Status and Availability of Insurance

	urban hukou, this city		urban hukou, not this city		rural hukou, this city		rural hukou, not this city	
	2010	2014	2010	2014	2010	2014	2010	2014
Urban residents' medical insurance	82.5	85.2	58.6	71.8	36.6	28.9	37.3	17.6
Urban residents' basic old-age insurance	71.8	70.7	50.3	57.9	25.6	18.7	22.2	12.6
Housing subsidy	42.2	30.6	34.9	35.1	11.8	7.9	11.7	8.9
Unemployment insurance	41.1	33.3	35.8	37.7	11.5	7.6	16.2	10.3
Commercial insurance	17.8	23.0	18.8	28.9	9.4	13.6	9.1	9.4
New rural cooperative medical insurance					67.0	74.2	58.3	72.8
Rural social security insurance					30.7	44.8	28.6	41.6

Source: Public Goods and Political Support Surveys.

65.2 percent would have difficulty submitting the paperwork necessary to be reimbursed for their expenses; and 65 percent would have difficulty being hospitalized in a timely fashion. This frustration with the cost and difficulty of finding care occasionally spills over into violence. Doctors have been attacked and even killed by patients angry at not being able to get the care they needed, or who feel they have been grossly overcharged. The lack of trust between doctors and patients came up repeatedly in focus groups with both officials and citizens. They thought doctors had no sense of ethics and cared only about money. They tried to trick patients into buying expensive services and medications, and often required bribes in order to provide good treatment.

As a result, survey respondents generally gave mediocre marks to the quality of healthcare in the cities where they lived. When asked about the city government's ability to control the cost of medicine, hygiene and disease control, community-based medical services, levels of medical insurance, and the construction of new medical facilities, the most common answer was "so-so." When asked about their overall level of satisfaction with the government's provision of medical care using a four-point scale (where 1 = very unsatisfied and 4 = very satisfied), the average score was 2.65, just above the midpoint.

In addition to the quality of the healthcare system itself, other personal qualities influenced the level of satisfaction with healthcare.[44] For example, there was a clear relationship between income and satisfaction with healthcare. The more a person could afford healthcare, the more satisfied they were with it. (Whether it is fair that the wealthy can get better healthcare because they can afford it is examined later.) Satisfaction with healthcare was also influenced by familiarity with it. The older a respondent was, the less likely they were to be satisfied. Younger people are generally healthier and less likely to have the kinds of chronic illnesses that plague seniors. They are also less likely to seek care when they are sick, and so have less direct experience with the healthcare system. The health of respondents also influenced the assessment of healthcare. Respondents identified their health as very good, pretty good, so-so, pretty bad, or very bad. As the respondents' quality of health declined, so too did their satisfaction with healthcare. However, actual use of the healthcare system did not have much of an impact on satisfaction. Over 80 percent of the respondents said they or their family members had used outpatient services in the previous two to three years, and one-third said they or family members had been hospitalized. Whether they had recent inpatient or outpatient care did not influence their level of satisfaction when other variables were controlled for. Migrant workers, who generally do not have access to public healthcare in the cities where they live, were no different from the rest of the respondents when these other variables were controlled for

---

[44] The following observations are based on a multiple regression analysis, in which income, age, quality of health, recent experience with the healthcare system, education, gender, and whether the respondent was a migrant are all controlled for.

(although they were much more likely to not answer this question, perhaps because they had no experience with the urban healthcare system).

Although most respondents had only middling satisfaction with the current healthcare system, most (61.2 percent) thought the situation was improving. Given the many and widespread complaints about healthcare in China, the perception that conditions are improving is an indication that the government's increased commitment to providing more and better healthcare is having its intended effect. However, that commitment began from a low point, and much more work remains to be done.

Public Satisfaction with Education

One consequence of the one-child policy is that most people do not have recent and direct experience with the public education system. In the Public Goods and Political Support Survey, barely one-quarter of survey respondents had children currently in school or who had graduated within the previous one or two years. Perhaps because of that, respondents see education as the least severe and most improved of all public policy issues, and where they are most satisfied with the government's work. It is also true that the government has been publicizing its increased spending on education and the expansion of opportunities to attend college, so the public satisfaction with the government's commitment to education also reflects to some extent the actual state of affairs. Compared to other types of public goods, education ranks high. But as we will see, there was less satisfaction with the government's general education policies than with the specific quality of education in local schools.

Among those who currently have children in school, satisfaction about particular aspects of public education is very high. Over 80 percent of parents with school-aged children were satisfied with their school's curriculum, the quality of teachers, and the school's facilities. There was somewhat less satisfaction (but still over 75 percent) with "teaching in line with the student's ability" (a Chinese idiom meaning that education should fit the needs of each individual student), extracurricular activities, and the reasonableness of school fees. In contrast, there was less satisfaction with the work of the government in providing education. All respondents, not just those with school-aged children, were asked about five specific education-related issues: management of school fees, educational fairness, the rationality of the curriculum, improvements in school facilities, and the quality of teachers. On each of these five issues, most respondents rated the government's work as either "so-so" or "good."[45] The average scores were between 3.2 and 3.5 on a five-point scale (1 = very bad and 5 = very good). Overall, these are passing but not stellar grades. Respondents with school-aged children—the ones with more recent and direct experience in these matters—were more likely to give slightly higher grades. Although education is seen as the least inadequate in the range of public goods shown in figure 4-3, there is clearly room for further improvement.

Focus group interviews echo these general sentiments. Access to education is uneven and unfair for several reasons. First, those without local *hukou* were not allowed to send their children to local schools without paying high levels of tuition, and in some cases, paying bribes to principals and teachers. Second, the quality of education varied markedly in different districts of the same city. Even those with local *hukou* had a difficult time getting their kids into the best schools if they did not live in the proper district. They either had to pay bribes or move to a district with better schools. Third, focus group participants—officials and ordinary people alike—complained that the quality of teaching had gone down, with teachers more intent on making money than on educating their students. With advancement to the best schools at the next level so dependent on test scores, they spent large sums of money on after-school cram classes in order to do well on the *gaokao* (高考, the national college entrance exam) and even on tests to get into high school. Parents in the Beijing, Wuhan, and Guangzhou focus groups paid 40,000 to 60,000 RMB (roughly $6,500–$9,700), in many cases equal to 50–70 percent of household income, per year on these prep classes and other education expenses. In Chongqing, the amount was lower, around 10,000 RMB per year.

Focus group parents with school-aged children, officials and ordinary people alike, thought recent government reforms had made the

---

[45] On the questions about the schools themselves, respondents were not given the option of answering "so-so." All respondents, not just those with school-aged kids, answered questions about the government's work. As a result, comparing satisfaction with schools to satisfaction with the government's work concerning education is a bit like comparing apples and oranges.

situation even worse. One official in Beijing said the government was full of slogans and policies without teeth. According to another, students from rural families have less chance today of going to first-tier colleges due to changes in the college entrance examination system. In the past, 30 percent of students at Peking University were from rural families, but now the percentage had dropped into the single digits. Focus group participants in Wuhan complained about the inequality of getting into the best colleges based on where people lived. Residents in Wuhan would have to score much higher on the *gaokao* in order to get into Peking University than Beijing residents. This group also said there was a recent trend for rural families to not send their kids to college because they could not get into the best schools and had to settle for low-paying jobs after they graduated. In 2013, the CCP Central Committee decided to implement a rotation system for teachers to try to alleviate the problem of students being unable to get into the best schools, but focus groups said this had so far been ineffective.

V. Fairness of Public Goods Provision

One of the sensitive issues accompanying the massive migration of people underway in China is who has access to public goods in the cities. Because of the *hukou* system, only people who are formally registered in a given city are entitled to send their children to local public schools and to be covered by medical insurance in the cities where they live. Others can attend local schools if they pass an entrance exam, pay higher school fees (which are unaffordable for most migrants), or have personal connections. Because only the state is legally entitled to deliver public education, migrant communities may not set up their own schools for their children; those that have tried have had their teaching materials confiscated and their schools bulldozed. Many migrant parents leave their children behind in their villages in the care of grandparents so they can go to school there. The main reason that local governments do not want to admit migrant children to local schools is financial: Spending on public education is primarily the responsibility of the local government, and many cannot afford to substantially increase the number of students enrolled in their schools without a commensurate increase in resources to pay for the additional teachers, materials, and administrative support required. As in many other policy areas, public education is a largely unfunded mandate passed down from the central government. Private schools exist, but they are few in number, and most migrants cannot afford their tuition and fees. Access to public education in China's cities therefore perpetuates the urban-rural divide, and more specifically the gap between rich and poor. The new regulation requiring local governments to spend 4 percent of GDP on education also reinforces the advantages of prosperous cities, which will spend more on education than less developed cities.

Despite the government's efforts to limit the ability of migrant children to attend local schools, public opinion is overwhelmingly on the side of the migrants. Among the respondents in the 2014 Public Goods and Political Support Survey, only 19.7 percent agreed it was "fair that migrant workers are frequently not permitted to go to school in this city." Even respondents who had their *hukou* registration in that city and were therefore entitled to send their children to local schools believed that restricting migrants was unfair. In contrast, most respondents (59.5 percent) believed it was "fair that people who are able to afford it can get a better education for their children." Put differently, twice as many people think that education based on *hukou* status is unfair (80.3) than think education based on wealth is unfair (40.5). As a question of social justice, most Chinese feel that access to education should not be based on place of birth; in that sense, education is seen as a basic birthright and should be available regardless of where people currently live. At the same time, they also feel that it is acceptable for wealthy families to pay to send their kids to higher-quality schools. Education based on *hukou* is zero-sum: Local residents are admitted, migrants are excluded. Education based on wealth is less restricted: Those who cannot afford better education are still entitled to public education in local schools.

Similarly, the availability of healthcare is also seen as a social justice issue. Should rich people be able to obtain better healthcare just because they can afford it? Almost two-thirds of the respondents (61.6 percent) say no. Access to healthcare can be a life-or-death issue, and most Chinese say it should not be based on ability to pay. This indicates strong public support for healthcare that is widely and evenly available. Compare this response to education: Almost 60 percent of the respondents said it was fair that rich people are able to give their children better educations, but an even larger percentage said it was not fair for them to get better healthcare. There is much greater public acceptance of inequality based on wealth in education than in healthcare.

Should migrants also be able to receive medical insurance in the cities where they currently live? Under current policy, most people with a rural *hukou* must return to their hometowns in order to receive care if they become ill or injured. This can be a major issue, because many of them live hundreds of miles away. Among the survey respondents, there is strong support for the general principle that migrants should be able to get at least a minimal level of medical insurance as urban residents. However, that support begins to fall when providing medical insurance to migrants results in fewer benefits for urban residents who are currently covered (see table 4-4). Not surprisingly, migrants are more likely to agree to each of these statements than those who have urban *hukou*. For example, on the fourth and most personal question, only 54.2 percent of those who have *hukou* in that city agreed, but 63.3 percent of the others agreed. Ironically, support declines even among those who would benefit the most (those who do not have urban *hukou* in the city where they live). Not only does support for medical insurance decline as the questions get more personal, the number of people who replied "don't know" also increased, indicating some doubt about the merits of providing medical insurance to migrants even though they agreed with the general principle, or perhaps an unwillingness to voice disagreement to a question about fairness. Nevertheless, in medical insurance as in education, there is widespread support for providing migrants the public goods they are currently denied.

The citizens' focus groups in Wuhan and Chongqing also complained that it was unfair that officials received better and cheaper medical care than ordinary people. Hospitals had special wards for officials, who also could get doctors' appointments whenever they wanted. In contrast, ordinary people could not get advance appointments and had to get in line at 2:00 or 3:00 a.m. in order to be seen by a doctor. Officials acknowledged that they got better healthcare than ordinary people, but they were still nostalgic for the past when they received healthcare for free.

A common theme in all the focus groups, citizens and officials alike, was that personal relationships—*guanxi* 关系—were the key to getting access to education, healthcare, and other public goods. They were cited as a source of inequality and unfairness, not the resourcefulness of people with good *guanxi*. For example, the inequalities in education

TABLE 4-4 Public Support for Medical Insurance for Migrants

The city government should have the obligation to guarantee that:	AGREE		DISAGREE		DON'T KNOW	
	2010	2014	2010	2014	2010	2014
all residents have a minimal level of medical insurance.	95.1	93.7	2.3	2.3	2.6	4.0
even migrants from outside the city also have a minimal level of medical insurance.	87.2	84.2	5.9	7.7	6.9	8.2
even migrants from outside the city have the same level of medical insurance as city residents.	79.9	74.5	11.8	15.1	8.3	10.3
even migrants from outside the city have the same level of medical insurance as city residents, even if this could lower the level of medical insurance I would have.	62.1	55.6	26.8	31.0	11.1	13.5

Source: Public Goods and Political Support Surveys.

started in kindergarten, when parents without good *guanxi* could not get their children into the best schools. In Chongqing, the citizens' focus group complained bitterly about the unfairness of using *guanxi* whenever people needed to solve a problem instead of following normal procedures. This practice of relying primarily on *guanxi* to get things done reflected the unfairness of contemporary society. Only in Guangzhou did participants in the citizens' focus group say *guanxi* was not necessary to handle *hukou* paperwork, make a doctor's appointment, or enroll children in school. For these routine things, following proper procedures was enough. But they also recognized that this was peculiar to Guangzhou, because even in other nearby cities (Shantou was specifically mentioned), *guanxi* was still the only thing that mattered.

VI. Performance Legitimacy

Besides their evaluations of individual public goods, how does the Chinese public evaluate the overall performance of the government? This is one aspect of performance legitimacy, based on what the government delivers (the legitimacy of the regime overall is examined in the next chapter). The survey data reveal some predictable patterns, but also some surprises.

First of all, there is a gap between the evaluation of the central government and the local governments, what I refer to as the "local legitimacy deficit." When asked about their level of satisfaction with the performance of the government on a 0–10 scale, respondents gave the central government an average score of 7.6, but local governments only 6.5. Across the full range of demographic characteristics, different groups of people are more likely to be satisfied with the work of the central government than they are with their local governments. This finding is consistent with previous research on China and is analyzed in more detail in chapter 5.

Second, public satisfaction with the government is also influenced by spending on public goods, especially for local governments.[46] The more local governments spend on education, healthcare, social welfare, and other forms of public goods, the more satisfied the people living in those cities are. Public goods spending also increases satisfaction with the center, but to a lesser degree. This is appropriate, since most money spent at the local level comes from local governments—the central government provides only 30 percent of public goods spending, far below international standards. And because local governments have lower levels of regime support to begin with, greater public goods spending increases support and trust in the local government, and also reduces the local legitimacy deficit.

---

[46] For more details on these points, see Bruce J. Dickson, Pierre F. Landry, Mingming Shen, and Jie Yan, "Public Goods and Popular Support in Urban China," *China Quarterly*, forthcoming. We use the 2010 data in this analysis because the Chinese government stopped reporting detailed information on public goods spending after 2007.

Third, age is closely correlated with satisfaction with the work of both the central and local governments. From these data, we cannot determine whether the difference is due to lifecycle effects, in which case the younger generations will become more satisfied as they grow older, or if this signifies a fundamental shift in public opinion, in which case the public will grow increasingly dissatisfied as younger generations replace older generations. We will need data from a much longer period of time to know for sure. But since the younger generations are also better educated, more likely to use the Internet, and more likely to engage in protests, their dissatisfaction represents a cause of concern for the Party. It cannot afford to wait and see if they will become more satisfied as they grow older.

Fourth, income is also highly correlated with satisfaction with the government's work. The higher respondents' family income (relative to others in their community), the more satisfied they were with the work of both the central and local governments. This is of course what the Party hopes for: that greater prosperity will produce performance legitimacy. At least on this indicator, that strategy is working. However, as chapter 5 will show, the link between prosperity and legitimacy is more tenuous than this issue alone would indicate.

Finally, several key characteristics are only weakly correlated with performance legitimacy. Those with high school and college degrees are less satisfied than those with lower levels of education, but the differences are not significant. Party members are slightly more satisfied than nonmembers, but again the difference is not significant. Most surprisingly, *hukou* status does not have a significant impact on satisfaction with the government's work. In part, this is because a person's *hukou* is also related to their age, income, and education, but even when *hukou* status is considered alone and other variables are not held constant, it is not a strong predictor of satisfaction with the government. Those with urban *hukou* in the cities where they live are the most satisfied overall, but the other types of respondents—those with rural *hukou* in the cities where they live and migrants from the countryside and other cities—are not statistically different. This seems hard to fathom, given the discrimination faced by those with rural *hukou*. It is most likely because the situation faced by many migrants, as bad as it is, is often better than the situation they left behind. In recent years, many migrants have been returning to the countryside after losing jobs in the cities and facing other kinds of hardships. Because my surveys were conducted only in China's cities, they do not capture the people who were so dissatisfied that they left the cities and returned to the countryside. For those who lived in the cities at the time of the surveys, *hukou* status alone did not determine how satisfied they were with the overall work of the government.

VII. The Politics of Public Goods Provision

As noted earlier in this chapter, there are several notable trends in public goods spending in China. First, there is tremendous variation in the amounts that city governments spend on public goods. Second, spending on public goods is highly correlated: Cities that spend large amounts on one type of public good also tend to spend large amounts on others. Third, the ability of city governments to provide public goods is determined by both the local level of economic development and the ability of the government to extract resources from the economy, primarily in the form of taxes. But this still leaves a question: Just because city governments are *able* to spend money on public goods, why are they *willing* to do so?

In a democratic context, the motivation for elected leaders to provide public goods is well established: It shows their ability to deliver the goods to their constituents and improves their likelihood of being reelected.[47] In large communities, politicians cannot offer personal favors to all voters because there are simply too many people. Of course, personal favors are given to some individuals, but usually in return for private benefits, such as donations or personal gifts. This exchange of favors is often seen as illegitimate, and in many cases is outright illegal. But in order to garner enough votes to be reelected, politicians in democracies tend to provide public goods that benefit the community as a whole.

But politicians in authoritarian regimes face different incentives. They are appointed, not elected, so they do not need to appeal to voters by providing public goods in order to keep their jobs. They are freer to seek power, privilege, and personal gain because they are not

[47] This contrast between democratic and authoritarian politicians is based on Bueno de Mesquita et al., *The Logic of Political Survival.* For other works on the impact of regime type on public goods provision, see note 2.

constrained by public opinion the way elected leaders are. They provide favors to their families and friends, such as plum jobs, lavish lifestyles, foreign education, and other goodies not otherwise available. At the top of the regime, the job security of incumbent leaders can be threatened more by insiders than by outsiders—by opponents within the regime rather than by the public at large. They have to nurture the continued support of their allies, often through appointments and promotions, and limit the potential threat posed by challengers, who have their own networks of allies. Under these conditions, it makes more sense for authoritarian leaders to provide private goods to their supporters, whom they depend on to remain in power, and provide fewer public goods to the population as a whole because it does not have a direct say in which leaders are in power.

China's leaders, however, are not following this logic. Beginning in the 1990s and especially in the 2000s, China's leaders have been committed to governing better and providing more public goods. This new commitment was prompted by several factors. First, existential threats to the public's well-being, such as the SARS health scare of 2003, compelled China's leaders to begin rebuilding the healthcare system after years of decline.

Second, the policy priorities among top leaders changed. The pro-growth strategies of the 1990s, most identified with Jiang Zemin and the so-called third generation of leaders, were partially supplanted by more populist policies under their successors, represented by Hu Jintao and Wen Jiabao. As Mark Frazier puts it, "Modern states that base part of their legitimacy on improving the well-being of the people must appear to be responsive to those who suffer declining living standards, and they must remain attentive to inequalities more generally."[48] During the 2000s, they placed more emphasis on improving incomes and living standards, especially in the countryside, and more generally narrowing the gap between rich and poor. It was during this decade that the cuts to public goods during the 1980s and '90s were reversed. The result was the dramatic growth in spending on public goods shown in table 4-1. This commitment has continued into the Xi Jinping era.

[48] Mark Frazier, *Socialist Inequality: Pensions and the Politics of Uneven Development in China* (Ithaca, NY: Cornell University Press, 2010), p. 26.

Upon becoming general secretary in 2012, Xi said the Chinese people "expect better education, more stable work, more satisfying incomes, more reliable social insurance, a higher standard of health services, more comfortable homes, a more beautiful environment. They hope that their children can grow up, work, and live better. The people's desire to live a good life is the entire purpose of our struggle."[49] *People's Daily*, the official newspaper of the Party, wrote in 2015, "doing good work for the welfare of the people is not a case in which mere enthusiasm will suffice: it also requires attention to methods, a grasp of tactics, and well-trained skills. Then and only then can we handle matters effectively; *then and only then can we use real achievements to win the support and approval of ordinary people . . .*" (emphasis added).[50]

Third, and relatedly, the basis for the Party's legitimacy began to diversify. Whereas the Party had emphasized economic growth and more specifically improving standards of living as its key goals in the 1980s and '90s, at the beginning of the 2000s, party leaders began to emphasize quality-of-life issues in addition to the material benefits of growth. This change in priorities found precedent in Mao's call to "serve the people" and also had parallels with the "people's livelihood" of Sun Yat-sen's "Three Principles of the People" from the 1920s and even earlier Confucian traditions.[51] Throughout the post-Mao period, and especially in recent years, the Party has turned its attention from ideological goals to economic and social development. It has been determined to rule, not simply reign.

The fourth reason for increasing spending on public goods was to support the Party's strategy for restructuring the economy toward domestic consumption and away from fixed asset investment and reliance

---

[49] "*Xi Jinping: renmin dui meihao shenghuo de xiangwang jiushi women de fendou mubiao*" (Xi Jinping: The People's Desire to Live a Good Life Is the Entire Purpose of Our Struggle), http://cpc.people.com.cn/18/n/2012/1116/c350821-19596022.html, accessed August 30, 2015.

[50] "*Xi Jinping 'siyao' shi minsheng gongzuo 'zhinan'*" (Xi Jinping's 'Four Musts' Are the 'Guide' to Work for the People's Welfare), *People's Daily*, March 13, 2015, http://opinion.people.com.cn/n/2015/0313/c1003-26686494.html, accessed August 30, 2015.

[51] Orville Schell and John Delury, *Wealth and Power: China's Long March to the Twenty-first Century* (New York: Random House, 2014).

TABLE 4-5 Domestic Savings Rates, 2013 (gross domestic savings as percent of GDP)

China	51.8
Low income	11.8
Lower middle income	22.4
Upper middle income	32.8
High income: OECD	20.0

Source: World Development Indicators.

on exports. China has one of the highest savings rates in the world, much higher than the averages for all income groups (see table 4-5). The expectation is that as the government provides more public goods, people will not have to save as much of their incomes for medical emergencies, retirement, and other uncertainties, and would therefore have more money available for spending on consumer goods. This is a long-term objective. The high propensity to save is almost a cultural characteristic and may not immediately change just because the government now spends more on education and healthcare. As noted throughout this chapter, out-of-pocket expenses can still be substantial, and the ability to pay remains a concern for most people.

However, the change in Beijing was mostly rhetorical. In China, most public goods spending comes from local coffers. Why are local leaders, who are appointed and not elected to their posts, willing to devote more resources to public goods? There are several good reasons. First, they wanted to avoid bad publicity that was the consequence of a low supply of public goods. For example, some schools that did not have enough money to pay teachers' salaries or buy school supplies resorted to commercial operations to the detriment of their educational missions. They forced students to work, building products that the schools then sold. In one tragic case, a school in Jiangxi was converted into a fireworks factory, with the principal and teachers as managers and the students as workers. When an accidental explosion occurred, over 40 children were killed. The original official story blamed a mentally ill man who allegedly brought explosives to the school, but subsequent investigations by reporters and a public security team sent from Beijing revealed that the school was being used to assemble fireworks. The provincial party secretary and governor—the two highest posts in the province—were fired several weeks later, presumably for misleading the central government about the cause of the blast and covering up the use of the school and schoolchildren to build fireworks.[52] In this and other cases, local leaders want to avoid bad publicity that can damage their careers. These stories are often covered in the local, national, and even international media, shedding a bad light on local leaders and their cities.

Local leaders are also sensitive to rankings and want to avoid the stigma of being seen as substandard. There are multiple rankings of cities in terms of their suitability for foreign investment, the provision of public goods, and the quality of governance.[53] Cities that rank high on these lists bring good publicity and praise for their Party and government leaders, and those that rank low risk a loss of face for their leaders.

City leaders have a second reason to spend more on public goods: By improving the quality of life, it can increase people's level of satisfaction and decrease the likelihood of popular protests. This is a powerful motivation for local leaders, who have to achieve three hard targets: promoting economic growth, enforcing the one-child policy, and maintaining political stability. If they fail to achieve these targets, they can be transferred, demoted, or even fired.[54] Most public goods

[52] Zixue Tai, *The Internet in China: Cyberspace and Civil Society* (New York and London: Routledge, 2012), pp. 244–251.

[53] See, e.g., *China: Governance, Investment Climate, and Harmonious Society: Competitiveness Enhancements for 120 Cities in China* (Washington, DC: World Bank, 2006); *China's Governance in Transition* (Paris: Organization for Economic Co-operation and Development, 2005); *2008 Report on Public Governance in China's Provincial Capital Cities* (Beijing: Unirule, 2009); *2010 Report on Public Governance in China's Provincial Capital Cities* (Beijing: Unirule, 2012).

[54] For the use of hard and soft targets to evaluate the work of local officials, see Kevin J. O'Brien and Lianjiang Li, "Selective Policy Implementation in Rural China," *Comparative Politics*, Vol. 31, No. 2 (January 1999), pp. 167–186; Maria Edin, "State Capacity and Local Agent Control in China: CCP Cadre Management From a Township Perspective," *China Quarterly*, No. 173 (March 2003), pp. 35–52; Susan H. Whiting, "The Cadre Evaluation System at the Grass Roots: The Paradox of Party Rule," in Barry Naughton and Dali L. Yang, eds., *Holding China Together: Diversity and National Integration in the Post-Deng Era* (New York: Cambridge University Press,

are seen as soft targets: Improving literacy, life expectancy, and environmental protection are all good if they can be achieved, but they are of less consequence in appointments and promotions than the three hard targets. But spending on public goods can have both direct and indirect consequences for political stability. On one hand, many local protests are triggered by the failure to deliver on past promises to provide public goods, such as housing, healthcare, and pensions to SOE workers. More spending in these areas can reduce the likelihood of protests. On the other hand, improvements in public goods can create more satisfaction with the overall quality of life, which in turn tends to make people more accepting of the status quo, more optimistic about future improvements, and less inclined to engage in protests.

A third reason to spend more on public goods is that it makes the city more appealing to foreign investors. Attracting foreign direct investment (FDI) is one indicator of promoting economic growth, and cities and counties compete with one another to land big contracts. Higher spending on public goods demonstrates local leaders' commitment to a well-educated and healthy labor force, reliable transportation, good infrastructure, and other goods and services that are attractive to foreign investors. In the 50 cities in the Public Goods and Political Support Survey, spending on public goods is highly correlated with levels of FDI in later years. Spending more on public goods can be a good investment in the growth of the local economy, which local officials need for their annual evaluations.

Providing public goods in China is not just the responsibility of the state; civil society is increasingly involved. As described in chapter 3, civil society groups—charity foundations, faith-based groups, and NGOs of all kinds—provide necessary goods and services to victims of natural disasters, those in need of legal advice, the poor, the disabled, and a range of other individuals and groups. Local officials who see the advantage of providing more public goods do not have to rely

2004), pp. 101–119; Pierre F. Landry, *Decentralized Authoritarianism in China: The Communist Party's Control of Local Elites in the Post-Mao Era* (New York: Cambridge University Press, 2008); Yongshun Cai and Lin Zhou, "Disciplining Local Officials in China: The Case of Conflict Management," *China Journal*, No. 70 (July 2013), pp. 98–119.

on their own resources; they can also partner with civil society groups to deliver public goods and services. Local governments have learned that NGOs have the resources to provide needed public goods, especially to disadvantaged groups like migrant workers, the elderly, and the disabled.[55] Central policy limits local governments' ability to increase revenue through taxes and fees, so NGOs help fill a variety of social needs. Although officials may be wary of civil society groups, they also recognize that they can play an important role in facilitating the provision of public goods. To the extent that this improves the quality of life, especially for targeted groups, then this cooperation can also lower the likelihood that dissatisfaction over public goods provision will lead to public protest. This reinforces the notion that serving the people through better governance is in the interests of local officials, who are evaluated in part on their ability to maintain political order.

* * *

Providing public goods—the ultimate example of serving the people—has become part of the Party's survival strategy. The Party has identified problems in the provision of public goods and taken steps to address them, but so far it has not been able to resolve them. Indeed, this is one of the tremendous challenges facing many developing countries: The push to modernize creates new needs for expanded public goods provision, and rising expectations make it difficult for governments to fully satisfy their societies. China is no exception. Rapid economic development is creating the need for a variety of public goods, education and healthcare in particular, while exacerbating other issues, such as the environment and economic inequality.

Several key themes emerge from this look at public goods provision in China. First, government spending on healthcare and education is typical of countries at China's level of economic development. It falls short of the advanced industrialized economies of the West, but that is

[55] Anthony J. Spires, "Contingent Symbiosis and Civil Society in an Authoritarian State: Understanding the Survival of China's Grassroots NGOs," *American Journal of Sociology*, Vol. 117, No. 1 (July 2011), pp. 1–45; Jessica C. Teets, *Civil Society under Authoritarianism: The China Model* (New York: Cambridge University Press, 2014).

not a fair comparison. China has the world's second-largest economy in aggregate terms, but in per capita terms—a better indicator of level of development—it is barely in the top 100. Public goods spending in China is comparable to other upper-middle-income countries, and its rate of growth in this regard is several times higher than in those countries. In comparative terms, its performance is relatively good, and it is getting better.

Second, there is tremendous variation in the amount of public goods spending over time and in different parts of the country. During the early part of the reform era through the 1990s, China's leaders were focused primarily on achieving high levels of economic growth and were less committed to the social welfare programs that characterized the Maoist era. When SOEs began to be restructured, sold off, or closed, many workers lost their jobs and the benefits that came with them. The "iron rice bowl" of lifetime job security, housing, education, medical care, pensions, and other benefits was suddenly taken away. Although China's leaders showed greater concern for public goods beginning in the early 2000s, we should not lose sight of a key point: The remarkable increase in public goods spending in China is in large part due to the decline in previous years. Recent increases in public goods spending are attempting to correct for past cutbacks in China's social safety net.

Not only is there significant change over time, but also dramatic regional variation in the provision of public goods in China. Some cities provide more public goods to their people than do other cities. This is not just a matter of priorities, with some cities emphasizing healthcare, and other cities education or different public goods. City governments that provide high levels of one type of public goods tend to provide large amounts of others. The explanation for this is straightforward: the more developed the local economy and the higher the local state's capacity to extract resources, the more it can provide public goods. It is not enough for the local economy to be prosperous. The local government must also be able to tap into that prosperity in order to provide more public goods.

Relatedly, the quality and quantity of public goods that individuals receive depend on where they live and where they work. Urban residents get a more generous amount of public goods compared to those in rural areas. Those who migrate from the countryside into the cities are generally excluded from the full range of public goods that urban residents receive. Because residency is formally determined by *hukou* status, those who move to the city but are unable to change their status from rural to urban remain outside the urban public goods system, even though they live in urban areas. In most cases, they are not entitled to send their children to local schools without paying fees and must return to their villages to be treated when they are injured or ill. Moreover, most migrants tend to work in the private sector where both wages and benefits are low. Those who work for SOEs tend to get higher wages and better benefits, but employment in the public sector has been steadily declining.

Third, the public gives middling grades to the public goods they receive. At the same time, there is also a recognition that the situation is generally improving. For the most part, this is consistent with the objective measures and comparative perspectives provided throughout the chapter: Public goods provision in China may be mediocre, but it is getting better, and most people are generally satisfied with the government's work in this area. China's leaders, mindful of the Tocquevillian paradox and the revolution of rising expectations, are determined to make improvements in public goods provision a source of regime legitimacy and not a cause for public dissatisfaction.

The CCP official who chastised me for suggesting that the Party's main goal was to remain in power (noted at the beginning of the chapter) was partially right: The Party may be increasingly focused on serving the people, but it is doing so as part of its strategy for survival. Does serving the people lead to greater popular support for the Party? What other parts of the Party's survival strategy increase or decrease regime support? Those questions are addressed in the next chapter.

5

Generating Support

AUTOCRATS MAY TRY TO generate popular support in order to help them remain in power, but do they get the results they want? This chapter analyzes the Party's survival strategy—a mix of repression, legitimation, and co-optation—in terms of its impact on levels of regime support and presents three key findings based on the two Public Goods and Popular Support Surveys used throughout this book. First, there are significant differences in levels of support and trust for central Party and government institutions and their local counterparts, what I refer to as the "local legitimacy deficit." Second, rising prosperity, normative values, and institutional ties to the state—when analyzed together instead of viewed in isolation—do not influence regime support in the way expected by conventional wisdom. For example, although most observers contend that the Party's legitimacy is based on economic growth, there is no relationship between levels of per capita GDP or economic growth and regime support. And although CCP members should be the base of support for the regime, CCP members are not so different from the rest of the population in their assessments of the regime at either the central or local levels. Third, the heavy hand of the state works in different ways to affect popular support for the regime. Both perceptions of corruption and personal experience with it have strong negative impacts on regime support. In contrast, encountering censorship online does not have the expected effect, largely because censorship primarily affects the youngest cohorts, who have less regime support to begin with. In short, the Party's survival strategy has major impacts on popular support for the regime, but not always in ways expected by conventional wisdom, or by the Party itself.

I. Indicators of Regime Support

Previous studies of regime support in China have consistently found two separate conclusions. First, levels of regime support are surprisingly high, especially given the frequent stories about political protests due to governance failures, environmental concerns, and corruption and malfeasance among Party and government officials. There are various ways to measure regime support. Like most abstract concepts, it is hard to pin down with a single indicator. Although most would accept the idea that political legitimacy is the acceptance of the status quo as part of the normal order of things, determining whether people accept the status quo is less clear-cut. Jie Chen's study of political support in Beijing measured support with six statements about the political system. Across three surveys in the 1990s, 75 percent or more of the respondents agreed with most of the statements, indicating their support for the current political system.[1] Tianjian Shi's analysis of Asian Barometer Survey data found that over 90 percent of respondents found national-level political institutions (the CCP, government, NPC, and PLA) to be "very trustworthy."[2] He also found that there was a significant gap between the trustworthiness of these national institutions, which are generally far removed from daily life, and local institutions, with which people are more likely to have personal experience (a gap we examine later). Even so, approximately

[1] The six statements were: (1) I am proud to live under the current political system. (2) I have an obligation to support the current political system. (3) I respect the political institutions in China today. (4) I feel that the basic rights of citizens are protected. (5) I believe that the courts can guarantee a fair trial. (6) I feel that my personal values are the same as those advocated by the government. See Jie Chen, *Popular Political Support in Urban China* (Stanford, CA: Stanford University Press, 2004), p. 23. These questions were based on the operationalization of political legitimacy suggested by Muller and Jukam; see Edward N. Muller and Thomas O. Jukam, "On the Meaning of Political Support," *American Political Science Review*, Vol. 71, No. 4 (December 1975), pp. 1561–1595.

[2] Tianjian Shi, "China: Democratic Values Supporting an Authoritarian System," in Yun-han Chu et al., eds., *How East Asians View Democracy* (New York: Columbia University Press, 2008), p. 229.

75 percent of people or more thought the local government, civil service, and local police to be either trustworthy or very trustworthy. A global survey conducted by Pew just before the international financial crisis in 2007 found that 86 percent of those surveyed in China believed the country was moving in the right direction, a more general but still positive indicator of support for the status quo; in contrast, just over 20 percent in the U.S. believed the same.[3] In the World Values Survey conducted in China in 2012, three-quarters or more said they had a great deal or a lot of confidence in the Party, the national government, and the NPC.[4] Each of these studies looks at regime support in different ways. But however it is measured, previous surveys show high levels of regime support.

The second consistent finding from previous research on political legitimacy in China concerns the distinction between the central and local levels of the state: When people evaluate the main political institutions and the people who work in them, the central ones are held in higher esteem than the local ones. This can be seen in a variety of answers in the Public Goods and Political Support Surveys.

- 78.5 percent said they trusted central leaders, but only 58.9 percent trusted local leaders in the 2014 survey.
- In 2010, 49.7 percent thought corruption was at least somewhat common among central officials, but 77.2 percent—over 50 percent more—thought the same for local officials. This changed in 2014, when China was in the midst of a high-profile anti-corruption campaign: The numbers jumped to 69.8 percent for central officials and 84.1 percent for local officials.[5] In both years, perceptions of the prevalence of corruption were notably higher for local officials than central ones.

[3] Pew Research Center, *The 2008 Pew Global Attitudes Survey in China: The Chinese Celebrate Their Roaring Economy, as They Struggle with Its Costs* (2008).

[4] Data taken from the online analysis section of the World Values Survey website, http://www.worldvaluessurvey.org/WVSOnline.jsp, accessed February 24, 2015.

[5] As might be imagined, this was one of the most sensitive questions in the survey and many respondents chose not to reply; in 2014, the non-response rate was 20.1 percent on local corruption and 29.4 percent on central-level corruption. The percentages reported here are based on those who did answer the questions.

- When asked about their levels of trust and support for the most important political institutions (the Party, the government, and the people's congresses), respondents consistently gave higher scores for the central institutions than their local counterparts, on average over 16 percent higher.

This local legitimacy deficit is consistent with a variety of previous studies of China.[6] It is in sharp contrast with the United States, where most people give higher approval ratings to local officials than to Congress or the president. Kent Jennings attributed this to greater responsiveness of local governments to popular concerns and greater ease in observing and evaluating what local governments do.[7] Among East Asian democracies, the pattern is the same: citizens in Japan, Korea, Taiwan, and the Philippines have higher levels of trust in local governments than national governments.[8] China stands out in having significantly lower levels of trust and support at the local level of government. However, the high levels of trust in the center may by partly illusory. Wang finds that most people have high trust in an "imaginary state" they never personally encounter, but have lower trust in the "real state" they have direct experience with at the local level.[9]

China's local legitimacy deficit is not only clear and consistent, it is easy to explain. First of all, central leaders are generally shielded from

[6] Tianjian Shi, "Cultural Values and Political Trust: A Comparison of the People's Republic of China and Taiwan," *Comparative Politics*, Vol. 33, No. 4 (July 2001), pp. 401–419; Tony Saich, "Citizen's Perceptions of Governance in Rural and Urban China," *Journal of Chinese Political Science*, Vol. 12, No. 1 (April 2007), pp. 1–28; Lianjiang Li, "Political Trust and Petitioning in the Chinese Countryside," *Comparative Politics*, Vol. 40, No. 2 (January 2008), pp. 209–226.

[7] M. Kent Jennings, "Political Trust and the Roots of Devolution," in Valerie Braithwaite and Margaret Levi, eds., *Trust and Governance* (New York: Russell Sage Foundation, 1998), pp. 218-244.

[8] Yun-han Chu, Larry Diamond, Andrew J. Nathan, and Doh Chull Shin, eds., *How East Asians View Democracy* (New York: Columbia University Press, 2008).

[9] Zhengxu Wang, "Political Trust in China: Forms and Causes," in Lynn T. White, ed., *Legitimacy: Ambiguities of Political Success or Failure in East and Southeast Asia.* (Singapore: World Scientific, 2005), pp. 113–139; see also Lianjiang Li, "The Magnitude of Trust in the Center: Evidence from Interviews with Petitioners in Beijing and a Local Survey in Rural China," *Modern China*, Vol. 39, no. 1 (2013), pp. 3–36.

bad publicity in the media. Before Xi Jinping became CCP general secretary in 2012, there was a norm that high-level officials were immune
from corruption investigations. This prevented one leader or faction
from accusing another (or even their families) of corrupt behavior.
When ministers, mayors, or party secretaries are charged with corruption, it is normally *after* they have lost a power struggle or been abandoned by their political mentors. Corrupt behavior is rarely the cause
of a political downfall. Even during Xi's anti-corruption campaign,
investigations have been politically motivated. Xi vowed to capture
both "tigers and flies" (i.e., both high- and low-level officials), and the
most prominent tiger was Zhou Yongkang, who had previously been
the internal security czar and a member of the Politburo's Standing
Committee, the inner circle of political power in China. More importantly, Zhou was a supporter of Bo Xilai, the charismatic Party secretary
of Chongqing whose public campaign to gain a seat on the Standing
Committee threatened the orderly leadership succession that had
been arranged in private. After Bo was fired from his post in 2012 and
imprisoned for corruption and covering up his wife's involvement in
the murder of a foreign businessman, Zhou allegedly attempted a coup
to exonerate Bo.[10] This challenge to the central leadership, and Xi in
particular, may have been the impetus for the anticorruption campaign
that followed, which focused on Zhou and many of his protégés.

Whereas central officials had previously been spared from corruption investigations, local officials were more vulnerable. Most exposés
of corruption, malfeasance, and illegal activities concern local officials.
This is true for the Internet, as well as the state-run media. Internet
criticism of central leaders is heavily censored, but stories and photos of
local misdeeds often go viral. This is by design: Central leaders prefer
to focus popular outrage against lower levels while deflecting it from
themselves. Media reports and CCP punishment of corruption normally involve local (county level or below) officials.

A second reason for the local legitimacy deficit concerns the policy
process. Central leaders frequently announce new policy initiatives,
but put the onus for implementing the policies, and more importantly

---

[10] Rumors of this attempted coup circulated widely in China and the China-
watching community. The Party has never commented on the rumor.

paying for them, on local officials. When local reality does not match central rhetoric, people are more prone to blame local officials for not delivering the promised goods and services rather than blame the center for imposing unfunded mandates. The center has also been known to announce a fine-sounding policy, but then direct local officials not to carry it out. For example, the Party has been promoting various channels for the public to articulate grievances, such as using the legal system, filing petitions, or appealing to higher levels to redress local problems. At the same time, it has directed local officials to maintain political stability (e.g., by not letting people in their jurisdictions travel to provincial capitals or Beijing to get their problems solved). Local officials will send police to prevent petitioners and protestors from traveling or take them into custody and force them to return home. When this happens, it is local leaders who get the blame, even though they are following orders from the center.

Local officials discussed the difficulty in complying with central directives during focus group interviews conducted in conjunction with the 2014 survey. A Beijing city official said that the central government was full of slogans, but its policies had no teeth. A social security official in Chongqing complained the center provided vague slogans and short-term campaigns, but not specific long-term guidelines. In Wuhan, an official working at a community services center complained that they could not convey local public opinion on public goods provision to higher levels of government. They had to spend most of their time catering to the whims of higher-level officials instead of the needs of the local people they were supposed to serve.

In measuring regime support in China, I use respondents' degree of trust and support in the main political institutions—the Party, the government, and the people's congress, or legislature—at both the central and local levels.[11] Conceptually, there is an important distinction between satisfaction with incumbent officials and the policies they

---

[11] Respondents were asked to indicate on a 0–10 scale how much they trusted the Party, the government, and the people's congress, China's main political institutions, and how much they supported them. There were a total of six questions for central institutions and six more for local institutions. These six questions were combined into a single index of regime support. In the analysis below, this index is standardized on a 0–100 scale to make it easier to interpret the results.

pursue, on one hand, and satisfaction with the system as a whole, on the other. David Easton first clarified this difference between *specific* support for leaders and their policies and *diffuse* support for the regime itself.[12] People may want a change of policy or even a change in individual leaders, but not of the political system as a whole. In practice, however, they are closely correlated. Those who support the incumbents are also likely to support the regime; conversely, those who do not support the incumbents may feel that the regime itself is to blame, and the only way to get better leaders and policies is to change the political system.

Measuring regime support in terms of trust and support of the main political institutions has two important advantages. First, it allows comparison of central and local levels of legitimacy. Do the factors that influence satisfaction with the central institutions have the same impact on local counterparts? Which factors account for the local legitimacy deficit? Second, it is a more intuitive measure of regime support for respondents. They are likely to have thought about whether they trust and support the main political institutions, but whether their personal values are represented by the Party and government may seem more abstract and harder to answer. In practice, though, the different ways of measuring regime support are highly correlated: Those who are satisfied with the overall work of the government also tend to trust and support China's main political institutions and feel that their personal values are well represented. Although diffuse and specific types of support are conceptually distinct, they are empirically closely related.

How valid are these responses? Do they reflect the genuine attitudes of respondents, or are they engaging in "preference falsification"— giving answers that they know not to be true, but are the politically correct responses given to strangers? After all, it would be natural for Chinese respondents to blur the truth on sensitive questions so that they do not face any potential retaliation for expressing critical views to pollsters whom they do not know. This is a well-known practice in authoritarian countries like China.[13] But there are several reasons

[12] David Easton, *A Systems Analysis of Political Life* (New York, NY: Wiley, 1965).
[13] Timur Kuran, "Now Out of Never: The Element of Surprise in the East European Revolution of 1989," *World Politics*, Vol. 44, No. 1 (October 1991), pp. 7–48. Kuran's seminal article was inspired by Vaclav Havel's essay "The Power of

why these assessments of regime support can be treated as reflecting the genuine attitudes of respondents. First of all, the respondents were promised anonymity in return for participating in the surveys. This is standard practice in survey work, designed to protect the identities and well-being of respondents. Survey research is increasingly common in China, and I am not aware of anyone who has been harmed for participating in a survey, except of course by enduring the tedium of sitting through an hour-long interview. Second, these are statements about the regime as a whole and are therefore less sensitive than questions about individual leaders. China does not allow approval ratings for political leaders, which are a staple of polling in other countries. The measures of regime support used here—trust and support in the Party, government, and legislature—are rough approximations of approval ratings, but are worded to avoid political sensitivities (figure 5.1). Third, survey researchers try to avoid questions that would likely elicit rote answers. As we shall see later, regime support is closely correlated with a variety of explanatory variables. As one of my former professors once put it, respondents may be lying, but they are lying in ways predicted by social science theory. Either they are very familiar with social science theory and answer accordingly, or they are giving answers that are close to their true opinions. While some may prefer to take these questions with a grain of salt, there is more than a grain of truth to them.

The next sections examine how the different elements of the Party's strategy for survival impact levels of regime support in China. These elements include improving material interests, promoting key political values, providing public goods, co-opting new elites into the CCP, and employing the heavy hand of the state, in particular corruption and censorship. In addition, other factors that are expected to influence regime support are also included. These factors include individual characteristics, such as age, education, gender, and *hukou* status. Put together, these various factors will provide a clear picture of what generates support for the Party and what undermines it.

the Powerless," which described how fear of reprisals made people living in communist countries exhibit support for the regime when in their hearts they did not, and as a result no one knew how many others shared their true feelings.

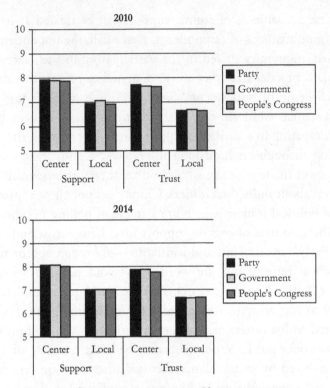

FIGURE 5-1 Levels of Regime Support in China, 2010–2014.
Source: Public Goods and Political Support Surveys.

II. The Impact of Rising Prosperity on Regime Support

The conventional wisdom among China watchers is that the Party's legitimacy is based primarily on economic growth. This assumption is repeated in most academic and journalistic accounts of sources of legitimacy in China. It is also the rationale behind the Party's commitment to economic modernization throughout the post-Mao era of reform and opening up. Chinese leaders were committed not only to the broad goals of economic modernization, but also to specific annual targets as well. Before the international financial crisis, Chinese leaders were determined to surpass a minimum target of 8 percent growth per year. In fact, economic growth averaged around 10 percent in these years. This rapid pace of growth had tangible signs, with new construction seemingly everywhere. Beginning in the 1990s, it was said that over half of the

TABLE 5-1 Income Gains (numbers in table are percentages)

	Family income now compared to five years ago is:		Expect family income five years from now to be:	
	2010	2014	2010	2014
Much better	8.0	10.3	13.6	15.1
Better	61.0	65.7	69.0	68.0
No difference	19.5	18.5	14.0	13.8
Worse	10.6	4.9	3.2	2.6
Much worse	.9	.7	.3	.4

Source: Public Goods and Political Support Surveys.

world's construction cranes were in China. Just as important, this rate of growth provided new jobs to the millions of workers joining the labor force each year. By keeping growth high and unemployment low, the benefits of growth were widely—although unequally—shared. In the early reform era, this was described as "reform without losers"; Because economic reform presented so many opportunities to so many people, there was little conflict between winners and losers and therefore little social turmoil.[14] Nearly everyone was better off. This changed with the beginning of SOE reform in the late 1990s, when tens of millions of people were laid off or forced into retirement (see chapter 4 for more discussion). Many of these workers were left destitute, stripped of the benefits and pensions they had relied on, and unable to find work in the private sector. In recent years, there have definitely been losers whose lives have been made worse as a consequence of ongoing economic reforms. But the vast majority of Chinese believe that their lives have gotten better, and even more are optimistic about the future (see table 5-1).

Asking people about their incomes can be a sensitive issue. Most do not like revealing precise information about how much they make, especially to strangers in the context of a public opinion survey. In the 2014 Public Goods and Political Support Survey, over 30 percent of

[14] Lawrence J. Lau, Yingyi Qian, and Gerard Roland, "Reform without Losers: An Interpretation of China's Dual-Track Approach to Transition," *Journal of Political Economy*, Vol. 108, No. 1 (February 2000), pp. 120–143.

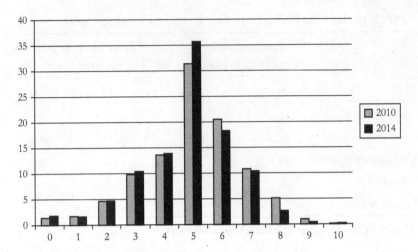

FIGURE 5-2 Level of Income Relative to Others in Community (low to high, percentages of respondents).
Source: Public Goods and Political Support Surveys.

respondents refused to say how much they made as individuals, and over 35 percent refused to give their family incomes. One alternative is to ask about incomes *relative to others in their community* (see figure 5-2). In some ways, this is a more relevant yardstick. People tend to assess their incomes not just in absolute dollar amounts (or yuan, in this case), but compared to what they perceive around them. Regardless of their actual incomes, are they keeping up with their neighbors? Asked this way, relative family incomes are distributed in a nice bell-shaped curve, centered on the midpoint (5). The vast majority of respondents are clustered in the middle (3–7).

Although Chinese leaders and China watchers alike expect that economic growth enhances the Party's legitimacy, modernization theory has the opposite perspective. It suggests that as the level of prosperity rises, countries are more likely to become democratic. Prosperity itself does not cause democratization, but the social changes that accompany economic modernization do. As countries modernize, they undergo industrialization, and workers move out of agriculture into manufacturing, because factory jobs tend to be higher paying than farming. This also leads to a demographic shift, as people move from the countryside into cities, where most factories are located. In cities, they are removed from their families and traditional ways of life and begin to mix and mingle with people from other backgrounds and other parts of the country. Education levels begin to rise because more jobs require basic literacy and math skills. As a result, scientific thinking replaces superstitious beliefs: Things happen not because of fate or capricious spirits, but because of cause and effect. The availability of the news media and other sources of information, combined with higher literacy, gives people a greater understanding of what is happening in their cities, their countries, and around the world. All of this makes people more aware of their current situation, better able to analyze it, better able to communicate their concerns, and better able to organize with those with similar grievances and goals. As society becomes less accepting of the status quo, people expect more accountability from their leaders, both their bosses and government officials. Awareness of their rights and the willingness to demand and defend them become the basis for democracy.

The correlation between economic development and democracy is well known: The richest countries are mostly democracies and the poorest countries are not. However, the causal connections between development and democracy have been the source of ongoing and often heated debate. The original perspective, and still the most popular, is that for each country, the process of development brings about democratization: The richer it gets, the more likely it is to transition from authoritarian rule to democracy. An alternative argument is that democratization can occur at any level of development, but is more likely to be successful at higher levels of development. In this view, something else triggers democratization—defeat in war, economic crisis, mass protest, elite conflict, etc.—but the prospects for democratization are better when a country is richer.[15] The eventual outcome is the same—rich countries tend to be democracies—but how this outcome occurs remains a contentious issue.

This is not just an academic debate; it has direct consequences in the real world. For decades, promoting democracy abroad has been

---

[15] A good summary of the argument with recent evidence is by Ronald Inglehart and Christian Welzel, "How Development Leads to Democracy: What We Know about Modernization," *Foreign Affairs*, Vol. 88, No. 2 (March-April 2009), pp. 33–48.

a primary goal of the U.S. and other Western countries. U.S. policies toward China in the post-Mao period have encouraged economic reform and trade with the expectation that these will facilitate democratization.[16] The expectations of modernization theory have underpinned this effort and led to policies promoting economic growth and free trade abroad. But if economic modernization does not cause democratization, but only makes it more likely to succeed when other events trigger it, then policy-makers should not expect that democratization will result from economic growth. There is little reason to think economic growth hurts the prospects for democratization, but there are strong doubts about whether it directly causes it. For countries that democratized after World War II, especially in the Third Wave and the post-communist transition, economic modernization was not a trigger; although higher levels of development did not by themselves make democratization more likely, they did make it more likely to survive.

The implication for China is clear: The level of per capita GDP is not a good barometer for potential democratization. The optimism inherent in the crude form of modernization theory—any country can become democratic if it becomes rich—is not the basis for good policy. In order to achieve policy goals, it is useful to know which tool is most likely to get the job done. There is no grand, unified theory of democratization. The prospects for democratization do not hinge on economic growth alone. To assume otherwise is to ignore the myriad ways that democratization comes about at all levels of development.

The insights of modernization theory have led to repeated predictions that China will soon democratize. Bruce Gilley argues that economic development has produced high levels of legitimacy in China at present, but is also leading to changes in political values that may require the Party to adopt institutional changes, specifically democratization, to accommodate popular demands.[17] Yun-han Chu and Yu-tzung Chang similarly found that a "culture shift" toward post-

[16] James Mann, *The China Fantasy: How Our Leaders Explain Away Chinese Repression* (New York: Viking, 2007).

[17] Bruce Gilley, "Legitimacy and Institutional Change: The Case of China," *Comparative Political Studies*, Vol. 41, No. 3 (March 2008), pp. 259–284.

modern values is undermining regime support in favor of democratization.[18] Henry Rowen boldly predicted that China would become "partly free" by 2015 and "fully free" by 2025, based on increases in education and economic growth.[19] Writing in 2005, Ronald Inglehart and Christian Welzel made a similar prediction on the same time frame: "We predict that China's socioeconomic liberalization process and its experimentation with local-level democracy will spill over to the national level so that China will make a transition to a liberal democracy within the next two decades" (i.e., by 2025).[20]

The Party and advocates of modernization theory have competing expectations about the impact of increased prosperity on the fate of the regime. The Party expects growth to legitimize the regime and prolong its rule, whereas modernization theory suggests that growth will undermine the Party's hold on power. The two views are not totally incompatible. Economic growth may legitimize the regime in the short run as standards of living rise and that translates into satisfaction with the regime. But adherents of modernization theory would suggest that in the long run, the economic and social changes underway in China will undermine support for the regime. In particular, modernization theory predicts that growth will ultimately undermine the Party by producing a middle class that will want more rights and freedoms than the Party has been willing to provide. As people begin to take prosperity and material interests for granted, they will develop "post-material" interests: Expectations not just of higher salaries, better housing, and creature comforts, but also of social equality and political freedom. Once their standards of living are secure, they will begin to care about

[18] Yun-han Chu and Yu-tzung Chang, "Culture Shift and Regime Legitimacy: Comparing Mainland China, Taiwan, and Hong Kong," in Shiping Hua, ed., *Chinese Political Culture 1989–2000* (Armonk, NY: M.E. Sharpe, 2001).

[19] Henry S. Rowen, "When Will the Chinese People Be Free?" *Journal of Democracy*, Vol. 18, No. 3 (July 2007), pp. 38–62. In predicting China's future, Rowen uses the Freedom House terminology for two of three regime types, the third being "not free." Since the start of Freedom House rankings, China has been in the not free category.

[20] Ronald Inglehart and Christian Welzel, *Modernization, Cultural Change, and Democracy: The Human Development Sequence* (New York: Cambridge University Press, 2005), pp. 190–191.

the quality of their lives, including a cleaner environment, more social justice, and a stronger say in the policies that affect them. In short, the "revolution of rising expectations" of the middle class may lead people to seek a more responsive and democratic government.

It is easier to talk about the impact of the middle class than to identify who belongs to it. Different people use different definitions for identifying the middle class, such as income, occupation, education, homeownership, urban residence, or some combination of these characteristics. These definitions overlap: White-collar managers tend to have higher educations, earn higher incomes, and live in cities. But they also yield quite different estimates of the size of the middle class, from a low of 10 percent of China's population to over 50 percent.[21] However, all agree that the middle class is growing, will continue to grow, and that the implications of its growth are worthy of attention. Rather than try to identify the members of the middle class among my survey respondents, I instead focus on the attributes associated with it, particularly income, education, *hukou* status, and age (because the middle class has only begun to emerge during the post-Mao era).

How can we test these competing expectations? The Party expects that improving standards of living should enhance its legitimacy. This includes higher levels of income and per capita GDP. Levels of regime support should be higher among the most prosperous individuals and in the most prosperous cities. In contrast, according to modernization theory, regime support should be lower in the more modern sectors of the country: Those who live in the richest cities, have higher education and professional (white-collar) jobs, and among the younger cohorts. Whereas older generations can appreciate how the present is better than the more distant past, younger ones have known only prosperity and progress and therefore take them for granted, and can be expected to develop other expectations.

---

[21] David S. G. Goodman, *Class in Contemporary China* (Cambridge, UK: Polity Press, 2014), pp. 92–121. See also Cheng Li, ed., *China's Emerging Middle Class: Beyond Economic Transition* (Washington, DC: Brookings Institution, 2010); and Jie Chen, *A Middle Class without Democracy: Economic Growth and the Prospects for Democratization in China* (New York: Oxford University Press, 2013).

These individual and aggregate measures of prosperity have different effects on regime support (the analysis below is based on a multivariate regression model; see appendix 2 for details). Both the level of family incomes (shown in figure 5-2) and the increase in family incomes have statistically significant positive impacts. However, neither per capita GDP nor GDP growth over the previous three years are correlated with trust and support at either the central or local levels. In American politics, scholars debate whether election results are driven by "sociotropic" voting or pocketbook voting: Do people care more about national economic conditions, or only whether their personal incomes are rising or falling? Even though people in China do not have the opportunity to elect their leaders, these survey data suggest that only pocketbooks drive regime support.

These findings do not match the expectations of modernization theory. Modernization may produce the anticipated effects in the future, but they are not very visible at present. However, this is only one aspect of modernization theory; others will be examined later. The Party's expectations are also only partially fulfilled by these findings. Only pocketbook factors have a positive impact on regime support at both the central and local levels. These results indicate that the beneficiaries of economic growth—when age, education, gender, *hukou* status, and other factors are held constant—have higher levels of regime support. Sociotropic factors—GDP levels and GDP growth—have minimal impact on regime support.

Many of the local protests that have rocked China in recent years are against the heavy-handed tactics that local officials use to pump up economic growth, including seizures of land and housing for redevelopment and projects that damage the environment. These tactics not only trigger NIMBY disputes as described in chapter 3, they also have a more widespread impact on public opinion. In recent years, the Party has been shifting to a new economic model with lower rates of economic growth and has simultaneously been publicizing the need for smarter growth, instead of faster growth, in order to adjust public expectations. Growth rates have declined since 2008, but most people report their incomes continued to rise and most remain optimistic about the future.

Even though family incomes are closely associated with regime support, this also points out a potential weakness in the Party's survival strategy. It indicates that pocketbook factors are a more important source of regime support than sociotropic factors, but that is predicated upon continued improvements in personal prosperity. If incomes stagnate or even decline, regime support is also likely to fall. There is a hint of such a scenario in figure 5-2. Survey respondents were asked to indicate their family income relative to their neighbors on a 0–10 scale. For those above the midpoint (6–10), the percentages were lower in 2014 than in 2010; more people put themselves at or below the midpoint (0–5) in 2014 than in 2010. People may see their incomes rising (see table 5-1), but they may also see it slipping, relative to their neighbors. The challenge for the Party is ensuring that incomes continue to rise even as aggregate growth begins to slow. Otherwise, it is likely to suffer lower regime support. Above all, these findings indicate why the Party's strategy for survival cannot be based on material factors alone.

Other aspects of modernization theory concerning age, education, and urbanization can also be tested with these survey data. There is a clear and strong relationship between age and regime support (see figure 5-3). Each generation feels less regime support than the one before it, with the youngest generation having an average level of regime support 13 percent below that of the oldest generation. From these cross-sectional data, we cannot tell if this difference is due to life cycle effects, in which attitudes change as people get older, or whether they reflect a

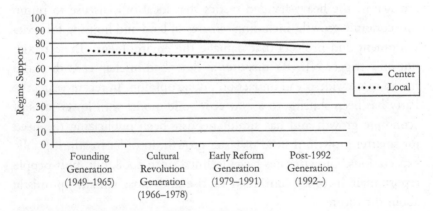

FIGURE 5-3 Age Cohorts and Regime Support.
Source: 2014 Public Goods and Political Support Survey.

more fundamental shift in political attitudes in China. Either way, the youngest cohort (which is also the best educated and the most "plugged in") is the least supportive of the regime at both the central and local levels. China is hardly unique in this regard: Young people are the most disaffected in most countries, and the most likely to engage in protest.

Modernization theory also predicts that those with higher levels of education will be less supportive of authoritarian rule, but the evidence from urban China is mixed. Those with a high school degree have higher regime support than those with less education, but the difference is not statistically significant. Those with a college degree have higher regime support, but only for the local level. Education alone is not a consistent and reliable predictor of regime support.

A third element of modernization theory concerns the consequences of urbanization. As people move to cities, they are exposed to new ideas and wider circles of people, live apart from much of their family and traditional social ties, and work in new sectors of the economy. This is expected to change their thinking on an array of political and social issues, and in particular create new demands for rights and freedoms and less acceptance of authoritarian rule. This social change is underway in China, but it has not yet had a strong effect on people's attitudes toward the regime that governs them. We can see this by focusing on the four types of *hukou* among the survey respondents: those with either urban or rural *hukou* in the cities where they live and those with urban or rural *hukou* who have migrated from elsewhere in China. Using the first and largest group (urban *hukou* in the cities where they live) as the reference group, none of the other groups have significantly different levels of regime support.

The weak relationships among education, *hukou*, and regime support do not fit the expectations of modernization theory, but they do not signal a rejection of the theory either. At best, we can conclude that levels of education and *hukou* status are weak predictors of regime support at the moment. Value change can be a long-term process, and the rapid increases in higher education and migration are quite recent. It may take considerably more time for their effects on political attitudes to be felt.

Although not central to modernization theory, the relationship between population size and regime support is also worth noting. As chapter 4 described, China is rapidly urbanizing, both as a consequence of rural to urban migration and the Party's policy of promoting ever bigger cities. If the size of a city's population is used as a proxy for urbanization, then the Party may be facing a dilemma: Larger cities may accomplish some policy goals, but support for the center is lower in the largest cities. Larger cities have also been the locations for anti-regime protests in other countries, which is another concern for the Party.[22] Will China remain stable as more and more people migrate into the cities and as already large cities turn into mega-cities? This may be the ultimate test of the Party's survival strategy.

III. Values and Regime Support

As the Party abandoned the Maoist goals of creating a communist utopia and downplayed its adherence to classic Marxist ideology, it sought other values to help legitimize its rule. Some Chinese officials are nostalgic for Maoist-era values. According to a local official in Wuhan, contemporary China lacks the faith and self-discipline that religion provides in other countries. Local governments promoting the "spirit of Beijing" or the "spirit of Wuhan" cannot fill this vacuum because "faith is something in our bloodline, not some spirit promoted by a certain administration or the party."[23] Lacking a shared religious tradition or ideology, the Party has begun cultivating nationalist sentiments, reviving Confucian sayings and practices, and drawing on the fear of political instability, a widely noted aspect of Chinese political culture. In a sense, as it became less communist, it tried to appear more Chinese.

Nationalism

By most accounts, nationalism has been on the rise in China in recent years. A lively debate remains underway over whether nationalism is nurtured and mobilized by the state[24] or has a popular base

[22] Jeremy L. Wallace, *Cities and Stability: Urbanization, Redistribution and Regime Survival in China* (New York: Oxford University Press, 2014).

[23] Focus group of party and government officials in Wuhan, November 23, 2013.

[24] Susan Shirk, *China: Fragile Superpower: How China's Internal Politics Could Derail Its Peaceful Rise* (New York: Oxford University Press, 2007); Suisheng Zhao,

independent of state actions.[25] Regardless of its origins, most agree that nationalism is a double-edged sword. While patriotism creates a sense of unity and shared identity, anti-foreign sentiments have led to repeated protests against Japan, the U.S., and other countries. These outpourings of anger become a cause of concern for the Party when criticisms against the actions of other countries turn into criticisms of the Chinese government for not doing enough to defend the country's interests.

Nationalism in modern China first blossomed during the May 4th movement of the early 20th century. In the Versailles treaty at the end of World War I, territory controlled by Germany in China was not returned to Chinese sovereignty but instead given to Japan, whose imperial ambitions would soon lead to greater encroachments in China and elsewhere in Asia. This was disillusioning to many in China, especially those who saw the Western ideals of democracy and science as China's future. But anger against the Western powers soon turned against the Chinese government when it was revealed that Chinese representatives at Versailles had approved the transfer of German concessions in China to Japan. Protests in China targeted Japanese ambitions, Western hypocrisy, and Chinese weakness in equal measures. This public outrage contributed to the downfall of the government at the time, and China entered into several decades of instability without a strong central government.

This is a vivid memory in China. Nationalist voices not only decry foreign actions against China, but also call on the government to take a stronger stand, implying that it is not doing enough to uphold Chinese interests in the face of foreign pressures and thereby questioning its legitimacy. As Andrew Nathan and Andrew Scobell have noted, nationalist protests are the only form of dissent tolerated by the Party.[26] It recognizes the risk of repressing nationalists, who represent a wider spectrum of public opinion than do democracy activists. At best, it tries

"A State-Led Nationalism: The Patriotic Education Campaign in Post-Tiananmen China," *Communist and Post-Communist Studies*, Vol. 31, No. 3 (September 1998), pp. 287–302.

[25] Peter Hays Gries, *China's New Nationalism: Pride, Politics, and Diplomacy* (Berkeley, CA: University of California Press, 2004); James Reilly, *Strong Society, Smart State* (New York: Columbia University Press, 2012).

[26] Andrew J. Nathan and Andrew Scobell, *China's Search for Security* (New York: Columbia University Press, 2012).

to channel the protests by signaling when they should end (often by text messages sent to all cell phone owners) and preventing the voicing of other political complaints during nationalist protests. Jessica Chen Weiss takes this a step farther and argues that the Party tolerates some nationalist protests to signal its resolve to foreign governments.[27]

In 1999, anti-American protests broke out across China after NATO planes bombed the Chinese Embassy in Belgrade, killing three journalists in the building. Protestors attacked the U.S. Embassy in Beijing with rocks and bottles. For several days, Ambassador James Sasser and other diplomatic staff were trapped inside the building, unsure of their safety. For a time, the Chinese government brought university students to the embassy in buses, giving each group a period of time to throw debris at it and chant slogans before they were put back on the bus and another group took their place. To some observers, this looked like the government was orchestrating and stage-managing the protests. More importantly, it was preventing them from escalating out of control. It limited how many protestors could be at the embassy and for how long. Within a few days, the protests ended, and Washington and Beijing quietly negotiated an agreement to pay for repairs of each other's embassies. The Party did not take a strong stand against the protestors, which would have likely turned public opinion against it, but it also did not allow protestors to operate on their own. This is part of the Party's dilemma: promoting nationalism without becoming a victim of it.

A more recent example came during 2012. China's ongoing dispute with Japan over islands in the East China Sea (known as Diaoyu in China and Senkaku in Japan) once again triggered anti-Japanese protests throughout China, which the Party did its best to contain. In several cities, police and soldiers cleared streets to create a route for marchers. "I need to lead the crowd and guide them to march in an orderly fashion," claimed one police officer in a blog post that was later removed.[28] The official state-run media carried warnings for the

---

[27] Jessica Chen Weiss, *Powerful Patriots: Nationalist Protest in China's Foreign Relations* (New York: Oxford University Press, 2014).

[28] Barbara Demick and Julie Makinen, "China Government's Hand Seen in Anti-Japan Protests," *Los Angeles Times*, September 20, 2012, http://articles. latimes.com/2012/sep/20/world/la-fg-china-japan-protests-20120921, accessed February 5, 2014.

public to avoid "irrational, violent anti-Japanese protests" and uphold the rule of law. Some protestors used the opportunity to carry signs of Chairman Mao, still seen by many in China as a symbol of national strength. These signs are an indirect critique of current leaders whose policies have allowed inequality and corruption to grow unchecked. Amid the signs denouncing Japan were some that read "the Diaoyu Islands belong to China, Bo Xilai belongs to the people." These signs—voicing support for a popular but controversial CCP leader who had recently been fired from his posts and was later sentenced for his involvement in the murder of a British businessman—were quickly confiscated and removed by the police, but still circulated widely on social media. The Party could tolerate anti-Japan slogans, but not popular support for a deposed leader.

The Party does not simply hope that the country's modernization will generate patriotism; it actively nurtures patriotism through the education system and recurring "patriotic education" campaigns for the population as a whole.[29] The goal is to create a closer link between individuals' self-identity and their country: Pride in China's achievements makes them feel prouder about themselves, and foreign criticism of China becomes a personal insult. China's leaders often say that statements by foreign leaders hurt the feelings of the Chinese people. As seen in table 5-2, that seems to be true: Over 80 percent of respondents in both the 2010 and 2014 surveys agreed that "When other people criticize China, it is as though they are criticizing me." This is a clear indicator that the self-identity of many Chinese is intimately tied to their country. The other questions in table 5-2 also show that the vast majority of Chinese take pride in their country's place in the world and prefer being a citizen of China more than any other country. Patriotism is a widely shared value in contemporary China.

---

[29] In a more coercive manner, it uses patriotic education programs to deter protests among minority groups, especially Tibetans. At the end of these programs, participants are forced to sign statements supporting Beijing's policies toward Tibet and denouncing the Dalai Lama. Those who refuse to sign have been imprisoned.

TABLE 5-2 Patriotic Sentiments in China (numbers in table are percentages)

	Strongly Agree		Agree		Disagree		Strongly Disagree	
	2010	2014	2010	2014	2010	2014	2010	2014
1. Even if I could pick any country in the world, I still want to be a Chinese citizen.	26.4	23.7	57.5	61.2	12.9	13.4	3.2	1.6
2. When other people criticize China, it is as though they are criticizing me.	21.6	20.0	58.8	60.8	16.4	17.3	3.2	1.9
3. Generally speaking, China is better than most other countries.	14.4	16.8	60.8	63.6	21.6	17.5	3.1	2.1

Source: Public Goods and Political Support Surveys.

In addition, the questions used to measure patriotism may be tapping into attitudes about Chinese culture, civilization, and ethnicity, not simply about the country, state, or government. The word "China" refers not only to a sovereign state or the incumbent regime but also to a shared identity of being Chinese. In that sense, pride in that shared identity is closely tied to regime support. The effect is likely interactive: Patriots are more likely to support the regime, but the accomplishments of the regime at home and abroad may also make people feel more patriotic. Pride in being Chinese is not simply about being a citizen of the PRC, but also being a part of the millennia-old Chinese civilization.

Patriotism and regime support are so closely correlated that patriotic sentiments may be more an indicator of regime support than a cause of it (see figure 5-4). It is often said that the terms nation, country, and state are not conceptually distinct in Chinese—the same words are used to convey different ideas. That is particularly relevant here, because people who criticize the Party or government are often accused—by the state as well as by fellow citizens—of being

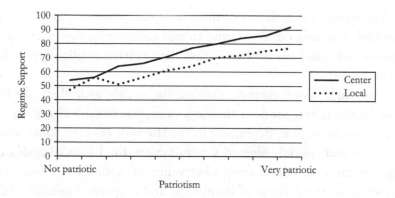

FIGURE 5-4 Patriotism and Regime Support.
Source: 2014 Public Goods and Political Support Survey.

anti-Chinese. This means the test of whether you are patriotic is whether you support the regime, and the test of whether you support the regime is whether you are patriotic.[30] The two are so closely entwined that dissidents have faced not just the state's repression but also society's reprobation.

Confucian Values

China has a long history of remonstration, people who point out the government's shortcomings in order to improve its performance. Like other types of critics and whistle-blowers, their critiques are not often welcomed by those who receive them. China has many examples of historical figures who told the truth to the emperor or other officials even though they expected to be punished for their uprightness—fired from their jobs and sometimes killed. This acceptance of authority is a primary feature of the Confucian heritage. Social relations are typically hierarchical in nature. Of the five great relationships, four are defined by positions of superior and subordinate status: between ruler and subject, father and son, husband and wife, and elder brother and younger brother. Only one is between equals (between friend and friend).

---

[30] This unquestioning acceptance of the status quo is by no means unique to China. In the not-too-distant past, "love it or leave it" was commonly used in the U.S. against antiwar demonstrators in the Vietnam era and in Brazil by the military dictatorship.

Challenges to the authority of those in higher positions can be seen as unfilial, and even traitorous, and treated accordingly. For that reason, critics and dissidents have a difficult time rallying public support for their causes.

Although Confucianism defined the state's orthodoxy during the imperial era, modern thinkers cast a more critical eye on its conservative nature. Beginning in the late 19th century, some intellectuals and officials blamed Confucianism for China's backwardness because it valued strict observance of traditional values and practices at the expense of innovation and progress. Especially during the May 4th era (roughly 1915–1921), some took the even more iconoclastic position that the solution to China's problems was to discard all Confucian tradition in favor of Western-style science and democracy. During the Maoist period, the Party tried to eradicate Confucian influences, particularly during the Cultural Revolution when the "Four Olds"—old customs, culture, habits, and ideas—were criticized. Art work, clothing, and books were looted from homes, schools, and museums and destroyed. Temples were demolished. The people who allegedly defended or at least symbolized the old ways were beaten and imprisoned. For much of the modern era, Chinese leaders tried to rid the country of the values and institutions that once defined it.

In the post-Mao period, Chinese leaders reversed course. While China was engulfed in recurring political campaigns, the "Asian Tigers"—South Korea, Taiwan, Hong Kong, and Singapore, each of them with Confucian traditions—experienced dramatic economic growth based on industrialization and foreign trade. Some even attributed Confucian values as a key to the success of the Asian Tigers. This is deeply ironic, since Confucianism had previously been blamed for the backwardness of East Asia, but was now offered as the reason for its success. Scholars who preferred this cultural explanation parsed the difference between Confucianism as a set of social norms emphasizing hard work, self-improvement, and a group orientation, and a political orthodoxy that insisted on conformity to past precedent, even when confronting unprecedented situations. Others rejected the cultural explanation in favor of institutions: close cooperation between government and business, labor repression, subsidized production, protectionist policies, a growing global economy, and U.S. protection.[31] Regardless of the merits of each side of the debate, there was some middle ground: It was now apparent that Confucianism was not incompatible with growth.

Whereas Mao and his supporters attacked Confucianism, post-Mao leaders have revived and promoted Confucian slogans to legitimize their policies. At the beginning of the reform era, "seek truth from facts" was the slogan for judging correct policies, not adherence to Marxism, Leninism, or Mao Zedong Thought, but actual results. The Party even changed the name of its ideological journal from *Red Flag* (*Hongqi*) to *Seek Truth* (*Qiushi*). The adoption of this phrase, originally dating from Ban Gu's *History of the Han Dynasty* (*Han Shu*) and perhaps earlier, was a sly strategy because it did not entail a complete rejection of Mao; he had the phrase written above the door to his home in Yan'an during the civil war years to show his pragmatic side. Its association with Mao legitimized its use by post-Mao reformers like Deng Xiaoping, who set about dismantling much of what Mao had created.

When Jiang Zemin was general secretary of the CCP (1989–2002), the Party's goal was to achieve "an economically comfortable society" (*xiaokang shehui* 小康社会), a phrase drawn from Confucius. The promise was not to create widespread wealth and prosperity, but to reach a more moderate standard of living. The phrase implied more comfortable lives, but not the crass commercialism that was also beginning around this time.

Despite this benign slogan, Jiang's policies led to growing economic inequalities. Whether comparing coastal and inland areas, cities and countryside, or individuals, the gap between rich and poor grew rapidly.

---

[31] This is not just an abstract theoretical debate; it also concerns whether the "East Asian Model" could be used in other countries. If culture was the key, then countries without Confucian traditions and similar collectivist values would have a difficult time duplicating Asian successes. But if the key was specific policies carried out by development-oriented institutions, they could be used virtually anywhere.

With those rising economic disparities came social tensions and public protests. As a result, when Hu Jintao replaced Jiang as CCP leader, he adopted a different Confucian slogan to emphasize his priorities: to promote a "harmonious society" (*hexie shehui* 和谐社会). He used more populist policies to raise incomes and living standards in rural and inland areas where the benefits of reform had been slow to be felt. In practice, achieving a harmonious society also had a coercive element: Threats to social harmony and political stability were harshly repressed. Those who ended up on the receiving end of this repression because of their writings, online statements, or involvement in public protests were "harmonized."

When Xi Jinping became general secretary in 2012, he adopted a new slogan: the "China dream." This is not a specifically Confucian expression, but it taps into the desire for national wealth and power originating in the late 19th century.[32] He did not identify exactly what the China dream was or how he would pursue it. During the following year, numerous academic conferences were held to flesh out its meaning.[33] Although the phrase sounds reminiscent of the American dream, its connotation is quite different. Whereas the American dream promises that anyone who works hard can be successful, the China dream is about the wealth and power of the country as a whole, not individual Chinese.[34]

As the Party downplayed reliance on Marxism-Leninism-Mao Zedong Thought as a guide to policy, it tried to resurrect more traditional Confucian values as a basis for its legitimacy. Students once again memorize Confucian essays. Confucius' hometown of Qufu has become a popular tourist destination. His birthday has become a national holiday. Confucian traditions of governance are also promoted and publicized, although not totally endorsed. Daniel Bell,

---

[32] Orville Schell and John Delury, *Wealth and Power: China's Long March to the Twenty-first Century* (New York: Random House, 2014).

[33] A special issue of the *Journal of Chinese Political Science* (March 2014) was devoted to defining and analyzing Xi's "China dream."

[34] In fact, before Xi began using this phrase, I often asked people if there was a Chinese phrase akin to the American dream about individual pursuit of economic and social advancement, because, clearly, people were working to achieve those goals in China. Everyone I asked said there was no such phrase.

a Canadian scholar teaching at Tsinghua University in Beijing, has attained a certain notoriety for promoting the idea of meritocracy as an alternative to democracy as a way of selecting leaders and governing the country.[35] The Party even uses Confucius Institutes around the world for building goodwill and creating "soft power."[36]

Confucian values remain prominent in contemporary China and were relatively stable across the years of the surveys (see table 5-3). These statements primarily refer to family relationships, although Confucian traditions also include political values such as meritocracy, subservience to authority, conformity to orthodoxy, and so on. What most of them share is a sense of hierarchy: Whether in personal relationships, families, or government, there are clear vertical lines of authority that should be preserved in order to maintain harmony. At the same time, acceptance of hierarchical relationships in one sphere does not automatically guarantee acceptance in other spheres. In the surveys, there is a relatively weak relationship between responses to the statements in table 5-3 and a statement equating family and government: "Government leaders are like the heads of family, we should obey their decisions," with which

[35] Daniel A. Bell, *The Age of Confucianism: Politics and Everyday Life in Contemporary China* (Princeton, NJ: Princeton University Press, 2010); *The China Model: Political Meritocracy and the Limits of Democracy* (Princeton, NJ: Princeton University Press, 2015).

[36] The CCP's efforts to create goodwill through its growing number of Confucius Institutes around the world have not always been successful. There has been backlash from faculty who feel that having Chinese government funding compromises academic freedom and invites self-censorship over the issues of Tibet, Taiwan, and human rights. Several universities have terminated their Confucius Institutes, and the Association of American University Professors in 2014 recommended that universities sever ties with Confucius Institutes unless governance guidelines were rewritten to give the universities complete control. See the critique by Marshall Sahlins, "China U.," *Nation*, November 18, 2013, http://www.thenation.com/article/176888/china-u#, and the rejoinder by my colleague Edward McCord, "Confucius Institutes: Hardly a Threat to Academic Freedom," *Diplomat*, March 27, 2014, http://thediplomat.com/2014/03/confucius-institutes-hardly-a-threat-to-academic-freedoms/, accessed April 2, 2015. For discussion of China's efforts to promote its soft power more generally, see David Shambaugh, "China's Soft-Power Push: The Search for Respect," *Foreign Affairs*, Vol. 94, No. 4 (July–August 2015), pp. 99–107.

TABLE 5-3 Traditional Confucian Values in Contemporary China (numbers in table are percentages)

	Strongly Agree		Agree		Disagree		Strongly Disagree	
	2010	2014	2010	2014	2010	2014	2010	2014
Even if parents' requests are unreasonable, the children should still comply.	7.4	7.6	35.0	33.4	51.4	50.1	6.2	9.0
If a dispute occurs, we should ask elders to decide what is fair.	11.3	11.9	54.8	54.0	31.4	30.0	2.5	4.2
Even if the mother-in-law is in the wrong, the son should encourage his wife to concede.	10.7	8.6	44.9	43.3	39.7	41.9	4.8	6.3

Source: Public Goods and Political Support Surveys.

56.4 percent of respondents agreed.[37] Not surprisingly, this question is closely correlated with regime support, but like patriotism, it is more likely an indicator of regime support than a cause of it.

While these values may be prominent, they are not equally shared among groups in contemporary China. In some cases, the variation is consistent with modernization theory. In the earlier discussion of material interests, we saw that many aspects of modernization theory did not have a direct effect on levels of regime support. However, here

[37] The three questions in table 5-3 have correlation coefficients of around 0.5 with each other, but only around 0.3 with the question equating heads of families and leaders of government.

we see them having an indirect effect. For example, those with higher levels of education, especially college degrees, are much less supportive of Confucian values. Younger cohorts, those who came of age in the post-Mao period and especially the post-Tiananmen years, are also less likely to hold Confucian beliefs. The relationship between income and Confucian values is also largely consistent with modernization theory. The relationship is U-shaped, with those at the low and high ends of the scale more likely to hold Confucian beliefs and middle-income respondents less likely to. Middle income is not synonymous with middle class, but the combined effects of education, age, and income on traditional Confucian values generally fit the expectations of modernization theory.

Urbanization is a key component of modernization theory, but here the survey results reveal an interesting pattern that puts a twist on the theory. Among the respondents in the 2014 survey, there was no difference between those with urban and rural *hukou*, but there was a clear difference between migrants and permanent residents. Rural migrants had lower levels of Confucian values than those who were born in the urban areas (which includes both holders of urban and rural *hukou*), and migrants from other cities had even lower levels. This may be because migrants are removed from their families and social networks, so the traditional political values become less salient for them. For some migrants, it may be that those who do not abide by traditional values are more inclined to migrate in the first place. Either way, the changing demographics in China may be reducing the importance of traditional Confucian values as both a social bond and a source of the Party's legitimacy.

Confucian values are positively correlated with regime support, but their effect washes out when patriotic values are held constant. Patriotic and Confucian values are only weakly correlated ($r = 0.24$), but their impact on regime support depends on whether they are viewed separately or together. Put differently, patriots have higher regime support regardless of whether or not they hold Confucian values, but Confucians only support the regime if they are also patriotic.

Fear of Instability

The CCP emphasizes that national unity and political stability are the prerequisites for other developmental goals, playing on the fear of chaos to generate support for suppressing real or imagined political threats. The CCP has utilized this preference for stability as one justification for one-party rule in China. The Party's recent determination to maintain a "harmonious society" speaks to this desire to suppress any organized opposition and enforce conformity to its way of thinking. For example, in May 2013, the CCP issued Document No. 9 that banned seven topics from discussion online and in classrooms: universal values, civil rights, civil society, press freedoms, judicial independence, past mistakes of the communist party, and the newly wealthy and political connected capitalist class. This ban was designed to prohibit the discussion of a wide range of political reforms. The CCP promotes social harmony and stability maintenance as the basis for economic and political development, and has also shown its willingness to impose harmony on those who might threaten it, and by extension challenge the CCP's right to rule.

To the extent that people are concerned with maintaining local order and national unity, and by extension see the CCP as able to achieve those goals, the more they are likely to support the continuation of the status quo. Conversely, one of the consequences of modernization is expected to be the decline of traditional values emphasizing stability and order with greater acceptance of social and political pluralism. The CCP's efforts to safeguard stability are unlikely to generate support among those who do not see the diversification of groups and ideas as an inherent threat to stability.

Fears of political instability remain strong in contemporary China (see table 5-4). Solid majorities agree that a multi-party system, organized groups, and public demonstrations pose real threats to stability. Combining these three questions into a single index shows that this fear of instability is positively correlated with regime support (although it is just shy of the conventional level of statistical significance [p=.052] for the local level): The more respondents are concerned that these developments are threats to China's stability, the more likely they are to support the regime (see figure 5-5).[38]

[38] The seemingly high level of regime support among those who have no fear of instability is misleading: less than 1 percent of respondents fall into this category, too few to draw solid conclusions.

TABLE 5-4 Fear of Instability in Contemporary China (numbers in table are percentages)

	Strongly Agree		Agree		Disagree		Strongly Disagree	
	2010	2014	2010	2014	2010	2014	2010	2014
If a country has multiple political parties, that could lead to social chaos.	9.9	13.7	50.4	53.5	35.0	29.2	4.8	3.7
Locally, if there were many groups with different points of view, that could influence local stability.	6.6	10.5	56.4	54.4	34.1	31.3	3.0	3.8
Demonstrations can easily turn into social upheaval, threatening social stability.	11.6	15.1	60.2	61.9	26.0	20.8	2.2	2.1

Source: Public Goods and Political Support Surveys.

IV. Political Reform and Regime Support

Chapter 4 described how local governments across the country have been experimenting with different types of consultations with society, in particular allowing online public comments on pending legislation and regulations, as well as consulting with the general public to help shape policy and budget priorities.[39] In 2014, Tsinghua University's Economic, Financial, and Governance Research Center issued an index that ranked almost 300 of China's largest cities in terms of their transparency. All

[39] Ann Florini, Hairong Lai, and Yeling Tan, *China Experiments: From Local Innovations to National Reform* (Washington, DC: Brookings Institution, 2012); Joseph Fewsmith, *The Logic and Limits of Political Reform in China* (New York: Cambridge University Press, 2013).

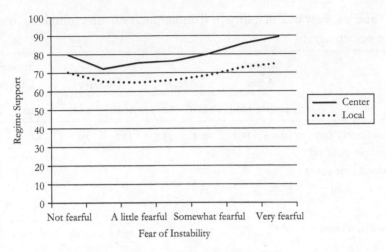

FIGURE 5-5 Fear of Instability and Regime Support.
Source: 2014 Public Goods and Political Support Survey.

cities in the Public Goods and Political Support Surveys are included in the index, which allows us to examine whether transparency influences regime support. It does not: The transparency of city governments is uncorrelated with regime support. Local political reforms may be making at least some cities more transparent and better governed, but they do not yet generate regime support in the way the Party intends.

V. Co-optation and Regime Support

Another way the Party attempts to generate support is by building institutional ties with key members of society, in particular when selecting people for Party membership. The Party's recruitment strategy has changed markedly over the years. In the early years, most Party members came from the "three revolutionary classes": peasants, workers, and soldiers. This made sense during the civil war years and when it was pursuing ideological goals after 1949, such as during the Great Leap Forward and the Cultural Revolution. During those times, ensuring political loyalty was a major factor in Party recruitment. But during other times, such as periods of economic recovery after the end of the civil war, the Great Leap Forward, and the Cultural Revolution, and especially during the post-Mao periods when the Party's main task was economic modernization, the Party favored professional skills and expertise in new members.

Ideally, CCP members would be both "red" and expert, but in practice, most were more one than the other, and the Party's criteria for recruitment tended to favor one over the other at different times. When the Party was pursuing ideological goals and waging class struggle, it emphasized political qualities, or "redness," including class background and loyalty to the Party in general and Mao in particular. During times of Maoist campaigns, such as the Great Leap Forward and the Cultural Revolution, the Party recruited large numbers of political activists who were considered red but typically did not have much professional expertise. They displayed their redness and political loyalty by active involvement in the Party's campaigns against supposed class enemies and "bourgeois" or feudal influences. In contrast, during periods of economic recovery after the Great Leap and the Cultural Revolution, the Party weeded out many of the activists recruited during those campaigns and focused instead on recruiting the kinds of people who had the managerial and technical expertise necessary to promote economic growth. In the post-Mao period, the Party's primary task was economic modernization, and it again shifted its recruitment strategy to attract the kinds of people it would rely on to promote growth. It adopted the "four transformations" policy in order to attract new members who were revolutionary, young, intellectual, and professional. In practice, the latter three were most important, because they contributed directly to the Party's goal of promoting modernization.

In annual reports of party recruitment (released just before the anniversary of the Party's founding on July 1), the emphasis on youth and education is prominent. By the end of 2014, the Party had grown to 87.8 million members. Among those recruited in 2014, over 80 percent were under 35 and almost 40 percent had college degrees. This is designed to reduce the average age of Party members and recruit those with the most up-to-date skills. As a consequence of these recruitment priorities, the composition of the CCP has become less proletarian over time. Two-thirds of Party members were workers or farmers in 1994, but ten years later in 2004, their share

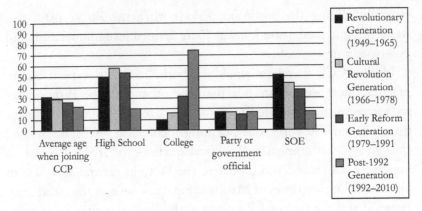

FIGURE 5-6 Characteristics of Party Members by Cohort (bars represent percentages, except for age when joining CCP).
Source: 2014 Public Goods and Popular Support Survey.

in the Party had declined to only 44 percent. By 2014 (the latest year this particular statistic is available), their share had fallen to just 38 percent.[40]

The changing priorities in Party recruitment are quite visible among the survey respondents (see figure 5-6). The age at which they joined the Party declined steadily, and the percentage with college degrees rose sharply. Among the youngest cohort, almost 75 percent had college degrees. The changing occupations of Party members are evident. Similar proportions of each cohort worked as Party or government officials (either currently or before they retired), but those who worked for SOEs fell sharply. Among the youngest cohort, only 17.2 percent worked for SOEs, compared to 51.4 percent for the oldest cohort. As is the case for the population as a whole, employment among the youngest cohort of Party members is diverse: 21.8 percent work in the private sector, 17.3 percent work for government-affiliated education, healthcare, science and technology, and cultural organizations, and 7.6 percent work for foreign enterprises or joint ventures. In addition, 17.3 percent were not employed, reflecting the difficulty for young and well-educated people to find appropriate jobs. In short, the Party of today is no longer

[40] The Party is concerned that it has become too large and too elitist. The number of new recruits dropped from 3.2 million in 2012 to 2.1 million in 2014. Since 2010, the annual reports on recruitment reveal a renewed interest in recruiting "workers on the front line of production" and downplaying college students and members of the "new social strata."

made up of peasants, workers, and soldiers—the "three revolutionary classes"—but represents a much wider segment of society.

Instead, the Party has focused on people in management, high-tech, and other white-collar careers. The "three revolutionary classes" have been replaced by the "three represents" slogan: The Party no longer simply represents the vanguard of the proletariat, but the advanced productive forces (a euphemism for private entrepreneurs and high-tech specialists), advanced culture, and the "fundamental interests of the overwhelming majority of the people of China." That is intentionally a very broad umbrella. The main purpose of the "three represents" was to give an ideological rationale for doing what local officials had been doing for years: recruiting capitalists into the Party, even though this was technically in violation of Party policy and totally contrary to Party traditions. What could be more incongruous than capitalists in the Party? But with the Party committed to promoting economic growth, it increasingly relied on the private sector to produce new jobs, new tax revenues, and above all new growth. In order to develop closer ties between the Party and the private sector, many local officials turned a blind eye to the official prohibition against recruiting private entrepreneurs into the Party. With the adoption of the "three represents" slogan, policy was catching up with practice.[41]

The status of private entrepreneurs remains a sensitive issue within the Party. No private entrepreneur has been a member of the Central Committee (the top 200 or so leaders in the party, elected every five years at a Party Congress, the most recent in 2012) or even its list of alternate members. Big business is represented on the Central Committee by heads of SOEs, not private enterprises. Before each Party Congress, there is speculation that a private entrepreneur will finally be added to the Central Committee, but so far that has not happened. The notion of having capitalists in the upper echelons of the Party must still rub too many Party leaders the wrong way. When it finally does happen, it will represent an important milestone in the Party's continuing evolution from a revolutionary

[41] For further discussion of the CCP's evolving relationship with private entrepreneurs, see my *Red Capitalists in China: The Party, Private Entrepreneurs, and Prospects for Political Change* (New York: Cambridge University Press, 2003); and *Wealth into Power: The Communist Party's Embrace of China's Private Sector* (New York and London: Cambridge University Press, 2008); see also Kellee Tsai, *Capitalism without Democracy: The Private Sector in Contemporary China* (Ithaca, NY: Cornell University Press, 2007).

vanguard party to a status quo ruling party. However, private entrepreneurs are well represented in China's legislative branch of the government, the National People's Congress and local people's congresses, but this branch is much less powerful than the executive branch and especially the CCP itself.

Above all, the Party has focused on college campuses as the main source of new members. Roughly 40 percent of new recruits are college students when they join the Party. At the time of the 1989 demonstrations in Tiananmen Square and elsewhere around the country, the Party paid little attention to recruiting college students. It preferred to wait until people had work experience to evaluate their credentials and political loyalty. As a result, the Party was not able to monitor campus life very effectively. In the years after the demonstrations, it changed its recruitment policies to emphasize college students. This allows it to bring college students into the Party when they are still works in progress and also gives the Party a stronger presence on college campuses, so it is less likely to be caught off guard again by a protest movement.

The Party wants to recruit from the best and the brightest, and therefore puts more emphasis on higher-ranked schools. At elite universities, up to half of graduate students are Party members by the time they get their degrees. At lower-ranked schools, the proportion of Party members among students is lower. This is an elitist (or some may describe it as a meritocratic) recruitment strategy. Party recruiters on college campuses have strict caps on how many students they can recruit each year. Whereas other officials are rewarded for exceeding certain goals, such as economic growth and attracting foreign investments, college recruiters cannot exceed their caps because the Party does not want to grow too rapidly. Only about one in six applicants is admitted to the Party.[42]

Why do people join the Party? It depends on whom you ask. Among Party members, the motivation to join depends on when they joined the Party. The changing incentives for joining the Party can be seen in the curved shape of the bars in figure 5-7. At the bottom of the figure, the oldest cohort—those who came of age before the Cultural Revolution began in 1966—are most likely to say that their desire to "serve the people" and their support of the Party and its mission

---

[42] Bruce J. Dickson, "Who Wants to Be a Communist? Career Incentives and Mobilized Loyalty in Contemporary China," *China Quarterly*, No. 217 (March 2014), pp. 42–68.

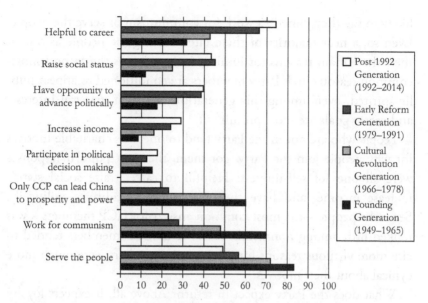

FIGURE 5-7 Why Do People Join the CCP? (bars represent percentages).
Source: 2014 Public Goods and Political Support Survey.

Please note: Respondents could give up to three reasons for joining the Party, so the numbers add up to more than 100 percent.

compelled them to join. Each successive cohort was less likely to claim these selfless motivations, with the Cultural Revolution generation just a bit less ideological in their reasons for joining. At the top of the figure, those who joined the Party in the post-Mao era are more likely to acknowledge that self-interest motivated their desire to join. For the post-1992 generation—the youngest cohort—"helpful to career" was by far the most common reason given for joining the Party. Older cohorts were sequentially less likely to acknowledge this as their motive for joining. Even for those in the founding and Cultural Revolution generations who joined when political criteria were the basis for admission, however, Party membership was seen as beneficial to career interests, though they needed to be covered with a veneer of selflessness.[43] The post-1992 generation was also the least

[43] Michel Oksenberg, "The Institutionalisation of the Chinese Communist Revolution: The Ladder of Success on the Eve of the Cultural Revolution," *China Quarterly*, No. 36 (December 1968), pp. 61–92; Bobai Li and Andrew G. Walder, "Career Advancement as Party Patronage: Sponsored Mobility into the Chinese Administrative Elite," *American Journal of Sociology*, Vol. 106, No. 5 (March 2001), pp. 1371–1408.

likely to say they joined to work for communism or serve the people. Even so, a near majority of them cited serving the people as one of their three main reasons for joining; in fact, it was the second-most-common reason cited. Party members are conditioned to appear public-spirited, even among this generation in which material interests and career goals are most prominent.

People who are not in the Party tend to offer less charitable motives for why people join the Party. For them, the most popular responses were all ones of self-interest: Helpful to career, raise social status, increase income, and have the opportunity to advance politically. Serve the people—the most common answer for CCP members—was ranked fifth among nonmembers. Whereas CCP members tended to cite more virtuous reasons for joining, nonmembers were much more cynical about their motives.

What does the Party expect in return? Above all, it expects loyalty from its members. Party members should be the core supporters of the regime, and their individual goals should be consistent with the Party's priorities. Political loyalty is still an important criterion for recruitment into the Party, but evaluating how loyal a potential recruit will be is a tremendous challenge. After the Party abandoned mass campaigns, people could not display their redness by participating in them. After it stopped emphasizing class background, belonging to one of the three revolutionary classes was no longer advantageous. Party recruiters on college campuses say they have to rely on exams and essays to discern the ideological viewpoints of potential members. However, this is complicated by the availability of essays for purchase online. Just as American professors struggle to determine how much of their students' papers reflect original thinking and how much is simply bought from a paper mill or copied from Wikipedia, party recruiters in China try to separate boilerplate language from genuine sentiments. An alternative indicator of an applicant's potential loyalty is pedigree: If one or both parents are CCP members, it is easier for an applicant to be admitted into the Party. Among the respondents in the Public Goods and Political Support Surveys, those who joined the Party in the post-Mao era were almost twice as likely to have a father who was a CCP member than those recruited in the Maoist era, when other tests of political loyalty were available.

The Party may expect loyalty, but that does not always translate into regime support. Most Party members have higher levels of regime support than nonmembers, but although the difference is statistically significant, it amounts to less than 5 percent. The patterns apparent in the population as a whole (for instance, lower levels of regime support in younger cohorts and a significant local legitimacy deficit) are just as apparent among Party members. These political insiders should be the most likely to express their support for the regime, whether genuinely or by preference falsification, but their assessments are similar to those outside the Party.

Even if the Party cannot always count on its members to be more loyal, it expects them to behave as if they are. It mobilizes Party members to participate in Party-sponsored activities in order to show their support—not just for the Party, but more importantly for other members of society. The Party expects its members to lead by example. For example, the Party organizes periodic elections for local people's congresses, the nominal legislative branch. These are not terribly competitive elections: No opposition parties exist, and even independent candidates are discouraged and in many cases prevented from running. Most people pay little attention because they realize that voting and the results of the elections are not very consequential. People's congresses are not an independent branch of government with the ability to check and balance the Party or government. For the most part, they approve the Party's nominations for government positions and vote the Party's bills into law. But the Party devotes a tremendous amount of time and energy to screen candidates, hold the elections, and publicize the results.[44] This is one aspect of how "socialist democracy" is practiced in China, and it allows the Party to claim that it represents the people. To be able to make this claim, it must ensure that a sufficient number of people vote, and so it mobilizes CCP members to do so. Party members are twice as likely as nonmembers to vote (53 percent compared to 23.2 percent in 2014). In the context of China's political system, voting

---

[44] Melanie Manion, "When Communist Party Candidates Can Lose, Who Wins? Assessing the Role of Local People's Congresses in the Selection of Leaders in China," *China Quarterly*, No. 195 (September 2008), pp. 607–630.

TABLE 5-5 Political and Civic Behavior among CCP Members and Nonmembers (percentages)

	CCP members		Nonmembers	
	2010	2014	2010	2014
Vote in people's congress elections	58.1	53.0	28.0	23.2
Donate money or goods	84.4	65.3	70.2	51.2
Collect donations or money for a social movement organization	20.3	12.8	12.3	8.0
Donate blood	19.1	25.0	12.6	18.2
Do volunteer work	11.4	20.5	7.8	14.7

Source: Public Goods and Political Support Surveys.

is less a form of participation and more a sign of support for the regime. Party members are expected to—and do—play their part.

Party members not only play a political role by voting, they are also expected to play a civic role by serving the people in various ways. After natural disasters, Party members are expected to take the lead in collecting charitable donations. Party and government offices compete against one another to see who can donate the most money and materials. Party members are also expected to volunteer their time in various ways, such as working in the hinterlands for a year after graduating from college or more routine activities such as planting trees or cleaning up trash in their neighborhoods. As seen in table 5-5, they are far more likely to do volunteer work, collect or donate money and goods, and even donate blood than are nonmembers. This is not just because CCP members are good citizens; it is better understood as "mobilized loyalty": The Party mobilizes its members to display their loyalty to the Party's mission publicly. To do otherwise would imply a lack of support for the regime. If Party members are not publicly engaged, the rest of the people have less reason to go along with the status quo. The Party expects loyalty from its members and mobilizes them to display it.

V. The Heavy Hand of the State Weighs Down Regime Support

Part of the Party's strategy for survival is designed to generate support. Other parts of that strategy are designed to stifle opposition, as described in chapter 2. Coercive tools are a hallmark of all authoritarian regimes, including China's, but they are costly. Not only do they require tremendous investments of manpower and money that could be put to better uses, they also risk undermining public support if used broadly instead of targeted at individuals and groups. In different ways, corruption, censorship, and the general repressive environment under Xi Jinping all diminish regime support.

Corruption

The corruption that has accompanied economic growth in China has been deeply unpopular. Most Chinese resent the extravagant spending by Party and government officials on banquets, automobiles, foreign travel, and personal luxuries, much of it paid for with gifts and bribes. They resent the favors given to families and friends of Party and government officials, and the haughty behavior of the *guan er dai* (官二代), the children of officials who seem to be exempt from the laws that govern the rest of society. In the focus group interviews conducted along with the public opinion surveys, people complained bitterly about the reliance on personal connections (*guanxi* 关系) to gain access to healthcare or get children enrolled in the top schools. Although *guanxi* is a key characteristic of traditional Chinese political culture, it is now seen as a primary source of inequality and unfairness, and not just as a resource for getting things done.

Attitudes about corruption are closely correlated with regime support: The more prevalent people think corruption is among central and local officials, the lower their regime support is (see figure 5-8). But just as satisfaction with public goods is an inexact factor for predicting regime support, so too are perceptions about corruption. Does the perceived prevalence of corruption lead to lower levels of regime support, or does low regime support create cynical perceptions of prevalent corruption? It is hard to untangle cause and effect, especially when one set of subjective attitudes is used to explain another. A better approach is to

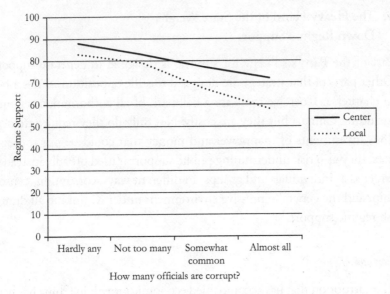

FIGURE 5-8 Perceptions of Corruption and Regime Support.
Source: 2014 Public Goods and Political Support Survey.

see how personal experience with corruption impacts regime support. In the 2014 survey, respondents were asked if they had given a bribe to an official (not including teachers, school principals, and doctors).[45] About one in five (19 percent) said they had. This personal experience paying a bribe has a clear impact on regime support (see figure 5-9), regardless of what other variables are held constant.

If corruption is so corrosive to the Party's legitimacy, why does the experience of paying bribes not have an even bigger impact on regime support? Part of the answer comes from who is paying the bribes. For some people, paying bribes undoubtedly makes them distrustful of Party and government officials. For others, it is a recognized way of getting things done. The post-Mao cohorts are almost twice as likely as older cohorts to have paid a bribe. Those with high levels of political and human capital—Party members and college graduates—are also more likely to have paid bribes. In other words, the people most likely to know how the system works are more likely to have paid bribes. If paying a bribe allows them to achieve their

[45] This question was not asked in the 2010 survey, so the results from 2014 cannot be compared.

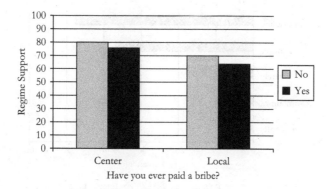

FIGURE 5-9 Corruption and Regime Support.
Source: 2014 Public Goods and Political Support Survey.

goals, they may be more cynical, but they also know how to make the system work for them.

Censorship

Controlling the flow of information is a trademark of authoritarian regimes. Autocrats limit what information they provide to their citizens and what information their citizens have access to through other channels. The Party uses the "Great Firewall" to censor information available to Internet users in China. What impact does censorship have on regime support? Think of censorship as a natural experiment, in which some people receive the treatment and others do not. In China, there are three groups in this experiment: those who encounter censorship on the Internet, those who use the Internet but do not experience censorship, and those who do not use the Internet (see figure 5-10).

How does the treatment of censorship influence the outcome of regime support?[46] Remarkably, experience with censorship has a mixed impact on regime support: It reduces regime support, but the effect is only statistically significant at the local level. This seems surprising, but it is explained by who gets censored and what their response is to it. First of all, some types of people are more likely to experience

[46] Questions about censorship were not asked in the 2010 survey, so the 2014 results again cannot be compared.

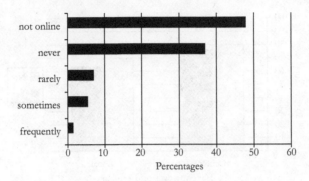

FIGURE 5-10 Frequency of Experiencing Censorship.
Source: 2014 Public Goods and Political Support Survey.

censorship than others. In a true experiment, the treatment—in this case censorship—would be randomly assigned to avoid one group or another from being overrepresented, which would bias the results. But Chinese are not equally likely to experience censorship. The people most likely to encounter censorship online are the youngest, best educated, and most prosperous people, attributes that are also correlated with regime support in different ways.

The second reason that censorship does not have the expected impact on regime support is that not everyone is bothered by it. When asked how they felt when they encountered censorship online, almost half said "it doesn't matter" (*wusuowei* 无所谓), suggesting that people have become accustomed to censorship and are not particularly bothered by it. But almost 40 percent were angered by censorship. This subgroup did have significantly lower regime support (see figure 5-11). But this is a small subgroup: Only 15 percent of respondents encountered censorship, and of these, only 40 percent were angry about it—this amounts to only 6 percent of all respondents.

* * *

Most elements of the Party's survival strategy have direct impacts on the levels of regime support, but not always in ways expected by the Party or outside observers. Contrary to the frequently noted claim that the Party's

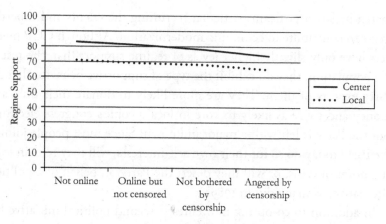

FIGURE 5-11 Censorship and Regime Support.
Source: 2014 Public Goods and Political Support Survey.

legitimacy is based primarily on economic growth, levels of per capita GDP and rates of GDP growth do not influence regime support. What *does* matter is individual incomes: The higher people's incomes and the more they say their incomes are rising, the more they support the regime at both the central and local levels. Although pocketbook factors influence regime support, sociotropic factors—per capita GDP and GDP growth—do not.

In addition to producing economic growth, the Party seeks support with the values it promotes and the way it governs. Whether the Party is producing nationalist sentiments or simply taking advantage of them, patriotism is a strong predictor of regime support: the more patriotic, the more support. Although many of China's post-Mao leaders, particularly current president Xi Jinping, have revived Confucian sayings and traditions, popular Confucian beliefs are not correlated with regime support when other factors are controlled for. The fear of instability, a frequently noted characteristic of Chinese political culture, is also strongly correlated with regime support. Although the Party receives criticism for the increased use of repression in recent years, the goal of maintaining stability still resonates with many in China.

A key part of the Party's survival strategy is the co-optation of new elites. The Party has changed its recruitment strategy over the years to match its larger goals, in particular recruiting the talents and expertise that can contribute to economic modernization. Although CCP members have only slightly higher levels of regime support than the rest of the population, they do exhibit the type of supportive behavior that the Party expects of them. They are more likely to donate their time and money and twice as likely to vote in local people's congress elections. But the Party is left with a major unknown: Since most people joining the Party today do so for their own self-interests, will they remain loyal at a point of crisis, or will they desert the Party on behalf of a political alternative, as many did in 1989?

In addition to co-opting new elites, a second political initiative has been introducing greater transparency into the policy process, especially at the local level. Despite these efforts, the degree of political transparency has almost no influence on regime support.

The Party's survival strategy is not just about generating support, it is also determined to eradicate opposition and, in recent years, even criticism. Repression is definitely a core part of its survival strategy, but it is both literally and figuratively costly. Repression comes in different forms, each with its own impact on regime support. Personal experience with corruption, namely giving bribes, lowers regime support. The Internet is often seen as a potential vehicle for political opposition and criticism, and so the Party censors the information available there. Censorship does not affect everyone the same way. Even though Internet users who are angry at being censored have lower levels of regime support, they represent only a sliver of the population. While other elements of the Party's strategy of survival may be generating support, the wider use of coercive tools is undermining that support to different degrees.

One of the key characteristics of regime support is the distinction people make between the central and local governments, what I refer to as the local legitimacy deficit. Regardless of how it is measured, whether individual or institutional, whether trust, support, or satisfaction, the same pattern is apparent: There is significantly higher support for the center than the localities. For the Party, the local legitimacy deficit may be a good thing. As long as people aim their frustration at local officials but continue to be satisfied with the leaders in Beijing, the likelihood of popular mobilization on behalf of regime change is low. But as the local legitimacy deficit declines—more specifically, if satisfaction with the central government falls to the level of local governments—then the legitimacy of the regime itself may be called into question. That is the ultimate dilemma for the Party: how to eliminate opposition without undermining support. By increasing the use of coercive tools, Xi Jinping may be jeopardizing the regime support he inherited.

6

Defining Democracy

FOR MOST OF THE post-Mao era, China watchers have been avidly look-ing for hints of democratization in China. The wide-ranging economic reforms that began in 1978 raised expectations (in China, as well as among outside observers) that political reforms would soon follow suit. Most observers predicted that an increasingly market-oriented econ-omy would be incompatible with China's one-party dictatorship, and that sooner or later, political reform would have to catch up with eco-nomic reform. But those expectations have not been realized. Despite wide-ranging economic reforms, political reforms have not kept pace. If political reform implies democratization, this view is accurate. But as shown in chapter 3, the Party has implemented a wide variety of politi-cal reforms that have changed relationships between state and society, even though they do not amount to democratization and were never intended to.

Why has the anticipated democratization in China gone unfulfilled? First and foremost, the Party has been opposed to such developments. Maintaining its monopoly on political power has been the most impor-tant element of its strategy for survival; opening up the political system to organized opposition is not part of the plan. But popular attitudes about democracy in China are also important. Although political and academic elites may debate the definition of democracy and its suitabil-ity for China, those debates are far removed from the perspectives of ordinary Chinese. As this chapter will show, most Chinese believe that the level of democracy has been steadily rising during the post-Mao era and that it will continue to rise in the future, and they are satisfied with the current level of democracy in China. For those reasons, they have little incentive to support efforts to promote immediate and thorough democratization, and are more inclined to wait for democracy to continue its gradual emergence. Democratic activists therefore not only face repression by the state, but indifference and even opposition from members of society. To understand why China has defied predictions of imminent democratization, we have to consider not only the Party's strategy for survival, but also societal perceptions about democracy in China.

I. Popular Movements for Democracy in China

In the post-Mao period, two episodes raised expectations of popular support for democratization. The Democracy Wall movement that began in 1978 occurred at a time when China's leaders were debating the initiation of economic reforms, the repudiation of Maoist social and political policies, and the rehabilitation of Party and government leaders who had been purged and imprisoned for opposing Maoist priorities. In order to show their support for reform and their opposition to Cultural Revolution policies, ordinary Chinese wrote hand-written posters decrying the excesses of the Cultural Revolution, lamenting their own suffering during those years, and criticizing Mao and other leaders responsible for those policies. They pasted their posters on a wall to the west of Tiananmen Square in downtown Beijing (this stretch of wall became known as "Democracy Wall"), gave interviews with foreign journalists, and reprinted the posters and wrote other essays in pamphlets they distributed for free to people who came to Democracy Wall. The beginning of this movement coincided with a high-level work conference of Party leaders in November-December that reassessed the policies of the past and decided on the initial set of reforms that were then officially ratified at the CCP's historic Third Plenum in December 1978. Some of these internal deliberations were leaked to Democracy Wall activists, who then wrote posters and essays criticizing CCP leaders who were resisting new reforms. This meeting also rehabilitated a number of Party veterans who had been fired from their posts and in some cases imprisoned over the past two decades. This convergence of voices inside and outside the Party criticizing the Cultural Revolution and supporting reform raised expectations for a broader political opening, but that hope soon faded. After reformers within the party leadership gained the upper hand against their opponents, they had less need for popular pressure to make their case. Once Democracy Wall writers moved beyond criticizing the past to arguing for truly democratic reforms to guard against future episodes of tyranny, and even suggesting that Deng Xiaoping himself could not be trusted with autocratic powers, the Party put an end to the movement. Deng identified "four cardinal principles" that were the basis of China's political system and that were off-limits to public debate: the socialist road, the dictatorship of the proletariat (later revised to be the people's democratic dictatorship), the leadership of the CCP, and Marxism-Leninism-Mao Zedong thought.[1] By delineating the Party's economic, political, and ideological principles in this way, Deng framed the Democracy Wall activists not as pro-reform supporters, but as regime opponents. Some of its most outspoken voices were arrested and imprisoned, and Democracy Wall itself was moved to the corner of an obscure park outside the downtown area. What began as an episode of collaboration between state and society ended without the democratization it seemed to promise.

The popular protests in Tiananmen Square and throughout China in 1989 were a more dramatic episode, had a more tragic ending, and left a longer-lasting memory. Although it is now often referred to as a pro-democracy movement, it did not start that way. Initially, protestors targeted corruption among party leaders and their families, inflation and the resulting decline in living standards, and a public funeral and memorial service for Hu Yaobang, whose death in April 1989 triggered the subsequent events. Hu held the top formal post in the CCP—general secretary—until January 1987, when he was forced to resign after losing the support of Deng Xiaoping and other Party leaders. From his death on April 16 to the tragedy of June 4, the movement picked up steam, gaining more and more supporters in public marches and broadening the scope of demands to include the resignation of

---

[1] Deng Xiaoping, "Uphold the Four Cardinal Principles," *Selected Works of Deng Xiaoping (1975–1982)* (Beijing: Foreign Languages Press, 1984), pp. 166–191.

Deng and other high-ranking leaders and the recognition of autonomous organizations for workers and students (a red-line issue for the
Party that would threaten its monopoly on political organizations).
People who worked in Party and government agencies and SOEs
joined the marches, carrying signs that identified where they worked.
The media began printing and broadcasting supportive stories about
the growing movement. Zhao Ziyang, who replaced Hu as general secretary in 1987, publicly sided with the protestors. These developments
signified support for the movement within the party-state itself, raising hopes for a democratic opening. The peaceful nature and dura-
tion of the movement, the signs of support from within the Party, and
the expectation that political reform would eventually catch up with
economic reform created growing optimism. However, demonstrators
and outside observers underestimated the power of high-level opposition to the movement.[2] Deng Xiaoping and other top leaders united
against Zhao and the demonstrators. Even if the movement was peaceful, even if it showed the tremendous popularity of calls for reform,
and even if many within the party-state were supportive, the hardliners
were unwilling to surrender the Party's monopoly on political power.
Their decision to impose martial law not only brought a violent end to
a peaceful movement, but also crushed hopes for a peaceful transition
to democracy in China.

II. How Democratic Is China?

Since 1989, there has been no sustained democracy movement with
broad popular support within China. China watchers in the media and
academic community continue to debate the prospects for democracy,
but hopes have dimmed over the years. The chance for a democratic
opening seems remote. The conventional wisdom among China watchers is that the political system has changed little during the reform era,
especially compared to the ambitious and extensive economic reforms.

---

[2] In the aftermath of the crackdown, Michel Oksenberg wrote an article that
began: "I am a chastened China watcher, as are many of my colleagues in universities and think tanks. Not since the Iranian revolution [of 1979] have the analysts
been so surprised by global developments of such strategic and social significance."
Newsweek, June 19, 1989.

This viewpoint is supported by international organizations that evaluate political characteristics of countries around the world. For example, Freedom House scores the levels of political rights and civil liberties around the world. From the time that it began reporting its scores in 1973, it has classified China as "not free." It has given China the lowest score for political rights every year since 1989, and the lowest or next-to-lowest score for civil liberties. Similarly, the Polity IV dataset, which measures a variety of political features over a long span of time, gives China a score of 0 for democracy in each year after 1949. Polity IV also measures the level of autocracy in a country on a 0–10 scale. In China, this peaked during the Cultural Revolution, when China had a score of 9, and has remained at 7 for the entire post-Mao period. This recognizes the difference between the Maoist and post-Mao eras, but also concludes that nothing significant has changed in China's political system since 1976. China watchers and other international observers generally agree that the PRC remains what it has been since 1949: a one-party authoritarian regime.

Despite these outside evaluations, the Chinese themselves report a dramatic increase in the level of democracy in China. The public opinion surveys used throughout this book suggest that most people in urban China believe the country is increasingly democratic and are optimistic that higher levels of democracy will be achieved in the near future. The surveys asked about levels of democracy at the times they were made (2010 and 2014), the recent past, and the near future, and the results run contrary to the conventional wisdom (see table 6-1).[3] For each point in time, respondents measured the level of democracy on a 0–10 scale. These scores were then condensed into four categories to make comparisons easier. Among survey respondents, over 70 percent agreed that there was a low level of democracy in the country at the beginning of the post-Mao era of reform. In the aftermath of the Cultural Revolution, and before the economic and political reforms of the post-Mao era got underway, this is an appropriate perception. The perceived level of democracy rose steadily in later periods. In the

[3] The results presented in table 6-1 are not unique to my surveys. See also Tianjian Shi, *The Cultural Logic of Politics in Mainland China and Taiwan* (New York: Cambridge University Press, 2015), esp. chapter 7.

TABLE 6-1 Changing Levels of Democracy in Contemporary China (0–10 scale; numbers in rows are percentages; boldfaced cells represent majority of public opinion for those years)

2010

Level of democracy in:	1979	Mid-1990s	Now (2010)	Five years from now (i.e., 2015)	U.S. 2010
Very high (9–10)	3.6	3.6	5.3	20.5	22.4
Somewhat high (6–8)	25.5	39.7	50.1	55.4	56.2
Somewhat low (3–5)	52.7	49.1	37.9	20.9	18.5
Little or none at all (0–2)	18.3	7.6	6.9	3.2	2.9
Average	4.4	5.2	5.7	6.8	7.0

2014

	1979	Mid-1990s	Mid-2000s	Now (2014)	Five years from now (i.e., 2019)	U.S. 2014
High	3	2.7	3.7	7.4	27.6	33.2
Somewhat high	21.4	31.4	42.7	51.7	55.5	52.5
Somewhat low	46.3	50.6	45.5	35.1	14.2	12.8
Little or none at all	29.2	15.2	8.2	5.7	2.9	1.5
Average	3.93	4.67	5.34	5.9	7.2	7.55

Source: Public Goods and Political Support Surveys.

mid-1990s, following the Tiananmen Square protests in 1989 and at the midpoint of the Jiang Zemin era, and then during the mid-2000s during the Hu Jintao-Wen Jiabao era (asked only in the 2014 survey), the percentage of those who believed China had become somewhat or highly democratic rose to almost 45 percent. By the time of the surveys in 2010 and 2014, this group rose even higher to between 55 and 60 percent, a clear majority. Remarkably, over three-fourths of respondents believed that China would be even more democratic within five years after the survey. If this were to be realized, China would be at a level of democracy on par with the U.S.! This reveals great optimism about the prospects for democracy in the country, or perhaps some cynicism about the level of democracy in the U.S.[4]

The contrast between the 2010 and 2014 surveys suggests the possibility for future dissatisfaction over the pace of democratization. In the 2010 survey, over 20 percent expected China to have a high level of democracy within five years. But in the 2014 survey, only 7.4 percent thought China had reached that point. This could make the Party vulnerable to the "revolution of rising expectations": If expectations for future improvements continue to rise but remain unmet, support for the status quo may diminish.

Is this view of a steadily more democratic China credible? People are often skeptical about public opinion data from China because they do not believe people will give honest answers, especially on politically sensitive questions like democracy. But if they are lying, they are lying in ways consistent with social science theory. Either Chinese survey respondents are aware of how Western social science theory predicts age, education, gender, income, and so on influence political attitudes and political behavior and respond accordingly—which of course is absurd—or their answers reflect the importance of those factors. As it turns out, the factors that typically influence political attitudes and political behavior in other countries also help to explain attitudes about democracy in China.

For one thing, the perception of rising democracy is not universally shared: Table 6-1 shows differences of opinion for each time period. For

[4] This latter point is not too surprising, given the negative views of the U.S. government prevalent in China, as well as the prolonged political stalemate in the U.S.

analytical purposes, the more salient question is whether the variation in responses for each time period is random or systematic in some way. One key factor is education. People with higher levels of education typically have more critical views on political matters. That is certainly true with evaluations of the level of democracy in China: Those with college degrees perceive lower levels of democracy than those with high school degrees or lower levels of education in earlier periods (see figure 6-1; the same patterns appeared in the 2010 survey, but only data from 2014 are shown to simplify the presentation). For the present period, those with college and high school degrees have identical evaluations, and both are lower than those with less education. In each time period, those with the lowest levels of education perceived higher levels of democracy. But education makes little difference in evaluating changes over time: Each group sees the level of democracy rising and expects it to continue to rise in the near future; moreover, the differences between the groups have narrowed over time.

Another factor that commonly influences political evaluations is age. People too young to have personal knowledge of past periods may not have the same reference points as those with longer memories, and therefore may have different evaluations of the past, present, and near future. If we divide the population into different cohorts based on their formative political experiences, we get four main cohorts: the founding generation (those who "came of age" [i.e., turned 16] before 1966), the Cultural Revolution generation (1966–1977), the early reform

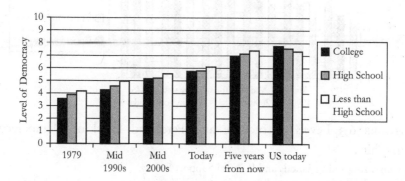

FIGURE 6-1 Levels of Education and Perceived Level of Democracy in China.

Source: 2014 Public Goods and Political Support Survey.

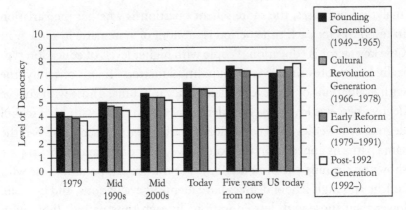

FIGURE 6-2 Age Cohorts and Perceived Level of Democracy in China.
Source: 2014 Public Goods and Political Support Survey.

generation (1978–1991), and the post-1992 generation (1992 and later). As figure 6-2 shows, older cohorts see more democracy at each point in time, but all four cohorts share the belief that China has become more democratic over time. The pattern is reversed for perceptions of U.S. democracy: The youngest see the most and the oldest see the least.

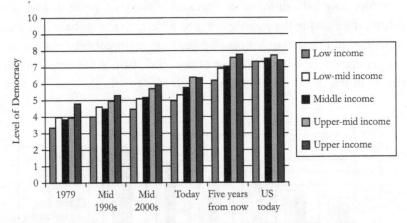

FIGURE 6-3 Levels of Income and Perceived Level of Democracy in China.
Source: 2014 Public Goods and Political Support Survey.

Level of income provides a sharper contrast (see figure 6-3). When evaluating the level of democracy now and in the recent past, respondents' household income has a consistent and strong effect. The higher the respondents' income, the more highly they evaluated the level of democracy—now, in the past, and in the future, and each income group sees the level of democracy steadily increasing. This is a recurring theme in Chinese political attitudes: The higher their income, the more highly they evaluate the status quo, and the more highly they are satisfied with it. Regarding the level of democracy in the U.S., all income groups had similar views.

Hukou status has a smaller but still notable impact, but the difference is not between urban and rural but between registered residents of the city (whether registered as urban or rural) and migrants to the city from other cities or the countryside. Most of the attention to China's migrant population focuses on those from the countryside, who are excluded from receiving healthcare, education, and other urban public goods in the cities where they live. But migrants from other cities may be just as excluded; this group reported the lowest level of democracy.

Other personal characteristics, such as gender and ethnicity, do not have a substantial impact on evaluations of the level of democracy: All have roughly the same level at a given point in time, and all perceive the level of democracy rising over time.

Not only do most Chinese see an increasingly democratic environment around them, they are generally satisfied with the level of democracy in their country (see figure 6-4). The patterns for level of

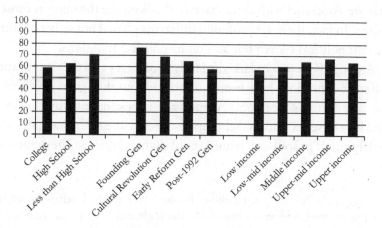

FIGURE 6-4 Satisfaction with Current Level of Democracy in China (percent satisfied or very satisfied).

Source: 2014 Public Goods and Political Support Survey.

education, age, and income are similar to those found for the perceived level of democracy: People with higher educations are less satisfied, older cohorts are more satisfied, and those with higher levels of income are generally more satisfied, although not in the same linear fashion as with education and age. More importantly, the majority in every category shown here is satisfied with the current level of democracy.[5] In short, these survey data indicate that most people in China see the level of democracy rising and believe that China is already somewhat if not highly democratic, and they are satisfied with the current level of democracy.

III. Definitions of Democracy

This presents a puzzle: If most outside observers see China as a one-party dictatorship, with few if any elements of democracy, why have the Chinese reached such different conclusions about how democratic their country is?

One reason is that democracy means different things to different people. As Tianjian Shi put it, "Studying people's aspirations toward democracy without carefully examining what democracy means to them would cause researchers to reach inaccurate conclusions about the relationship between people's support for democracy, regime change, and democratic consolidation."[6] We should not assume the meanings that are associated with democracy in the West are the same as those in China. In fact, there are profound differences based not only on China's current political system but also on its political traditions.

Among Western scholars who study democracy and democratization, different definitions have been put forward, but they generally agree on the core features. For some, democracy is best defined by the use of elections to select leaders. Schumpeter offered one of the first (and most widely cited) procedural definitions of democracy: ". . . the democratic

---

[5] Respondents were given a choice between very satisfied, relatively satisfied, not too satisfied, and very unsatisfied. The high and low options received few responses (less than 5 percent for every category of respondent), so very satisfied and relatively satisfied were combined to simplify the presentation.

[6] Shi, *The Cultural Logic of Politics*, p. 220.

method is that institutional arrangement for arriving at political decisions in which individuals acquire the power to decide by means of a
competitive struggle for the people's vote."[7] In short, leaders are chosen through popular elections. Huntington used a similar definition
in order to identify which countries were or were not democracies: A
country can be considered democratic when "its *most powerful collective
decision makers* are selected through fair, honest, and periodic elections
in which candidates freely compete for votes."[8] China has elections for
village leaders, village councils, and delegates to people's congresses at
the local level, but few outside observers believe that China therefore
qualifies as a democracy, and few Chinese point to village elections as
proof that it is democratic. That is why Huntington and others specified that democracies elect the "most powerful collective decision makers," not just local leaders. Przeworski agreed that elections were the
core characteristic of democracies, but with a twist: They were a means
of "institutionalizing uncertainty": "Democracy is a system in which
parties lose elections. There are parties: divisions of interest, values
and opinions. There is competition, organized by rules. And there are
periodic winners and losers."[9] It is the uncertain outcomes of elections
that are key: Incumbents cannot count on remaining in office past the
next election (despite the well-known advantages of incumbency), and
challengers cannot despair that they will forever be locked out. The
institutional arrangements of democracy—parties, competition, elections—guarantee and protect the uncertainty.

Others have been critical of this procedural definition. At best, elections may be a necessary but not sufficient characteristic of democratic
regimes. It is hard to imagine a modern democracy without elections,
but other elements must also be present. According to Dahl, democracy
requires not only competitive elections and the right to participate in
them, but also other rights and freedoms, such as the freedom to form

[7] Joseph A. Schumpeter, *Capitalism, Socialism, and Democracy* (New York:
Harper & Row, 1942), p. 269.

[8] Samuel P. Huntington, *The Third Wave: Democratization in the Late Twentieth
Century* (Norman, OK: University of Oklahoma Press, 1991), p. 7, emphasis added.

[9] Adam Przeworski, *Democracy and the Market: Political and Economic Reforms
in Eastern Europe and Latin America* (New York: Cambridge University Press,
1991), p. 10.

and join organizations, freedom of expression, alternative sources of information, and "institutions for making government policies depend on votes and other expressions of preferences."[10] Diamond provides a more succinct synopsis: "[D]emocratic structures will be mere facades unless people come to value the essential principles of democracy: popular sovereignty, accountability of rulers, freedom, and the rule of law."[11] By identifying these additional features of democracy, it is even more apparent that China falls short of the mark. And yet most Chinese think otherwise. Why?

Elite Definitions of Democracy in China

China's political leaders and intellectual elites have been debating the meaning of democracy and its suitability for China since the late 19th century. The Chinese word for democracy, *minzhu* (民主), has itself changed in meaning. As Chinese thinkers began to study Western countries, forms of government, and philosophical writings, they quickly realized that most of them were quite different from China's traditions. In order to translate key concepts, they needed proper terms. In some cases, they created new Chinese words that sounded like the Western equivalents (e.g., *baliman* 巴厘满 for parliament [later replaced by *yiyuan* 议院 as the preferred translation]) and captured the meanings of the Western terms (*huoche* 火车 [fire car] for train), or appropriated an existing Chinese word but gave it a new meaning. That was the case for *minzhu*. To capture the meaning of the Western concept of democracy, its original meaning—the chief of the people—was transformed into an entirely new meaning: The people are chiefs.[12] This change in meaning also introduced ambiguity: The word connotes both popular sovereignty (power from below) and leadership (power from above).

---

[10] Robert A. Dahl, *Polyarchy: Participation and Opposition*. (New Haven, CT: Yale University Press, 1971), p. 3.

[11] Larry Diamond, *The Spirit of Democracy: The Struggle to Build Free Societies throughout the World* (New York: Times Books/Henry Holt and Co., 2008), p. 20.

[12] Federico Masini, "The Formation of Modern Chinese Lexicon and Its Evolution Toward a National Language: The Period from 1840 to 1898," *Journal of Chinese Linguistics*, Monograph Series No. 6 (1993), p. 144.

As Chinese elites debated the propriety of democracy in China, one of the recurring themes was that democracy would make the country stronger.[13] Liang Qichao was an influential advocate of democracy in the late 19th and early 20th centuries who called for political reform as a means to strengthen the state and unify society. He saw an ongoing struggle between nations that threatened to overwhelm and even eliminate China, as both a nation and a race. The goal of democracy was not to promote individual rights and interests, but make the state stronger. Liang assumed that the interests of state and society were in harmony, and he did not see the potential for conflict between them. He advocated a constitutional government that would encourage political participation by wider segments of society. This, he claimed, would not only be good for society but would also protect against challenges to the domestic order. A constitution would eliminate what Liang saw as the three main sources of political instability: It would outline the rules for leadership succession, which would eliminate political struggle; it would delimit the authority of officials, which would minimize their ability to accumulate more power for themselves; and it would provide channels for political participation, giving society an opportunity to voice their complaints and not resort to rebellion to show their displeasure. "Thus," Liang concluded, "a constitutional form of government can never suffer from disorder."[14]

Liang's rationale for adopting democracy in China was to make the state strong enough to defend China against international threats, not to protect Chinese society from domestic dictatorship. In fact, Liang later abandoned democracy as the solution to China's problems in favor of "enlightened despotism." After visiting the United States in 1903, he despaired that the Chinese people were too divisive and too politically passive to be ready for democratic government. An autocratic leader, committed to the public's well-being, would educate society on how to be good and active citizens before granting them the rights and freedoms inherent in democracy. Liang's goal was to make China strong and modern; both democracy and

---

[13] The best discussion of this theme is in Andrew J. Nathan, *Chinese Democracy* (Berkeley, CA: University of California Press, 1985).

[14] Quoted in Nathan, *Chinese Democracy*, p. 55.

despotism were means for achieving those ends. This goal of making China internally unified and externally strong would find echoes in more contemporary debates on the propriety of democracy in China.

The contemporary debate over democracy in China has included its definition and core components, as well as its suitability for China. China's leaders have not shied away from discussing the prospects of democracy in China. Wen Jiabao, who served as prime minister from 2003 to 2013, was the most outspoken advocate for democracy among high-level leaders. "When we talk about democracy," he once said, "we usually refer to the three most important components: elections, judicial independence, and supervision based on checks and balances."[15] And he was quite enthusiastic that this type of democracy was not only possible but also fully compatible with China's conditions:

> China should take its own path in enhancing democracy. We never view socialism and democracy as something that is mutually exclusive. As a matter of fact, we see a high degree of democracy and well developed legal system as the inherent requirement of socialism and a key important feature of a mature socialist system. We are fully capable of building China into a country of democracy and rule of law under socialist conditions. We should explore ways to develop democracy with Chinese characteristics in light of China's particular conditions. We should focus on efforts to promote economic development, protect lawful rights and interests of the people, fight corruption, increase public trust in government, strengthen government functions and enhance social harmony. And we should continue the reform in the political system by expanding democracy and improving the legal system. This will enable other members of the international community to better appreciate and accept the path of development taken by the Chinese people.[16]

[15]   Quoted in Cheng Li, "Assessing China's Political Development," in Cheng Li, ed., *China's Changing Political Landscape: Prospects for Democracy* (Washington DC: Brookings Institution, 2008), p. 9.

[16] ."Our Historical Tasks at the Primary Stage of Socialism and Several Issues Concerning China's Foreign Policy," *Renmin ribao*, February 27, 2007 *China Daily* published an English summary: http://www.chinadaily.com.cn/china/2007-03/03/content_818952.htm, accessed November 8, 2013.

Other Chinese leaders have not been as supportive of this version of democracy.[17] Deng Xiaoping set limits on permissible political reforms at the beginning of the reform era. In March 1979, he emphasized "four cardinal principles" that defined Party rule: socialism, proletarian dictatorship, CCP supremacy, and Marxism-Leninism-Mao Zedong Thought. None of these principles is remotely democratic. This speech marked the effective end of the Democracy Wall movement of 1978–79 and set limits on public debate in later years. In 1986, he rejected any suggestion of checks and balances, which would limit the autonomy of the Party. "In reforming our political structure we must not imitate the West, and no liberalization should be allowed. Of course our present structure of leadership has certain advantages. For example, it enables us to make quick decisions, while if we place too much emphasis on a need for checks and balances, problems may arise."[18] In more recent years, these sentiments have become more explicit. Even though China's leaders talk about democracy constantly, they rarely define the term, other than to say that China's democracy will be unlike what is practiced in the West. Wu Bangguo, who was chairman of the National People's Congress (China's legislature) while Wen was prime minister, was adamant that China could never adopt Western-style democracy:

> On the basis of China's conditions, we have made a solemn declaration that we will not employ a system of multiple parties holding office in rotation; diversify our guiding thought; separate executive, legislative and judicial powers; use a bicameral or federal system; or

[17] Wen became more outspoken in his support for wide-ranging political reforms, including greater democracy in China, during his final years in office. Some believed that this reflected his genuine frustration with the slow pace of reform during Hu Jintao's leadership (2002–2012), but others thought it was primarily an effort to shape his own historical legacy and reputation. He found few supporters for his reform initiative, and some of his speeches were not even covered in the Chinese media (e.g., his speech to the United Nations and interview with Fareed Zakaria on CNN, both in 2010). Among the current leaders in China, none are identified as Wen's protégé.

[18] Deng Xiaoping, "On the Reform of Political Structure, September–November 1986," *Selected Works, Vol. 3: 1982–1992* (Beijing: Foreign Languages Press, 1994).

carry out privatization. . . . Different countries have different systems of laws, and we do not copy the systems of laws of certain Western countries.[19]

This sweeping rejection of Western political and economic institutions became known as the "five no's" and reinforced the view that political reform had stalled in China.

Xi Jinping has preferred to talk about "consultative democracy," a phrase coined by Li Junru of the Central Party School.[20] In September 2014, at the 65th anniversary of the Chinese People's Political Consultative Conference (a largely symbolic body that meets each spring in tandem with the National People's Congress), Xi said, "There are various ways to realize democracy. We should neither stick to one model nor claim that there is a universal one." Instead of adopting liberal democracy, Xi said the Party would consult selectively with different parts of society on different kinds of issues. "The whole of society will be consulted about the interests of the whole country while people in a certain area will be consulted about local affairs and a certain group of people will be consulted about affairs relevant to their interests," he said.[21] This speech kicked off a propaganda campaign to promote the advantages of consultative democracy in China. As in chapter 3, this is another manifestation of consultation without accountability, and it falls well short of the Western concept of democracy.

When Party leaders talk about democracy, they often refer to inner-party democracy. This allows Party members to have some say in which leaders are selected for top positions, but it does not meet the standard for democracy that most outsiders have in mind. For example, every five

---

[19] Wu Bangguo, "Full Text: Work Report of NPC Standing Committee (2011)," GOV.cn, last modified March 18, 2011, http://english.gov.cn/official/2011-03/18/content_1827230_6.htm, accessed October 29, 2013,

[20] David Shambaugh, *China's Communist Party: Atrophy and Adaptation* (Berkeley, CA, and Washington, DC: University of California Press and Woodrow Wilson Center Press, 2009), pp. 122–123.

[21] "China Hails Consultative Democracy on 65th Anniversary of Political Advisory Body," *Xinhuanet*, September 21, 2014, http://news.xinhuanet.com/english/china/2014-09/21/c_133660577_2.htm, accessed August 24, 2015.

years, the CCP convenes a National Party Congress, and its main task is to elect a Central Committee, a body of about 200 people who represent the top leadership in the Party. In the past, the Central Committee was elected by acclamation; all nominees were unanimously elected. In recent years, however, the CCP has introduced a smidgen of choice. At the 2012 National Party Congress, there were 221 nominees for the 205 seats on the Central Committee, a difference of roughly 8 percent. At the local level, some Party leaders have experimented with allowing Party members to vote for local leaders. From an outside perspective, these examples of inner-party democracy may seem inconsequential, but in the Chinese context, they represent a change from past practices, in which the higher levels of the Party bureaucracy appointed people to fill lower-level posts. The new practices allow for some degree of consultation and choice without threatening the Party's hold on power, because all posts of any political significance continue to be held by Party members.

Among China's contemporary scholars and public intellectuals, there is a similar debate on the meaning and practice of democracy. To make sense of this debate, it helps to distinguish those who favor liberal democracy, which is practiced in the U.S. and many other former U.K.-settled countries and emphasizes political and economic freedoms, from those who advocate social democracy, which is more common in Western Europe and emphasizes political and economic equality, and especially from those who reject both variants of democracy.

The liberal perspective was most prominent in the 1980s.[22] In the early post-Mao years when economic and political reforms were being debated and implemented, the liberal critique of authoritarianism and emphasis on a limited state had definite appeal. Their support for economic liberalization was seen as not only important in its own right, but also important for the emergence of liberal democracy in China. In the 1990s, liberal intellectuals were repressed by the Party for their support for and involvement in the 1989 demonstrations. Many fled from China, and those that remained found it difficult to get their views published. At the same time, they also faced criticism from other intellectuals. In the 1980s, the main debate was between those who

[22] Joseph Fewsmith, *China since Tiananmen: From Deng Xiaoping to Hu Jintao*, second edition (New York: Cambridge University Press, 2008), esp. Part II.

were for and against reform, but in the 1990s, a new alternative gained prominence: political, economic, and social instability brought on by the collapse of the regime. The existential threat posed by the 1989 demonstrations, combined a few years later with the collapse of the Soviet Union and the economic and social turmoil that ensued, made political leaders and critical intellectuals aware of a possibility that had seemed unthinkable just a few years earlier. Other perspectives, emphasizing the strengthening of state capacity, gained popularity at the expense of liberalism. In addition, the liberal critique of China's authoritarian regime was deemed unpatriotic by other intellectuals, a very serious charge at a time when nationalism was also rising in the country. As a result of the twin sources of state repression and intellectual trends, liberals in China were criticized and marginalized in the 1990s.

Although liberal democracy lost popularity to other groups, it never fully lost its appeal. Its priorities were captured in "Charter 08," an online petition calling for wide-ranging political reforms:

> Democracy: The most fundamental meaning is that sovereignty resides in the people and the government elected by the people. Democracy has the following basic characteristics: (1) The legitimacy of political power comes from the people; the source of political power is the people. (2) Political control is exercised through choices made by the people. (3) Citizens enjoy the genuine right to vote; officials in key positions at all levels of government must be the product of elections at regular intervals. (4) Respect the decisions of the majority while protecting the basic human rights of the minority. In a word, democracy is the modern public instrument for creating a government "of the people, by the people, and for the people."[23]

One of Charter 08's primary authors was Liu Xiaobo, who had previously spent over 18 months in prison for his involvement in the 1989 demonstrations. He was arrested soon after Charter 08 was posted online and later sentenced to 11 years in prison on December 25, 2009. Given the importance of the Christmas holiday in most Western countries,

---

[23] "Charter 08, Human Rights in China," last modified December 9, 2008, http://www.hrichina.org/content/238, accessed October 4, 2013.

the timing of the announcement was not likely a coincidence. Liu received the Nobel Peace Prize in 2010, but it went unclaimed. Liu was in prison, and his wife was prevented from leaving China to accept the award in his honor.

Yu Keping is one of China's best-known public intellectuals and advocates of democracy. He was deputy director of the Central Compilation and Translation Bureau of the Central Committee of the CCP and later became the director of the Center for Chinese Government Innovations at Peking University (as mentioned in chapter 3). He is best known for his essay "Democracy Is a Good Thing," in which he described democracy as "the best political system for humankind."[24] Like many Western scholars, Yu sees the competitive election of top leaders as the essence of democracy. According to Yu, "Democracy, no matter what form it takes, is defined by the free election of political leaders. Hence democratization will mean enlarging the scope of people's political choices so as to move from less competition to more competition."[25] But he treads a fine line between advocating democracy while also upholding Party rule. He and others in his center look for ways to achieve democracy within the confines of the existing regime, but this search is akin to squaring a circle: It cannot be done without changing its basic structure. While some see this vision as quixotic, he represents a liberal perspective within the Party.

Many Chinese intellectuals criticize the liberal democratic perspective as being unsuitable to China. Like Liang Qichao, they argue that what China needs most is a strong state to protect it from international pressures, guide economic development, and alleviate income inequality. The goal of democracy is to make China strong and modern. They have less concern for potential conflict between individual and collective interests, and when there is a conflict, they are sure the collective will prevail.

[24] Yu Keping, *Democracy Is a Good Thing: Essays on Politics, Society, and Culture in Contemporary China* (Washington, DC: Brookings Institution, 2009), p. 4. For more background on Yu, see Andrew Jacobs, "A Chinese Official Praises a Taboo: Democracy," *New York Times*, July 24, 2010, http://www.nytimes.com/2010/07/24/world/asia/24beijing.html?pagewanted=all&_r=0, accessed October 8, 2013.

[25] Yu Keping, "Ideological Change and Incremental Democracy in Reform-Era China," in Cheng Li, ed., *China's Changing Political Landscape: Prospects for Democracy* (Washington DC: Brookings Institution, 2008), p. 57.

In contrast, Western thinkers assume there is a conflict between state and society and between individual and collective interests. Democratic institutions are designed to protect society from a potentially despotic state. Democratic constitutions and rule of law are designed, in part, to protect individual interests while also balancing them against collective interests. Sometimes individual interests prevail, and sometimes collective interests do. Institutional design is the key to the outcome. But Chinese democrats have been less bothered by the potential for conflict between interests. Democracy should strengthen the state, harmonize relations between state and society, and eliminate conflict within society.

Promoting a strong state runs contrary to the goals of liberal democracy, which emphasize political and economic freedoms and therefore a small state with limited regulatory powers. This alternative perspective is often referred to as the "New Left" (even though the people who are categorized as part of the New Left generally reject the label). One of its most prominent voices belongs to Wang Hui, a professor of Chinese language and literature at Tsinghua University and a prolific writer on political and social trends and intellectual history in China. Unlike the other Western and Chinese scholars noted before, Wang sees democracy as not just electoral procedures and political freedoms, but also desired policy outcomes:

> In the contemporary context, people usually mean two things when they talk about democracy, that is, democracy as a political institution, and democracy as a form of society. The former includes universal suffrage, protection of individual rights, freedom of speech, pluralism, etc., while the core of the latter is equality, which is mainly embodied in social security, access to public goods by all members of society, and redistribution. The combination of the two becomes the so-called social democracy.[26]

This social democratic emphasis on equality and well-being is similar to the Chinese concept of *minben* 民本, which literally means "the people

---

[26] Wang Hui, "*Daibiaoxing de duanlie: Fansi weilai de minzhu jincheng*" (Break of Representativeness: Reflections on Future Democratic Process), aisixiang.com, last modified January 3, 2011, http://www.aisixiang.com/data/38172.html, accessed October 4, 2013.

as the base." This ancient Confucian concept argues that the goal of good government is to serve the interests of the people. Common prosperity and social stability serve the public well-being and in turn legitimate the state.[27] Social democracy, like *minben*, establishes priorities for the work of the government. As a consequence of these priorities, social democratic countries tend to have much lower levels of income inequality than liberal democracies. To oversimplify, liberal democracies privilege economic *growth* by promoting political and economic freedoms, whereas social democracies privilege *equity* by narrowing the gap between rich and poor, in large part through collective bargaining, a progressive tax system, and the expansive provision of public goods, such as healthcare, education, and other social welfare programs. For Wang Hui, it is the pursuit of greater equity that should be the top priority, not simply the holding of free and fair elections. This new left perspective was of particular influence during the Hu-Wen era, when the concern for more equality and social justice rose within the top leadership.

A third perspective adopts some elements of liberal and social democracy, but rejects the necessity of democratic procedures to achieve desired political and social goals. Pan Wei, a political science professor at Peking University, defines democracy strictly in terms of elections, but for very different reasons:

> [T]he periodic election of top leaders is the core characteristic of all democracies, and all definitions include it, although they disagree on other features. . . . [O]ther key factors, such as checks and balances and freedoms of speech, press, assembly, and association should be excluded, *for they can be obtained without elections of top leaders.*[28]

---

[27] Enbao Wang and Regina F. Titunik, "Democracy in China: The Theory and Practice of *Minben*," in Suisheng Zhao, ed., *China and Democracy: Reconsidering the Prospects for a Democratic China* (New York and London: Routledge, 2000), pp. 73–88.

[28] Pan Wei, "Toward a Consultative Rule of Law Regime in China," in Zhao Suisheng, ed., *Debating Political Reform in China: Rule of Law vs. Democratization* (Armonk, NY: M.E. Sharpe, 2006), p. 7, emphasis added. This perspective gave rise to a lively debate among Chinese and Western scholars, some of which are included in *Debating Political Reform in China*.

Pan wants to limit the definition of democracy to elections because he believes the other institutional features often attributed to democracy are possible in other forms of government as well. Like Yu Keping and others, he accepts elections as the essence of democracy, but unlike them, he dismisses the desirability of democracy. He argues instead that other political institutions are more desirable. From his perspective, what China needs most is rule of law, and that can be achieved without having to first establish democratic elections. He also wants to "exclude ends, which are often attached to definitions. All forms of polity claim noble ends, and the declared noble ends serve to mythologize a polity and ignore its means."[29] In this, he is alone among Chinese intellectuals on ignoring outcomes.[30] For most democracy advocates from the late 19th century to the early post-Mao era, making China a democracy was a means to a larger end: making the state strong. Pan does not deny the importance of making the state strong, just as he does not reject the importance of rule of law, checks and balances, and various political freedoms (press, speech, organization, and so on); rather, he believes that all of them are achievable without the popular election of top leaders. From his perspective, the primary difference between democracies and autocracies is their methods of leadership selection, not other institutions or political outcomes. He is in favor of the goals of social democracy—greater equality, more state involvement in the economy, more public goods—but believes that they can and should be achieved without democracy.

A full assessment of the Chinese debate over democracy is outside the scope of this book.[31] But two points deserve emphasis. First, democracy as defined by China's political leaders and intellectual elites mirrors

[29] Pan, "Toward a Consultative Rule of Law Regime in China," p. 7.

[30] In distinguishing between results and institutional requirements, Pan's perspective is reminiscent of Philippe C. Schmitter and Terry Lynn Karl, "What Democracy Is . . . and Is Not," *Journal of Democracy*, Vol. 2, No. 1 (Summer 1991), pp. 75–88.

[31] For the broader debates, see Nathan, *Chinese Democracy*; Fewsmith, *China since Tiananmen*; Cheng Li, ed., *China's Changing Political Landscape: Prospects for Democracy* (Washington, DC: Brookings Institution, 2008); He Li, "Chinese Intellectual Discourse on Democracy," *Journal of Chinese Political Science*, Vol. 19, No. 3 (September 2014), pp. 289–314.

Western definitions. Some are skeptical that democracy is necessary, suitable, or even preferable in China. They either add other institutional factors to show why they are unsuited to China, or exclude them (Pan Wei) to show that they can be achieved in non-democracies as well. Second, the elite discussion in China has little in common with the popular understanding of democracy.

Popular Definitions of Democracy in China

To most Western observers and Chinese elites, competitive, free, and fair elections are the sine qua non of democracy. Elections alone do not a democracy make, but it is hard to imagine a true democracy without them. Rule of law, freedom of the press, freedom of speech, freedom of assembly, civil liberties, and civil rights are also crucial elements of a democratic political system. But all of these are absent in China, or if not absent, then in short and unpredictable supply. To understand why most Chinese believe their country is increasingly democratic and are satisfied with the level of democracy, we need to find out what democracy means to them.

In the Public Goods and Political Support Surveys, respondents were asked the following question: "Everybody talks about democracy, but in your view, what does 'democracy' actually mean?" Rather than asking respondents to choose between various definitions, the question was open-ended, allowing them to describe what democracy meant to them. In order to analyze these definitions, similar answers were coded into separate categories. Their answers were quite varied, as can be seen in figure 6-5. Some people gave more than one definition, in which case each definition was coded into the proper category (as a result, the percentages in figure 6-5 add up to more than 100 percent).

Although competitive elections may be the litmus test of democracy for Western observers and Chinese elites, they are less consequential for ordinary Chinese. Only 3.1 percent of the respondents in 2010 and 2.9 percent in 2014 mentioned elections when they defined democracy ("everybody votes," "the majority rules," "right to elect and be elected").[32] Some respondents mentioned other formal institutional

---

[32] These quotes are taken from the definitions of democracy given by the survey respondents.

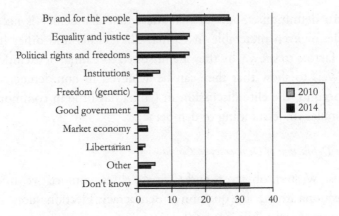

FIGURE 6-5 Popular Definitions of Democracy in Urban China (percent who defined democracy with each term).
Source: Public Goods and Political Support Surveys.

elements of democracy, such as rule of law, a multiparty system, and the presence of a legislature.[33] These responses were combined into a single category ("institutions"), and still less than 5 percent of respondents in 2014 defined democracy in this way.

Political rights and freedoms are often part of the definition of democracy, and many of the survey respondents agreed. The categories "equality and justice" and "rights and freedoms" have some overlap, but they differ in terms of relationships between state and society. Responses coded as rights and freedoms concerned the vertical relationships between the state and society: "the opportunity and right to tell the government their views," "ordinary people can speak, be respected,

[33] Some people referenced the National People's Congress, China's legislature. At the most basic level (rural townships and urban districts), delegates are directly elected by the people, but delegates of higher-level people's congresses are indirectly elected (e.g., provincial people's congresses appoint delegates to the National People's Congress). Indirect elections violate one of the basic elements of liberal democracy, but people's congresses do pass laws and to some extent oversee the government by approving the CCP's nominees for official positions and receiving annual reports on the work of the government. On paper, the Chinese political system resembles a parliamentary system, but the concentration of power in the CCP and the process by which delegates are chosen for higher-level people's congresses (selected, not elected) demonstrate why organization charts and blueprints do not always reflect how a system operates.

and express their views whenever they like," and "people enjoy the right to information." In contrast, answers coded as equality and justice concerned horizontal relationships within society, with an emphasis on how one individual compares with another: "everyone is treated equally," "ordinary people can enjoy the same rights and interests," and "to be more equal in terms of income, housing, and employment." Rights and freedoms and equality and justice are often complementary, but the distinction between freedom *from* the state and equality *among* citizens is an important one, and one that many of the Chinese respondents made when defining democracy. Approximately 15 percent defined democracy in terms of rights and freedoms, and another 15 percent defined it in terms of equality and justice; less than 2 percent defined it in both ways.

Less than half of the Chinese respondents, therefore, offered definitions of democracy that were similar to the standard definitions employed in both the West and China. That is one reason why most believe that China is already at least somewhat democratic, that it is increasingly so, that they are satisfied with the current level of democracy, and are optimistic about even higher levels in the near future. The most common response, given by 27.6 percent of the respondents, was a government that was governed by and for the people. This category includes answers such as "the people and the government are interdependent," "the people are the master," "listen to the people," and "government policies reflect public opinion," as well as references to Sun Yat-sen's "Three Principles of the People," in particular about public well-being.[34] This category emphasizes the government's responsiveness to public opinion and the interests, power, or authority of the people. It concerns what leaders should do, but not how they are chosen. More importantly, it suggests that the public's interests and the state's interests are fundamentally in harmony (or at least should be). In that sense, it is as similar to the traditional notion of *minben* as the modern concept of *minzhu*.[35] Modern thinkers like Liang Qichao also

[34] This was the slogan coined by Sun Yat-sen in the early 20th century. The three principles are nationalism, democracy, and the people's livelihood.

[35] For a comparison of liberal democracy and *minben*, see Shi, *The Cultural Logic of Politics*, pp. 196–201.

asserted the shared interests of the rulers and the people, assuming that both would hold collective well-being above individual (and therefore selfish and destructive) interests. The purpose of democracy, as seen by many Chinese, is to strengthen the state so that it can better provide for the common well-being of the people and the nation as a whole; it is not to limit the state's authority in order to protect individual rights and freedoms or to adjudicate between competing interests.

The category "good government," offered by 3.2 percent of the respondents, has some overlap with "by and for the people," but the focus here is on how the government operates and the quality of leaders and officials. People who defined democracy in terms of good government said that "the government should be open to the people as much as possible," "politics should be open and transparent," and there should be "no corruption." For people who defined democracy in this way, the emphasis was on the character of leaders and transparent decision-making, but not on how leaders should be chosen or what rights society should enjoy.

Other definitions were given by similarly small numbers of respondents. About 4 percent said democracy meant "freedom" in a generic sense, without specifying what kinds of freedoms. Just under 3 percent referred to the presence of a market economy and the achievement of economic results; ironically, this was more common for rural migrants and others with low incomes. Less than 2 percent defined democracy as managing one's own affairs, having autonomy from the government and others, being free to do what one wants, and similar sentiments that fall into the category of "libertarian." There were also a few general comments that were hard to otherwise categorize, some positive ("it is good for China, and won't lead to chaos," "peace and stability"), some negative ("the common people can't handle democracy," "too much freedom is bad for China, it can lead to chaos"), and some neutral or ambiguous ("democracy is a kind of system," "it doesn't mean anything").

Not only did the opportunity to define democracy yield a wide variety of answers, it also stumped many of the respondents. In fact, "don't know" was the second most popular answer (25.4 percent) in 2010, and the most popular (33 percent) in 2014. Another 9 and 2.1 percent in 2010 and 2014, respectively, simply refused to answer. In other words, over a third of the respondents in the survey failed to offer any definition of democracy at all.

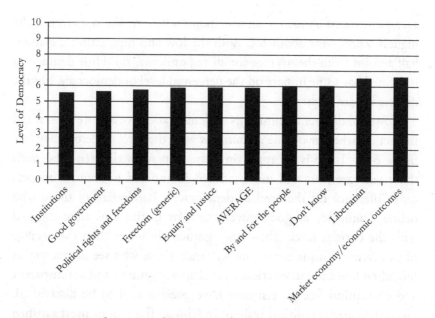

FIGURE 6-6 Definitions of Democracy and Perceived Level of Democracy in China.

Source: 2014 Public Goods and Political Support Survey.

IV. How Definitions Matter

Given that Chinese respondents offered such a variety of definitions for democracy, do these differences matter? If we asked the same question of Americans, the French, Germans, or others living in a democracy, we would likely also get a range of responses, and many of them would be similar to the ones given by the Chinese.[36] But do these different definitions also help us understand why most Chinese believe they already have a high degree of democracy and are satisfied with it?

Different definitions of democracy do have some influence on people's perceptions about the level of democracy in contemporary China, but they vary within a fairly narrow band (see figure 6-6). At the low end of the scale, those who defined democracy in terms of good government or formal institutions (elections, parties, rule of law) had an

[36] Russell J. Dalton, Doh C. Shin, and Willy Jou, "Understanding Democracy: Data from Unlikely Places," *Journal of Democracy*, Vol. 18, No. 4 (October 2007), pp. 142–156.

average score of about 5.5 on a 10-point scale. At the upper end, the highest scores were about 6.5. Both the low and high scores are about half a point from the average for all respondents, 5.9. How democracy is defined has some impact on the perceived level of democracy, but the differences are slight.

However, different definitions of democracy have a more substantial impact on whether people are *satisfied* with the level of democracy (see figure 6-7). There is an approximately 40 percent difference between those who are least and most satisfied (compared to about a 20 percent difference for the level of democracy). Barely half of those who define democracy as good government or institutions were satisfied with the current level. These are significantly lower than the average of 65 percent. This is easy to understand: Those who see democracy as including free and fair elections, a multiparty system, and a transparent and corruption-free government have good reason to be dissatisfied, given the current political realities in China. The groups most satisfied with the level of democracy in China defined democracy in terms of libertarian values or a market economy and economic outcomes, but these groups only account for 1.3 and 2.9 percent, respectively, of all

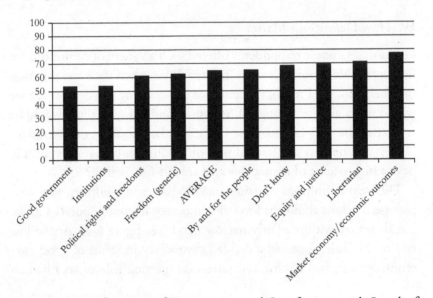

FIGURE 6-7 Definitions of Democracy and Satisfaction with Level of Democracy in China (percent satisfied or very satisfied).

Source: 2014 Public Goods and Political Support Survey.

respondents. Remarkably, those who chose not to offer a definition also reported a high level of satisfaction: Almost 70 percent of those who gave "don't know" as their answer were satisfied with the current level of democracy, even though they could not say what it meant to them. This is undoubtedly due to the somewhat abstract notion of what democracy means in a country where it is not fully practiced. But as we will see, it is also due to the kinds of people who did not define their understanding of democracy.

How democracy is defined in China has some impact on the perceived level of democracy and an even bigger impact on how satisfied people are with that level. More importantly, it has an impact on their political and social behavior. Let's take voting for starters, since most outside observers see voting as an essential component of democracy (even though, in Chinese cities, voting is largely limited to the lowest level of the people's congress system, the nominal legislature). Voting is not a particularly common practice for urban Chinese: Only 15 percent of respondents voted in the most recent election in their cities, and only another 11 percent reported they had ever voted in a previous people's congress election. Most people do not highly value the work of their people's congress, are not aware of what it does, and do not even know who their delegate is.[37] Those who defined democracy as good government or institutions were the most likely to vote compared to others in the survey, and those who defined it with libertarian terms or "don't know" were least likely to. The likelihood of voting is not solely determined by definitions of democracy, of course. When we control for common determinants of political behavior—such as age, education, gender, income, and in the Chinese case, membership in the CCP— only the "good government" group is significantly (in both a statistical and substantive sense) more likely to vote than others.

[37] Kevin J. O'Brien, "Agents and Remonstrators: Role Accumulation by Chinese People's Congress Deputies," *China Quarterly*, No. 138 (June 1994), pp. 359–380; Melanie Manion, "Chinese Democratization in Perspective: Electorates and Selectorates at the Township Level," *China Quarterly*, No. 163 (September 2000), pp. 764–782; Young Nam Cho, *Local People's Congresses in China: Development and Transition* (New York: Cambridge University Press, 2009). After discussing the weak role of the people's congress system in class, one Chinese student came to my office the next day to say he did know who his delegate was: It was his mother!

Looking at other types of behavior reveals a similar pattern. Those who defined democracy as good government were the most likely to contact officials, most likely to criticize local government, and the second most likely to discuss national affairs on the Internet. In contrast, the "don't knows" were the *least* likely to contact officials, least likely to criticize local government, and the second least likely to discuss national affairs on the Internet. Although it is true that the good government group is relatively small, only 3.2 percent of the sample, that is to be expected: The most politically active people in any country tend to be a small subset of the overall population. But this group is distinctive: It reports the second-lowest level of democracy in China, is the least satisfied with the current level of democracy, and is most likely to contact officials and criticize local government. The don't knows are the mirror opposite: Not only are they a much larger group (a third of the respondents), but they are also among the most satisfied with the level of democracy and the least likely to vote, contact officials, use the Internet to discuss national affairs, or criticize their local governments, and—to add two more examples—the least likely to know the names of the current prime minister or the mayor of their city. In short, the good government group is the most politically active, and the don't knows are the least active. Who belongs to these groups? What other attributes do people in these two groups share that might give us further insight into their political perspectives, political behavior, and even potential for political change in China?

In survey research, "don't know" can be an ambiguous reply. It may mean that respondents truly do not know, or it may hide the fact that they do not want to give an answer. The question may be politically sensitive, or respondents may be unwilling to reveal their true feelings to a stranger. Defining democracy is an example where "don't know" is probably the honest answer. Compared to others in the survey, the don't knows have less interest in national affairs, less education, and less confidence in their own ability to understand politics or influence the actions of local officials, what political scientists refer to as political efficacy. They are less likely to know the current prime minister or their city's mayor (even when controlling for *hukou* status). They are satisfied with the status quo and not inclined to try to change or influence it, but it is probably more accurate to describe them as complacent or acquiescent rather than overt regime supporters.

The Party depends on a large proportion of the population to be complacent, and the don't knows fit the bill. Ruling parties, like business organizations, cannot cope with a sudden upsurge in demands; they need a balance between criticism and complacency, between activism and apathy. Too little, and they lack meaningful feedback on their performance and can become despotic, unresponsive, or just lazy, becoming less popular or legitimate as a result; too much, and they can become quickly overwhelmed by the range and intensity of demands, which are not necessarily compatible, and are unable to respond effectively and in a timely manner.[38] Efforts to mollify one group may only further inflame another. Attempts to suppress all voices may create sympathy for those who bravely aired their complaints and may even motivate others to join the chorus. The Chinese political system is not designed to accommodate much political participation, and the don't knows make few demands on it. They are political outsiders; they are less likely to be CCP members, have a high school or college education, or believe in their own political efficacy. In other words, they lack the political capital and political skills necessary to navigate the state successfully. They do not expect much from the Party and government, and are unlikely to get much in return.[39]

The good government types are more likely to be political insiders. Compared to the other respondents, they are more likely to be CCP members, to have a college education, and to be male. These are the preferred attributes for Party and government officials. They have a higher sense of their political efficacy. They are less satisfied with the work of the local government and have the connections and skills to interact with the state more effectively. As previously noted, they are also the most politically active and the least satisfied with the current level of democracy. All of which raises a provocative question: Are they potentially subversive or simply politically savvy?

[38] Albert Hirschman, *Exit, Voice and Loyalty: Responses to Decline in Firms, Organizations, and States* (Cambridge, MA: Harvard University Press, 1970).

[39] This is reminiscent of Putnam's discussion of the importance of social capital in making democracy work, and intentionally so. In addition to the other attributes already mentioned, the don't knows have fewer social contacts and less trust in party and government officials at any level, and even less trust in their colleagues and classmates.

In his forecast of China's democratic future, Bruce Gilley predicts that the most likely path of democratization in China is for democratic advocates to emerge within the Party itself, transforming the political system in the process.[40] These data give some support to that possibility. At a minimum, they suggest that democrats have sympathizers within the state, even though other parts of the state are engaged in repressing democratic activists. In previous episodes of democratic activism, protestors knew they had potential allies among Party and government officials. During the Democracy Wall movement of 1978–79, Deng Xiaoping and other top leaders made oblique statements to indicate their support for protestors who wrote pamphlets and wall posters criticizing the practices of the Cultural Revolution and emphasizing the need for political reform. Party officials also leaked documents detailing internal Party deliberations to show that the demands made on Democracy Wall had echoes within the Party. Some of these leaked documents were then posted on Democracy Wall for the public to read.

During the 1989 demonstrations in Tiananmen Square, support within the state for popular protests was revealed in much more public ways. People from Party and government organs joined the marches, carrying signs that identified what unit they worked for. The official media began printing and broadcasting supportive stories. These actions by key parts of the Party-state revealed the deep split within the Party about how to respond to the escalating protests. In the end, however, this sympathy was not enough to shape the outcome. Eventually, the protestors' demands were denied, many of their leaders ended up in prison or in exile, and many protestors and innocent bystanders were killed or injured when the regime imposed martial law on June 4. Many of the officials who supported the protestors lost their jobs, most notably Zhao Ziyang, who was general secretary of the CCP when the 1989 protests began but lived the rest of his life under house arrest.[41]

[40] Bruce Gilley, *China's Democratic Future: How It Will Happen and Where It Will Lead* (New York: Columbia University Press, 2004); "Democrats Will Emerge," *Current History* (September 2007), pp. 245–247.

[41] See his memoir *Prisoner of the State*. The preface describes the dramatic story of how Zhao made tape recordings of his political experiences and hid them in his granddaughter's toy chest. The tapes were not discovered until after he died, and they were smuggled out of China to Hong Kong, where they were transcribed and published in both Chinese and English editions.

Are those who define democracy as good government potential agents of change or defenders of the status quo? They are already political insiders and have the attributes needed to be successful within the current regime: They are well-educated male CCP members with a strong sense of political efficacy. They know the system better than most and therefore recognize the low level of democracy and are less satisfied with it. They are a relatively small group, but they are the most politically active and the most politically connected. Because of this, their voices carry more weight than their numbers alone might justify.

Will they defend the status quo or defect when a democratic opening appears? This is a crucial question, not just for China watchers (and for theories of regime change more generally), but also for the Party itself. Maintaining the loyalty of political insiders is a crucial challenge for any regime, even more so for authoritarian regimes.[42] There are undoubtedly democracy supporters within the CCP and government bureaucracies, but it is impossible to know how many there are. That is why the participation of CCP and government units in the 1989 demonstrations was such a revelation. It showed that the discontent and desire for change was widespread throughout society and even within the state. But it also showed how limited their impact was when faced with the determination of Party leaders to preserve the Party's political monopoly.

In the years after the 1989 demonstrations, the Party has used recurring campaigns to reemphasize the leading role of the Party and the need to identify and repress threats to its continued rule. It has stressed the need for Party members, and especially officials, to follow the prevailing Party line. Above all, it has avoided a public display of political differences among Party leaders. It does not want to give even the appearance of a split, lest activists once again be emboldened to press for change and seek the support of one faction of the leadership. Maintaining Party unity and mobilizing the loyalty of Party members are key parts of the Party's strategy for survival.

There are undoubtedly democratic supporters among China's political elite, but whether they are numerous enough, powerful enough, and skilled enough to guide regime change is impossible to know in

---

[42] Bruce Bueno de Mesquita, Alastair Smith, Randolph M. Siverson, and James Morrow, *The Logic of Political Survival* (Cambridge, MA: MIT Press, 2003).

advance. Despite the hopes of many, the alternative to authoritarianism is not always democracy. When an authoritarian regime falls, it is often replaced by another form of authoritarianism. Political openings in much of the former Soviet Union and during the Arab Spring in 2011 did not lead to stable democracies, but rather to political turmoil and new autocrats, some of whom came out of the old regime. Political insiders in China have no incentives to reveal their democratic aspirations, and they probably do not even have a reliable estimate of how many like-minded people they can count on for support. This is what Timur Kuran refers to as "preference falsification": In situations where it is dangerous to reveal one's true preferences, people will frequently offer politically correct statements and actions, even though they do not genuinely support them. Because so many do this, people with similar preferences are not aware of each other's existence, are unable to estimate how widespread their preferences are, and as a result cannot cooperate to achieve their preferred outcomes.[43] It is only during rare moments of political opening that they come to realize that many others share their views.

With the notable exceptions of Zhao Ziyang and Wen Jiabao, other Party and government leaders toe the Party's line. Debates about political reform focus on improving the political system, not replacing it. To go further is to risk the loss of a job or even be sent to prison. Even attempts to discuss the benefits of constitutional government have been repeatedly nipped in the bud. Advocates of constitutionalism hoped it would be a more neutral topic than political reform and therefore more acceptable, since both the CCP and the government have formal constitutions, but others within the Party leadership were not so easily fooled. They recognized the implications of openly debating constitutional reform, which at a minimum would delimit the Party's authority and could even entail a change of regime altogether. Rather than risk another wave of pro-reform sentiments from society, as occurred in 1978–79 and 1989, Party leaders preferred to end the debate. In 2013, the CCP gave college professors a list of topics related to constitutional

[43] Timur Kuran, "Now Out of Never: The Element of Surprise in the East European Revolution of 1989," *World Politics*, Vol. 44, No. 1 (October 1991), pp. 7–48.

government that were now forbidden from even classroom discussion, including universal values, citizen rights, civil society, judicial independence, and freedom of the press (the other two topics were the capitalist class in China and the Party's past mistakes). The Party is determined to prevent challenges to its monopoly on political power, even to the point of blocking oblique discussions of constitutional government, a proxy for discussing political reform.

Supporters of Western-style democracy certainly exist in China and even in the Party. But China's recent political history shows how difficult it is for these sentiments to sway China's leaders. And the experiences of other countries (e.g., in the former Soviet Union, the Middle East, and Northern Africa) show that widespread public support for regime change often gets hijacked by political elites. The Party's strategy for survival is defined above all by its determination to prevent any organized opposition to its rule. This, combined with the widespread belief in society at large that the country is increasingly democratic, leaves little space for democracy activists to operate. Even if these activists could rally public opinion to their side, and even if this would lead to regime change, there is good reason to doubt whether Western observers or Chinese elites would recognize the new regime as truly democratic. The transition from authoritarianism does not necessarily lead to democracy.

* * *

Although most outside observers agree that China remains a one-party authoritarian regime, most Chinese perceive dramatic improvements in their political environment. Despite the absence of political rights and freedoms that most people living in democratic countries take for granted, China is more open today than it was in the Maoist era, despite the political tightening that began in 2008. The Party continues to monitor and repress any potential threat to its hold on power, but for most people in China, the state is less intrusive than in the Maoist era, and the range of freedoms, though not complete, is broader than in the recent past. Foreign governments, international organizations, and nongovernmental groups criticize China for political repression and human rights violations. However, this criticism is often resented not only by the

Party, but also by many ordinary Chinese as well. The criticism does not recognize the greater political openness in China and is not in accord with what Chinese see as rising levels of democracy in their country.

As this chapter has shown, the discrepancy between the conventional wisdom that China lacks democracy and the popular assessment that China is increasingly democratic is simply explained: Ordinary Chinese define democracy in distinctive ways, different from both the Western understanding of democracy and even the elite discourse within China about the meaning of democracy and its suitability for China. If most Chinese believe that the country has become more democratic and will continue to do so in the future, they are less inclined to push for greater democracy, and they even see democracy activists as reckless troublemakers.

This is not meant to suggest that the definition of democracy should change to fit different situations, or that the popular Chinese definitions of democracy are just as valid as the ones generally held by democracy scholars inside and outside of China and even by Chinese leaders. But it does suggest that the weak popular support for democracy activists in China can be explained by how democracy is understood by their fellow citizens.

Democracy advocates in China not only face harassment, prison, and even exile by the state, they also face indifference from society at large and criticism from their fellow dissidents. When Liu Xiaobo won the Nobel Peace Prize in 2010, interviews with ordinary Chinese found that many were unfamiliar with him, and many of those who were familiar with him either felt he had not accomplished anything worthy of the Nobel Peace Prize or thought his efforts to promote democracy in China were misguided. Even fellow dissidents criticized him for being too moderate. The title of his most recent collection of writings, *No Enemies, No Hatred*, symbolized for his critics the problem with his low-key, non-confrontational style. Even though he has been a committed advocate of democratization in China, has been monitored, arrested, and imprisoned for much of his adult life because of his political beliefs, and has won acclamation from the international community, he has limited sympathy and support within China.

This skepticism is targeted not only against democracy activists, but also other prominent people who publicly support democracy. One example is the online reaction to pro-democracy statements by Zhang Xin, the CEO of SOHO China, a very successful high-end real estate developer based in Beijing. In an interview on the CBS news program "60 Minutes" in 2013, she said, "if you ask [Chinese] one thing, everyone craves for is what? It's not food. It's not homes. Everyone craves for democracy. I know there's a lot of negativities in the U.S. about the political system, but don't forget, you know, 8,000 miles away, people in China are looking at it, longing for it."[44] She was heavily criticized online by people who thought she was rich, out of touch, and presumptuous to speak for all Chinese. She and her husband "made billions of dollars themselves, and then told us it was meaningless to pursue cars, houses and money—'why do you need food? Democracy alone would be enough.'"[45] For lots of Chinese, material interests still outweigh the potential advantages of democratic rule.

Those who promote democracy in China are in a lonely place: They face opposition from the state and do not enjoy much sympathy or support from society. Contrast this with figures such as Andrei Sakharov, Vaclav Havel, Aung San Suu Kyi, and most of all Nelson Mandela: They spent much of their adult lives in prison, house arrest, or exile, but they were seen—within their own countries and around the world—as heroic figures fighting for democracy and justice. When political change happened, Havel and Mandela became presidents in their countries, Sakharov and Suu Kyi led the opposition in parliament. There is no one in China who comes close to their stature, no one who enjoys widespread public support, and no one who is seen as the symbol of a deeper democratic sentiment within China. Without that sympathy and support, China's democracy movement will remain small and fragile, with little chance of influencing the regime's actions or public opinion.

In my conversations with many Chinese, including those born and raised in the U.S., I often hear that China is not ready for democracy because it is too poor, too rural, and too culturally backward. This is

---

[44] See the transcript of the interview at http://www.cbsnews.com/news/zhang-xin-chinas-real-estate-mogul-03-03-2013/5/, accessed July 15, 2015.

[45] This and other criticisms are available at http://bbs.tianya.cn/post-worldlook-1201752-1.shtml, accessed July 15, 2015.

an implicit endorsement of modernization theory, which suggests that as countries become more urban, better educated, and prosperous, they are more likely to become democratic.[46] Until recently, China has ranked low on each of these indicators of modernity, but the situation in China is rapidly changing. Compared to other countries around the world, China has now reached the upper-middle ranks of per capita GDP, a level at which other countries successfully democratized. The majority of its people now live in cities, and the urban population is expected to surpass 70 percent by 2025. With that demographic shift has come a change in the labor structure: The proportion of people who depend on agriculture for their livelihoods has steadily declined, while those who are engaged in industry and especially the service sector have grown. Levels of education, access to information, and interactions with foreign countries are all increasing steadily. None of these guarantees a democratic transition, but at a minimum, it can be said that there are fewer obstacles to Chinese democracy than in the past.[47] What remains, however, is the Party's opposition to democratization and the popular misconception that democratization is already underway.

[46] There is a vast literature on this topic and an ongoing debate about whether modernization actually causes democratization or if the two processes are simply correlated without having any causal links between them. A good summary of the argument with recent evidence is Ronald Inglehart and Christian Welzel, "How Development Leads to Democracy: What We Know about Modernization," *Foreign Affairs*, Vol. 88, No. 2 (March–April 2009), pp. 33–48.

[47] Andrew Nathan, "Chinese Democracy: The Lessons of Failure," in Zhao, ed., *China and Democracy*, pp. 21–32.

7

Will the Party Survive?

AUTHORITARIAN PARTIES LIKE THE CCP have two main goals. First, they seek to hold on to power by eliminating real and perceived threats. Some threats come from inside the regime and are handled through occasional purges and, more recently in China, by corruption investigations. Other threats come from outside the regime, including dissent, public protests, and efforts to organize collective action for political or religious purposes. These threats are handled with a combination of repression, censorship, and control over individuals and groups. The Party has handled both types of threats successfully so far. It exhibits a high degree of elite unity, especially since the 1989 demonstrations revealed divisions among the top Party leadership. It maintains its monopoly on political power and faces no viable opposition. In many ways, it is the quintessential one-party regime.

The second goal of the CCP and other authoritarian parties is to generate popular support in order to achieve developmental goals without relying exclusively on repression. Repression is expensive: It requires staffing a large repressive apparatus, diverts resources from other regime goals, and risks alienating potential regime supporters when used too broadly. If the regime can achieve its goals through cooperation instead of repression, it will be more sustainable in the long run. In the post-Mao period, the Party has sought popular support in a variety of ways. It has provided more opportunities for individuals and groups to participate in the policy-making process, the result being increased consultation but without accountability and therefore should not be mistaken for democratization. It has tolerated and encouraged some civil society organizations, even partnering with some to provide valued social welfare services. At the same time, it has repressed other civil society groups that may criticize or challenge the regime and its policies. It has increased spending on public goods, such as healthcare and education, although the availability of affordable healthcare and quality education remains uneven. Migrant workers, who make up roughly a quarter of the urban population, typically cannot receive healthcare or send their children to local schools in the cities where they live. Above all, it has promoted rapid economic growth that has raised incomes and living standards for most Chinese. To different degrees, each of these efforts has generated some degree of popular support for the Party. Most Chinese are optimistic that their incomes will continue to grow and the level of democracy will rise in the near future. The Party enjoys a high degree of performance legitimacy, even though people are often frustrated by policy failures like food safety and pollution, and angry about the corruption and malfeasance of Party and government officials.

Although it has been generally successful in generating popular support, each of these endeavors subjects the Party to a crucial dilemma: What is beneficial in the short run may be costly in the long run. It has opened new channels for participation in the policy process. As people become accustomed to these opportunities for participation, they may not be content with simply offering their opinions but will expect more accountability. Do officials actually listen to them? Do they abandon their preferred policies when they do not accord with public opinion? Consulting the public may raise expectations for more influential participation in the future. Similarly, encouraging the noncritical realm of civil society (also known as civil society I), which is focused on economic, social, and cultural issues, may provide cover for more politically oriented groups in the critical realm of civil society (civil society II). Individuals and organizations that work on non-sensitive issues, such as job training, adult literacy, or disaster relief, can easily become critics of the government's poor performance in these areas. Increased spending on public goods can reveal the inequalities in their distribution: Some localities spend much more than others, and individuals living in the same city can be excluded from receiving public goods. Greater attention to social welfare can lead to greater concern for social justice when welfare benefits are not equally distributed. Expectations of higher incomes and increased levels of democracy may prove difficult to satisfy. One indicator of this is already apparent: In sharp contrast to the conventional wisdom that economic growth is the primary source of the Party's legitimacy, economic growth is not correlated with public satisfaction with the work of the government or regime support more generally. Even if the Party does not face organized opposition at present, it may be undone by the revolution of rising expectations. But so far this is mostly hypothetical. The Party does face opposition, but expectations are not rising on a wide enough scale to threaten its hold on power.

I. Prospects for Regime Change in China

Understanding the Party's strategy for survival and the public's response to it is the key to understanding the prospects for regime change in China. When regime change does occur, it normally happens in one of three ways.[1] The first mode of regime change is a state-led transformation, in which members of the incumbent authoritarian regime initiate changes that bring about a new regime. This tends to be the most peaceful mode of change, because the regime is stronger than the opposition and can initiate change without being forced. In some cases, as in South Korea, Taiwan, and Brazil, it leads to a relatively peaceful and successful transition to democracy. But in other cases, as in Russia and other former communist countries, it is like putting old wine into new bottles. The elites of the old regime become the leaders of the new authoritarian regime and the result falls far short of democracy.

The second mode of regime change is a society-led revolution. This kind of transition is the most dramatic type of regime change, often pitting an idealistic public rising up to seek political freedom against a regime equally determined to hang on to power. Because of this confrontational posture, they are often violent, with uncertain prospects for democracy. When the regime uses overwhelming force to suppress

---

[1] Actual transitions often have elements of more than one form of regime change, and scholars and practitioners debate over which dynamic was most important.

a social uprising, as in China in 1989, the regime survives. Even when a movement topples a dictator, as in Egypt in 2011, the new regime may not be democratic. But sometimes the revolution succeeds: In the Philippines and Argentina, popular movements deposed dictators, and new democracies were established.

The third mode of regime change is a pacted transition in which leaders of the authoritarian regime and the opposition negotiate the terms of transition. This type of regime change is most likely to lead to successful democratization, as in Poland and South Africa. The negotiations themselves require cooperation and compromise, the essence of democratic governance, and create a solid basis for building a new democratic regime. It is also a relatively rare style of democratization. Authoritarians do not like to surrender power, and democrats dislike compromising with dictators. When successful, however, the result is more likely to be a stable and lasting democracy than the other types of regime change.

Which is most likely in China? Bruce Gilley predicts a state-led transition when CCP elites realize that clinging to dictatorship will not save them, and democratization provides the best opportunity for them to remain in power.[2] So far, Party elites have shown no sign of this shift in thinking. While the Party seems to be responsive to public opinion, it is only when its survival is not at stake that it is willing to compromise. When the life of the Party is on the line, or when it faces a popular movement that it defines as a threat to its survival, as in 1989 or the Falun Gong spiritual movement, the Party has chosen to crack down rather than concede.[3] Democrats may eventually emerge from within the CCP, but if they exist, they must remain in deep cover for the time

[2] Bruce Gilley, *China's Democratic Future: How It Will Happen and Where It Will Lead* (New York: Columbia University Press, 2004).

[3] Yongshun Cai, *Collective Resistance in China: Why Popular Protests Succeed or Fail* (Palo Alto, CA: Stanford University Press, 2010); Xi Chen, *Social Protest and Contentious Authoritarianism in China* (New York: Cambridge University Press, 2012). Dan Slater and Joseph Wong have an intriguing argument about when the CCP might choose to cede power in order to survive, based on examples of one-party regimes in Taiwan, South Korea, and Indonesia. See their "The Strength to Concede: Ruling Parties and Democratization in Developmental Asia," *Perspectives on Politics*, Vol. 11, No. 3 (September 2013), pp. 717–733.

being. Any hint that they are democrats in hiding would undoubtedly get them ousted from the inner circle.

A pacted transition is perhaps the least likely form of transition, given the current political realities in China. The Party has been so successful at suppressing any political opposition that it has no one with whom it could negotiate, even if it wanted to. More importantly, China lacks a democratic activist with the stature of Nelson Mandela, Aung San Suu Kyi, or Vaclav Havel, someone with broad-based popular support who is seen as the face of the opposition and the voice of society. There is no one outside the Party who would overwhelmingly win a popular election, if one could be held. Without an opposition leader with an organization and popular base, any negotiated transition would lack legitimacy.

Although not a likely scenario, a society-led revolution still seems to be more likely than the other two modes of regime change.[4] Because the Party has so consistently defended its political monopoly, refusing to tolerate any organized opposition much less negotiate with one, a state-led or pacted transition seems unlikely given China's current political realities. For the reasons described throughout this book, I do not think a revolution is likely. When people see their incomes rising, believe that their country is becoming increasingly democratic, and see the state finally starting to grapple with the provision of more and better public goods, often in partnership with a vibrant civil society—this is not a context in which revolution is to be expected.

We should not assume that democracy is the inevitable alternative to communist rule in China. This is the implicit starting point for most of the literature on prospects for regime change in China.[5] These forecasts for China's democratization overlook two crucial factors: international experience and domestic viewpoints.

---

[4] I have made this argument in the past; see *Democratization in China and Taiwan: The Adaptability of Leninist Parties* (London and New York: Oxford University Press, 1997); and "The Future of the Chinese Communist Party," in Jae Ho Chung, ed., *Charting China's Future: Political, Social, and International Dimensions* (Lanham, MD: Rowman & Littlefield, 2006).

[5] See, e.g., Cheng Li's "The End of the CCP's Authoritarian Resilience? A Tripartite Assessment of Shifting Power in China," *China Quarterly*, No. 211 (September 2012), pp. 595–623.

Recent experience shows that regime change more often than not does not result in democracy but in a new type of authoritarianism, or at best a hybrid regime with a semblance of democratic institutions but authoritarian practices. A study of authoritarian regimes concluded that "when dictators fall, they are most often replaced by other dictators." Even when the autocrat was overthrown by a popular revolt or civil war, the result was democracy in less than half the cases between 1950 and 2012.[6] We should not assume that democracy is the automatic alternative to authoritarianism.

Most alarming is that these new authoritarian and hybrid regimes are not just the result of political elites hijacking the democratization process, but rather a response to public opinion as well.[7] The recent examples of Vladimir Putin and Hugo Chávez show that strong leaders can repress their opponents, silence independent media, squeeze civil society groups, and threaten the rights and freedoms they are sworn to uphold, while enjoying popular support for doing so. In Egypt, the military coup that ousted the democratically elected President Mohammed Morsi had widespread popular support. For many, the experience of democratization has meant economic uncertainty, social insecurity, and political fragmentation. One response to such a situation is nostalgia for the authoritarian past and support for a strong leader. This is a troubling reality for those who promote democratization: Too often the fruits of their labors are as bad as or even worse than the problems they were trying to solve.

The experiences of former communist countries in Europe present a cautionary tale for China. For the Party, the experience of the former Soviet Union showed the folly of trying to engage in political reforms without first modernizing the economy, and the danger of incorporating society into efforts to reform the state.[8] Outside observers often

[6] Andrea Kendall-Taylor and Erica Frantz, "How Autocracies Fall," *Washington Quarterly*, Vol. 37, No. 1 (Spring 2014), pp. 35–47. See also Milan W. Svolik, *The Politics of Authoritarian Rule* (New York: Cambridge University Press, 2012).

[7] This is the key insight of Fareed Zakaria's *The Future of Freedom: Illiberal Democracy at Home and Abroad* (New York: Norton, 2004).

[8] David Shambaugh, *China's Communist Party: Atrophy and Adaptation* (Berkeley, CA, and Washington, DC: University of California Press and Woodrow Wilson Center Press, 2009).

speculate about which of China's leaders may be like Gorbachev. For China's leaders, this is surely the kiss of death: Gorbachev is not seen as a successful reformer in China (or in Russia for that matter), but rather a naïve politician who caused the downfall of his party and the disintegration of his country. The end of communism also led to the dissolution of Yugoslavia and Czechoslovakia. National unity is a priority in China, and the fates of these countries suggest the potential risks of regime change. Most of the former Soviet republics did not become democratic after gaining independence, but instead developed new forms of authoritarian rule.

Just as China's leaders are wary of following Gorbachev's example, post-communist Russia does not offer Chinese society a better alternative. The transition from communism in Russia meant economic devastation. As the economy shrank during the 1990s, people lost their jobs and saw their lifetime savings evaporate when the government devalued the ruble. Life expectancy dropped from 70 years in 1985 to 59 years in 2005 as alcoholism and other health issues took their toll. During these same years, the Chinese economy boomed, and living standards improved. Russia has never regained the superpower status of the former Soviet Union. From China's perspective, whatever political benefits that were gained by the end of communism were offset by the accompanying economic and diplomatic costs.

Regime changes in the Middle East and North Africa also show the uncertainty of democratization. The U.S.-led invasion of Iraq that deposed Saddam Hussein did not produce a stable government, much less a consolidated democracy. The Arab Spring did not lead to democratization but to ongoing political, economic, and social turmoil. Of the many countries affected by the Arab Spring, only Tunisia became democratic. Other countries ended up with new authoritarian leaders (Egypt) or devolved into violence and chaos (Syria, Libya, Yemen). China's leaders were worried that the popular uprisings in the Middle East and North Africa (MENA) might spread to China, and they increased censorship of the Internet and repression of society to preempt any such ripple effects. This proved to be an overreaction. MENA is too far away geographically and too dissimilar culturally to snowball into China. The underlying economic and social conditions that motivated the Arab Spring were also quite different from the situation in

China. As in other cases of political change around the world, people in China were interested but not inspired by the protests that rocked the Arab world in 2011.

The experience of Asian democracies is also worrisome in different ways for China's leaders and society. Japan is the oldest democracy in Asia, but it has been economically stagnant for over 20 years, a real cause of concern in China now that its own economic growth has begun to slow. Given the historical animosity and competing territorial claims of the two countries, few Chinese see Japan as a suitable role model. In South Korea, two former presidents were convicted of corruption and treason (Chun Doo-hwan and Roh Tae-woo), and another committed suicide while under investigation for bribery (Roh Moo-hyun). This is not a track record that China's leaders want to emulate.

Taiwan is ethnically and culturally closest to China, but its democratization seems not to have inspired many Chinese. They may be curious about elections and other political developments on Taiwan, but few envy them. On one hand, they are amused by frequent scuffles and fistfights in the legislature. On the other hand, they are concerned that Taiwan's democratization may lead to a declaration of independence by Taiwan. Most Chinese accept the government's claim that Taiwan is part of China and will eventually be reunited with it. Support for independence on Taiwan and a growing Taiwanese identity distinct from the Chinese mainland make peaceful reunification more unlikely. The "sunflower movement," in which college students occupied the legislative building to protest a bilateral trade agreement between China and Taiwan, reflected the growing opposition in Taiwan to closer cross-straits ties. The first president from the Democratic Progressive Party, Chen Shui-bian, was elected in 2000, and his two terms in office were marked by growing tensions with China and even the U.S. over Taiwan's international status. After leaving office, he was imprisoned for corruption (seen by his supporters as politically motivated). For all these reasons, most Chinese have not seen Taiwan's democratization as a precedent for them. However, it does suggest that Chinese culture is not incompatible with democracy, as some have claimed.

A second challenge for democratizers in China comes from domestic public opinion. Most Chinese think China is already democratic, are satisfied with the current level of democracy, and are optimistic about rising levels of democracy in the near future. These sentiments are based on different definitions of democracy than are common in the West, but they shape public attitudes about democracy just the same. Just as incrementalism has been the style of economic reform, people in China might prefer to remain on the path of gradual democratization. Such complacency may be misguided—democratization rarely comes about through incremental changes, but more often at critical junctures—but it nevertheless complicates the challenge of those promoting democracy in China. They face not only the opposition of the Party, which recognizes that democracy requires the loss of its political monopoly; they also face apathy and even resistance from within society. Why rock the boat when the present seems better than the past and the future looks to become better still?

Although many Chinese may be unhappy with many aspects of the political system they are currently living in, they are not convinced that democracy provides a preferable alternative. Western-style democracy as currently practiced is seen as deficient, a viewpoint shared by many in the West. Political stalemates in the U.S. and Europe prevent consensus on pressing policy issues. Most Western democracies have been experiencing declining trust and confidence in political and social institutions, and as a result participation in them have declined.[9]

All things considered, the status quo seems not so bad to many Chinese. On one hand, there is no viable and preferable alternative: Each of the available alternatives is seen as flawed in some way. On the other hand, most people in China are genuinely optimistic about the future. They recognize that their incomes and standards of living have risen in recent years and expect their incomes to continue to grow in the years ahead. Most Chinese also see the level of democracy increasing, are satisfied with the current level of democracy, and expect that level to rise even further in the near future. This is not a scenario under which regime change is likely, and calls for regime change are unlikely to get much popular support. For those who are committed to bringing democracy to China, this must be discouraging. Not only do they encounter repression from the state, they also face indifference

[9] Robert Putnam, *Bowling Alone: The Collapse and Revival of American Community* (New York: Simon & Schuster, 2000).

from society. Although private entrepreneurs are often seen as the natural allies of democracy, in China, they have been skeptical that democracy would bring advantages.[10] This skepticism was nicely stated by Zhang Dazhong, founder of Dazhong Electronics, one of China's leading retailers of home electronics: "How fast can China change politically? Too fast is no good either. Say we have a democracy like India's now, then we may not have stability and efficiency. On the whole I'm pretty comfortable with the present pace of change."[11] Like many others in China, Zhang is willing to be patient for political change in order to preserve the economic benefits of the present regime.

But unexpected events often bring about change, whether it is wanted or not. The 1989 protests in Tiananmen Square were not expected or planned, even by the participants. The Arab Spring of 2011 was triggered by a random event. If a policewoman in Tunisia had not slapped a street vendor in public, the wave of protests that spread throughout the Arab world may never have begun. A similar triggering event is possible in China, but it will most likely take observers and even participants by surprise. The contingent nature of regime change makes pinpoint predictions, often based on straight-line projections, risky and even pointless.

It is much easier to explain events than to predict them. If regime change does occur in China, we will point to changes in several key indicators to explain what happened: the growing influence of civil society, a slowing economy, revelations of corruption, societal reactions to growing repression, the atrophy of the CCP, etc. If regime change does *not* happen, we will point to the current levels of each of those indicators: the weakness of civil society, continued prosperity, performance legitimacy, state capacity, the adaptability of the Party, and other aspects of "authoritarian resilience." We currently have theories that

[10] Bruce J. Dickson, *Red Capitalists in China: The Party, Private Entrepreneurs, and Prospects for Political Change* (New York: Cambridge University Press, 2003); Kellee Tsai, *Capitalism without Democracy: The Private Sector in Contemporary China* (Ithaca, NY: Cornell University Press, 2007); Jie Chen and Bruce J. Dickson, *Allies of the State: Democratic Support and Regime Support among China's Private Entrepreneurs* (Cambridge, MA: Harvard University Press, 2010).

[11] Quoted in Jianying Zha, *Tide Players: The Movers and Shakers of a Rising China* (New York: New Press, 2010), p. 38.

explain authoritarian durability, and we have different theories that explain regime change. But there is no grand, unified theory of regimes that can explain both change and continuity. The factors that allow regimes to survive are not necessarily the same factors that cause them to perish. Regime change is often contingent on exogenous shocks that neither outside observers nor inside participants anticipate.

II. The Consequences of Regime Change in China

While debating the likelihood of regime change in China and how it may happen, we should also consider what would come after. One possibility is a conventional Western-style liberal democracy, with multiple parties, free and fair elections, rule of law, and the full range of rights and freedoms that are seen as integral to democratic governance. This is the scenario that most advocates of regime change in China have in mind. But there are several challenges to this optimistic scenario, in addition to the factors previously noted. In order for democracy to survive, a country's leaders must be committed to democratic institutions and practices, not just pay lip service to them. That is an untested proposition in China, and it is unknowable in advance. Whether a democratically elected president or prime minister comes from among current Party leaders or emerges from within society, the true test of the new leader and the new regime will be a commitment to democracy. A related challenge is the relatively small size and low popular support for China's dissidents, including those in exile abroad. Dissidents within China are isolated, their voices muted by the Party's censorship and repression, and their support limited within society. Even dissidents in exile lack cohesion, instead competing with each other for visibility and stature.

The limited popular demand for democracy is also a potential obstacle to successful democratization in China. Most Chinese believe that China is increasingly democratic and are optimistic that the level will continue to rise in the future. They are therefore willing to wait for further democratization and do not support overthrowing the status quo. The Party has been so successful in repressing threats to its monopoly on political power that China lacks a well-organized opposition, an individual who symbolizes the popular desire for change, or even an autonomous civil society capable of challenging the Party's rule. A successful democratic transition will be less likely without a strong and popular political opposition. These challenges are formidable, although not insurmountable. Democracy has taken root in countries where people once thought it impossible, including World War II-era Germany and Japan. Commitment to democracy is not a necessary prerequisite for democratization, but it can be learned by practicing democracy. If it is not learned, democracy is unlikely to survive.

Another possible result of regime change is national disintegration, either as local strongmen try to assert their control over parts of the country's territory against the central state, or as regions declare their independence as new and sovereign states. China has recent experience with both of these developments. In the early 20th century, after the fall of the Qing dynasty, China underwent a prolonged period of division, first during the warlord era of the 1910s and '20s, and then during the prolonged civil war between the nationalist government and the CCP, which ended in 1949. This period of divisiveness reinforced the cultural fear of chaos and instability. The Party's ability to unify the country, expel foreign influences, and restore order was one of its signal achievements, which it continues to emphasize today to bolster its popular legitimacy.[12] Regime change in China could lead to democratization, but it could also produce prolonged instability and uncertainty within China that would destabilize the East Asian region.

The Party repeatedly claims that "without the CCP, there would be no New China." More importantly, there is no other organization, informal or formal, with the capability of governing the country and holding it together. In an odd way, that might be the bottom line for questions of regime support: Just as Louis XV reportedly said, "après moi, le deluge," so too does the CCP imply that if it were to be removed, China could crumble. Popular concerns for maintaining stability make

---

[12] The restored order was short-lived, as Chairman Mao launched repeated political campaigns to alter the status quo, above all in the riotous Cultural Revolution. In the post-Mao era, CCP leaders have been committed to maintaining political stability and have been willing to use whatever force is necessary to do so.

people risk-averse, especially when other examples of regime change—Russia, Egypt, Libya—present examples of economic, political, and social decline.

Maintaining national unity also means denying regional aspirations for autonomy and independence. China's leaders have suppressed challenges to Chinese control by Tibetans and Uighurs in Xinjiang over their territories. While these actions have led to international criticism, they are generally popular within China. Most Han Chinese are not sympathetic to calls for religious freedom, and even resentful of the preferential treatment given to ethnic minorities in college admissions and other pursuits (similar to opposition to affirmative action programs in the U.S.). Even China's democratic activists accept the Party's claim of sovereignty over these regions. Some years ago, a Washington-based think tank organized an informal meeting between exiled dissidents and Tibetans. Despite their shared opposition to the Party, the two groups had little other common ground. The dissidents did not support the Tibetans' desire for independence, and the Tibetans were less interested in how the rest of China was governed. The meeting ended quickly, with little left to discuss.[13] Democratization can trigger ethnic mobilization for autonomy and independence, which in turn may prompt nationalist leaders to take a strong stand in defense of the country's borders in order to bolster their popular support.[14] Even if China becomes a democracy, it is unlikely that a newly elected government would grant independence to either Tibet or Xinjiang.

Democratization in China also has implications for Taiwan. Although few countries now have formal diplomatic ties with Taiwan, most provide tacit recognition, including unofficial embassies and consulates. The U.S. maintains consular functions with the American Institute in Taiwan, whose director has ambassadorial status and whose staff are often "on leave" from the U.S. foreign service. The U.S. government is officially committed to the peaceful resolution of Taiwan's international status, whether reunification with the mainland or formal independence, as long as both China and Taiwan agree on the

[13] The meeting was described to me by one of its organizers.
[14] Edward Mansfield and Jack Snyder, *Electing to Fight: Why Emerging Democracies Go to War* (Cambridge, MA: MIT Press, 2007).

outcome. Much of the political support for Taiwan in the U.S. is based on its symbolic status as a "free" country resisting pressure from the communist government in China.[15] If China were to become democratic, the international support for Taiwan's status quo would likely evaporate. That support is predicated on the desire to protect Taiwan and its almost 25 million people from the authoritarian regime now in Beijing. If that regime is replaced by a democracy, international support for Taiwan may change as well. In the past, some democratic activists in China argued that one incentive for democratization was that it would lead to Taiwan's reunification with the mainland. That argument never gained much support, but it may well prove to be correct.

III. Rethinking the Conventional Wisdom on China

These findings should cause us to rethink the conventional wisdom on the Party and the political environment in China. First of all, a common assumption is that economic growth is the main source of the Party's legitimacy. Throughout the post-Mao era, China's leaders have placed top priority on achieving economic modernization through the "reform and opening" policies. They have launched market-oriented economic reforms and increased integration with the global economy. This has resulted in rapid growth and rising living standards across the country, but also the attendant problems of uneven development, environmental degradation, a growing gap between rich and poor, and public protests over land grabs, unpaid severance and retirement packages, and other types of dislocations caused by rapid growth. Although rising living standards have produced regime support in the short run, looming challenges exist going forward. China is now attempting a transition from an economic model based on building infrastructure and assembling goods for export to one based on domestic consumption.

---

[15] This was also true when Taiwan was under authoritarian rule. After the end of the Chinese civil war, the remnants of the KMT-led Republic of China government retreated to Taiwan. It continued to claim it was the legitimate government of all of China and had diplomatic ties with the U.S. and most other Western countries. It was informally referred to as "Free China," as opposed to the PRC on the mainland.

In the U.S., scholars and pundits debate whether sociotropic or pocket-book factors (national economic trends or individual prosperity, respectively) most influence public opinion and especially voting. A similar distinction between sociotropic and pocketbook factors exists in China. Pocketbooks are primary: The more individuals believe their incomes are rising, the more they support the regime. But sociotropic factors have little influence on public opinion: Levels of per capita GDP and economic growth rates are not correlated with regime support. This is not the simple story that the conventional wisdom is based on.

The second common assumption about Party rule in China is that it is based primarily on repression. Repression is real, and in recent years, it has been ratcheted up to address real and perceived threats to the Party. It has targeted dissidents, religious groups, and ethnic minorities that are critical of the regime and seek more political and religious freedoms. But the repression has been somewhat paradoxical. Censorship over the Internet has expanded, but the number of Chinese online has also grown, and many of them find clever ways of getting around the Great Firewall. Repression is unquestionably part of China's political system, as it is for all authoritarian regimes, and its full impact cannot be measured with survey data alone. But the Party's survival strategy is a combination of both carrots and sticks. We need to have an understanding of both in order to assess its future prospects.

A third part of the conventional wisdom is that the Party is incapable of change. Many observers believe that the Party has been slow to respond to the rapidly changing economic and social environment in China and too reliant on outdated slogans and practices. While it may have been slow to change, it has been more adaptable than it is often given credit for. Its recruitment strategy has shifted away from the "three revolutionary classes"—workers, farmers, and soldiers—to incorporate the newly emerging urban elites, including college students and private entrepreneurs. Because these new elites join for their own material interests, they are not necessarily loyal supporters of the regime. Their continued support for the regime, even as political insiders, may be contingent on those material interests, or even on their sense of what is right and proper. The Party has continued to propagandize about the mass line, but now interacting with the masses involves not just listening to individuals but also working with NGOs.

It has been experimenting with adding more consultation and transparency into the policy process. Although it has stopped short of being fully accountable to the public, it has opened new channels for political participation. It continues to rely on its network of Party cells to monitor what is happening in the Party itself, and it has adapted its Party-building efforts to now include private firms, NGOs, and other new social organizations. While it has not eliminated patronage as the source of career advancement in the Party and government bureaucracies, it has introduced more meritocratic methods for evaluating the performance of officials and determining which ones are promoted.[16] It has modified some of its most unpopular policies, such as the one-child policy and the *hukou* system, even though it has not fully abandoned them. And some of its other unpopular practices—such as its censorship technology and expansion of the coercive apparatus—are in their own way indicators of adaptability, although not liberalization. In short, the Party has not been a passive bystander to the economic, social, and technological changes taking place in China, but it is adapting in fits and starts, sometimes creating new openings, at other times finding new ways to keep areas closed off.

The fourth aspect of conventional wisdom that needs to be rethought is that China has no civil society. The Party has pressured and closed some NGOs, but the overall number of NGOs has continued to grow. It has also begun partnering with local NGOs to provide public goods and social welfare services, especially to disadvantaged groups like rural migrants, the disabled, and the elderly. It is frequently stated that China does not have a civil society, but that is only partly true. It lacks the type of politically oriented groups that are critical of the status quo and could pose a challenge to the Party. But it has over half a million formally registered NGOs, and several times that number of unregistered

---

[16] There remains a lively debate over whether competence or connections determines promotions. Andrew J. Nathan, "Authoritarian Resilience," *Journal of Democracy*, Vol. 14, No. 1 (January 2003), pp. 6–17; Pierre F. Landry, *Decentralized Authoritarianism in China: The Communist Party's Control of Local Elites in the Post-Mao Era* (New York: Cambridge University Press, 2008); Victor Shih, Christopher Adolph, and Mingxing Liu, "Getting Ahead in the Communist Party: Explaining the Advancement of Central Committee Members in China," *American Political Science Review*, Vol. 106, No. 1 (February 2012), pp. 166–187.

NGOs that are active in a variety of economic, social, cultural, and environmental issues. These are the types of civil society groups that are said to enhance the stability of democratic regimes by providing useful services to their members and the wider public, building political trust, and improving the quality of governance.[17] If Chinese NGOs perform a similar function in China, they may prove to enhance the surviv-ability of the Party rather than pose a threat to it. Rather than being opposed to the regime, many Chinese NGOs are partners with it.

The findings of this book also challenge a final element of conven-tional wisdom concerning China: that the people have lost trust in their leaders and grown impatient for political change. While there is widespread frustration with the cost of healthcare, access to the best schools, safety of the food supply, and quality of the environment, there is also the perception that things are generally getting better. Many recognize that some of these problems are the natural consequences of rapid growth, which takes some of the heat off Party and government officials. Despite these well-known and widespread problems, the over-all satisfaction with the work of the government remains high. In cities that govern better by providing more public goods, regime support is higher and the local legitimacy deficit—the gap between satisfaction with the central and local governments—narrows. This is a good incen-tive for governing better.

Contrary to reports that people in China have grown impatient for political change, most Chinese see their political system as already at a relatively high level of democracy and becoming increasingly demo-cratic, and they are optimistic about higher levels in the future and sat-isfied with the level as it currently exists. While this may seem puzzling to outside observers and even as proof that the Chinese public has been duped by Party propaganda or is dishonest in survey responses, the key is in recognizing how democracy is defined in China. Whereas the West defines democracy largely in terms of institutional arrangements—competitive parties, free and fair elections, rule of law, protection of rights and freedoms—most Chinese define democracy in terms of outcomes: providing for the needs of society and raising standards

[17] Robert Putnam, *Making Democracy Work: Civic Traditions in Modern Italy* (Princeton, NJ: Princeton University Press, 1993).

of living. Rather than be impatient for change, most Chinese see it already happening. As a result, most Chinese are not sympathetic to calls for democratic change, whether from foreign leaders or domestic dissidents, because they think the country is already fairly democratic and likely to become more so in the near future. This presents a real challenge for supporters of liberal democracy: They and their listeners are using the same words but have different understandings of those words. China's dissidents not only face oppression from the state, they must also overcome indifference from society, even suspicion that they are doing the bidding of foreign countries.

However, one warning sign for the Party is corruption, one of the most corrosive issues for support and trust in the regime. The anticorruption campaign launched by Xi Jinping after becoming general secretary in 2012 has had an interesting impact on public opinion: Though most people now see the situation improving, they also believe that more officials are corrupt than they thought before the campaign. This is a significant dilemma facing Xi and the Party: The anticorruption campaign may be good for Xi's image, but it is bad for the Party's reputation. Many believe that Xi's campaign is politically motivated, designed to intimidate potential opponents within the Party and not to address corrupt practices themselves. If more and more Chinese reach this conclusion, then the campaign will be bad for both Xi and the Party he leads. It is not just perceptions of corruption that matter. Those who have personal experience with corruption—such as the one in five respondents in the 2014 survey who reported they paid bribes to Party and government officials—have lower levels of regime support than the rest of the population. Corruption breeds cynicism, which is detrimental to regime support.

These adaptations may prove to be short-term fixes that buy the Party some more time but only postpone a later fall. But people have been predicting the demise of the CCP for decades, and yet it still remains in power in China and does not face a viable alternative. Like most large organizations (and with almost 90 million members, it is surely one of the largest in the world), it may be resistant to change and slow to respond to new challenges. But it does adapt, perhaps not efficiently and completely, but more than enough to survive.

The Party's willingness and ability to adapt make resorting to repression all the more perplexing. As the scope of repression grows, it risks antagonizing many of the people who support it or at least are indifferent to it. Wider repression tends to spark stronger resistance.[18] The Party may be squandering the resources it has instead of taking advantage of its strengths. This is the ultimate dilemma facing all authoritarian regimes: What is the proper mix of control and cooperation necessary to remain in power? This question has motivated numerous scholarly studies, without a clear consensus. It is not clear what mix is optimal or which specific tools enhance the survivability of a regime.[19]

The challenges the Party faces are real and serious, but it has been able to cope with past challenges. Its future may seem doubtful, but its past survival in the face of steep odds suggests that we should not dismiss the Party's ability to adapt to new ones. China specialists have been predicting the demise of the Party since the beginning of the post-Mao period over 35 years ago, and yet it remains in power and, by many measures, more solidly in power than in the past.

IV. The Future of the CCP and Its Implications

The fate of the CCP has important implications for both theory and practice. China is a paradigmatic case of authoritarian resilience and durability, but it is rarely included in comparative studies of authoritarian regimes. It is a traditional one-party authoritarian regime at a time when more scholarly attention has focused on hybrid regimes like the one in Russia, where some democratic institutions exist, such as parties and elections, but are inhibited by the state's authoritarian tactics.

---

[18] Evgeny Finkel, "The Phoenix Effect of State Repression: Jewish Resistance during the Holocaust," *American Political Science Review*, Vol. 109, No. 2 (May 2015), pp. 339–353.

[19] Ronald Wintrobe, *The Political Economy of Dictatorship* (New York: Cambridge University Press, 2000); Bruce Bueno de Mesquita, Alastair Smith, Randolph M. Siverson, and James Morrow, *The Logic of Political Survival* (Cambridge, MA: MIT Press, 2003); Jennifer Gandhi and Adam Przeworski, "Authoritarian Institutions and the Survival of Autocrats," *Comparative Political Studies*, Vol. 40, No. 11 (November 2007), pp. 1279–1301; Jennifer Gandhi, *Political Institutions under Dictatorship* (Cambridge, UK: Cambridge University Press, 2008); Milan Svolik, *The Politics of Authoritarian Rule* (New York: Cambridge University Press, 2012).

When the Chinese case does not fit prevailing theories, the tendency is to treat China as a unique outlier rather than adjust the theories to accommodate it. It may be just one case, but it is too big a case to ignore so easily. For their part, China specialists have long been criticized for not contributing enough to political science theory. We are often content to more fully understand changes occurring within China and theorize about them, with only passing references to the generalizability of our findings.[20] As a result, we also contribute to the marginalization of China in the study of politics.

Even though scholars have been reticent about generalizing from the Chinese experience, other autocrats have been willing to adopt its strategies for survival. In Hungary, the president has patterned his crackdown on civil society groups after the CCP's actions. In Vietnam and to some extent Cuba, communist leaders are introducing economic reforms while upholding Party control. In a number of African countries, China provides a model for promoting rapid growth with continued state control over leading areas of the economy (and often directly with Chinese economic support). In Iran and other countries, governments are trying to limit the inflow of foreign ideas by replacing the Internet with a type of intranet with mostly domestic content. Scholars should be as flexible generalizing from the Chinese case as authoritarian leaders elsewhere are.

* * *

Popular views on China in the U.S. are often one-dimensional and fail to capture the everyday life experiences of most people in China. Compared to the examples of Western liberal democracies, China lacks many of the rights and freedoms that we take for granted. Compared to China's own past, it is in some ways freer than ever, although with caveats. People have opportunities to move to other parts of the country in order to find better jobs, but the *hukou* system still institutionalizes inequality. People may find better jobs, but still find it difficult to access

---

[20] Mea culpa: I have more articles published in area studies journals than in disciplinary and policy journals.

healthcare or send their children to local schools. More people have access to the Internet, even though the Great Firewall limits what they can see and read. The number of registered NGOs has surpassed half a million and continues to grow, even though the Party has increased pressure on groups and individuals who it believes pose a threat to its monopoly on political power. At the local level, policy-makers consult with a wide range of local society, but they are still not accountable to them. At the national level, interested groups and individuals can comment on pending legislation and policy reforms, even though those comments are not revealed publicly. These diverse trends are also reflected in public opinion. Anger and frustration are commonly expressed on social media, but they may represent the most disaffected rather than the population as a whole. Public opinion surveys also capture these individuals, but they reveal that much larger segments of society accept the status quo and even support it.

The challenges to forecasting China's future are the countervailing trends of development and decay, adaptability and atrophy, reform and regression. As observers of China, we need to be able to keep more than one idea in our heads at the same time, especially when those ideas are contradictory rather than complementary. Just as the Party has updated how it interacts with society, China watchers in the academic and policy worlds must also update their assumptions about the Party's style of governance, interactions between state and society, and the prospects for political change in China.

APPENDIX I

Survey Design

THE DATA PRESENTED IN this book come from two waves of a survey implemented in China during 2010 and 2014. This was not a panel survey, but the same cities were used in both waves in order to keep the local context as constant as possible. The survey was a nationwide probability sample of urban areas, including the provincial-level municipalities (Beijing, Tianjin, Shanghai, and Chongqing), provincial capitals, and prefecture-level cities. This pool of over 280 cities was stratified using per capita GDP. A sample of 50 cities was selected using the probability proportionate to size (PPS) method, meaning that cities with large populations had a higher probability of being selected than smaller cities. Equivalent numbers of cities were selected from each of three strata (high, medium, and low levels of per capita GDP). Within each city, a district was selected as the primary sampling unit using the PPS method, based on the number of housing units in each district. Each PSU was divided into 30" by 30" squares using GPS technology, and from this grid, three squares were selected as secondary sampling units using the PPS method, with the number of households as the measure of size.[1] Within each secondary sampling unit, three sub-squares

---

[1] For more details on using GPS technology in sampling, see Pierre F. Landry and Mingming Shen, "Reaching Migrants in Survey Research: The Use of the Global Positioning System to Reduce Coverage Bias in China," *Political Analysis*, Vol. 13, No. 1 (Winter 2005), pp. 1–22.

(roughly 90 meters square) were selected as tertiary sampling units with a simplified random sampling method. Among all the occupied residential units within the selected sub-squares, 60 equidistant residential units were selected. Finally, on the basis of a Kish grid, individuals within each selected residential unit who had lived there for at least six months and were between the ages of 18 and 80 were chosen as respondents and interviewed face-to-face. The 2010 survey had a total of 3,874 respondents, and the 2014 survey had 4,128 respondents. The same basic questionnaire was used in both waves of the survey, although additional questions on timely issues—such as food safety, censorship, and corruption—were added in 2014.

The actual implementation of the survey was conducted by the Research Center for Contemporary China of Peking University, under the supervision of Shen Mingming, Yang Ming, Yan Jie, and Chai Jingjing. All the interviewers for this project were currently enrolled college students in the targeted provinces and cities. RCCC supervisors trained the interviewers and monitored their work daily.

In addition to the surveys, a series of focus group interviews were conducted in four cities: Beijing and Wuhan in 2013, and Guangzhou and Chongqing in 2014. In each city, separate focus groups of officials and local residents were organized. The officials were mostly from departments involved in the provision of public goods, such as public health, education, social security, food and drugs, environmental protection, construction, and transportation, as well as civil affairs and public security. The groups of local residents included a mix of occupations (including unemployed people and migrant workers), ages, and backgrounds. These interviews were conducted by the RCCC research team that was sent to each city.

APPENDIX 2

THE ANALYSIS OF REGIME support in chapter 5 is based on a multivariate analysis using both original survey data and city-level statistics. Because there are both individual and city-level statistics, I use a mixed-effects general linear model. The results of the regression models are below, presenting regression coefficients and standard errors. Two models are presented, one for the central level of the state and the other for the local level.

	Center		Local	
	Coeff.	s.e.	Coeff.	s.e.
1. Material				
Level of income	.396*	.172	1.821***	.210
Retrospective income gains	2.460***	.383	2.518***	.463
Per capita GDP (1000 RMB)	.009	.015	.049	.027
GDP growth (2009–2012)	−5.343	2.756	−3.335	4.909
2. Normative				
Nationalism	8.094***	.530	8.401***	.644
Confucian family values	.007	.461	.016	.559
Fear of instability	2.725***	.497	1.167	.601
3. Institutional				
CCP member	1.423*	.715	2.199**	.866
Local Government transparency	.001	.009	−.001	.016

(*continued*)

Continued

	Center		Local	
	Coeff.	s.e.	Coeff.	s.e.
4. Repression				
Paid bribes	-2.341**	.678	-3.898***	.820
Experienced censorship	-.834	.724	-2.585**	.878
5. Demographic controls				
Cultural Revolution generation	-2.401**	.839	-1.890	1.021
Reform generation	-3.362***	.866	-3.792***	1.053
Post-1992 generation	-5.721***	.911	-4.316***	1.108
College	.761	.904	2.311*	1.098
High	-.871	.625	-.124	.758
Male	-.254	.516	-1.644**	.624
Rural resident	-1.458	.776	-.194	.943
Rural migrant	1.077	.966	2.217	1.170
Urban migrant	.428	1.147	.959	1.401
Han	1.647	1.457	1.517	1.774
6. Geographic controls				
Population	-.013***	.003	-.004	.005
Urban hierarchy	7.396***	2.022	4.985	3.600
Coastal	-3.912	2.145	-2.069	3.836
Northeast	-2.765	2.690	.179	4.802
Central	-5.434**	1.835	-7.020*	3.269
City effects	14.921	3.677	53.243	11.629
Constant	99.784***	3.831	71.655***	5.805
No. of individuals	3538		3512	
No. of cities	50		50	
LR test vs. linear model:	chibar^2 (01) = 130.38		chibar^2(01) = 397.15	
	prob(chibar^2) = .000		prob(chibar^2) = .000	

* $p < .05$, ** $p < .01$, *** $p < .001$.

BIBLIOGRAPHY

2008 Report on Public Governance in China's Provincial Capital Cities (Beijing: Unirule, 2009).

2010 Report on Public Governance in China's Provincial Capital Cities (Beijing: Unirule, 2012).

An Evaluation of and Recommendations on the Reforms of the Health System in China: Executive Summary (Beijing: State Council Development Research Council, 2005).

Balla, Steven J., "Information Technology, Political Participation, and the Evolution of Chinese Policymaking," *Journal of Contemporary China*, Vol. 21, No. 76 (April 2012), pp. 655–673.

Barnett, Robert, "Tibet," in William A. Joseph, ed., *Politics in China: An Introduction*, second edition (New York: Oxford University Press, 2014), pp. 401–427.

Baum, Richard, "The Road to Tiananmen: Chinese Politics in the 1980s," in MacFarquhar, ed., *Politics of China*, pp. 340–471.

Becker, Jeffrey, *Social Ties, Resources, and Migrant Labor Contention in Contemporary China: From Peasants to Protestors* (Lanham, MD: Lexington Books, 2014).

Bell, Daniel A., *The Age of Confucianism: Politics and Everyday Life in Contemporary China* (Princeton, NJ: Princeton University Press, 2010).

_____, *The China Model: Political Meritocracy and the Limits of Democracy* (Princeton, NJ: Princeton University Press, 2015).

Bellin, Eva, "The Robustness of Authoritarianism in the Middle East," *Comparative Politics*, Vol. 36, No. 2 (January 2004), pp. 139–157.

Bernstein, Thomas P. and Xiaobo Lü, *Taxation without Representation in Contemporary Rural China* (New York: Cambridge University Press, 2003).

Brady, Anne-Marie, *Marketing Dictatorship: Propaganda and Thought Work in Contemporary China* (Lanham, MD: Rowman & Littlefield, 2009).

Brownlee, Jason, *Authoritarianism in an Age of Democratization* (New York: Cambridge University Press, 2007).

Bueno de Mesquita, Bruce and George W. Downs, "Development and Democracy," *Foreign Affairs*, Vol. 84, No. 5 (September/October 2005), pp. 77–86.

Bueno de Mesquita, Bruce, Alastair Smith, Randolph M. Siverson, and James Morrow, *The Logic of Political Survival* (Cambridge, MA: MIT Press, 2003).

Cai, Yongshun, *Collective Resistance in China: Why Popular Protests Succeed or Fail* (Palo Alto, CA: Stanford University Press, 2010).

Cai, Yongshun and Lin Zhou, "Disciplining Local Officials in China: The Case of Conflict Management," *China Journal*, No. 70 (July 2013), pp. 98–119.

Chan, Anita, Richard Madsen, and Jonathan Unger, *Chen Village: Revolution to Globalization*, third edition (Berkeley, CA: University of California Press, 2009).

Chang, Gordon, *The Coming Collapse of China* (New York: Random House, 2001).

Chang, Leslie T., *Factory Girls: From Village to City in a Changing China* (New York: Spiegel and Grau, 2009).

Chen, Jie, *Popular Political Support in Urban China* (Stanford, CA: Stanford University Press, 2004).

_____, *A Middle Class without Democracy: Economic Growth and the Prospects for Democratization in China* (New York: Oxford University Press, 2013).

Chen, Jie and Bruce J. Dickson, *Allies of the State: Democratic Support and Regime Support among China's Private Entrepreneurs* (Cambridge, MA: Harvard University Press, 2010).

Chen, Xi, *Social Protest and Contentious Authoritarianism in China* (New York: Cambridge University Press, 2012).

Cheng, Tiejun and Mark Selden, "The Origins and Social Consequences of China's Hukou System," *China Quarterly*, No. 139 (September 1994), pp. 644–668.

China: Governance, Investment Climate, and Harmonious Society: Competitiveness Enhancements for 120 Cities in China (Washington, DC: World Bank, 2006).

China's Governance in Transition (Paris: Organization for Economic Co-operation and Development, 2005).

Cho, Young Nam, *Local People's Congresses in China: Development and Transition* (New York: Cambridge University Press, 2009).

Chu, Yun-han and Yu-tzung Chang, "Culture Shift and Regime Legitimacy: Comparing Mainland China, Taiwan, and Hong Kong," in Shiping Hua, ed., *Chinese Political Culture 1989–2000* (Armonk, NY: M.E. Sharpe, 2001).

Chu, Yun-han, Larry Diamond, Andrew J. Nathan, and Doh Chull Shin, eds., *How East Asians View Democracy* (New York: Columbia University Press, 2008).

Cook, Sarah, *The Politburo's Predicament: Confronting the Limitations of Chinese Communist Party Repression* (New York: Freedom House, 2015).

Dahl, Robert A., *Polyarchy: Participation and Opposition*. (New Haven, CT: Yale University Press, 1971).

Dai, Qing, *Wang Shiwei and "Wild Lilies": Rectification and Purges in the Chinese Communist Party, 1942–1944* (Armonk, NY: M.E. Sharpe, 1994).

Dalton, Russell J., Doh C. Shin, and Willy Jou, "Understanding Democracy: Data from Unlikely Places," *Journal of Democracy*, Vol. 18, No. 4 (October 2007), pp. 142–156.

Deng Xiaoping, *Selected Works of Deng Xiaoping, 1975–1982* (Beijing: Foreign Languages Press, 1984).

Diamond, Larry, "Thinking about Hybrid Regimes," *Journal of Democracy*, Vol. 13, No. 2 (April 2002), pp. 21–35.

_____, *The Spirit of Democracy: The Struggle to Build Free Societies throughout the World* (New York: Times Books/Henry Holt and Co., 2008).

Dickson, Bruce J., *Democratization in China and Taiwan: The Adaptability of Leninist Parties* (London and New York: Oxford University Press, 1997).

_____, *Red Capitalists in China: The Party, Private Entrepreneurs, and Prospects for Political Change* (New York: Cambridge University Press, 2003).

_____, "The Future of the Chinese Communist Party," in Jae Ho Chung, ed., *Charting China's Future: Political, Social, and International Dimensions* (Lanham, MD: Rowman & Littlefield, 2006).

_____, *Wealth into Power: The Communist Party's Embrace of China's Private Sector* (New York and London: Cambridge University Press, 2008).

_____, "Who Wants to Be a Communist? Career Incentives and Mobilized Loyalty in Contemporary China," *China Quarterly*, No. 217 (March 2014), pp. 42–68.

Dickson, Bruce J., Pierre F. Landry, Mingming Shen, and Jie Yan, "Public Goods and Popular Support in Urban China," *China Quarterly*, forthcoming.

Distelhorst, Greg, "The Power of Empty Promises: Quasidemocratic Institutions and Activism in China," *Comparative Political Studies*, forthcoming.

Duckett, Jane and Ana Inés Langer, "Populism versus Neoliberalism: Diversity and Ideology in the Chinese Media's Narratives of Health Care Reform," *Modern China*, Vol. 39, No. 6 (November 2013), pp. 653–680.

Easton, David, *A Systems Analysis of Political Life* (New York, NY: Wiley, 1965).

Economy, Elizabeth, *The River Runs Black: The Environmental Challenge to China's Future*, second edition (Ithaca, NY: Cornell University Press, 2010).

Edin, Maria, "State Capacity and Local Agent Control in China: CCP Cadre Management From a Township Perspective," *China Quarterly*, No. 173 (March 2003), pp. 35–52.

Eggleston, Karen, "*Kan Bing Nan, Kan Bing Gui*: Challenges for China's Healthcare System Thirty Years into Reform," in Jean C. Oi, Scott Rozelle, and Xueguang Zhou, eds., *Growing Pains: Tensions and Opportunity in China's*

Transformation (Palo Alto, CA: Walter H. Shorenstein Asia-Pacific Research Center, Stanford University, 2010).

Fewsmith, Joseph, *China since Tiananmen: From Deng Xiaoping to Hu Jintao*, second edition (New York: Cambridge University Press, 2008).

_____, *The Logic and Limits of Political Reform in China* (New York: Cambridge University Press, 2013).

Finkel, Evgeny, "The Phoenix Effect of State Repression: Jewish Resistance during the Holocaust," *American Political Science Review*, Vol. 109, No. 2 (May 2015), pp. 339–353.

Fishkin, James S., Baogang He, Robert C. Luskin, and Alice Siu, "Deliberative Democracy in an Unlikely Place: Deliberative Polling in China," *British Journal of Political Science*, Vol. 40, No. 2 (April 2010), pp. 435–448.

Florini, Ann, Hairong Lai, and Yeling Tan, *China Experiments: From Local Innovations to National Reform* (Washington, DC: Brookings Institution, 2012).

Foley, Michael W. and Bob Edwards, "The Paradox of Civil Society," *Journal of Democracy*, Vol. 7, No. 3 (July 1996), pp. 38–52.

Ford, Caylan, "Tradition and Dissent in China: The Tuidang Movement and Its Challenge to the Communist Party," master's thesis, George Washington University, 2011.

Frazier, Mark W., *Socialist Inequality: Pensions and the Politics of Uneven Development in China* (Ithaca, NY: Cornell University Press, 2010).

_____, "Popular Responses to China's Emerging Welfare State," in Peter Hays Gries and Stanley Rosen, eds., *Chinese Politics: State, Society, and the Market* (London: Routledge, 2010), pp. 258–274.

Gandhi, Jennifer, *Political Institutions under Dictatorship* (New York: Cambridge University Press, 2008).

Gandhi, Jennifer and Adam Przeworski, "Authoritarian Institutions and the Survival of Autocrats," *Comparative Political Studies*, Vol. 40, No. 11 (November 2007), pp. 1279–1301.

Gerring, John, Strom C. Thacker, and Rodrigo Alfaro, "Democracy and Human Development," *Journal of Politics*, Vol. 74, No. 1 (January 2012), pp. 1–17.

Gilley, Bruce, *China's Democratic Future: How It Will Happen and Where It Will Lead* (New York: Columbia University Press, 2004).

_____, "Democrats Will Emerge," *Current History* (September 2007), pp. 245–247.

_____, "Legitimacy and Institutional Change: The Case of China," *Comparative Political Studies*, Vol. 41, No. 3 (March 2008), pp. 259–284.

_____, "Democratic Enclaves in Authoritarian Regimes," *Democratization*, Vol. 17, No. 3 (June 2010), pp. 389–415.

Gilley, Bruce and Heike Holbig, "The Debate on Party Legitimacy in China: A Mixed Quantitative/Qualitative Analysis," *Journal of Contemporary China*, Vol. 18, No. 59 (March 2009), pp. 337–356.

Goodman, David S. G., *Class in Contemporary China* (Cambridge, UK: Polity Press, 2014).

Greenfeld, Karl Taro, *China Syndrome: The True Story of the 21st Century's First Great Epidemic* (New York: HarperCollins, 2006).

Gries, Peter Hays, *China's New Nationalism: Pride, Politics, and Diplomacy* (Berkeley, CA: University of California Press, 2004).

Guo, Gang, "Party Recruitment of College Students in China," *Journal of Contemporary China*, Vol. 14, No. 43 (2005), pp. 371–393.

Haggard, Stephan and Robert R. Kaufman, *Development, Democracy, and Welfare States: Latin America, East Asia, and Eastern Europe* (Princeton, NJ: Princeton University Press, 2008).

Halperin, Morton H., Joseph T. Siegle, and Michael M. Weinstein, *The Democracy Advantage: How Democracies Promote Prosperity and Peace* (New York: Routledge, 2010).

Han, Enze, *Contestation and Adaptation: The Politics of National Identity in China* (New York: Oxford University Press, 2013).

Harding, Harry, *China's Second Reform: Reform after Mao* (Washington, DC: Brookings Institution, 1987).

He, Baogang and Stig Thøgersen, "Giving the People a Voice? Experiments with Consultative Authoritarian Institutions in China," *Journal of Contemporary China*, Vol. 19, No. 66 (September 2010), pp. 675–692.

He, Baogang and Mark Warren, "Authoritarian Deliberation: The Deliberative Turn in Chinese Political Development," *Perspectives on Politics*, Vol. 9, No. 2 (Summer 2011), pp. 269–289.

Heath, Timothy R., *China's New Governing Party Paradigm: Political Renewal and the Pursuit of National Rejuvenation* (Burlington, VT: Ashgate, 2014).

Heilmann, Sebastian, "From Local Experiments to National Policy: The Origins of China's Distinctive Policy Process," *China Journal*, No. 59 (January 2008), pp. 1–30.

_____, "Policy Experimentation In China's Economic Rise," *Studies in Comparative International Development*, Vol. 43, No.1 (March 2008), pp. 1–26.

Heilmann, Sebastian and Elizabeth J. Perry, eds., *Mao's Invisible Hand: The Political Foundations of Adaptive Governance in China* (Cambridge, MA: Harvard University Asia Center, 2011).

Heydemann, Steven, "Upgrading Authoritarianism in the Arab World," Brookings Institution, Analysis Paper No. 13 (October 2007).

Hildebrandt, Timothy, *Social Organizations and the Authoritarian State in China* (New York: Cambridge University Press, 2013).

Hirschman, Albert, *Exit, Voice and Loyalty: Responses to Decline in Firms, Organizations, and States* (Cambridge, MA: Harvard University Press, 1970).

Horsley, Jamie P., "Public Participation in the People's Republic: Developing a More Participatory Governance Model in China" (2009), unpublished paper.

Hu Angang, *China in 2020: A New Type of Superpower* (Washington, DC: Brookings Institution, 2011).

Huang, Yasheng, *Capitalism with Chinese Characteristics: Entrepreneurship and the State* (New York: Cambridge University Press, 2008).

Huntington, Samuel P., *The Third Wave: Democratization in the Late Twentieth Century* (Norman, OK: University of Oklahoma Press, 1991).

Hurst, William, *The Chinese Worker after Socialism* (New York: Cambridge University Press, 2009).

Inglehart, Ronald and Christian Welzel, *Modernization, Cultural Change, and Democracy: The Human Development Sequence* (New York: Cambridge University Press, 2005).

_____, "How Development Leads to Democracy: What We Know about Modernization," *Foreign Affairs*, Vol. 88, No. 2 (March-April 2009), pp. 33–48.

Jennings, M. Kent, "Political Trust and the Roots of Devolution," in Valerie Braithwaite and Margaret Levi, eds., *Trust and Governance* (New York: Russell Sage Foundation, 1998), pp. 218–244.

Jing, Yijia, "The One-Child Policy Needs an Overhaul," *Journal of Policy Analysis and Management*, Vol. 32, No. 2 (Spring 2013), pp. 392–399.

Kendall-Taylor, Andrea and Erica Frantz, "How Autocracies Fall," *Washington Quarterly*, Vol. 37, No. 1 (Spring 2014), pp. 35–47.

Kennedy, John James and Yaojiang Shi, "Rule by Virtue, the Mass Line Model and Cadre-Mass Relations" in Shiping Hua, ed., *East Asian Development Model: The 21st Century Perspectives* (New York: Routledge, 2015).

Kennedy, Scott, *The Business of Lobbying in China* (Cambridge, MA: Harvard University Press, 2005).

King, Gary, Jennifer Pan, and Margaret E. Roberts, "How Censorship In China Allows Government Criticism But Silences Collective Expression," *American Political Science Review*, Vol. 107, No. 2 (2013), pp. 326–343.

Kornreich, Yoel, Ilan Vertinsky, and Pitman B. Potter, "Consultation and Deliberation in China: The Making of China's Health-Care Reform," *China Journal*, No. 68 (July 2012), pp. 176–203.

Kuran, Timur, "Now Out of Never: The Element of Surprise in the East European Revolution of 1989," *World Politics*, Vol. 44, No. 1 (October 1991), pp. 7–48.

Lam, Willy Wo-Lap, *Chinese Politics in the Era of Xi Jinping: Renaissance, Reform, or Regression?* (New York and London: Routledge, 2015), esp. chapter 3.

Lampton, David M., *Following the Leader: Ruling China, from Deng Xiaoping to Xi Jinping* (Berkeley, CA: University of California Press, 2014).

Landry, Pierre F., *Decentralized Authoritarianism in China: The Communist Party's Control of Local Elites in the Post-Mao Era* (New York: Cambridge University Press, 2008).

Lau, Lawrence J., Yingyi Qian, and Gerard Roland, "Reform without Losers: An Interpretation of China's Dual-Track Approach to Transition," *Journal of Political Economy*, Vol. 108, No. 1 (February 2000), pp. 120–143.

Lee, Ching Kwan, *Against the Law: Labor Protests in China's Rustbelt and Sunbelt* (Berkeley, CA: University of California Press, 2007).

Lee, Hong Yung, *From Revolutionary Cadres to Party Technocrats in Socialist China* (Berkeley, CA: University of California Press, 1990).

Levitsky, Steven and Lucan Way, *Competitive Authoritarianism: Hybrid Regimes after the Cold War* (New York: Cambridge University Press, 2010).

Li, Bobai and Andrew G. Walder, "Career Advancement as Party Patronage: Sponsored Mobility into the Chinese Administrative Elite," *American Journal of Sociology*, Vol. 106, No. 5 (March 2001), pp. 1371–1408.

Li, Cheng, *China's Leaders: The New Generation* (Lanham, MD: Rowman & Littlefield, 2001).

_____, "Assessing China's Political Development," in Cheng Li, ed., *China's Changing Political Landscape: Prospects for Democracy* (Washington DC: Brookings Institution, 2008).

_____, "The End of the CCP's Authoritarian Resilience? A Tripartite Assessment of Shifting Power in China," *China Quarterly*, No. 211 (September 2012), pp. 595–623.

Li, Cheng, ed., *China's Emerging Middle Class: Beyond Economic Transition* (Washington, DC: Brookings Institution, 2010).

Li, He, "Chinese Intellectual Discourse on Democracy," *Journal of Chinese Political Science*, Vol. 19, No. 3 (September 2014), pp. 289–314.

Li, Lianjiang, "Political Trust and Petitioning in the Chinese Countryside," *Comparative Politics*, Vol. 40, No. 2 (January 2008), pp. 209–226.

_____, "The Magnitude of Trust in the Center: Evidence from Interviews with Petitioners in Beijing and a Local Survey in Rural China," *Modern China*, Vol. 39, no. 1 (2013), pp. 3–36.

Lieberthal, Kenneth, "The 'Fragmented Authoritarianism' Model and Its Limitations," in Kenneth Lieberthal and David M. Lampton, eds., *Bureaucracy, Politics, and Decision Making in Post-Mao China* (Berkeley, CA: University of California Press, 1992).

Lieberthal, Kenneth and Michel Oksenberg, *Policy Making in China: Leaders, Structures, and Processes* (Princeton, NJ: Princeton University Press, 1988).

Lord, Winston, "China and America: Beyond the Big Chill," *Foreign Affairs*, Vol. 68, No. 4 (Fall 1989), pp.1–26.

Lorentzen, Peter, Pierre F. Landry, and John Yasuda, "Undermining Authoritarian Innovation: The Power of China's Industrial Giants," *Journal of Politics*, Vol. 76, No. 1 (January 2014), pp. 182–194.

Lust-Okar, Ellen, "Divided They Rule: The Management and Manipulation of Political Oppression," *Comparative Politics*, Vol. 36, No. 2 (January 2004), pp. 159–179.

Lynch, Marc, "After Egypt: The Limits and Promise of Online Challenges to the Authoritarian Arab State," *Perspectives on Politics*, Vol. 9, No. 2 (June 2011), pp. 301–310.

Lynch, Michael, *Mao* (London and New York: Routledge, 2004).

McGregor, Richard, *The Party: The Secret World of China's Communist Rulers* (New York: HarperCollins, 2010).

Magaloni, Beatriz, *Voting for Autocracy: Hegemonic Party Survival and Its Demise in Mexico* (New York: Cambridge University Press, 2008).

Manion, Melanie, "Introduction: Reluctant Duelists—The Logic of the 1989 Demonstrations and Massacre," in Michel Oksenberg, Marc Lambert, and Lawrence Sullivan, eds., *Beijing Spring 1989: Confrontation and Conflict* (Armonk, NY: M.E. Sharpe, 1990), p. xli.

_____, *Retirement of Revolutionary Cadres in China: Public Policies, Social Norms, Private Interests* (Princeton, NJ: Princeton University Press, 1993).

_____, "Chinese Democratization in Perspective: Electorates and Selectorates at the Township Level," *China Quarterly*, No. 163 (September 2000), pp. 764–782.

_____, *Corruption by Design: Building Clean Government in Mainland China and Hong Kong* (Cambridge, MA: Harvard University Press, 2004).

_____, "When Communist Party Candidates Can Lose, Who Wins? Assessing the Role of Local People's Congresses in the Selection of Leaders in China," *China Quarterly*, No. 195 (September 2008), pp. 607–630.

Mann, James, *The China Fantasy: How Our Leaders Explain Away Chinese Repression* (New York: Viking, 2007).

Mansfield, Edward and Jack Snyder, *Electing to Fight: Why Emerging Democracies Go to War* (Cambridge, MA: MIT Press, 2007).

Masini, Federico, "The Formation of Modern Chinese Lexicon and Its Evolution Toward a National Language: The Period from 1840 to 1898," *Journal of Chinese Linguistics*, Monograph Series No. 6 (1993), p. 144.

McCarthy, Susan, "Serving Society, Repurposing the State: Religious Charity and Resistance in China," *China Journal*, No. 73 (July 2013), pp. 48–72.

McCord, Edward, "Confucius Institutes: Hardly a Threat to Academic Freedom," *Diplomat*, March 27, 2014.

Mertha, Andrew, "'Fragmented Authoritarianism 2.0': Political Pluralization in the Chinese Policy Process," *China Quarterly*, No. 200 (December 2009), pp. 995–1012.

Muller, Edward N. and Thomas O. Jukam, "On the Meaning of Political Support," *American Political Science Review*, Vol. 71, No. 4 (December 1975), pp. 1561–1595.

Nathan, Andrew J., *Chinese Democracy* (Berkeley, CA: University of California Press, 1985).

_____, "Chinese Democracy: The Lessons of Failure," in Suisheng Zhao, ed., *China and Democracy: Reconsidering the Prospects for a Democratic China* (New York and London: Routledge, 2000), pp. 21–32.

_____, "Authoritarian Resilience," *Journal of Democracy*, Vol. 14, No. 1 (January 2003), pp. 6–17.

Nathan, Andrew J. and Bruce Gilley, *China's New Rulers: The Secret Files* (New York: New York Review Books, 2001).

Nathan, Andrew J. and Andrew Scobell, *China's Search for Security* (New York: Columbia University Press, 2012).

Naughton, Barry, *The Chinese Economy: Transitions and Growth* (Cambridge, MA: MIT Press, 2007).

O'Brien, Kevin J., "Agents and Remonstrators: Role Accumulation by Chinese People's Congress Deputies," *China Quarterly*, No. 138 (June 1994), pp. 359–380.

———, "Implementing Political Reform in China's Villages," *Australian Journal of Chinese Affairs*, No. 32 (July 1994), pp. 33–59.

O'Brien, Kevin J., ed., *Popular Protest in China* (Cambridge, MA: Harvard University Press, 2008).

O'Brien, Kevin J. and Lianjiang Li, "Selective Policy Implementation in Rural China," *Comparative Politics*, Vol. 31, No. 2 (January 1999), pp. 167–186.

———, *Rightful Resistance in Rural China* (New York: Cambridge University Press, 2006).

O'Brien, Kevin J. and Suisheng Zhao, eds., *Grassroots Elections in China* (New York and London: Routledge, 2010).

Oksenberg, Michel, "The Institutionalisation of the Chinese Communist Revolution: The Ladder of Success on the Eve of the Cultural Revolution," *China Quarterly*, No. 36 (December 1968), pp. 61–92.

———, "Confessions of a China Watcher," *Newsweek*, June 19, 1989.

Osburg, John, *Anxious Wealth: Money and Morality among China's New Rich* (Palo Alto, CA: Stanford University Press, 2013).

Pan Wei, "Toward a Consultative Rule of Law Regime in China," in Zhao Suisheng, ed., *Debating Political Reform in China: Rule of Law vs. Democratization* (Armonk, NY: M.E. Sharpe, 2006).

Pan, Philip P., *Out of Mao's Shadow: The Struggle for the Soul of a New China* (New York: Simon and Schuster, 2008), pp. 247–267.

Parish, William L. and Martin King Whyte, *Village and Family in Contemporary China* (Chicago: University of Chicago Press, 1977).

Pei, Minxin, *China's Trapped Transition: The Limits of Developmental Autocracy* (Cambridge, MA: Harvard University Press, 2006).

———, "Is CCP Rule Fragile or Resilient?" *Journal of Democracy*, Vol. 23, No. 1 (January 2012), pp. 27–41.

Perry, Elizabeth J., "Labor Divided: Sources of State Formation in Modern China," in Joel Migdal, Atul Kohli, and Vivienne Shue, eds., *State Power and Social Forces: Domination and Transformation in the Third World* (New York: Cambridge University Press, 1994).

———, "Studying Chinese Politics: Farewell to Revolution?" *China Journal*, No. 57 (January 2007), pp. 1–22.

Pew Research Center, *The 2008 Pew Global Attitudes Survey in China: The Chinese Celebrate Their Roaring Economy, as They Struggle with Its Costs* (2008).

Pierson, Paul, "The New Politics of the Welfare State," *World Politics*, Vol. 48, No. 2 (January 1996), pp. 143–179.

Przeworski, Adam, "Some Problems in the Transition to Democracy," in Guillermo O'Donnell, Philippe C. Schmitter, and Laurence Whitehead, eds., *Transitions from Authoritarian Rule, Vol. 3: Comparative Perspectives* (Baltimore, MD: Johns Hopkins University Press, 1986).

———, *Democracy and the Market: Political and Economic Reforms in Eastern Europe and Latin America* (New York: Cambridge University Press, 1991).

Przeworski, Adam, Michael E. Alvarez, Jose Antonio Cheibub, Fernando Limongi, *Democracy and Development: Political Institutions and Well-Being in the World, 1950–1990* (New York: Cambridge University Press, 2000).

Putnam, Robert, *Making Democracy Work: Civic Traditions in Modern Italy* (Princeton, NJ: Princeton University Press, 1993).

_____, *Bowling Alone: The Collapse and Revival of American Community* (New York: Simon & Schuster, 2000).

Reilly, James, *Strong Society, Smart State* (New York: Columbia University Press, 2012).

Ross, Michael L., "Does Oil Hinder Democracy?" *World Politics*, Vol. 53 (April 2001), pp. 325–361.

Rowen, Henry S., "When Will the Chinese People Be Free?" *Journal of Democracy*, Vol. 18, No. 3 (July 2007), pp. 38–62.

Sahlins, Marshall, "China U.," *Nation*, November 18, 2013.

Saich, Tony, "Negotiating the State: The Development of Social Organizations in China," *China Quarterly*, No. 161 (March 2000), pp. 124–141.

_____, "Citizen's Perceptions of Governance in Rural and Urban China," *Journal of Chinese Political Science*, Vol. 12, No.1 (April 2007), pp. 1–28.

_____, *Providing Public Goods in Transitional China* (New York: Palgrave Macmillan, 2008).

Schell, Orville and John Delury, *Wealth and Power: China's Long March to the Twenty-first Century* (New York: Random House, 2014).

Schmitter, Philippe C. and Terry Lynn Karl, "What Democracy Is . . . and Is Not," *Journal of Democracy*, Vol. 2, No. 1 (Summer 1991), pp. 75–88.

Schumpeter, Joseph A., *Capitalism, Socialism, and Democracy* (New York: Harper & Row, 1942), p. 269.

Schwarz, Jonathan and Shawn Shieh, eds., *State and Society Responses to Social Welfare Needs in China: Serving the People* (New York and London: Routledge, 2009).

Sen, Amartya, *Resources, Values, and Development* (Oxford, UK: Blackwell, 2004).

Shambaugh, David, "China's Propaganda System: Institutions, Processes and Efficacy," *China Journal*, No. 57 (January 2007), pp. 25–58.

_____, *China's Communist Party: Atrophy and Adaptation* (Berkeley, CA, and Washington, DC: University of California Press and Woodrow Wilson Center Press, 2009).

_____, "The Coming Chinese Crackup," *Wall Street Journal*, March 6, 2015.

_____, "China's Soft-Power Push: The Search for Respect," *Foreign Affairs*, Vol. 94, No. 4 (July-August 2015), pp. 99–107.

_____, *China's Future* (Cambridge, UK: Polity, 2016).

Shi, Tianjian, "Cultural Values and Political Trust: A Comparison of the People's Republic of China and Taiwan," *Comparative Politics*, Vol. 33, No. 4 (July 2001), pp. 401–419.

_____, "China: Democratic Values Supporting an Authoritarian System," in Yun-han Chu et al., eds., *How East Asians View Democracy* (New York: Columbia University Press, 2008), p. 229.

_____, *The Cultural Logic of Politics in Mainland China and Taiwan* (New York: Cambridge University Press, 2015).

Shi, Yaozhong and John J. Kennedy, "Delayed Registration and Identifying the 'Missing Girls' in China," *China Quarterly*, forthcoming.

Shih, Victor, Christopher Adolph, and Mingxing Liu, "Getting Ahead in the Communist Party: Explaining the Advancement of Central Committee Members in China," *American Political Science Review*, Vol. 106, No. 1 (February 2012), pp. 166–187.

Shirk, Susan, *China: Fragile Superpower: How China's Internal Politics Could Derail Its Peaceful Rise* (New York: Oxford University Press, 2007).

Shue, Vivienne, "Legitimacy Crisis in China?" in Peter Hays Gries and Stanley Rosen, eds., *Chinese Politics: State, Society, and the Market* (New York: Routledge, 2010), pp. 41–68.

Simon, Karla W., *Civil Society in China: The Legal Framework from Ancient Times to the "New Reform Era"* (New York: Oxford University Press, 2013), pp. 323–324.

Slater, Dan, *Ordering Power: Contentious Politics and Authoritarian Leviathans in Southeast Asia* (New York: Cambridge University Press, 2010).

Slater, Dan and Joseph Wong, "The Strength to Concede: Ruling Parties and Democratization in Developmental Asia," *Perspectives on Politics*, Vol. 11, No. 3 (September 2013), pp. 717–733.

Smith, Graeme, "The Hollow State: Rural Governance in China," *China Quarterly*, No. 203 (September 2010), pp. 601–618.

Solinger, Dorothy J., *Contesting Citizenship in Urban China: Peasant Migrants, the State, and the Logic of the Market* (Berkeley, CA: University of California Press, 1999).

_____, "Labour Market Reform and the Plight of the Laid-Off Proletariat," *China Quarterly*, No. 170 (June 2002), pp. 304–326.

Spires, Anthony J., "Contingent Symbiosis and Civil Society in an Authoritarian State: Understanding the Survival of China's Grassroots NGOs," *American Journal of Sociology*, Vol. 117, No. 1 (July 2011), pp. 1–45.

Steinfeld, Edward S., *Forging Reform in China: The Fate of State-Owned Industry* (New York: Cambridge University Press, 1998).

Stockmann, Daniela, *Media Commercialization and Authoritarian Rule in China* (New York: Cambridge University Press, 2012).

Svolik, Milan W., *The Politics of Authoritarian Rule* (New York: Cambridge University Press, 2012).

Tai, John W., *Building Civil Society in Authoritarian China: Importance of Leadership Connections for Establishing Effective Nongovernmental Organizations in a Non-Democracy* (New York: Springer, 2015).

Tai, Zixue, *The Internet in China: Cyberspace and Civil Society* (New York and London: Routledge, 2012).

Teets, Jessica C., "Let Many Civil Societies Bloom: The Rise of Consultative Authoritarianism in China," *China Quarterly*, No. 213 (March 2013), pp. 19–38.

_____, *Civil Society under Authoritarianism: The China Model* (New York: Cambridge University Press, 2014).

Teiwes, Frederick C., "Establishment and Consolidation of the New Regime," in Roderick MacFarquhar, ed., *The Politics of China*, second edition (NY: Cambridge University Press, 1997), pp. 5–86.

Thelen, Kathleen, "How Institutions Evolve: Insights from Comparative Historical Analysis," in James Mahoney and Dietrich Rueschemeyer, eds., *Comparative Historical Analysis in the Social Sciences* (New York: Cambridge University Press, 2003), pp. 208–240.

Thompson, Drew, "China's Health Care Reform Redux," in Charles W. Freeman III and Xiaoqing Lu, eds., *China's Capacity to Manage Infectious Diseases: Global Implications* (Washington, DC: Center for Strategic and International Studies, 2009), pp. 59–80.

Thornton, Patricia M., "The New Life of the Party: Party-Building and Social Engineering in Greater Shanghai," *China Journal*, No. 68 (July 2012), pp. 58–78.

_____, "The Advance of the Party: Transformation or Takeover of Urban Grassroots Society?" *China Quarterly*, No. 213 (March 2013), pp. 1–18.

Tong, Yanqi, "State, Society, and Political Change in China and Hungary," *Comparative Politics*, Vol. 26, No. 3 (April 1994), pp. 333–353.

Tsai, Kellee S., *Capitalism without Democracy: The Private Sector in Contemporary China* (Ithaca, NY: Cornell University Press, 2007).

Tsou, Tang, *The Cultural Revolution and Post-Mao Reforms: A Historical Perspective* (Chicago: University of Chicago Press, 1986).

Walder, Andrew G., *Communist Neo-Traditionalism: Work and Authority in Chinese Industry* (Berkeley, CA: University of California Press, 1986).

_____, "The Party Elite and China's Trajectory of Change," *China: An International Journal*, Vol. 2, No. 2 (September 2004), pp. 189–2009.

Wallace, Jeremy L., *Cities and Stability: Urbanization, Redistribution and Regime Survival in China* (New York: Oxford University Press, 2014).

Wang, Enbao and Regina F. Titunik, "Democracy in China: The Theory and Practice of *Minben*," in Suisheng Zhao, ed., *China and Democracy: Reconsidering the Prospects for a Democratic China* (New York and London: Routledge, 2000), pp. 73–88.

Wang, Fei-ling, *Organizing through Division and Exclusion: China's Hukou System* (Palo Alto, CA: Stanford University Press, 2005).

Wang, Shaoguang, "Changing Models of China's Policy Agenda Setting," *Modern China*, Vol. 34, No. 1 (January 2008), pp. 56–87.

Wang, Zhengxu, "Political Trust in China: Forms and Causes," in Lynn T. White, ed., *Legitimacy: Ambiguities of Political Success or Failure in East and Southeast Asia.* (Singapore: World Scientific, 2005), pp. 113–139.

Wedeman, Andrew, *Double Paradox: Rapid Growth and Rising Corruption in China* (Ithaca, NY: Cornell University Press, 2012).

Weiss, Jessica Chen, *Powerful Patriots: Nationalist Protest in China's Foreign Relations* (New York: Oxford University Press, 2014).

White, Gordon, Jude Howell, and Shang Xiaoyuan, *In Search of Civil Society: Market Reform and Social Change in Contemporary China* (Oxford, UK: Oxford University Press, 1996).

White, Tyrene, "Domination, Resistance, and Accommodation in China's One-Child Campaign," in Elizabeth J. Perry and Mark Selden, eds., *Chinese Society: Change, Conflict, and Resistance*, second edition (London and New York: Routledge, 2003).

_____, "Population Policy," in William A. Joseph, ed., *Politics in China: An Introduction*, second edition (New York: Oxford University Press, 2014), p. 394.

Whiting, Susan H., "The Cadre Evaluation System at the Grass Roots: The Paradox of Party Rule," in Barry Naughton and Dali L. Yang, eds., *Holding China Together: Diversity and National Integration in the Post-Deng Era* (New York: Cambridge University Press, 2004), pp. 101–119.

Wintrobe, Ronald, *The Political Economy of Dictatorship* (New York: Cambridge University Press, 2000).

World Health Report 2000: Health Systems: Improving Performance (Geneva: World Health Organization, 2000).

Wright, Teresa, *Accepting Authoritarianism: State-Society Relations in China's Reform Era* (Palo Alto, CA: Stanford University Press, 2010).

Xi Jinping, *The Governance of China* (Beijing: Foreign Languages Press, 2014).

Yang, Dali L., *Remaking the Chinese Leviathan: Market Transition and the Politics of Governance in China* (Stanford, CA: Stanford University Press, 2004).

Yu Keping, "Ideological Change and Incremental Democracy in Reform-Era China," in Cheng Li, ed., *China's Changing Political Landscape: Prospects for Democracy* (Washington DC: Brookings Institution, 2008).

_____, *Democracy Is a Good Thing: Essays on Politics, Society, and Culture in Contemporary China* (Washington, DC: Brookings Institution, 2009).

Yusuf, Shahid, Kaoru Nabeshima, and Dwight Perkins, *Under New Ownership: Privatizing China's State-owned Enterprises* (Palo Alto, CA, and Washington, DC: Stanford University Press and World Bank, 2006).

Zakaria, Fareed, *The Future of Freedom: Illiberal Democracy at Home and Abroad* (New York: Norton, 2004).

Zha, Jianying, *Tide Players: The Movers and Shakers of a Rising China* (New York: New Press, 2010).

Zhao, Suisheng, "A State-Led Nationalism: The Patriotic Education Campaign in Post-Tiananmen China," *Communist and Post-Communist Studies*, Vol. 31, No. 3 (September 1998), pp. 287–302.

INDEX

Numbers in **boldface** refer to tables; numbers in *italics* refer to figures.

Administrative Litigation Law
  (ALL), 115–16
adult literacy, 173
Ai Weiwei, 44
air pollution, 186–87
Alipay, 152
All-China Federation of Industry
  and Commerce (ACFIC), 133, 145
All-China Federation of Trade Unions,
  133, 137, 139–140
All-China Women's Federation
  (ACWF), 133, 143, 148
anti-American protests (1999), 234
anti-corruption campaigns, 34, 86–88,
  90–92, 94–95, 218, 318
Anti-Rightist Campaign, 35–36
Arab Spring (2011)
  democratization and, 22, 296, 307–8
  repression in China and, 40, 42, 44–45
  triggering event for, 310
Argentina, 304
Asia Foundation, 145
Asian Barometer Survey, 215–16
Asia-Pacific Economic Cooperation
  (APEC), 40

Association of American University
  Professors, 241n36
authoritarian resilience, 19–24, 310–11,
  319–320
autocrats
  censorship and, 60, 257
  China's example to, 320
  Liang Qichao and, 275
  popular support and, 214,
  public goods and, 165,

Balla, Steven J., 65
Ban Gu, 239
Beijing Internet Association, 69
Beijing Olympics (2008), 40,
  42, 55
Belgrade, 234
Bell, Daniel A., 240–41
Bloomberg News, 63
Bo Xilai, 85–86, 87, 218, 235
Brady, Anne-Marie, 20
Brazil, 303
Buddhism, 48
budget transparency, 104–5
Bueno de Mesquita, Bruce, 12, 184

Bush, George W., 25–26
business associations, 140

Catholicism, 48–49, 50, 51, 133–34
censorship, 7, 26
    challenges of, 32–33
    Internet and: Arab Spring and,307;
        criticism of central leaders and,
        218; Great Firewall and, 64–69,
        70–72, 257; outsourcing and,
        69–71; personal experience with,
        71-73, **72–73**, 257–58, *258*; regime
        support and, 214, 260
    mechanisms for, 60–61
    media control and, 61–63
    regime support and, 214, 254,
        257–58, *259*, 260
Central Discipline Inspection
    Committee (CDIC), 84–85, 86,
    89, 94–95
Central National Security
    Commission, 87
Chai Jing, 69
Chang, Gordon, 17
Chang, Yu-tzung, 226–27
charities, 132–33
Charter 08 (online petition), 42,
    124, 280–81
Chávez, Hugo, 306
Chen, Jie, 13, 215
Chen, Xi, 20
Chen Guangcheng, 80–81
Chen Liangyu, 85
Chen Shui-bian, 308
Chen Xitong, 85
Chen Yun, 90
Cheng Yizhong, 76
China Charity Federation, 132
China Charity Festival, 145
China Democracy Party, 38–39
"China Dream" (slogan), 99–100, 103
China Merchants Bank, 152
China National Petroleum
    Corporation, 88

China Women's Development
    Foundation, 132–33
China Youth Daily (newspaper), 62
Chinese Academy of Social
    Sciences, 94
Chongqing
    Bo Xilai in, 85-87, 218
    hukou reforms, 77-78
    public goods in, 142-43, 168, 190-93,
        198, 201-2
Christianity, 48–51, 133–34
Chu, Yun-han, 226–27
Church of Almighty God (Eastern
    Lightning), 50–51
civil society groups
    assessment of, 123–27, *125*
    case studies: Fuping Development
        Institute,146–48; One
        Foundation, 151–54; Rural
        Women Knowing All, 143–46;
        Smile Angel Foundation, 148–150
    conventional wisdom on, 16, 316–17
    different views of within the
        state, 127–28
    migrant workers and, 131, 143–44,
        145, 147–48, 211, 316
    party building and, 154–161
    public goods provision and, 210–11
    repression of, 124, 126–27
    restrictions and regulation of, 10–11,
        97, 135–141, 161–63, 302–3
    societal responses to, 141–43, *142*
    types of, 123–27, **127**, 128–135
    See also Charter 08 (online
        petition); Falun Gong (spiritual
        movement)
Clinton, Bill, 25
Communist Youth League, 139–140
Confucian values
    "harmonious society" as, 47
    minben as, 282–83
    regime support and, 13–14, 232,
        237–243, **242**, 259
Confucius Institutes, 241

consultative authoritarianism, 20
consultative democracy, 278
co-optation
    civil society and, 158–160
    regime support and, 3, 14–15,
        246–253, *248*, 259–260
corruption
    anti-corruption campaigns and, 34,
        86–88, 90–92, 94–95, 218, 318
    assessment of, 90
    charities and, 132–33
    consequences of, 89–90, 318
    effects of, 83–84, 92–93
    history of, 34, 84–89
    personal experience with, 198, 256-57
    public opinion on, 91–92, **92–93**,
        255-56, *257*
    regime support and, 214, 254–57,
        256-57, 260
Cuba, 319
Cultural Revolution
    Confucian values and, 238
    co-optation and, 246
    Democracy Wall movement and,
        263–64, 294
    mass line and, 98–99
    as national trauma, 27–28
    repression and, 36
Cyberspace Administration of
    China, 69

Dahl, Robert A., 273–74
Dalai Lama, 48, 54–57, 59–60
deliberative polling, 105–7
democracy in China
    assessment of, 265–272, **267**,
        269–271
    conventional wisdom on, 16–17
    elite definitions of, 274–285
    as *minzhu*, 274
    public opinion on, 266–271, **267**,
        289–299, *289–290*, 308–10
    popular definitions of, 285–88, *286*,
        289–290, 298

popular movements for, 36–37,
    263–65, 277, 294, 299
    Western definitions of democracy
        and, 26–27, 272–74, 308–9
Democracy Wall movement (1978–79),
    36–37, 263–64, 277, 294
"democratic consultation"
    meetings, 107–8
democratization
    consequences of, 311–14
    conventional wisdom on, 317–18
    modernization theory and, 224–232,
        299–300
    modes of regime change and,
        303–4, 306
    predictions and prospects of, 17–19,
        21–29, 262–63, 304–5, 307–11
    U.S. policies and, 225–26
Deng Xiaoping
    Confucian values and, 239
    "Four Cardinal Principles" and, 37,
        264, 277
    "Four Modernizations"
        and, 99–100
    mass line and, 100
    one-child policy and, 79
    popular movements for democracy
        and, 36–37, 264–65, 277, 294
    Tibet and, 54
Diamond, Larry, 6, 274
Diaoyu Islands dispute, 234–35
dictator's dilemma
    censorship and, 67-68,
    corruption and, 90-92, 318
    explained, 3
    nationalism and, 234
    repression and16, 261, 319
    rising expectations and, 28, 96, 302
    urbanization and, 232,
Distelhorst, Greg, 116
domestic savings rates, 207–8, **208**
donations, 134, 253
Downs, George W., 184
Duckett, Jane, 112–13

East Turkestan Independence
    Movement, 58
Eastern Lightning (Church of
    Almighty God), 50–51
Easton, David, 220
economic modernization
    democratization and, 224–232
    income and, 176–78
    regime support and, 8–9, 222–23
    repression and, 36–37
"Economically Comfortable Society"
    (slogan), 239
education
    co-optation and, 249–250
    democratization and, 225
    government spending on, 167–69,
        168, 170–71, 181–85, *183*
    in Maoist era, 172–73, 181
    perception of democracy and, 269,
        269, 271–72
    public assessments of, 190–91,
        193, 197–99
    regime support and, 231, 243
    restricted access to, 74, 77, 198–200
Egypt, 22, 304, 306, 307
elections
    concept of democracy and,
        283–84, 285
    Party members and, 252–53
environment and environmental issues
    civil society and, 128
    Under the Dome and, 69
    Internet and, 69, 186–87
    NIMBY disputes and, 118–120
    nongovernmental organizations
        and, 128, 131
    public assessments of, 190, 192
Environmental Protection Agency, 69
European Union (EU), 145
Exxon Mobil, 145

faith-based organizations, 129, 131
Falun Gong (spiritual movement), 41,
    52, 124

family-planning policies. *See* one-child
    policy; two-child policy
fear of instability, 232, 243–44, *245*,
    254, 259
Federation of Social Organizations, 139
Fewsmith, Joseph, 23
financial crisis (2007–2008), 39,
    42, 176
Fishkin, James S., 10, 105
"floating population." *See* migrant
    population
focus groups, 4, 255, 324
    on central government, 190-91,
        219, 232
    on education, 198-99
    on *guanxi*, 201-2, 255
    on healthcare, 193-95
    on NGOs, 142-43
    on public goods, 168, 190-93
food safety, 185–86, 191–92
Ford Foundation, 130, 145
foreign direct investment (FDI), 210
"Four Cardinal Principles,"
        37, 264, 277. *See also*
        Marxism-Leninism-Mao Zedong
        Thought
"Four Comprehensives"
        (slogan), 99–100
"Four Modernizations"
        (slogan), 99–100
Francis, Pope, 57
Frazier, Mark W., 206
Freedom House, 61, 227n19, 266
Freezing Point (supplement), 62
Fuping Development Institute, 146–48

Gang of Four, 40
Gao Zhisheng, 41–42
Gates Foundation, 130
Germany, 145
Gilley, Bruce, 21, 23, 226, 294, 304
Gini coefficient, 177
Global Governance Indicators, 90
Google, 71

Gorbachev, Mikhail, 306–7
government spending
    central and local governments and,
        129–130
    democracies and, 167
    on education, 167–69, **168**, 170–71,
        181–85, *183*
    on healthcare, III, 167–69, **168**,
        170–71, 178–181, *179*
    on public security, 43, 170–71
government-organized
        nongovernmental organizations
        (GONGO), 133
Great Firewall, 64–69, 70–72, 257
Great Leap Forward, 98–99, 246
Green Dam Youth Escort
        (software), 64
guanxi (personal relationships),
        201–2, 255
Guangzhou
    guanxi in, 202
    NIMBY disputes in, 118-19
    political reform in, 115
    public goods in, 142-43, 190-94, 198
Guo Boxiong, 88
Guo Meimei, 132

Harding, Harry, 20
"Harmonious Society" (slogan), 47,
        64–65, 99–100
Havel, Vaclav, 220–21n13, 299
He, Baogang, 10, 20
Health Care System Reform
        Coordination Small
        Group, III–14
health insurance program, 180–81,
        194–96, **195**, 199, 201
healthcare
    government spending on, III,
        167–69, **168**, 170–71, 178–181, *179*
    in Maoist era, 173
    public assessments of, 190–91,
        193–97, **195**
    reform of, III–14

restricted access to, 33, 74, 77, 199,
        200–201, **202**
    Smile Angel Foundation and,
        148–150
Hildebrandt, Timothy, 134–35
Hirschman, Albert, 47
History of the Han Dynasty (Han Shu)
        (Ban Gu), 239
homosexuality, 129
Hong Kong, 238
house churches, 50–51, 94, 133–34
housing, 74, 188, 190. *See also hukou*
        (household registration system)
Hu Angang, 103
Hu Jintao
    Confucian values and, 240
    corruption and, 85
    economic reforms and, 177–78
    "Harmonious Society" and,
        64–65, 99–100
    mass line and, 100, 162–63
    public goods provision and, 206
    repression and, 32, 39, 43
    "Scientific Development"
        and, 99–100
Hu Yaobang, 40, 264–65
Huang Wan, 87–88
Huang Yusheng, 87–88
hukou (household registration system)
    access to public goods and, 78,
        131, 166, 196–97, 198–201, **202**,
        204–5, 212–13, 271, 302
    description of, 73–74
    education and, 198–200
    insurance coverage and, 194–96, **195**
    in Maoist era, 173
    as means of population
        control, 7, 33
    reforms of, 77–78
    See also migrant population
human development, **170**, 173
Hundred Flowers Movement,
        35–36, 98
Hungary, 319

Huntington, Samuel P., 273
Hussein, Saddam, 307

income
    Confucian values and, 243
    economic reforms and, 176–78
    inequality and, 177
    perception of democracy and,
        270–72, 270
    Public Goods and Political Support
        Survey, **223**, 224
    regime support and, 9, 214,
        222–232, 258–59
Inglehart, Ronald, 227
Innovations and Excellence in Chinese
    Local Governance Program,
    109, 139
instability, 232, 243–44, 245, **254**, 259
Instagram, 67–68
Institutional Reform and Functional
    Transformation Plan, 140
International Monetary Fund, 167n4
Internet
    Arab Spring and, 44, 307
    censorship and: Arab Spring and,307;
        criticism of central leaders and, 218;
        experience with, **72–73**, 257–58, 258;
        Great Firewall and, 64–69, 70–72,
        257; regime support and, 214, 260
    environmental issues and, 69, 186–87
    penetration of, 32, 64
    public opinion on policy issues
        and, 110–14
    use of, 61, 66, 67–68, **68**
    as window on public opinion, 4
Iran, 319
Iraq, 307
Ireland, 145
Islam, 48

Japan, 145, 217, 233, 234–35, 308
Jasmine Revolution, 42
Jennings, M. Kent, 217
Jet Li One Foundation Charity Fund,
    132, 151-53

Jiang Jiemin, 87
Jiang Zemin
    Chen Xitong and, 85
    Confucian values and, 239–240
    Falun Gong movement and, 52
    mass line and, 100
    public goods provision and, 206
    "Shanghai Gang" and, 180n23
    "Three Represents" and, 99–100, 158
    Xu Caihou and, 87
Jiang Zhaohua, 106
The Jungle (Sinclair), 186

Kadeer, Rebiya, 59–60
Khrushchev, Nikita, 99
Korea, 217
Kuran, Timur, 220–21n13, 296

labor unions, 131. *See also* All-China
    Federation of Trade Unions
Lai Hairong, 23
land-reform programs, 35
Langer, Ana Inés, 112–13
Lao Niu Foundation, 152
legitimacy, 1, 15, 96–97, 203-4, 207,
    215–16.
    sources of, 8-15
    See also regime support
Lenin, Vladimir, 99
Li, Cheng, 20–21, 22–23
Li, Jet, 151–54
Li Chuncheng, 87
Li Dongsheng, 87
Li Junru, 278
Li Keqiang, 92
Li Yapeng, 148–150
Li Yuanchao, 89, 117
Liang Qichao, 275–76, 281, 287–88
Libya, 22, 307
Lieberthal, Kenneth, 20
life expectancy, 173, 186
Ling Jihua, 88
literacy, 173
Liu Xia, 42
Liu Xiaobo, 42, 280–81, 298

local legitimacy deficit, 203, 214,
    216–220, 252, 260–61
Louis XV, King of France, 312
loyalty, 251–53

Ma Daqin, Thaddeus, 50
Mandela, Nelson, 299
Manion, Melanie, 37
Mao Yushi, 146-47
Mao Zedong
    repression and, 34–36
    "serve the people" slogan and,
        164–65, 207
    See also Marxism-Leninism-Mao
        Zedong Thought
Maoist era (1949–1976), 6, 172–73,
    181, 238
Maoming, 120
Marx, Karl, 35
Marxism-Leninism-Mao Zedong
    Thought
    Confucian values and, 239–240
    Deng Xiaoping and, 264, 277
    Falun Gong movement and, 52
    mass line and, 97–104
    repression and, 37
mass line
    advantages of consultative approach
        and, 104–5
    concept of, 96–104, 161
    Internet and, 110–14
    NIMBY disputes and, 117–120, 121
    Open Government Information
        and, 115–17
    policy priorities and, 105–10
    public opinion on government
        responsiveness, 122–23
    regime support and, 9–11
    significance of, 121–22
    See also civil society
mass organizations. See
    government-organized
    nongovernmental organizations
    (GONGO)
May 4th movement, 233

McGregor, Richard, 19, 117
"mega-tigers," 86–89
melamine, 185
Meng Xuenong, 180n23
micro-finance, 146–47
Microsoft, 145
middle class, 227-28, 243
migrant population
    access to public goods and, 78,
        131, 166, 196–97, 198–201, **202**,
        204–5, 212–13, 271, 302
    civil society groups and, 131, 143–44,
        145, 147–48, 211, 316
    Confucian values and, 243
    democracy and, 288
    history of, 75–77
    hukou reforms and, 77–78
    private sector and, 175–76, 213
    size of, 75
    See also hukou (household
        registration system)
Migrant Women's Club, 143–44, 145
Mill, John Stuart, 23
minben, 282–83, 287–88
Ministry of Propaganda, 61
minzhu, 274, 287–88
mobilized loyalty, 253
modernization theory, 224–232,
    242–43, 298–99
Morsi, Mohammed, 306

Nathan, Andrew J., 19, 38-39n8, 233–34
National Bureau of Statistics, 89
national unity, 312–13
nationalism
    anti-American protests and, 234
    Diaoyu Islands dispute and, 234–35
    May 4th movement and, 233
    regime support and, 13, 232–37,
        237, 259
natural disasters, 134, 253
New Citizen's Movement, 40–41, 45
"New Left," 86, 282-83
New York Times (newspaper), 63
News China, 145

nongovernmental
    organizations (NGOs)
    assessment of, 123–27, *125*
    conventional wisdom on, 316–17
    environmental issues and, 128, 131
    party building and, 154–160
    restrictions and regulation of, 10–11,
        41, 97, 135–141, 161–63
    societal responses to, 141–43, *142*
    types of, 128–131
"not in my backyard" (NIMBY)
    disputes, 117–120, 121

Oksenberg, Michel, 265n2
Olympic Games (Beijing 2008),
    40, 42, 55
One Foundation, 132, 151–54
one-child policy, 7, 33–34, 78–83
Open Constitution Initiative
    (OCI), 41
Open Government Information
    (OGI), 115–17
"Open Up the West" program, 55, 57
Orange Revolution, 42
Overseas NGO Management Law, 141

Pan Wei, 283–84
Panchen Lama, 56
party building, 96, 154–160, 161. *See
    also* mass line
Party members
    co-optation and, 3, 158–160,
        246–253, *248*, 259–260
    on democracy and democratization,
        293, 295–96
    political and civic behavior of,
        252–53, **255**, 260
party-organized nongovernmental
    organizations (PONGOs), 160
Patriotic Catholic Association,
    50, 133–34
patriotic education campaigns, 235
Pei, Minxin, 18, 21

People's Daily (newspaper)
    anti-corruption campaign
        and, 94–95
    on civil society, 103
    on corruption, 90–91
    Under the Dome and, 69
    on mass line, 102
    as official newspaper, 32
    on regime support, 207
    trust in, 67
People's Liberation Army (PLA),
    1, 88, 95
Perry, Elizabeth J., 19
Pew Research Center, 216
Philippines, 217, 304
Poland, 304
political fear, 45–48, *46*, **49**
political reforms. *See* democratization;
    mass line
Polity IV, 266
pollution, 186–87
popular authoritarianism, 20
population control
    mechanisms for, 7, 33–34, 73
    one-child policy and, 7, 33–34, 78–83
    See also hukou (household
        registration system)
populist policies, 85, 113, 206
poverty alleviation, 147–148,
    188–89, *189*
Practical Skills Training Center, 145
preference falsification, 220, 296
private property, 35
private sector, 154–160, 175–76
Propaganda Department, 61–62,
    67, 69–70
Protestantism, 48–49, 51, 133–34
proxy servers, 65
Przeworski, Adam, 28, 273
public goods
    compared to other countries,
        166–69, **168**, 211–12
    fairness of provision of, 199–202

migrant workers and, 78, 166,
    196–97, 199–201, **202**, 204–5,
    271, 302
nongovernmental organizations
    and, 129–130
performance legitimacy and, 203–5
politics of, 11–13, 205–11, 302
public assessments of, 187–199,
    189, 213
regional disparities in,
    170–72, 212–13
"serve the people" slogan
    and, 164–65
Tocquevillian paradox and, 165–66
variation over time in, 172–187, 212
See also education; environment
    and environmental issues; food
    safety; healthcare
Public Goods and Political Support
    Surveys
anonymity and, 221
on censorship, 71–73, **72–73**, *258–59*
on Confucian values, 241–42, **242**
on co-optation, 247–48, *248*, *251*
on corruption, 91–92, **92–93**,
    255–57, *256–57*
on democracy and
    democratization: age cohorts and,
    269–270, *270*, 271–72; definitions
    of, 285–293, *286*, *289–290*; education
    and, 269, *269*, 271–72; income and,
    270–72, *270*; perceived levels of,
    266–272, **267**, *271*, *289–290*
design and implementation of,
    3–5, 323–25
on fear of instability, 243–44,
    245, **254**
on government officials, 122–23, *123*
impact of repression on,
    45–48, *46*, **49**
on income, 223–24, **223**, *224*,
    230–31, 243
on nationalism, 235–37, **236**, *237*

on nongovernmental organizations,
    142, *142*
on public goods: age cohorts and,
    188–190, 205; on education,
    197–99, 200; fairness of provision
    of, 200–201; general assessment
    of, 187–193, *189*; on healthcare,
    190–91, 193–97, **195**, 200–201,
    202; performance legitimacy
    and, 203–5; regional disparities
    in, 170–72
on regime support: age cohorts
    and, 230–31, *230*; censorship
    and, *259*; co-optation and,
    248; corruption and, 255–57,
    256–57; education and, 231;
    fear of instability and, 243–44,
    245, **254**; local legitimacy
    deficit and, 216–17; measures
    of, 219–221; nationalism and,
    236–37, *237*; overview, *222*;
    political reform and, 245;
    population size and, 232;
    urbanization and, 231
on trust in media, 65–66, *66*
reliability of, 4, 220-21, 268
public opinion
advantages of consutative approach
    and, 104–5
on government
    responsiveness, 122–23
Internet and, 110–14
NIMBY disputes and, 117–120, 121
Open Government Information
    and, 115–17
policy priorities and, 105–10
significance of, 121–22
public security
civil society and, 127
government spending on,
    43, 170–71
public assessments of, 192–93
Putin, Vladimir, 306

Red Cross Society of China, 132, 149, 151, 152
red hat enterprises, 155
regime change
    consequences of, 311–14
    modes of, 303–4, 306–7
    prospects for, 304–5, 306–11
    See also democratization
regime support
    age cohorts and, 230–31, *230*
    censorship and, 214, 254, 257–58, *258–59*, 260
    Confucian values and, 13–14, 232, 237–243, **242**, 259
    conventional wisdom on, 15–17, 314–19
    co-optation and, 14–15, 246–253, *248*, 259–260
    corruption and, 214, 254–57, *256–57*, 260
    education and, 231, 243
    fear of instability and, 232, 243–44, *245*, **254**, 259
    future and fate of CCP and, 319–321
    impact of rising prosperity on, 8–9, 214, 222–232, 258–59
    indicators of, 215–221, *222*
    local legitimacy deficit and, 214, 216–220, 260–61
    multivariate analysis of, **326–27**
    nationalism and, 13, 232–37, *237*, 259
    political reform and, 245
    population size and, 232
    strategies for, 1–3, 5–7, 28–30, 301–3
    transparency and, 260
    urbanization and, 231
    See also legitimacy, mass line; public goods
religion and religious freedoms, 48–51, 313
religious organizations, 133–34
repression
    civil society groups and, 124, 126–27
    conventional wisdom on, 15–16, 315

cost of, 7–8, 31–32, 301, 318–19
cyclic nature of, 39–45, 93–95
Falun Gong movement and, 41, 52, 124
history of, 3, 34–39
public opinion on, 45–48, *46*, **49**
religious freedoms and, 48–51
Tibet and, 53–57
Xinjiang and, 53–54, 57–60
    See also population control;
        Tiananmen Square protests (1989)
rights defense lawyers, 40–42, 45, 162–63
Rowen, Henry S., 227
Rural Women Knowing All (organization), 143–46
Rural Women Knowing All (magazine), 143, 145
Russia, 131, 303, 306–7

Sakharov, Andrei, 299
SARS (severe acute respiratory syndrome) crisis (2003), 179–180, 206
Sasser, James, 234
Schumpeter, Joseph A., 272–73
"Scientific Development" (slogan), 99–100
Scobell, Andrew, 233–34
self-censorship, 70
Senkaku Islands dispute, 234–35
"serve the people" (slogan), 164–65, 207. *See also* public goods
Seventeen Point Agreement, 54
severe acute respiratory syndrome (SARS) crisis (2003), 179–180, 206
Shambaugh, David, 18–19, 23–24
Shanghai
    family planning in, 81
    hukou reforms in, 78
    NGOs in, 156–57, 159–61
    NIMBY dispute in, 118
"Shanghai Gang," 180n23

Shen Dongshu, 146–47
Shenzhen, 139, 152
Shi, Tianjian, 22, 23, 215–16, 272
Shirk, Susan, 17–18
Shouwang Church (Beijing), 51
shuanggui (double designation), 89
Sichuan earthquakes (2008 and 2013),
    44n14, 132, 134, 144, 152–54
Sinclair, Upton, 186
Singapore, 238
Smile Angel Foundation, 148–150
social democracy, 282–83
social justice, 302–3
social order, 190
social organizations. *See*
    nongovernmental
    organizations (NGOs)
South Africa, 304
South Korea, 238, 303, 308
Southern Media Group, 62–63, 67, 76
Soviet Union, 99, 296
Stalin, Joseph, 99
state-owned enterprises (SOEs)
    co-optation and, 247–49
    in Maoist era, 172
    reforms of, 173–75, 223
Stockmann, Daniela, 63
"Strike Hard" campaigns, 58
Summer Olympic Games (2008),
    40, 42, 55
Sun Liping, 38
Sun Yat-sen, 207, 287
Sun Zhigang, 76
sunflower movement, 308
Suu Kyi, Aung San, 299
Syria, 22, 307

Taiwan, 131, 217, 238, 303, 308, 313–14
Tang Min, 146
Taoism, 48
Teets, Jessica C., 20
Tencent Charitable Foundation, 152
Thøgersen, Stig, 20
Thornton, Patricia M., 160

"Three Principles of the People," 207
"Three Represents" (slogan),
    99–100, 158
Three-Self Patriotic Church, 133–34
Tiananmen Square protests (1989)
    anniversaries of, 40, 141
    repression of, 1, 37–38, 264–65
    as unexpected and unplanned,
    294, 310
Tibet, 40, 53–57, 235n29, 313
"tigers," 86–89
Tocquevillian paradox, 165–66
torture, 89–90
tourism, 186
transparency, 104–5, 260
Transparency International, 90
transportation, 190–91
Tsou, Tang, 32
Tunisia, 22, 42, 307, 310
Tutu, Archbishop Desmond, 57
21st Century Business Herald
    (newspaper), 67
two-child policy, 33, 81–82

Uighurs. *See* Xinjiang
Ukraine, 42
Under the Dome (documentary
    film), 69
UNESCO (United Nations
    Educational, Scientific and
    Cultural Organization), 145
Unirule (think tank), 109–10
United Bank of Switzerland, 149
United Nations (UN), 58, 149
United States
    anti-American protests and, 234
    Chen Guangcheng and, 80–81
    civil rights movement in, 130–31
    East Turkestan Independence
        Movement and, 58
    foreign policy of, 24–26
    Iraq and, 307
    Rural Women Knowing All and, 145
    Taiwan and, 313–14

urbanization, 178, 224–25, 231, 243, 271. *See also* migrant population

Vanke Foundation for Public Welfare, 152
Vantone Foundation for Public Welfare, 152
Vatican, 50
Versailles treaty. *See* May 4th movement
Vietnam, 319
virtual private networks (VPNs), 65
volunteering, 134, 253

Wang, Shaoguang, 10, 23
Wang, Zhengxu, 217
Wang Bao'an, 89
Wang Hui, 282–83
Wang Qishan, 165–66
Wang Shiwei, 34–35
Wang Youcai, 38–39
WeChat, 70
Weibo, 70
Weiss, Jessica Chen, 234
Welzel, Christian, 227
Wen Jiabao, 63, 177, 206, 276, 296
Wenling, 10, 105–7, 108
Women's Federation, 139–140
Wong, Faye, 148
World Bank, 83, 90, 130, 145, 167–68
World Development Indicators, 83
World Health Organization (WHO), 111
World Values Survey, 216
World War I. *See* May 4th movement
Wu Bangguo, 277–78
Wu Qing, 144
Wu Zhiping, 144

Xi Jinping
anti-corruption campaign and, 34, 86–88, 90–92, 94–95, 218, 318
"China Dream" and, 99–100, 103
Confucian values and, 240, 259
on consultative democracy, 278
foreign media on, 63
"Four Comprehensives" and, 99–100
mass line and, 100–101, 109, 162–63
public goods provision and, 206–7
repression and, 32, 39, 45, 51
Tibet and, 56
urbanization and, 178
Xie Lihua, 144, 145
Xinhe, 107–8
Xinhua, 67
Xinjiang, 53–54, 57–60, 94, 313
Xu Caihou, 86–87, 88
Xu Wenli, 38–39
Xu Zhiyong, 41

Yahoo, 71
Yanan rectification, 34–35
Yang, Dali L., 19, 23
Yemen, 22, 307
Yongji Fuping Small-Sum Loan Company, 146–47
Yu Keping, 109, 281, 284

Zeng Qinghong, 89
Zhang Dazhong, 310
Zhang Wenkang, 180n23
Zhang Xin, 298–99
Zhao Ziyang, 38, 40, 265, 294, 296
Zhou Bin, 87–88
Zhou Enlai, 40
Zhou Yongkang, 86–88, 218